LEVINAS'S ETHICAL POLITICS

LEVINAS'S ETHICAL POLITICS

MICHAEL L. MORGAN

INDIANA UNIVERSITY PRESS

Bloomington and Indianapolis

This book is a publication of

Indiana University Press
Office of Scholarly Publishing
Herman B Wells Library 350
1320 East 10th Street
Bloomington, Indiana 47405 USA

iupress.indiana.edu

The paper used in this publication
meets the minimum requirements of
the American National Standard for
Information Sciences—Permanence
of Paper for Printed Library
Materials, ANSI Z39.48–1992.

Manufactured in the
United States of America

Library of Congress
Cataloging-in-Publication Data

Names: Morgan, Michael L., [date],
author.
Title: Levinas's ethical politics /
Michael L. Morgan.
Description: Bloomington : Indiana
University Press, 2016. | Series:
The Helen and Martin Schwartz
lectures in Jewish studies | Includes
bibliographical references and index.
Identifiers: LCCN 2015046060 | ISBN
9780253021069 (cloth : alk. paper) |
ISBN 9780253021106 (pbk. : alk.
paper) | ISBN 9780253021182 eb
Subjects: LCSH: Levinas, Emmanuel. |
Ethics. | Political science—
Philosophy. | Political ethics.
Classification: LCC B2430.L484
M674 2016 | DDC 172.092—dc23
LC record available at http://
lccn.loc.gov/2015046060

1 2 3 4 5   21 20 19 18 17 16

To my brother, Fred
RABBI, TEACHER, SCHOLAR

CONTENTS

PREFACE

Readers of Emmanuel Levinas will not proceed far in their study of his writings and his thought without coming across the criticism that his central idea about the face-to-face relation and interpersonal responsibility is irrelevant—to our daily lives, to social relations, and to politics. About ten years ago, in the course of writing *Discovering Levinas,* I cited the off-hand comment of Richard Rorty to this effect: that Levinas's face-to-face is of no public, political, or social importance at all—simply a "mere nuisance."[1] This virtually gratuitous criticism of Levinas is but the most flamboyant and striking example of an objection regularly leveled against Levinas's highly abstract and seemingly mystifying expressions and ideas. Unlike Rorty, who gave no indication of actually having read and studied Levinas with care and sympathetically, there are others who have and who still come away with such a criticism. To the student of Levinas, the criticism of his irrelevance to daily life and especially to social and political life hovers as a constant worry—or what ought to be. It certainly was for me, and while I was convinced that it was mistaken, it took a good deal of time for me to gather up the will and the effort to try to confront it head-on.

The immediate stimulus was a conversation with Seyla Benhabib in New Haven in the fall of 2012. At the time Seyla was immersed in the controversy in Germany over Judith Butler and the awarding of the Adorno Prize and, at the same time, was in the process of writing a critical review of Butler's *Parting Ways: Jewishness and the Critique of Zionism.* At lunch we talked about both, and I was surprised at Seyla's willingness to accept Butler's interpretation and use of Levinas and in fact to endorse it. To me, Butler was clearly confused, if not manipulative, and I left lunch convinced that one day soon I ought to take up the whole issue of Levinas's political relevance. I had read Howard Caygill's influential book, and I knew Simon Critchley's work well. And I was familiar with the many objections to Levinas's purported Eurocentrism and his embarrassing comments on China and other cultures. But I felt that a more generous reading that was nonetheless serious and not simply fawning admiration had yet to be given. My conviction was nursed along by ongoing discussion of Levinas and politics with Carmen Dege, then a graduate student working with Seyla and someone who knew Levinas's writings and had strong views about the issues. Carmen sat in on my course at Yale on Levinas, and we talked all semester long about the political implications of Levinas's ethical insight. We also discussed at length drafts of Seyla's review, which eventually was published in *Constellations*.[2] I left Yale in the spring of 2013 for the University of Toronto and a reading group on Levinas, where I continued to think about ethics and politics in Levinas, sharing thoughts with Sol Goldberg, Simone Chambers, and others. When Jeff Veidlinger, then director of the Borns Jewish Studies Program at Indiana University—my home for nearly thirty-five years—invited me to deliver the Schwartz Lectures at Indiana in the spring of 2014, I decided without much deliberation that I had a subject, and in March and April of that year I gave two lectures, "Tears the Civil Servant Cannot See," one on ethics and politics in Levinas, the other on Levinas on Zionism and the State of Israel. These have become chapters 1 and 2 of this book, which is an expanded version of those lectures.

Levinas calls his way of thinking a form of Platonism. It is a claim that could easily be misunderstood. Platonism, after all, is a multidimensional and complex tradition, with many facets and richly diverse. To understand what Levinas means, however, we need to focus on the *Republic* and especially on book 6, where the ultimate subject of study and the preeminent locus of the order of nature and society is called the Form of the Good. To Levinas, this Platonic formulation stands for the primacy of the ethical for all human experience and the determinative role that the ethical plays vis-à-vis our cognitive achievements and our social and political goals. As Levinas looks back to Husserl, Heidegger, and the tradition of Western philosophy, he takes Plato to have stood for this commitment to the centrality or primacy of the good, of ethics and morality, and he sees his own thinking to be a twentieth-century return to this affirmation.[3] Moreover, his return to this Platonism is made all the more salient and urgent by the fact that it is a determinative feature of a philosophical reorientation not only to the tradition of Western philosophy but also to twentieth-century society and culture, to modernity, and to recent historical events. For Levinas's Platonism is as much about life as it is about thought, indeed more so, for it is the core of his response to the century of atrocities, horrors, and suffering that he associates with World War I, the rise of totalitarianisms and fascisms, the discovery, use, and threats of nuclear weapons, ongoing genocides, and so forth—all of which is represented by the metonymy, the Holocaust, Auschwitz, the death camps. It is the central thesis of Richard J. Bernstein's essay on Levinas and radical evil that all his thought is a response to Auschwitz and the Nazi death camps, and there is some truth in such a claim.[4] What interests me here is the point that for Levinas, philosophy and ethics are a response to life, to the particular historical and political events that constitute concrete experience. Levinas's claim about his Platonism, then, is not an endorsement of a kind of world-denial or Gnosticism; Levinas does not admire the Plato of the *Phaedo* in this respect. To be sure, the face of the other person is one—perhaps the central—exemplification of transcendence in human experience. But transcendence for Levinas is not beyond the world and history; rather it is in it, for it is present in all face-to-face human encounters and relations. And it is the fulcrum of the ethical, which is also present foundationally in all human experience. This is Platonism; it is Levinas's Platonism, and it speaks directly to all those who object that Levinas's thinking is irrelevant and a "mere nuisance."

The Belgian filmmakers Jean-Pierre and Luc Dardenne are deeply influenced by Levinas. Their most recent film, *Two Days, One Night*, an extraordinary accomplishment, is, on my reading, a compelling expression of a Levinasian ethical sensibility. The film begins on a Friday, when Sandra, who has recently been released from a hospital where she has been treated for depression and has been on leave from her job at a small factory, is informed by a co-worker and friend that Sandra has lost her job. While she has been on leave, the owner and foreman have

determined that they can make do with one less employee, and on that
Friday they had asked the sixteen employees to vote on whether they
would prefer to receive their annual bonuses of 1,000 euros each or forgo
their bonuses so that Sandra can return to work. Sandra discovers that
the vote was fourteen to two in favor of receiving the bonuses, but she
is also told that the foreman had influenced some of the employees by
threatening them that the owner wanted to let someone go and if it is
not Sandra, it would be one of them. With her friend's encouragement
and her husband's, Sandra is moved to report the irregularity and ask the
owner to take a new vote, this time a secret ballot, on Monday, giving her
the weekend to talk with her co-workers in order to solicit their support.
The owner agrees, and the movie is then taken up largely with Sandra's
individual encounters with each of her co-workers as she explains the
situation and asks for their support.

In each case, as she travels around the city seeking out each of her
co-workers, Sandra pleads with each to sacrifice his or her bonus for her,
and in the course of these extraordinary encounters, we learn—and she
learns—both about them, their situations and motives and needs, and
about her, about the strain, the sense of embarrassment, and the sense
of gratitude at times and frustration at others—which even leads her to
attempt suicide. Ultimately, on Monday morning, the vote is conducted
once more, and the vote is a tie. There is no majority in her favor. But
the owner offers her a choice: to finish her leave of absence and then to
return to work, when he will not renew the temporary contract of one of
her co-workers, a person who in fact had decided to support her and yet
feared for his own position. Sandra chooses to reject the offer—which
she explains to the owner is in effect a choice between her own job and
that of the temporary contracted co-worker; she will not choose her own
well-being over his. As she leaves the factory, she calls her husband to tell
him that they have won.

What we have in the Dardenne film is a depiction of how the encounters between us, in the most ordinary of circumstances, such as those
that concern our livelihood and also our character, our economic, social,
and psychological lives, expose the dialectic between our personal needs
and investments and our concern and responsibilities to others. The
setting for the film is the present, with its economic challenges, high un-

employment, the influx into Europe of foreign workers, and the psychological strains attendant to globalization and ethnic and racial tensions. As Sandra encounters the company's owner, her husband, and each of her co-workers, the economic and emotional nuances of the lives of each are disclosed and come into conflict with one another. Again and again Sandra tells her co-workers that she has not created the situation; she is not to blame. Some become angry; some show remorse about having voted against her; some stand firm regarding their own needs; some recant; and so forth. In the end, Sandra becomes the agent—the option becomes hers, and she chooses immediately—virtually spontaneously—to sacrifice for the other and to take that to be a victory. But just as important for us, the viewers, is all we learn about the complexity of conditions, the very particular needs, attitudes, and commitments of each of her co-workers as each is presented with the option to sacrifice for Sandra or not. In some cases, the issue seems to be one of self-interest pure and simple, but just as often—indeed more often—the co-worker is being asked to weigh his or her responsibilities to others—a husband or wife and family—over against his or her responsibility or sense of generosity toward Sandra.

However, beyond the details of the Dardenne film and the details of their other films, many of which exhibit Levinasian themes in very telling ways, is the simple point that in the end Levinas's conception of interpersonal responsibility, of turning to the other and responding to the claim the other makes upon each of us, is not an abstraction. It is concrete, particular, unremarkable, and ordinary. It occurs in the everyday, and hence insofar as it involves an ethical claim, that claim is part of all of our lives—personal, social, and political.[5] *Two Nights, One Day* makes this point with a restrained but unavoidable power. The situation that Sandra faces, of being let go from work, is utterly common; the struggles we have in deciding between giving to one person or to another, between obligations to friends and to family—all this is utterly ordinary, as is the psychological and economic situation facing Europeans today. And yet in the working out of those decisions, of encounters between those who are vulnerable and in need and those who are called upon to reach out and give, we see Levinas's insight in action, in the complexity and nuance of everyday life. The film portrays the engagement between ethics and the political in Levinas in a most mundane and common setting and yet in one that exposes its compelling character and its importance for us.

In this book, I take this concreteness of Levinas seriously, this worldliness and involvement in the ordinary, but I also address more particularly the various ways in which his ethical insight about our fundamental responsibility to others provides a standard by which our social and political institutions, policies, and practices can be considered and evaluated. I argue that ethics is the lever of social and political critique for Levinas. Who we are is deeply normative, and hence being who we are amounts to coping with the complexity of the claims made of us, responding to the normativity of the other person's very being, the claims of their neediness, their dependencies, their vulnerability. Politics, when viewed within such a framework, will look different from how it is regularly viewed, both by those who treat politics as largely a matter of power and violence and by those who treat it as serving to protect us and our rights.

Since Levinas does not have a systematic social or political philosophy, this book is not organized so as to display a linear argument or deduction of the political from some foundation or initial situation or premises. Rather I begin with the two Schwartz Lectures, which introduce a variety of themes, texts, and ideas. I then, in subsequent chapters, pull on various threads that are present in the tapestry of those first chapters. I discuss in some detail the crucial texts in which Levinas introduces the notion of the "third party" and with it the complexity of social and political existence. I consider Levinas's views on liberalism and on democracy. I take up how concrete economic and political issues are raised in his Talmudic lessons. I examine what he has to say about Zionism as the movement within Judaism to establish and organize a state based on the notions of responsibility and concern for others. I give a close reading and critical analysis of the notorious interview after the Lebanon War in 1982, when Levinas is asked about the Israeli treatment of the Palestinians and seems to avoid responding and to fail his own principles. I place Levinas in conversation with some important recent developments in Western political philosophy and political theory, and I examine a number of the most compelling critics of his work and his thinking. My strategy, then, is to illuminate a region of Levinas's work, where ethics and politics interact with one another, and to do so by shedding light from a number of directions. At the end, the result is not a thesis or precise conclusion as much as it is an overall picture or portrait, or, to alter the metaphor slightly, it is the identification of a set of motifs as they are present in a mural or panorama.

I want to thank a number of people who have played important roles in the development of my thinking about Levinas and especially about these ethical and political matters. First, of course, I want to thank Seyla Benhabib for provoking me to think through what Levinas has to say and what he contributes to our thinking about social and political matters. We have kept up a conversation, largely by e-mail, about these issues, and I hope she will find the result of some interest, although I doubt that I will convince her completely. I also thank Carmen Dege for many conversations during that semester at Yale; Carmen always took Levinas very seriously and yet at the same time worried about what in the end his thinking could provide for political theory and for political life. Second, Sol Goldberg, Simone Chambers, and the other participants in our Levinas reading group have been a great sounding board for my thoughts about Levinas. Sol, in particular, has been a wonderful conversation partner on these issues ever since we first met; I am sure that many of his insights and suggestions have found their way into my work and into my views on Levinas, too often for me to cite him and in ways that I may hardly notice now. I always leave our conversations—whether in person or over the phone or by e-mail—with new ideas, concerns, and suggestions to consider. Third, an older debt goes to Joshua Shaw, who wrote his dissertation under my direction on this very issue, the political implications of Levinasian ethics. Over a period of several years, we met constantly, talked about Levinas and moral and political philosophy, and read texts together. His book, *Emmanuel Levinas and the Priority of Ethics: Putting Ethics First*, published in 2008, is an outstanding examination of various dimensions of the issue of Levinas's understanding of the ethical contribution to the political. An older debt is to Simon Critchley and Robert Bernasconi, both of whose work has meant so much to me over the past two decades. I also want to thank a more recent student, Kevin Houser, whose dissertation is a creative implementation of Levinasian ideas; Kevin's work on reasons and the second person, in the light

of a Levinasian understanding of the ethical, is an exemplary effort to
explore problems in moral philosophy and moral psychology in the light
of Levinas's conception of the face-to-face.

As I was preparing for the Schwartz lectures, I was invited to give
talks on Levinas in which I tried out some of the ideas now presented
in the first two chapters of this book. On one occasion, at Berkeley, I
received very helpful and critical comments from Marty Jay and Jay
Wallace, and on another, at UCLA, David Myers provided very valuable
suggestions, as did Todd Presner. Subsequently Marty and I have carried
on an exchange about Levinas's comments in the famous interview after
Sabra and Shatila; he is not the only one who finds me too charitable and
who will doubtless remain unconvinced by my reading of that interview
and Levinas's intentions behind his participation in it. Indeed, when I
think about that interview and talk with people about it, I always have
Marty's criticisms in mind. Finally, when I gave the Schwartz Lectures,
there were some excellent comments, especially after the initial lecture
on the relation between ethics and politics in Levinas's thinking; I want
to thank especially Bill Scheuerman, who is a regular conversation partner about political theory and political philosophy; Milton Fisk, whose
question about the lack of a social theory in Levinas unfortunately has
no clear answer; and Jordi Cat.

On Israel and Zionism, I have been helped by a number of people
who have clarified to me their own views, have argued and debated
with me, and have given me guidance about what to read and where,
on the web, to keep up with the most recent discussion. My preeminent
guide in these matters, as well as on so much else, has been Shaul Magid.
Shaul possesses a rare combination of capacities that make his advice
and counsel exemplary. His thinking expresses passion and critical engagement, combined with extraordinarily wide reading, fairness and
openness, and unlimited energy. I cannot thank him enough for all that
our conversations have meant to this work and to me. Allan Arkush gave
me good advice on various readings and in particular pointed me to the
material on the legislative efforts to enact a bill on Israel as a Jewish and
democratic state published on the website *Marginalia*. For several years,
I have read the work of Ruth Gavison, and when we finally met, I found
Ruth to be as intense and yet generous, as careful and thoughtful and

engaged, as I had expected—indeed more so. For her guidance and for generously sharing with me an English translation of her Hebrew book on Israel as a Jewish and democratic state at a crucial moment, I want to express my thanks. I also thank Chaim Gans for his outstanding book *A Just Zionism* and for memorable conversations during and after his visit to Stanford in the fall of 2013, when I was teaching there. I am also grateful for his sharing with me versions of his translation of his Hebrew book *A Political Theory for the Jewish People* prior to its publication by Oxford University Press. It was my good fortune that during my semester at Stanford, my friend Sam Fleischacker was at the Center for Advanced Study in the Behavioral Sciences, working on a project on Zionism. Sam and I met often during that fall and talked about his work and mine and especially papers of his on peoplehood and nationality and on territorial issues connected with Israel and Zionism. While at Stanford, Mira Wasserman and I met weekly to read and examine Gans's book on Zionism, and as in the past, I found this opportunity to talk with Mira and explore texts of common interest tremendously helpful. Finally, I want to thank Mike Walzer for providing me with a copy of a paper of his on Israel and democracy and for his various papers and essays on Israel and Zionism.

The chapter on Levinas and messianism originally appeared in a volume that Steve Weitzman and I edited, entitled *Rethinking the Messianic Idea in Judaism*, and I want to thank Martin Kavka, who responded to the paper when it was first presented at a conference at Princeton, and then for written versions of his comments on Levinas and messianism. Some of Martin's reading of Levinas, which differs from my own, can be found in his paper in that same volume. I also thank Steve Weitzman, then director of Jewish Studies at Stanford and now director of the Katz Center at the University of Pennsylvania, for the invitation to teach at Stanford, which proved such an important period for me as I was working on this material. I also thank Jeff Veidlinger, then director of Jewish Studies at Indiana and now at the University of Michigan, for the invitation to present the Schwartz Lectures at Indiana University, which form the core of this book and in which series this book appears. I thank too John Efron at Berkeley and David Myers at UCLA for invitations to present some of this material at their respective universities. Finally, I thank Marty Schwartz and his wife Helen, now deceased, for their generosity, intellectual engagement, and vision that led to the establishment of the Schwartz Lecture series and the impressive contributions that have resulted from it.

When this project was in its final stages, I received especially helpful advice and direction from two directions. First, I was invited to spend a month in Melbourne by Kevin Hart, Nick Trakakis, Robyn Horner, and their colleagues at the Australian Catholic University, where I was privileged to deliver the Simone Weil Lecture on the themes of this book. In the course of my visit, I received valuable comments and advice from Kevin, Nick, and Robyn and also from Jean-Luc Marion, Richard Colledge, and others who attended the lecture and with whom I had valuable conversations during the month in Australia. Second, while I was in Australia, I received an extremely helpful set of comments on a draft of the book from Stephen Mulhall, and in response to Stephen's suggestions, I revised, cut, and reorganized the draft into its present form. I am confident that I have failed to do justice to the help provided during this valuable period, but the present book, I think, is substantially better as a result of the goodwill and insights of these friends and colleagues.

There is nothing that I write and nothing that I think about that I do not discuss with my very close friends and philosophical conversation partners, Paul Franks, Benjamin Pollock, and Sol Goldberg. I value and am constantly enriched by my friendships with all three, and this book, as is the case with all I do these days, is better and philosophically richer because of our conversations and our ongoing correspondence. Even though I am here writing about Levinas and not Fichte or Kant or Hegel or Rosenzweig or Heidegger, there is more of these three of my friends in this book than I could possibly identify. In the end, of course, I would not want to burden any of them with my unclarities or confusions or mistakes, but I hope it is to their credit when I say that much that is good here has been made good or better by my ongoing conversations with them.

This book is about philosophy, Judaism, and life—very ordinary life and political life. As I have been writing, I have paid due attention—albeit I am sure insufficient attention—to the lives of my family members. I have enjoyed watching Gabby, Sasha, Tyler, and Halle learn and play and grow—with their laughter and joy, their cleverness and intensity, their frustrations and thrills. Their parents—Sara, Deb, and Adam—are a constant source of pride and wonder; they are not only our grandchildren's caretakers, although I am sure they may believe that we think of them in these terms, they are mostly our wonderful children, whom we love. Aud and I have recently celebrated our fiftieth anniversary. If I am the philosopher in our little family, she is my anchor in life and my constant reminder of what it all means. What we do, we do together, which is my *mazel*, my great good fortune.

PART ONE

Overview

ONE

TEARS THE CIVIL
SERVANT CANNOT SEE
Ethics and Politics

THE PROBLEM

How does Emmanuel Levinas understand the relationship between the domain of responsibility or the ethical, on the one hand, and the domain of justice or the political, on the other? Broadly speaking, many commentators have argued that Levinas has a story to tell about this relationship that is informative, serious, and compelling; critics, however, claim that whatever Levinas has to say about the matter is unclear and unhelpful. It betrays a weakness in Levinas's thinking and its implausibility or its irrelevance or both.

In his paper "The Possibility of an Ethical Politics: From Peace to Liturgy," John Drabinski begins his account by noticing that at least some criticism of Levinas is leveled against the primacy of the biblical tradition and his Hebraism. This is tantamount to claiming that what prevents Levinas from developing his political thought is a one-sided attention to the primacy of the ethical for our lives and too great a dependence on the Bible, religion, and Judaism. Drabinski identifies Gillian Rose as one among several critics of this kind, and he notices too a host of passages in Levinas's own writings that seem to take the face-to-face and responsibility as a disturbance of the political and as opposed to it.[1] But, at the same time, Drabinski is surely right to point out that this criticism fails to take seriously Levinas's frequent claims that Europe is both "the Bible and the Greeks," ethics and politics. Any one-sided reading of Levinas that leads to anarchism or asceticism is surely mistaken.[2] What Drabinski stakes out is a position between dismissing the political as secondary or derivative and privileging the political at the same level as the ethical. As he puts it, the singularity of the face and the universality of law open up a gap between the two; politics is necessary and yet opposes the ethical. The face signifies without context; the face as citizen is the political, which contextualizes the face.[3]

By the ethical or the domain of responsibility or the regime of charity, Levinas is referring to the normative character of the particular face-to-face relationships that underlie and ground all of human social experience.[4] This ethically normative claim for acknowledgment, acceptance, and care for the other person is a dimension of all human experience, and it is both determinative of how we ought to live and a transcendental condition for every aspect of our lives. Alternatively, by the political or the domain of justice, Levinas sometimes intends to pick out all of our everyday experience, from the most ordinary perceptual experience to the most organized, institutionalized behavior, from the most individual conduct to the most general or abstract thinking and action. At other times, however, Levinas has in mind by the political the narrower domain of those institutions, laws, policies, and practices that organize our everyday lives as citizens of a state or as subjects of a particular government. This narrower conception of the political is clearly a subdivision of the larger, more embracing conception, so that the problem for Levinas of understanding how the ethical is related to governmental policies and conduct or legal and juridical practices is not independent of how we understand more broadly what special role or roles the transcendental structure of interpersonal encounter plays in our everyday lives. As a result, there are going to be similarities between what the ethical means for the political in the narrow sense and what it means for religious institutions, culture and art, and other modes of everyday life, as well as for everyday life in general.

Another distinction useful to make at the outset is that between political life and political theory. On the one hand, for Levinas, by and large, the issue that he takes to be raised by worrying about how the ethical, as he understands it, or the order of charity is related to the political domain or the order of justice is a matter of concrete experience. How do our fundamental responsibilities to other persons have an impact on our political lives—on our institutions, our policies, our laws, and our political conduct, as individuals or as a society? On the other hand, there is another question that might be asked, certainly by philosophers: does Levinas have a political philosophy? Does Levinas think that we can derive particular guidance about how we understand the authority, role, and character of political institutions from the belief that human existence is determined fundamentally by our infinite responsibilities one to another or that it is grounded in concern for the other person? Does his central insight about human social existence help us to understand what the political order is and how it ought to be organized? I will say something about what Levinas's conception of the ethical means for both—political life and political theory.

As I proceed, I will be drawing on what Levinas himself says and what he chooses to discuss. Therefore, at times I will be discussing political conduct and institutions, and at times political theory; I will simply follow Levinas's lead. Moreover, I will at times use the analogy between political life and institutions and non-political ones, based on the thought that politics in the narrow sense is one of a number of different domains within our everyday lives, all of which have a similar relationship to the ethical foundation of all human experience, as Levinas sees it.

To begin, let us consider two questions that Levinas will have to answer: One is the question, what grounds the normative authority of those duties and ideals that constitute our moral lives? The other is, how is the ethical domain of our lives related to the authority and forms of our political lives? These are Platonic questions. In Western philosophy and in Western culture, since antiquity, there have been a variety of answers to both questions. Some have argued that the authority, form, and goals of our moral lives are dictated by divine will, others that they are shaped by their foundation in human nature or human rationality and agency. Some have believed that political life is natural and continuous with moral considerations and obligations, while others have sought to make political life independent of any particular conception of what it is to live a good life. Levinas, in the end, takes our human condition to be a continuous one. Religious, moral, and cultural experience are not utterly separated one from the other, and both are related to our political lives, and all are somehow responsive to the ethical core of our existence.

As Sam Fleischacker has reminded me, modern philosophers, from Hobbes to Rawls and beyond, have sought to segregate our conceptions of political authority and forms of political life from our orienting religious and moral conceptions of life, for theoretical and historical reasons. But this tendency failed to impress Levinas. In a sense, modern political philosophy has attempted to ground political philosophy in human nature or rationality and to make it impartial or neutral with respect to substantive, deep conceptions of what is valuable and worthwhile about human life. With this strategy comes a marked separation between the public and the private and much else. Justifying the state in this fashion is an attempt to free the state from partisan—religious, moral, nationalist—advocacy and to avoid the risk of "wars of religion," as it were. For Levinas, however, although such efforts do have benefits, they also free political life from an incontrovertible grounding in our ethical sensibility and leave open options that can easily—as history has shown us—decline into horrific results, totalitarianisms and fascisms. The challenge he must meet, then, is to expose our unqualified opposition to such horrors and at the same time to show how arguing for the continuity between normative foundations and political life, for their interrelationship, does not simply land us back in a situation that risks intolerance and conflict, social and political. To do this, he finds the multiplicity of moral, religious, and other comprehensive views to be grounded ultimately in something single and common, a structure that we all share as part of all of our interpersonal lives. But does Levinas's strategy succeed? Is the ethical dimension he identifies substantial enough and yet not too substantial? How does it determine but not distort the political? And what are the benefits and the disadvantages of his efforts to meet this challenge? In the end what kind of relationship does exist between our fundamentally ethical existence and political life?

THE SOLUTION

Often, in the 1980s, in interviews and elsewhere, when the topic of the ethical and the political arose, Levinas was fond of referring to a Talmudic text to clarify their relationship.[5] It can serve as a kind of emblem of their interrelation, and examining it will facilitate our effort at clarifying how he conceived of the ethical-political relationship. The passage occurs in the Babylonian Talmud, Tractate Rosh Ha-Shanah, at 17b–18a; let me begin with my own account. A question is addressed to Rabban Gamaliel about an apparent contradiction between two biblical verses,

Deuteronomy 10:17, "who does not lift up [His] countenance," and Numbers 6:26, "The Lord shall lift up His countenance unto you." The text then records a story or parable that is intended to clarify the situation: Two men arranged a loan before the king, the recipient swearing on the king's life to repay the loan. But when the time came to make the repayment and the borrower did not pay, he sought to excuse himself before the king. The king said, "I accept your excuse, but go and obtain forgiveness from your neighbor." The Talmud takes this distinction between offenses against God and those against one's neighbor to apply to the original conflict between the two verses. With regard to offenses against Him, God may show favor and forgive or excuse the misconduct, but not with regard to offenses against one's fellow human being. But in fact, Levinas ignores this explanation and focuses solely on what the Talmud says next: that this explanation was generally accepted until Rabbi Akiba taught, "One text refers to God's attitude before the final sentence, the other to His attitude after the final sentence." And Levinas takes Akiba to have meant that we should distinguish the application of the principles of justice impartially, with no attention to the particularity of the claimant, from the act of mercy, which comes after the judgment is given and attends to the particularity of the claimant and his petition, his request for forgiveness.

As I read the text and in particular the way in which the parable is intended to dissolve the apparent contradiction, the traditional explanation appears to be relying on a customary distinction between sins committed against God and sins committed against other persons; this distinction calls to mind its use in Tractate Yoma regarding repentance and what sins require the prior request for forgiveness from others whom one has wronged. This is one framework in which the parable is understood. But, on the other hand, Akiba is relying on a different distinction, that between divine justice (*middat ha-din*) and divine mercy (*middat ha-rahamim*). Levinas's own reading follows Akiba but in a very distinctive way.

It is clear from the four occasions on which Levinas introduces the text—and there may very well have been more—that he takes the text, the point of the story or parable, to apply to or to exemplify in some way his own understanding of ethics and politics, the order of responsibility and the order of justice, as he calls them.[6] On his reading, the central theme of this Talmudic passage is captured in Akiba's alternative account of the meaning of the story about the sinner's appeal to the king for forgiveness. It is clear that Levinas takes this account to refer not to divine action literally but rather to the judgment of the court, both its verdict and the sentencing that follows that verdict. Moreover, Levinas takes the guilty verdict to be got by the strict application of principles of justice, and the judgment that follows, the merciful forgiveness that weakens or lightens the sentence on the guilty borrower, to be the result of responding with very particular sensitivity and compassion to the sinner's appeal for forgiveness. In short, justice must not forgive the borrower's having failed to pay the debt, but mercy can lighten the sentence on him, given his appeal for forgiveness. As Levinas himself puts it, "Do not look at the face before the verdict. Once the verdict has been given, look at the face."[7] This is how Levinas reads the "before" and "after" of Akiba's interpretation, that is, before and after the court's judgment about his actual guilt or culpability. To generalize, the state's responsibility is to apply laws fairly and uniformly, with generality, but even then, once the verdict is issued, there is still room for "humanity," or what Levinas calls the "possibility of or appeal to something that will reconsider the rigor of always rigorous justice."[8] This he calls a "surplus of charity or of mercy." "This," he says, "is how the necessity of the State is able not to exclude charity."[9] The distinctive circumstances concerning the borrower do not matter to the judgment against him; if he failed to repay the debt, he is culpable. But when it comes to the sentence to be exacted of him, various features of the situation become relevant. These all apply to him distinctively and include, in particular, the fact that he sought the forgiveness of the court and perhaps the unique financial and personal circumstances that prevented him from repaying the loan and led him to tender his excuse. At this stage, the court can take these distinguishing factors into consideration; it can, that is, "look at [the borrower's] face."

Moreover, this reading suggests that the regime of justice recognizes its own imperfection, and so in allowing for mitigation or mercy, it already acknowledges its own incompleteness and hence is "already questioning the State." It is in this sense that acknowledging the repentant sinner and his appeal for forgiveness and then lightening the sentence in response to this appeal constitute an act of mercy within justice and not outside of it. As Levinas puts it, "This after-verdict, with its possibilities of mercy, still belongs—with full legitimacy—to the work of justice."[10] In broader terms, the political, mediated by an appreciation of responsibility, is self-critical, or the ethic of responsibility does not simply criticize the state *ab extra,* or from the outside; rather its role within the domain of justice or the political leads justice to appreciate its own limitations. Levinas calls this "justice with a bad conscience."[11]

Why have I taken so long with Levinas's references to this Talmudic passage? The standard approach to Levinas's understanding of the political and its relation to the ethical is by way of his notion of the third party and the way in which he argues that the "entrance" or inclusion of the third party into our social lives requires forms of classification, distinction, comparison, and measurement that constitute justice and lead to the development of general principles, practices, and institutions. We will get to this in a moment. The reason I have begun with this Talmudic comment, however, is that it allows us to see, before we turn to Levinas's more systematic discussion, what he is aiming at and what that theoretical or systematic account is intended to accomplish. To be sure, the Talmudic discussion does not express a doctrine; it points to an illuminating case, one intended to be suggestive and instructive. So let us ask: what do Levinas's references and his interpretation of this text tell us about the relation between charity or mercy, as he calls it, and justice and the state?

First, we learn that for Levinas justice involves applying general principles fairly and impartially, regardless of who the particular agents are. And justice involves laws, the courts, and the other institutions of the state whose goal is to organize social life with an attention to this sort of just treatment. Second, justice and the state are necessary. We cannot live without them. Human existence involves both everyday experience and a transcendental dimension of responsibility for other persons; each depends upon and limits the other. Third, justice is, however, limited and imperfect; not attending to the particularity of individuals is a strength of the principles and institutions of justice, but it is also a weakness. Although justice must not pay attention to individuals, it can easily lead us to forget that the reason to order social life is to help us to deal with each other as individuals, as particular persons. Fourth, even within the regime of justice there are opportunities for such responsiveness, moments or occasions when we can, within just practices, turn to and respond to individuals as individuals. We can call this "mercy" or "charity" or generosity or concern or sensitivity; it is a way that our fundamental responsibility to other persons is expressed in the midst of our public, everyday lives. Finally, we can develop a critique of political practices and institutions from the point of view of charity or responsibility to others, but we can also develop a critique from the point of view of justice. Justice can recognize its own weaknesses, imperfections, or limitations and criticize itself, so to speak. In short, one can engage in political critique both from outside of the state and from within it.

These remarks merely sketch how the ethical and the political are interrelated in Levinas's thinking. We now need to turn to the terms he uses and the analysis he develops to elaborate and clarify this sketch.

THE ARGUMENT AND ITS CLARIFICATION

The central text in which Levinas examines the relationship between the responsibility of each person to every other person and our everyday lives occurs in a section late in his 1974 book *Otherwise Than Being*. I will set aside this technical discussion for a later chapter, however, and use instead an alternative strategy to present his account.

Levinas ends the crucial section "Being and Beyond Being" with the sentence "Philosophy is the wisdom of love at the service of love." What is true of philosophy is also true of politics. It is an understanding of love—of human responsibility, concern for the other, and justice—in the service of that human responsibility and justice. And beyond this, politics is the institutional implementation, the policies and regulations, of justice in the service of shaping a just and humane life for all its members. In *Otherwise Than Being* this is as far as Levinas goes toward characterizing the political and its relation to ethics.[12] With this account in hand, then, we can ask what Levinas's philosophy contributes to understanding everyday morality and political life. Can we derive precise principles of political life? Does Levinas's conception of justice and the face-to-face provide a standard for judging political regimes and practices? Does it recommend some forms of constitution and reject others? Does it help us to make particular normative proposals?

One way to begin to answer these questions and to bring into sharper focus Levinas's account is to turn to some of Levinas's interviews, where he responds to questions about precisely these matters. In "The Paradox of Morality," an interview given in 1986 to three graduate students from the University of Warwick, Levinas says that justice, which involves calculation, is "inseparable from the political," and he associates it with "the terrible task" of comparing people. All of this, he points out, arises within "Greek logic and Greek politics." "Everything that I say about justice comes from Greek thought, and Greek politics, as well. But it [justice or politics] is, ultimately, based on the relationship to the other, on the ethics without which I would not have sought justice. Justice is the way in which I respond to the fact that I am not alone in the world with the other."[13]

These remarks recall features of the account from *Otherwise Than Being*. What underlies or organizes human social experience is the very particular relationship that each of us has to each and every other self. That face-to-face, as he calls it, is characterized by the claim of the other on the self, the way the other person's needs or vulnerability targets the self and puts the self into question; the other person pleas for acknowledgment and assistance and demands it as well. But while this relational nexus occurs within every interpersonal relationship, it is accompanied by a vast array of other modes of relation. Moreover, each of us is not faced only with one other person at any given moment; rather we are never "alone in the world with the other," as he says in this interview. There is always a third party or person, and a fourth, and on and on—innumerable others. And each of these others is face-to-face with me and face-to-face with each and every other, in a complex, infinitely arrayed network. This network makes up our social lives, and politics, in the narrow sense, is one set of categories, structures, practices, policies, and institutions that organizes that network. We are, among many other things, citizens. And insofar as justice is concerned, impartiality and fairness of treatment and distribution, this political order is one domain in which justice is a virtue. It is a word, for Levinas, for what the infinite responsibility of the face-to-face—that is, charity and mercy and generosity—becomes in this ramified and complex network, in our ordinary political lives. Justice is responsibility in action.[14]

In this interview, Levinas also says that justice and the face-to-face are opposites. He says elsewhere that justice involves comparing incomparables, and this is another way of saying that the generality and commonality that mark justice are not true of the face-to-face, which is utterly particular. Still, they are related. Justice emerges from our responsibility to the other. As he puts it, "Everything terminates in justice."[15] That is, since we are always in a world with innumerable others, all of our interpersonal relations are at the level of politics and justice. The way we relate to others in terms of general categories, principles, roles, and institutions is unavoidable; our lives are filled out with such relationships and the experiences we have in terms of them.

But, Levinas asks, if everything ends with justice and if justice is the "opposite" of the face-to-face dimension of our interpersonal lives, "why tell this long story about the face?"[16] He gives three reasons, which go some way to answering the questions I asked. The first reason, he says, "is that it is ethics which is the foundation of justice," and then he explains that justice is not the last word; we always seek better and better justice, and this is what the liberal state seeks to accomplish.[17] To put this in slightly different terms, we need justice because of our responsibility to meet the needs of others; justice is a way of orchestrating responsibility for others in a complex society. That is what justice is for, so to speak.[18] And it is always a matter of degree. The best type of political regime is the one that does the best job of being just, of orchestrating our interpersonal responsibilities in such a complex network.[19] Here and in many other places Levinas calls it "the liberal state," and as we shall see, he also calls it "democracy." We ought to ask why he uses these expressions and why it is just these that best pick out the regime capable of the highest degree of justice, but for the moment let us defer these questions.

The second reason for telling a long story about the face-to-face is that justice is violent. Clearly this comment is connected with his saying that justice is a "terrible task."[20] This can be taken in a couple of different ways. On the one hand, justice is terrible because every decision to help one person involves not helping another, to some degree and in some way. No just decision or action comes without compromise. On the other hand, justice always involves treating people generically, as Levinas says, as representing a category or a type; it always means failing to take into consideration very particular features or actions or claims. Levinas associates the necessity of this violence, then, with the imperfection of just regimes and the fact that they must always seek to mitigate that violence and to do a better job of designing and employing practices and policies that care for people, are humane and responsive, and so forth. Here Levinas uses the word "democracy" to refer to the type of regime that recognizes its own limitations of this kind. As he puts it in "In the Name of the Other":

> By admitting its imperfection, by arranging for a recourse for the judged, justice is already questioning the State. This is why democracy is the necessary prolongation of the State. It is not one regime possible among others, but the only suitable one. This is because it safeguards the capacity to improve or to change the law by changing ... tyrants, these personalities necessary to the State despite everything. Once we choose another tyrant, we imagine, of course, that he will be better than his predecessors. We say this with each election![21]

In addition to advocating democracy, Levinas here alludes to the Talmudic text we have discussed, for he puts his point by referring to a juridical setting: "When the verdict of justice is pronounced, there remains for the unique I that I am the possibility of finding something more to soften the verdict. There is a place for charity after justice."[22] The use of the expressions "verdict" and "softening the verdict" together with the reference to "a place for charity *after* justice" surely suggests his interpretation of Akiba's explanation of how to understand the parable of the guilty borrower.

Levinas's third reason is that the face-to-face calls attention to the fact that in every situation there is a "moment," as it were, when each of us as a unique I "can find something else which improves universality itself." He then gives the example that "the abolition of the death penalty certainly results from that."[23] In a sense, this reason can be understood to combine elements of the earlier two: the fact that justice is imperfect and can always be made better and the fact that this can involve the particular agent's acting with generosity or compassion or sensitivity to others as individuals. Here too we have an allusion to the Talmudic passage and the idea of forgiveness and having opportunities for repentance and a change of heart. Not only does justice or the political regime recognize its own limitations; each particular citizen also is capable of critique and of moments of charity or humanity.

These reasons for spending so much time telling his story about the face-to-face and the order of responsibility, as he sometimes calls it, might be summarized by saying that Levinas's conception of the ethical does indeed provide a standard or an ideal in terms of which political practices and institutions should be evaluated. Or, in other words, Levinas's philosophy does provide a type of social and political critique. He gives a very helpful description in "The Paradox of Morality" when he says:

> That is the great separation that there is between the way the world functions concretely and the ideal of saintliness of which I am speaking. And I maintain that this ideal of saintliness is presupposed in all our value judgments. There is no politics for accomplishing the moral, but there are certainly some politics which are further from it or closer to it. For example, I've mentioned Stalinism to you. I've told you that justice is always a justice which desires a better justice. This is the way that I will characterize the liberal state. The liberal state is a state which holds justice as the absolutely desirable end and hence as a perfection. Concretely, the liberal state has always admitted—alongside the written law— human rights as a parallel institution. It continues to preach that within its justice there are always improvements to be made on human rights. Human rights are the reminder that there is no justice yet. And, consequently, I believe that it is absolutely obvious that the liberal state is more moral than the fascist state, and closer to the morally ideal state.
>
> There is a utopian moment in what I say; it is the recognition of something which cannot be realized but which, ultimately, guides all moral action. This utopianism does not prohibit you from condemning certain factual states, nor from recognizing the relative progress that can be made. Utopianism is not a condemnation of everything else. There is no moral life without utopianism— utopianism in this exact sense that saintliness is goodness.[24]

The face-to-face or the order of responsibility to the other Levinas here calls "saintliness."[25] It is impossible to realize it in one's life, certainly politically. But our states can be closer or further from that ideal. There are states that aim at justice and do better or worse jobs of accomplishing it, and there are states that ignore or defy justice. Levinas notes the role that human rights play as a "reminder" or "sign" of how well a society is doing with regard to this ideal, to saintliness. It is no wonder that the best states are liberal ones and democracies.[26]

Here, then, we have the same double form of critique that we mentioned earlier, a critique within justice itself, insofar and as part of its own recognition of its limitations. This is "the very excellence of democracy, whose fundamental liberalism corresponds to the ceaseless deep remorse of justice, legislation always unfinished, always resumed, a legislation open to the better."[27] And there is a critique from the individual who criticizes the state and seeks, insofar as he or she can, to respond to particular others with concern and humanity. The point of both forms of critique is to expose where justice and the state fail to serve the particularity of each person and those persons who are often neglected or ignored—the poor, the stranger, minorities, and the destitute.[28]

In other terms, it makes a difference on what foundation that state is built and in terms of which it is constructed and shaped. Levinas does not develop a political theory regarding how political authority arises and how political obligation is derived from a ground of normativity. But he does believe that the state organizes human conduct and hence that its character is determined by what is the point or significance of human life. In short, as he says on several occasions, "it is then not without importance to know if the egalitarian and just State in which man is fulfilled ... proceeds from a war of all against all, or from the irreducible responsibility of the one for all, and if it can do without friendships and faces."[29] In the course of the interviews with Philippe Nemo, published as *Ethics and Infinity*, Levinas makes the same point; he puts it in terms of what limits what: "Does the social, with its institutions, universal forms and laws, result from limiting the consequences of the war between men, or from limiting the infinity which opens in the ethical relationship of man to man?" He glosses this question by describing such a limitation as politics being "checked and criticized starting from the ethical."[30]

Annabel Herzog is right to focus on these formulations.[31] Levinas should be understood as holding that political institutions, policies, and conduct must be evaluated and criticized in terms of how well or how poorly they take seriously and facilitate our basic social normativity, our responsibilities to respect and act in behalf of the rights of others. One of the challenges facing anyone trying to make sense of these matters in Levinas's thinking is to spell out, with some sense of concreteness and precision, how this process might work. That is a project for us to take

up in subsequent chapters. It is sufficient to note that it is a process that
is best carried out within liberal democracies, and although Levinas,
early in his career, was critical of liberalism, he later came to endorse it
regularly and for very specific reasons.[32]

Levinas, that is, argues that the best forms of political regime are
liberal states and democracies.[33] They have two features that he believes
are essential to states that are expressive of the deep ethical character of
human existence. First, they seek to be just—that is, to protect human
rights; and second they are aware of the limitations or imperfections of
the justice they accomplish. Such regimes are organized so that they are
open to revision; they know that they can always be better than they
are, that their justice can always be more just.[34] Critique of both kinds
is essential to such revision, to the order of justice becoming better and
better. Furthermore, liberal democracies leave room for humane and
caring conduct by individuals, as well as altering their programs and
policies to be more just and humane.[35] To clarify these two dimensions,
in one place, Levinas makes note of the role of elections in this respect,
and in another he focuses on the special role of human rights in liberal
states as an indication of their effort to care for others.[36] The role of
elections is obvious; it is one way that democratic governments express
critique and undergo change. Moreover, it is founded on the fact that
the plurality of demands of other people requires representation and
the institutions of representation. As Levinas says in "Diachrony and
Representation," where he introduces institutions, courts, and political
organization as dimensions of the "order of rationality," "This [plurality
of other persons] is the call to re-presentation that ceaselessly covers over
the nakedness of the face, giving it content and composure in a world."[37]
In one sense, "representation" here means conscious cognitive depiction
in ideas, thoughts, and statements, but in another, it means the kind of
representation we associate with elections of delegates to a congress or
parliament. Both the election of such representatives and their deliberations about matters of policy and law are constitutive of the democratic
process of seeking justice and modifying laws and policies to achieve
that justice.[38]

By the discourse of human rights, I take Levinas to mean that the
language of human rights marks off domains of need that make claims

on us all—food, shelter, security and protection, opportunities for self-expression and productivity, a healthy environment, medical care, and more. To be sure, there may be a tendency to treat human rights as matters of protecting *ourselves* from harm and intrusion and therefore as focused on freedom and individual self-expression. But Levinas takes rights differently. He thinks of them as signs of domains of dependency, and primarily he thinks of others as having rights toward us. The real subject of human rights is each and every person as the *other* person vis-á-vis each of us; they are claims that others make of each of us. To protect and respect the rights of others is to express our concern for them.[39]

ETHICS AND POLITICS IN THE REAL WORLD

In the legal and juridical world, governed by considerations of justice, there is still room for mercy and humanity, for a very particular response to the claims of the other person—given his or her state of mind and conduct. Repentance is not an excuse for committing a crime, but it does make a difference—or it can. The ethical dimension of our lives provides us with an ideal or standard in terms of which social and political critique can take place, by citizens as members of the state or even agents of its institutions and by individuals as radical critics. But what, in practice, might this mean? What kind of critique? What kind of difference would mark a Levinasian critique and distinguish it from other forms of critique—liberal critique based on a rights discourse and others? As Levinas himself puts it, as I have said, it is of some importance that our social and political institutions are founded on charity and responsibility and not on a war of all against all. Justice and the state are necessary not in order to limit natural cruelty or violence, but rather to express and realize mercy and concern for others in our social lives.[40] But, we might ask, of what importance is it? What is omitted by a Hobbesian picture? What does it fail to see and to attend to? What is left out, as Herzog puts it? What does Levinas have in mind?[41]

To conclude, let me point to a mode of critique with which we might usefully compare what Levinas has in mind, if only in broad outline.

Levinas's conception of ethical critique, as we might call it, is similar to what Avishai Margalit calls a critique based on issues of honor, decency, and the avoidance of humiliation.[42] Margalit distinguishes between evaluating a society in terms of how just it is and judging it in terms of how effectively it avoids humiliating its own citizens and others.[43] Justice is about fairness, impartiality, and equal treatment, while decency is a matter of self-respect and the avoidance of humiliation. In a sense, justice requires that we not show special favor to individuals, while decency tells us to pay attention to the other person's worth or value as the particular person he or she is.[44] Injustice involves doing injury by failing to treat someone fairly, while humiliation involves another kind of injury by failing to treat someone with respect so that he or she feels humiliated. Levinas's commitment to the primacy of responsibility to others may share substantive features with Margalit's interest in decency and the avoidance of humiliation, but what interests me here is their formal similarities. In a sense, Levinas and Margalit are interested in how a society can be judged by something that is different from and perhaps deeper than the justice of its institutions. As both seek to expose this dimension that is beyond justice, I think the greatest difference between Margalit's conception and Levinas's is that for the latter, it is the needs of others and their dependency on us that matter most to us and make us infinitely responsible to and for others, while for Margalit the emphasis is not positive but negative. For him, the decent society treats people with respect, where this carries the special meaning of avoiding humiliation—treating others as less than human and in a degrading manner. Such avoidance means not doing others extreme injury or harm of special kinds.[45] Levinas warns us never to let justice prevent us from treating individuals with a very particular sense of concern and responsibility. Margalit also warns that we ought never allow justice to seem sufficient or to distract us from treating others with appropriate respect. For him, as important as it is to be fair and even-handed, it is equally if not more important not to act toward others in such a way that they feel humiliated and degraded by how they are treated—even if that treatment is just.[46] As we turn to Levinas's comments on Zionism and the State of Israel, then, we are looking for something akin to Margalit's style of critique, a mode of critique that does not ignore justice but turns on other, and for Levinas deeper, considerations for judging the state's conduct and policies.[47]

In this book I have begun the process of clarifying how Levinas distinguishes between ethics and politics and how he understands their interrelationship. Our existence, complex and social, has both of these dimensions, and they are mutually interdependent. Nonetheless, our ethical responsibilities to one another make demands on us that enable and justify both institutional and extra-institutional critique of our political institutions in the narrow sense. What this means, as Levinas says in a famous remark in the discussion following his paper "Transcendence and Height" in 1962, is that there are tears that the civil servant cannot see.[48] In one sense, insofar as the civil servant represents the order or domain of justice, the political order, he or she simply cannot attend to such tears. They are outside his purview. In another sense, however, they are tears of particular persons, each with his or her particular needs and concerns, worries and suffering, that need to be and ought to be seen. It is one purpose of the ethical critique of political institutions to disclose those tears and to see to it that a way is found to see them and respond to them—with humanity and concern. This disclosure is not only the job of critique; it is also what makes our societies and our civil institutions humane and caring settings in which to live.

Levinas believes that there is a general need for the ethical critique of political practices. But, given his distinctive views about Judaism and about Zionism, the need for such critique is especially strong with regard to the Jewish state. In the next chapter, I will turn to this subject and the controversies that have swirled around Levinas's engagement with it.

TWO

JUDAISM, ZIONISM, AND THE STATE OF ISRAEL

In two places in his writings on Zionism, Levinas comments on concrete historical events in Israel's career.[1] One is the visit of Anwar Sadat to Jerusalem and the Knesset in 1977 and the subsequent treaty between Israel and Egypt, and the second is the massacre in the refugee camps Sabra and Shatila in 1982, at the end of the Lebanon War, and the Israeli response to those events. Briefly put, Levinas praises Sadat's action as an extraordinary ethical gesture that transcends normal political conduct and led to a diplomatic event of major significance. With regard to the complicity in the massacres in Lebanon, although it has not been altogether clear to everyone, he appears to remain silent regarding the victims of the massacres but explicitly applauds the Israeli call for a board of inquiry and for those responsible to be held accountable.[2] These are two occasions, then, on which Levinas comments and that call for some kind of ethical judgment regarding political conduct.

Levinas's understanding of Zionism and the State of Israel and these two moments of critical comment are intrinsically interesting. But my purpose is not to explore them in order to clarify the Jewish dimension of Levinas's thought. Rather it is to use these two incidents as evidence or illustrations of how he thinks the human condition as fundamentally ethical is related, as a ground of critique, to our political lives. What, in short, do Levinas's comments on Zionism tell us about how ethics is related to political conduct and institutions?

Zionism means many things, among them a historical movement that dates from the nineteenth century and sought to establish a modern Jewish state as a Jewish homeland. Zionism is also a variety of ideological views that were invoked, in one way or another, by those involved in the historical movement to establish a modern Jewish state and that continue to be the primary set of political views of many Israeli citizens about their own state. Levinas takes the ethical dimension of our existence as social beings to provide a ground of critique in terms of which our everyday decisions and conduct can be judged; it also provides the ground for political critique of any and all political regimes, of which the State of Israel as a Zionist regime is one. In this sense, our infinite responsibilities to others and the caring for others, what Levinas at times calls charity or love, can result in a direct critique of the State of Israel. But according to Levinas this teaching—that as human beings we are infinitely responsible one for another—is central to Jewish texts and Jewish tradition; it is the core of what it means to be Jewish. For this reason, the ethical dimension of human existence also results in an indirect critique of the State of Israel, for it provides a standard for judging how well or how poorly that state is a Jewish state. As a political philosophy, that is, Zionism or whatever is the dominant or determinative political view of the State of Israel should incorporate the central Jewish teaching that all human existence ought to be shaped by our responsibilities toward others. The State of Israel, then, is subject both to direct and indirect ethical critique. Moreover, insofar as one of its founding grounds is the Jewish people's protection and security, a ground rooted in various forms of anti-Semitism and then in an overwhelming way by the Nazi extermination program and the Holocaust, the State of Israel will necessarily give rise to tragic problems concerning its responsibilities and concern for its own security and well-being and also the security and well-being of others whom it has displaced and dislocated. The tension between a people's accomplishing its own security and protection and its serving the needs and respecting the rights of other peoples with whom its own project may come into conflict is a frequent, if not ubiquitous, feature of modern states and their growth, development, and change. These overall conditions are the background for Levinas's remarks about two incidents in the State of Israel's political history.

These two moments of critique, however, can only be understood against the background of Levinas's understanding of Zionism, which in turn is grounded in his view of Judaism. Levinas, in the early 1950s, takes Jewish identity to involve a sense of responsibility for others; this is the view of the Bible, the Talmud, and of other sources such as Rabbi Hayyim of Volozhin, the disciple of the Vilna Gaon, who wrote, in his *Nefesh Ha-Hayyim*, that the Jew is responsible for the whole of creation. Moreover, this same identity is "expressed in a more tolerable way by Zionism," even if it runs the risk of "becoming confused with nationalism."[3]

Perhaps the early essay that best clarifies what Levinas thinks about Zionsim and its relation to Judaism is a piece from 1951, "The State of Israel and the Religion of Israel."[4] It is a review of a collection of articles by Israeli authors on religion and the state. In it Levinas makes note of a conflict between Judaism, concerned as it is with justice, and the modern state, with its emphasis on human freedom, leisure, and security. Furthermore, modern states, with their universality of purpose and function, have contributed to the decline of particular religions, for while religions are particular and clerical, the state is universal and humanistic. Given this situation, what is the special role of the State of Israel for Judaism? Levinas's answer has two parts. First, he views Judaism in his own particular way: in Judaism the "belief in God [does not] incite one to justice—it *is* the institution of that justice." Moreover, this justice is not an "abstract principle" but rather "the possibility for a man to see the face of an other." In short, Levinas interprets religious language so that it in fact points to the face-to-face as human responsibility and the justice that issues from it. Second, the State of Israel "finally offers the opportunity to carry out the social law of Judaism. . . . [Until now] it was horrible to be both the only people to define itself with a doctrine of justice, and to be the meaning incapable of applying it." He calls this the "heartbreak and the meaning of the Diaspora." After centuries of statelessness, without the opportunity to realize its special purpose, to apply its sensibility for justice, now, in the twentieth century, there is the opportunity to do so. Levinas summarizes this role and this justification for what Zionism means when he says that "the contrast is between those who seek to have a State in order to have justice and those who seek justice in order to ensure the survival of the State."[5] That is, "justice is the *raison d'être* of the State: that is religion."[6]

From this early date, then, Levinas believes regarding Zionism that ethics and politics are related as a founding ideal of justice and the reality in which that ideal needs to be implemented. This conception, as he realizes, is a form of Platonism, but it is a realistic Platonism, realistic both because he thinks that it can be realized and because he thinks that the ideal of justice is not an abstract or otherworldly ideal. Rather it is a dimension of our social lives that is always present in the real world and yet must be cultivated, disclosed, and become operative, as it were, as the guiding standard for political life. This is the very precise task of Zionism, to put the laws of justice into practice, to construct a just state. There is no other reason for Zionism, no other justification.[7] All the rest is mythology—or politics, that is, a matter of self-protection or survival. Hence, to the degree that Zionism addresses this task, it is genuine and serious; to the degree that it ignores that task or fails at it, Zionism is a distortion and irresponsible. Levinas seems serious about such judgments. Zionism receives no blanket endorsement from him; like any political regime, it can succeed or fail to one degree or another. And Zionism has not always succeeded; it risks lapsing into a mere "political event."[8]

These critical judgments about Zionism do not diminish the importance of the State of Israel in Levinas's eyes. In a paper from the late 1960s, Levinas could say that "the State of Israel . . . constitutes the greatest event in modern Judaism" in the sense that it provides the Jewish people with a flesh-and-blood, real opportunity to sacrifice itself to its destiny, to put its commitment to responsibility and justice into practice.[9] Levinas calls this "dying for an idea," making national sovereignty into moral sovereignty, and taking the risk that comes with it.[10] The early Zionists had a dream; they faced "desert and swamp" and dreamed of "milk and honey."[11] Levinas acknowledges and appreciates how much the ideal or the destiny of Zionism has adjusted to reality and must face all that this adjustment has meant. As a state, Israel has been "reduced to political categories." "Its builders found themselves abruptly on the side of the colonialists. Israel's independence was called imperialism, the oppression of native peoples, racism."[12] Levinas is disturbed by this. He is critical of all the material prosperity, the luxuries and hedonism, the indulgence and more. But all this he calls "carnal Israel," and he weighs it against the real purpose of Jewish identity, to take the reins of government and to create a just and humane society to the degree that it can.

The final section of the collection *Beyond the Verse*, entitled "Zionisms," includes three essays that deal with this task and this challenge.[13] In the foreword to the volume, Levinas describes the subtle and intimate connection he sees between ancient themes and current, modern realities. He makes these points: First,

> the three studies grouped together under the title "Zionisms" aim merely to show how the historical work of the State, which it is not possible to do without in the extremely politicized world of our time, a work of courage and labour which claims to be secular, is impregnated in Israel, from the beginning, and progressively, with young thoughts, but thoughts which issue from the Bible; how the continuation and development of this biblical culture showed itself to be inseparable from the temporal ends of the State, and extended beyond those ends.[14]

This connection between the central teaching of biblical culture—responsibility and justice—and the institutions and policies of the modern state is unbreakable. The State of Israel is about the humanity of man, as Levinas puts it. He calls this "Israel's unrepentant eschatology," an odd expression for some, so unabashedly religious and messianic.[15] That is, the historical work of the Jewish state is to be Jewish, which is to be just and humane, and this is what it means to feel and be responsible for the future one hopes to exist for others, all others.

Levinas's second point is that this aspiration, this central justifying commitment, is sorely threatened by "the conflict between Israel and the Palestinians or Israel and the Arabs." "It is," he admonishes, "time to take the heat out of such adversity."[16] Could Levinas be more explicit that the conflict that has been and continues to be so enflamed and so horrific is incompatible with the heart of Zionism and the heart of Judaism? Could he be more specific that the goal of Israel must be peace and that peace is "inseparable from the recognition of the other in the love of one's neighbor taught by the Scriptures?" And here he points at the Jews who utterly confuse the election of the Jewish people with pride and misplaced self-righteousness: "Is being chosen a scandal of pride and of the will to power, or is it moral conscience itself which, made up of responsibilities that are always urgent and non-transferable, is the first to respond, as if it were the only one to be called?"[17] The Palestinians are indeed the responsibility of Israel; similarly all that has befallen the Jewish people is an Arab responsibility. Both sides must acknowledge this and each other. In 1981, when this foreword was written, Levinas affirms what he had written in 1963, prior to the Six-Day War and the Yom Kippur War: a call for the Arab peoples to recognize Israel as a Jewish state and a conviction that Israel would respond with "brotherly zeal" toward the Palestinian people. Israel needs the recognition of the Arab world, and the fundamental idea of "political Zionism . . . is the necessity for the Jewish people, in peace with its neighbours, not to continue being a minority in its political structure." This, he says, is a "historical necessity" to prevent the "attack and murder of Jews in the world."[18] He implies, but does not say, that other nations, the Arab nations included, must respect that necessity and the reasons for it, but at the same time Israel must recognize the needs of its Palestinian neighbors.

Still, he ends on this note about what the Arab world must recognize as Israel's responsibility to her own citizens and people, and he defends this concern against those who might argue that his view of responsibility to and for the other might make no room for such a thing:

> I think of the last words of the verse from Genesis 30:30: "Now when shall I provide for my own household also?" In the biblical context they can mean neither that a self vowed, of itself, to others, is making a simple and sharp claim for its own interests, nor that the essential structure of the self is being denied. I think that in the responsibility for others prescribed by a non-archaic monotheism it reminds us that it should not be forgotten that *my* family and *my* people, despite the possessive pronouns, are my "others," like strangers, and demand justice and protection. The love of the other—the love of one's neighbour. Those near to me are also my neighbours.[19]

Responsibility, the face-to-face, is who I am; it is my selfhood toward each and every other. This responsibility must be as aware of the needs and vulnerabilities of those close to the self as it is of the needs and vulnerabilities of those who are not, indeed of one's enemies. Simply because someone is a friend or a spouse or a cousin does not mean that they are not an other person. This is not self-interest, Levinas says; it is acknowledging need when the need is urgent and help is deserved. Of course, this deep sense of responsibility toward one's own people does have consequences. As I indicated earlier, it is the sense of urgency about this need for protection and security for the Jewish people that, together with a historical claim to a specific land, has brought with it the tragedy and the conflict between the State of Israel and the Palestinian people.

The litmus test—certainly one litmus test—for a just and humane society and state with a religious or ethnic majority that is organized around the priority of that majority is how it deals with minorities within. There are many varieties of democratic states currently in existence in the world, and only one aims at being impartial in its constitutional and legal rights and privileges, that is, the United States. All the others have a place for a privileged group or collectivity, a state religion or ethnic group. Israel is one of those. And in Israel's case, the status of women, non-Haredi Jews, migrant workers, Mizrahi Jews, and Arab citizens is problematic, as is the relation between Israel itself and its Arab neighbors. The conflicts between Israel and the Palestinians are well-known, if not in detail at least in general. And the same holds for conflicts between Israel and certain of her Arab neighbors—Iran, Syria, Lebanon, and Egypt among them. This is the general theme that Levinas addresses in "Politics After!," which appeared in *Les Temps modernes* in 1979. The specific event that stimulated Levinas's reflections was the visit of Anwar Sadat of Egypt to Jerusalem on November 19, 1977, an event that Levinas takes to be of momentous significance and that he considers heroic and courageous. It gives him an opportunity to comment on a decisive political action and to evaluate it in terms of its importance for the prospects of peace, in this case for peace between Israel and her Arab neighbors.

What, then, is the significance of Sadat's trip? Levinas is unrestrained in his praise: "His trip has probably been the exceptional transhistorical event that one neither makes nor is contemporaneous with twice in a lifetime." Why? What did Sadat's trip make possible? What kind of an act was it? Levinas says, "For a moment, political standards and clichés were forgotten, along with all the deceitful motives that a certain wisdom attributes even to the gesture of a man who transcends himself and raises himself above his cautiousness and precautions."[20] He then asks what Sadat understood about Zionism; did he see behind the imputed imperialism and the apparent militarism? And did he understand "the opportunities opened up through friendship with Israel—or simply through already recognizing its existence and entering into talks—and all the prophetic promises that are hidden behind the Zionist claim to historical rights and its contortions under the political yoke?" What should we make of these passages? They could mean that Levinas takes Sadat's gesture, his trip, to have defied personal wariness and political judgments about its negative political repercussions. That is, he could mean that Sadat himself acted on ethical and moral motives, reaching out to Israel in friendship, in defiance of his Arab colleagues. He does, after all, ask what Sadat understood about Israel and what opportunities presented themselves. On the other hand, Levinas could mean that whatever Sadat's own motives, it is possible—easy?—to forget or set aside political principles and questions about whether Sadat acted honestly or not and to interpret his action as grand and important, as an audacious and bold act. With regard to Sadat's state of mind, Levinas is not wholly clear or committal. Cynically, he could be claiming only that we can understand his action morally; generously, he could be saying that Sadat himself saw in Israel "a State which will have to incarnate the prophetic moral code and the idea of its peace" and sought to reach out to her.[21] On either reading, however, Levinas makes the point that the trip, as a gesture toward Israel and reconciliation with her, "opened up the unique path for peace in the Near East, if this peace is to be possible at all." In other words, the gesture expresses the claim that "peace is a concept which goes beyond purely political thought."[22] There is political peace, the cessation of war and conflict, and there is a deeper, ethical peace, a fraternal sense of community, of mutual recognition, respect, and concern.[23]

What does Levinas's assessment of the importance of Sadat's trip tell us about the relation between ethics and politics? On the one hand, Levinas emphasizes that Zionism makes possible political opportunities for Judaism, and these must be to implement her sense of prophetic morality—understood in terms of Levinas's conception of Judaism as an austere humanism—and hence to create institutions and laws whose purpose is the just and humane treatment of everyone. On the other hand, Levinas does distinguish between ethical or spiritual motives and political or prudential ones. There are political acts and ethical ones. Sadat's action can be understood as a political error, or it can be seen as a bold moral gesture. That is, the evaluation of Sadat is ambivalent about how to treat the ethics-politics relationship. Politics can be viewed as a deficient mode of conduct; it can also be viewed as necessary and unavoidable. If deficient, one ought to aspire to transcend it; if necessary, one ought to aim at the most humane and just political practices possible.

If my reading of Levinas's essay is correct, then on either reading of ethics and politics, ethics must be implemented and acted upon to the greatest degree possible. Ethics should either replace politics or correct it. In either case, ethics is relevant and significant; ethical responsibility is normatively primary. One ought always seek to determine what responsibilities to others are most compelling and require the greatest attention one can provide, and this applies personally and collectively, to one's society as a whole.

Let me now turn to the famous interview following the massacres at Sabra and Shatila. There may be no more controversial comments associated with Emmanuel Levinas than his remarks during a radio interview, broadcast on Radio Communauté on September 28, 1982, in the wake of the massacres in the refugee camps in West Beirut. The interview was conducted by Shlomo Malka, and the interviewees were Levinas and Alain Finkielkraut. A transcript was published in *Les Nouveaux Cahiers*, but its notoriety, certainly for English-speaking audiences, was accelerated by the publication of an English translation, included by Seán Hand in his *The Levinas Reader*, published in 1989.[24]

The massacre occurred over four days, September 15–18, 1982, and resulted in the slaughter of Palestinian and Lebanese men, women, and children, numbering anywhere from eight hundred to several thousand.[25] Ariel Sharon and the Israeli military had asked the Christian militiamen to clear out PLO terrorists and Palestinian guerillas from the camps, although there was a long-standing hatred between the Phalangist Christians and the Muslim occupants of the camps. By Friday, September 17, it was known by Israeli military officials that a slaughter was under way, but the Phalangists were permitted to remain until Saturday morning, and the massacre continued. No distinction was made between guerilla fighters, women, children, and the elderly.

In response to the efforts of Menachem Begin to dismiss charges of Israeli complicity in the massacres, a number of peace movements, Peace

Now (Shalom Achshav) in particular, organized a massive rally in Tel Aviv on September 25. It was estimated that 350,000 to 400,000 people gathered in the plaza before City Hall in Tel Aviv. The rally was reported to have been the largest in Israeli history, and in the course of the many speeches given, there were calls for the establishment of a board of inquiry into responsibility for the events and numerous cries for Begin and Sharon to resign.[26] By September 28 Begin had in fact appointed a board of inquiry under the leadership of the chief justice of the Supreme Court, Yitzhak Kahan. By this time, Thomas Friedman had (on September 25) published a long and detailed article in the *New York Times* on the details of the four-day massacre, and on that same day reports of the Tel Aviv rally were widely circulated.

This was the situation when Malka, Finkielkraut, and Levinas met for their radio interview. It was less than two weeks after the massacres had occurred. Begin's resistance and the internal criticisms of him and his government in Israel were known, and reports were widespread of the massive rally in Tel Aviv. The board of inquiry was appointed that very day.[27]

In his influential book *Levinas and the Political*, Howard Caygill argues that on the critical issue Levinas is silent. That critical issue is the Israeli treatment of Palestinians, in this case Palestinian refugees living in the camps. Does Levinas or does he not condemn the Israeli military, which introduced Phalangists into the camps purportedly to clear out fedayeen and then looked on and allowed the slaughter of hundreds of Palestinians and Lebanese Shiites, of being complicit in the massacre?

Levinas's first comment is that upon hearing about the massacre, our response is one of having a sense of responsibility toward the victims. He does emphasize that this response comes whether or not one is guilty. Responsibility is prior to any determination of who is guilty and who is innocent and independent of who are the guilty parties. Each of us is responsible for each and every other person, and therefore when there is such suffering and horror, each of us should feel responsible. Now this may seem to avoid the issue of guilt and hence the issue of indicting the Israeli military for its part in the slaughter, but it is surely no more than an effort to try to set the stage, so to speak, and to point out that any judgment about innocence or guilt must be grounded on this point of view, the perspective of unlimited individual responsibility for each and every other person.

Levinas's next point—this time in response to Alain Finkielkraut—is to point to the fact that the majority of Israeli Jews felt this responsibility and articulated it, expressed it. They did this by marching in the streets and by calling for a board of inquiry. Levinas calls this an "ethical reaction." Moreover, it is hard not to take Levinas's response as an *endorsement* of that reaction, even though he continues, at this point, to talk about the Israeli response and not his own.

When taken to extremes, Levinas then says, ethics and politics are contradictory. At least part of what this means is that there are times when the political conduct of a state, to defend itself and maintain security, reaches moral limits. This is not, Levinas says, an abstract or philosophical issue; it arises in lived experience, and, he notes, this situation in the refugee camps in Lebanon may be one of those moments that mark such a limit. To me, these remarks are clearly an expression of Levinas's judgment that the events at Sabra and Shatila constitute a moment when political expediency and political conduct, typically organized for order and deterrence and defense, are put into question. Here moral considerations, and this means considerations about what each of us owes others, intercede or interrupt the everyday, normal political fabric and tear it apart. The political comes under a judgment of where it has failed, where it leads to suffering and atrocities and deserves to be criticized and where the agency, the military at least, deserves censor and criticism. Hundreds of thousands of Israelis made this point through their actions; they were not tempted to avoid taking responsibility but accepted it and acted on it by calling for a board of inquiry that would take the military and the government to task.

It is not much later in the interview, however, that Shlomo Malka initiates the most controversial exchange. He charges Levinas to answer whether or not the enemy, the Palestinians, do not deserve special attention, since for Israelis they are the most other, politically speaking. Here Levinas makes a central point, and it is indeed a conceptual one about his way of thinking. He notes that he is using the expression "other" in a different sense from Malka. For him, the other is the neighbor, and this expression refers no less to someone close to you, one's family or kin, than it does to those far from you or even opposed to you, a threat to you.

All these are others; indeed, every other person is the other to whom and for whom one is responsible. "Neighbor" does not refer to *everyday* proximity. It does not necessarily mean those who are not in your community or group; it is not only the "widow, the stranger, and the orphan."[28] Levinas here puts it this way: "The other is the neighbour, who is not necessarily kin, but who can be." Earlier, in response to Finkielkraut, he had said "my people and my kin are still my neighbours."[29] The point is the same. We should not confuse the everyday, historical, or political use of the expression "other," where it might be taken to refer to those outside one's group and most of all one's enemies, and the ethical meaning, where it refers to all those other than the self and hence all to whom and for whom one is responsible, including those near to you. In the political sense, otherness may come in degrees; in the ethical sense, it does not.

To me, then, the point of Levinas's comments in this interview is that ethics and politics, in the narrow sense, can come into conflict, and when they do, the ethical should take priority. As Finkielkraut—correctly in my view—interprets Levinas's comments, "We're now witnessing a passionate examination of the contradictions between ethics and politics, and of the necessity, that is both vital and almost impossible, of conforming the demands of collective action to fundamental ethical principles."[30] Levinas underscores this summary when he says, "Ethics will never, in any lasting way, be the good conscience of corrupt politics—the immediate reactions we've witnessed these last few days prove it; and transgression of ethics made 'in the name of ethics' is immediately perceived as a hypocrisy and as a personal offense."[31] I would contend that Levinas is being very clear here that any attempt to defend the Israeli army's action and to justify it would constitute this kind of "hypocrisy" and "offense." If the political and military decisions are flawed and even horrific, there can be no ethical justification for them. Moreover, this is the judgment of the majority of Israelis themselves and one that Levinas himself shares. It is expressed in the call for a governmental board of inquiry that will make clear who was responsible for the massacres in the refugee camps and who should be punished for their part in the events that took place.

I am not sure what critics of Levinas expect of him in such a situation. To be sure, acknowledging and endorsing a general sentiment of responsibility and making a judgment of the Israeli military's culpability are not, in and of themselves, an expression of compassion or sympathy for the victims of the massacres. Nor does Levinas, anywhere in this interview, articulate explicitly such compassion or sympathy with the Palestinian people.[32] But Levinas's conception of the ethical is about responsibility, acceptance, and concern; it is not by itself about compassion or mercy as feelings or reactive emotions. It is an ethical matter and not a psychological one. And in this particular interview, he chooses to focus on how the Israeli reaction to the massacres is itself an expression of how the ethical and the political come into conflict and how the ethical must take priority. In short, Levinas focuses on Israel and her citizens and not on the victims of the slaughter. His decision is a point worth making and underscoring.[33] Even if there were military and political reasons for standing by and permitting the Phalangist slaughter, such complicity deserves and received moral censor and outrage, both within and outside of Israel itself.

What is true of those events might very well be true too of many moments in the Israeli treatment of the Palestinian inhabitants of Gaza and the West Bank and indeed of Arab Israelis and others. Ethics can never be the "good conscience of corrupt politics," as Levinas put it. For him, ethics involves always being sensitive to the needs of the other person, even when carrying out policies and programs that appear to have overall justifications but lead to injury, suffering, and humiliation. At times, there will not appear to be any question that the policies or conduct is or has been wrong; at other times, not all will see this. But for Levinas the determining considerations must always turn on how individual persons are treated as part of the program or conduct and hence how effectively such policies or conduct express our responsibilities to others in all their particularity.[34] For Zionism and for Israel, politics is never enough, nor is the land—with its stones and wood; more is needed, and that more is responding to others with concern and respect.

Few agree with me about Levinas's responses. Howard Caygill's critical remarks on Levinas's comments in this interview are among the most complete and most harsh that we have. Let me focus on what Caygill says about Levinas's response to Malka's question about the Palestinians and whether they are, as the enemies of Israel, the most other and hence, by implication, deserving of the most concerned acceptance and aid. He describes Levinas's answer this way: "Faced with this un-avoidable question that went to the heart not only of his philosophy but also of his political judgment, Levinas's reply is chilling and, to use his idiom, opens a wound in his whole œuvre."[35] He then quotes Levinas's reply, which we have discussed above. Caygill's terms raise a number of questions. Why exactly should we—and Levinas—take Malka's ques-tion to go "to the heart not only of his philosophy but also of his political judgment"? And why is Levinas's reply "chilling"? Does it in fact "open a wound" in his entire project? What follows in Caygill's account can only impress the reader as a cascade of confusions and errors, all aimed at vilifying Levinas for his response.

Caygill does in fact see what Levinas is saying in the first words of his response, but he then makes a crucial mistake. He realizes that Levinas is distinguishing here between the ethical other and the political other or "between empirical and transcendental others," as he puts it. And he sees the possibility that Levinas is referring in his response to the empirical other, what I would call the political other, or other persons in everyday experience. He calls this an "apologetic response" and suggests instead that "a harder thought is that Levinas's claim is rigorously consistent with his philosophy."[36] He says this, he argues, because Levinas must accept the inevitability of war. But what does he mean by "rigorously consistent"? And what are we to make of this criticism?

As we have observed, Levinas's answer is composed of two parts. In the first, he calls attention to what he means by confronting the face of the other person and that the other person here is the ethical other, or the other who makes a claim on me and to whom and for whom I am responsible. In the second part, however, he introduces the third party, and this means that we are in the regime of justice, as he calls it, in the domain of ordinary life. Here the other person is classified, thematized, compared, and such. This is clearly the everyday self, what Caygill calls "the empirical self." It is as certain as can be that here Levinas is in fact talking about such others, everyday others. Only here are there enemies; only here is there any question of degrees of responsibility and justice, and so forth. When Caygill argues that to be "rigorously consistent" Levinas would have to be talking in this second stage about the transcen-dental or ethical other, he is simply distorting not only what Levinas says here but also his overall thinking. Caygill worries who is the neighbor and who is attacking whom. But this is completely clear; indeed can there be any doubt? When your neighbor attacks another neighbor and even acts unjustly—when as a Jew, he sees Israelis attacking Palestinians or vice versa—then there is the issue of who is a friend, who an enemy, who is just, and who unjust. That is, all such discriminations and classifications are matters of how in everyday life the plurality of our social situation occurs and how the various parties, all of whom one is responsible for and to, engage with one another. This is simply an articulation of what Levinas says in more abstract terms in *Otherwise Than Being* and in essays like "Peace and Proximity."[37] All of Caygill's questions, the intent of which seem to be to make what is clear confused and unclear, lead to the suggestion that the Palestinian is not an other at all or is not the Israeli's other nor indeed the Jew's other. This indictment, which is wholly incoherent, is made by Judith Butler when she charges Levinas with saying that the Palestinian has no face. For Levinas, however, while it is one thing to say that in everyday life we act toward particular people with greater or lesser responsibility, it is another to say that there are particular others toward whom we have no responsibility at all, and this latter is impossible in Levinas's view of human social relations and human existence. Drawing such a conclusion, then, should be a reductio of Caygill's line of thinking and not a conclusion worthy of anyone's attention. For Levinas, everyone's relationship with each and every other person is one of responsibility but also one of claim and petition; we are all others in the ethical or transcendental sense.

Caygill's unwillingness to follow up on the clarity of the distinction between empirical and transcendental others, between ethical and political others, leads him to a further confusion. He next charges that the problem of knowing who is right or wrong, just or unjust simply "reduces ethics to the problem of knowledge." But this knowledge, he argues, must be ethical and not simply "of tactical or strategic utility." And if so, then it makes it that much harder, he says, "to identify in the other an enemy."[38] Once again, Caygill takes Levinas to be talking about the face-to-face as a transcendental structure, when, as we have seen, the course of the argument makes it clear that Levinas is talking about the everyday or political domain, where discriminating between friend and enemy, just and unjust, and so forth are made and where the important knowledge is about how to respond to others, what to judge and what to do, and not about "moral knowledge" of what right and wrong are in any everyday sense. In all cases in everyday affairs, what is just and unjust and so forth is a matter of judgment based on weighing responsibilities, resources, and a host of other situational considerations. Caygill takes Levinas to be utterly confused about the underlying or primordial structure that grounds moral normativity, but he is not. Levinas is very careful to distinguish it from the much more contextual judgments we make in everyday life and which, in this case, were made by the hundreds of thousands of Israelis who called for a board of inquiry and by doing so leveled an ethical charge against military and political conduct.

No commentator's criticisms of Levinas and what Levinas says about the treatment of other persons and what it means in a political setting, especially what it means for evaluating Zionism, have been more strident than those of Judith Butler. Consider, for example, Butler's infamous and widely discussed appropriation of Levinas in her anti-Zionist critique of Zionism.[39] Let me defer for a later chapter a detailed examination of Butler's reading of Levinas and focus here on the summary of her view in the introductory chapter to *Parting Ways: Jewishness and the Critique of Zionism*. Butler does see that for Levinas "we are bound to those we do not know, and did not choose, and . . . these obligations are, strictly speaking, precontractual." She glosses this claim as meaning that "Levinas . . . gave us a conception of ethical relations that make us ethically responsive to those who exceed our immediate sphere of belonging and to whom we nevertheless belong, regardless of any choice or contract."[40] This point is surely correct; it is what I have meant by saying that each of us is related to each and every other person as infinitely responsible. Butler then claims, however, that Levinas himself betrays his own principle by denying such relationships to members of certain groups. Utterly misreading passages from Levinas's writings, including the interview we just discussed about the massacres in Sabra and Shatila, she claims that Levinas restricts the face-to-face to those within the orbit of Western European culture, Judeo-Christian and Greco-Roman, as it were. Specifically, she claims that Levinas denies that the Palestinian has a face. Indeed, she goes on to argue, this is precisely where Hannah

Arendt is both similar to Levinas in principle and more consistent in detail, for Butler takes Arendt to say that "cohabitation is not a choice, but a condition of our political life," which Butler takes to mean what Levinas means by relating to all others in terms of the face-to-face.[41] But, in Butler's eyes, Arendt never "betrays" or qualifies the universality of this principle, and it lies behind her understanding of genocide and her opposition to the creation of nation-states that involves dispossession of existing populations. In short, Levinas leads Butler in the right direction but ultimately fails to be consistent; Arendt proves to be a more reliable and authentic guide.

But this is to misread Levinas's remarks and his writings as falling into parochialism with regard to the Palestinians in particular. It may be that there is a Eurocentricism to Levinas, but if this is true, it occurs at the level of everyday, historical and political judgments and conduct, and not at the transcendental or philosophical level. As we saw, in the interview with Finkielkraut, Levinas wanted to underline how different the political and ethical orders are from one another and how, when events bring them into conflict, the ethical must take priority. Rather than speak to any rejection or ignoring of the Palestinian refugees in the camps in Lebanon, this point underscores why Israelis and so many others had every reason to come to their defense and to charge with complicity the Israeli army. But such a judgment would have required careful deliberation about all the features of the events that were relevant to considering whose needs and whose rights were significant and what injuries were inflicted and in what ways. It is not hard to imagine what led Butler to such an a priori, uncharitable reading of Levinas and to such a positive one of Arendt. Surely it was her own sympathies for the Palestinian people and her inflammatory and highly critical attitude toward Zionism that led Butler to emphasize what she took to be Levinas's betrayal and Arendt's constancy.[42] But, as Seyla Benhabib has shown clearly and convincingly, Butler misreads what Arendt means by plurality, and as I have tried to make clear, her reading and appropriation of Levinas can only be seen as biased and unsympathetic.

Unlike Butler and Caygill, then, Levinas grasps the tragedy of the Israeli-Palestinian situation and yet will not abandon the State of Israel to unrealistic principles. He is unafraid to judge the state harshly for failures to meet its ethical responsibilities but at the same time to appreciate the unavoidability of its political foundations. His writings on Zionism, on the Jewish core of the State of Israel, on the legacy of Judaism, and on the ethical character of human existence all testify to these convictions.

Levinas, then, is a defender of the State of Israel and of Zionism, but he is also a critic, both of Israel as a state and of Israel as a Jewish state. In a review of several books on the State of Israel and Zionism, the political theorist Alan Wolfe distinguishes between those he calls "liberal critics" and those he calls "leftist critics." "Liberals," he says, "accept Israel's legitimacy, search for ways that it can respect the rights of its non-Jewish citizens, and believe that the only viable future for the country is a two-state solution, one primarily Jewish, the other primarily Palestinian." "Leftists," on the other hand, "view Israel's creation in 1948 as an outgrowth of European colonialism, insist that as a Jewish state its character is inevitably racist, and lean toward the eventual creation of one state containing both Jews and Arabs." To Wolfe, liberals include Gershom Gorenberg and Peter Beinart, and we might add others like Ruth Gavison and Chaim Gans.[43] As leftists he names Gabriel Piterberg and Judith Butler, and he might have included any number of anti- or post-Zionists. For a variety of reasons, it may not be easy to locate Levinas as a member of either camp or of any identifiable political group to the right or left of them. Clearly, he has a deep appreciation for the role that Zionism has played and ought to play both politically and ethically for Jews and for all humanity; he has high praise for its many achievements. But at the same time, he was aware of Israel's failings and of the challenges it has yet to meet in anything like a satisfactory way. However, he said little of detail about these matters, and this leaves us with a more complex task than simply locating him in a political cubbyhole. That task is to consider seriously the social, political, religious, and moral decisions that have been made within Israeli life, to reflect on the reasoning of advocates and critics alike, and only then to clarify how a Levinasian conception of the ethical responsibilities we have for one another might lead to judgments about these matters and in what ways such judgments might differ from those based on political considerations of a pragmatic or tactical kind or on liberal principles based on traditional conceptions of human rights and responsibilities.

Liberal criticisms of Israel's policies and practices toward the Palestinians are typically framed in terms of a rights discourse; Israel is
charged with infringing the human rights of Palestinians in the territories and of Arab Israelis and other minorities within Israel herself.[44] Here
I cannot turn to any particular cases to ask what a Levinasian critique
might look like; to do so would involve empirical and historical considerations that are now beyond our scope. But we can say two things about
how Levinasian considerations would lead to a distinctive response.

First, we should recall that Levinas does not eschew rights discourse,
but the critical point is what it means for him. The typical rights vocabulary, embedded in the Western political tradition, is oriented around the
protection of the individual's property and liberty; it is subject-oriented
and grounded in a conception of the primacy of the individual. The new
rights discourse, stemming from Grotius, Hobbes, Locke, and others, is
an expression of the idea of protection, and basic human rights are those
domains of the individual's life—her needs and interests and characteristics—that require universal and absolute protection from interference
and injury by others. For Levinas, on the other hand, such protections
and the subject's decisions and interests they guard are present but not
primary; prior to them are the needs we all have to live and flourish
and the very particular ways in which those needs call upon each and
every one of us to serve them, to be responsible for them. That is, as
I said above, Levinas takes rights language to express our infinite responsibilities to and for other persons. Only when the rights-protection
apparatus of the state is ordered so as to facilitate and implement interpersonal responsibilities is it fitting and legitimate. This is the first point
to remember in comparing Levinasian critique with that based on the
question of rights.[45]

The second point is that the protection of rights, like all institutions
and programs, always involves compromise. Rights discourse expresses
concerns at the everyday level, and so it applies to policies and practices
that are organized to treat others in general. In the case of human rights,
charges can be made that rights to equal treatment, to respect, to property or free speech, and so forth are being systematically infringed. For
Levinas, such systematic infringements can be understood as organized
failure to accept and care for particular other persons; it means that there

is generalized lack of respect and concern for others. At first glance, one might say that every such case deserves censor and critique. But this is not so. All laws, policies, and practices involve some level of negotiation and compromise regarding responsibilities to and for others and concern for them. In Levinasian language, there are many "neighbors," near and far, and one cannot act on all of one's infinite responsibilities to everyone. Every particular decision and action involves compromises, and every general program or policy projects such compromises over many cases and into the future. Simply because a particular other person is harmed by something we do or because a group of others are harmed by a policy we put into practice does not mean that the action or the policy is deserving of criticism and its agents deserving of censor or indictment. The question must be whether the particular action or the particular policy can or cannot be deemed to be acceptable and even desirable once the needs and interests and demands of all the relevant parties are considered. Determining this involves clarity of description, honesty, discrimination, and comparison, and an abiding interest in responding with respect and concern toward each and every person. For every action and every policy one should ask: Is this as close as I or we can come to acting toward others with the greatest responsibility—respect and concern—for each and every person involved in any way in what I am about to do or what we are about to prescribe? Could we find a better policy or perform a more humane and benevolent act? Could we be more responsive to the other's claim upon me? Furthermore, does this policy make room for opportunities to reach out to particular others, even while its general program requires that all of us stand at a distance from all others?[46] Privileging these sorts of questions, I would argue, may or may not yield the same results as asking whether a policy or conduct infringes the rights of a particular group; there is certainly no necessity that it will. What needs to be determined is what is positively accomplished and what opportunities for particular acts of "kindness or mercy or charity" remain open.[47] In Margalit's terms, can the procedures of justice permit us to avoid humiliation and disrespect?

We have seen that for Levinas, the best form of state is a liberal democracy. This ideal ought to be the political ideal of every society and hence of every nationality. It is doubly true of Zionism and the State of

Israel. We can easily see why. Such a state would protect rights and hence would acknowledge individual needs and the importance of addressing them; it would encourage taking responsibility for the lives and well-being of its citizens, treat others in a humane and sensitive way, insofar as that is possible, and do what it could to acknowledge the particular needs and suffering of its citizens. Moreover, such a state would be open to revision and change and would recognize its own "imperfection," its perfectability. This means several things: that a liberal democracy would always seek to revise laws and policies so that they are more and more just; that it would always be attentive to the particular needs and suffering of its citizens even when they are being treated fairly according to the laws of the state; and that it would recognize that even the best laws and policies treat citizens generically and not individually and hence that the state must make room for and even encourage acting in response to individual suffering and pain. It would seek to have just laws and aim at impartiality and fair treatment for all, even if it only approximated such a goal, and also to appreciate its intrinsic limitations regarding responding to individual need.

But Levinas takes Judaism as the ideology of the Jewish people to be specially attuned to recognizing all people's infinite responsibilities to one another and therefore to acting in humane and caring ways. It is in Judaism's interest to cultivate such an attitude on everyone's part, to encourage such conduct, and to create—when it has the opportunity—institutions and policies that are as considerate, humane, and benevolent as they can be. Moreover, it is especially in the interest of Judaism, when given the opportunity for territorial and political self-determination, to create a democratic and Jewish state.[48] That is what Levinas takes Zionism ideally to be, the movement to take that opportunity and hence to realize such a state to the greatest degree possible.[49] As early as 1951, but three years after the reestablishment of the Jewish state, Levinas said this as explicitly as one would want:

> The thing that is special about the State of Israel is not that it fulfils an ancient promise, or heralds a new age of material security (one that is unfortunately problematic), but that it finally offers the opportunity to carry out the social law of Judaism. The Jewish people craved their own land and their own State not because of the abstract independence which they desired, but because they could then finally begin the work of their lives. Up until now they had obeyed

the commandments, and later on they fashioned an art and a literature for themselves, but all these works of self-expression are merely the early attempts of an
overlong adolescence. The masterpiece has now finally come. All the same, it was
horrible to be both the only people to define itself with a doctrine of justice, and
to be the meaning incapable of applying it. The heartbreak and the meaning of
the Diaspora. . . .

   It is in this way that the political event is already outstripped. And ultimately,
it is in this way that we can distinguish those Jews who are religious from those
who are not. The contrast is between those who seek to have a State in order to
have justice and those who seek justice in order to ensure the survival of the
State.[50]

This is Levinas's Zionism: not about fulfilling ancient historical promises
or gaining material security, it is the quest for a just and humane society.
After a long adolescence spent without the resources to create and build
what it most desired, the Jewish people has arrived at its maturity, and
the Jewish state is—he says in 1951—its masterpiece. We are now more
than sixty years later. Could there be any doubt that Levinas today would
be less satisfied, less optimistic? Surely his conscience would temper
such adulation and praise. It would urge him to remind its citizens and
supporters that at risk is the core of the state's being, the very austere
humanism or difficult freedom that is the heart of Judaism itself and
indeed of all human experience.

PART TWO

Philosophical Articulation

THREE

THE THIRD PARTY

Transcendental Ethics and Realistic Politics

Suppose we take the human condition primarily to involve the self or subject, on the one hand, and the world, on the other. The philosophical project of articulating the structure of human experience would be the characterization of all the ways in which self and world are related and interrelated. If so, then there are surely going to be relations that account for the way the self is related to nonhuman constituents of the world—from sense perception, observation and analysis, belief, and knowledge to desire, various modes of appetite and aversion, and so forth. And there will also be a host of relations such as the physical ones (e.g., the subject is far from the object, near the object, to the left or right of it) and social and economic ones (e.g., the subject is the owner of the object, is the occupant of the object, is using the object, has just paid for the object). With regard to human beings in the world, too, there will be a complex set of relations and relationships—momentary or briefly continuing relations, such as the subject's being angry with another subject, and ongoing relationships, such as the subject's being the father or mother of the other subject or the teacher of the subject. Let us take Levinas to be aware of all of this and to include it within the broad domain of human experience, which he would take Heidegger to have called the being of Dasein, and we might call the domain of ordinary, everyday human existence. Levinas's distinctive claim is that an account of all of these aspects or dimensions of human relatedness to the world is by and large what we think of as our existence as natural beings, but it is incomplete and inadequate to characterize the totality of human experience. Something significant is here omitted, and it is what broadly we might call, after Wilfrid Sellars, the "space of reasons" or what we might refer to as the dimension of evaluative normativity, especially moral normativity. In *Otherwise Than Being*, with special reference to language, Levinas calls the former aspects of our natural existence "the Said," and he calls the dimension or aspect that brings with it or introduces into human existence this evaluative normativity and especially moral normativity "the Saying." The latter, of course, is the descendant of the face-to-face of Levinas's earlier writings, and it is what he has called the relation with "transcendence" and "enigma" and the relation with the infinite, the face, and so much else.[1]

Levinas's central task in *Otherwise Than Being* is to develop a clear and defensible account of how the Said and the Saying are related to one another and in a way that does not ultimately risk assimilating the Saying to the Said. That is, what Levinas needs is an account of how the relational (transcendental) ground of our moral normativity is distinct from and yet related to our everyday lives. The problem of how ethics is related to politics, for him, is one dimension of this larger problem. His second goal in this work of 1974 is to explore and clarify how the self and the other person, or the transcendent, the face, are related such that we can understand in terms of it how the Said and the Saying are related. This involves a richer account of selfhood and subjectivity than Levinas has thus far provided. All of this, then, is the background for his systematic or philosophical account of how our social and political lives are related to the ethical foundation of human existence. It is the background of what I have called his conception of ethical critique of the political. This formulation, while not his, and schematic as it is, may be helpful as we proceed to that philosophical account, but not before we have said something about the more general problem of how the Said and the Saying are related, as Levinas sees it.[2]

One vehicle that Levinas employs to clarify this relationship between the ethical relation, or face-to-face, and our ordinary lives (the Said) is to compare it to the relation between philosophy and skepticism. Those familiar with Levinas will recognize immediately that part of the reason that Levinas frames this latter relationship in this way is to highlight the temporal relation between assertions of knowledge and skeptical doubts raised regarding the possibility of such knowledge. That is, in Levinasian terminology, the comparison is drawn to introduce the notion of diachrony and the way in which the Saying and the Said are absolutely diachronous, as I like to put it. What Levinas means, in this instance, is that the moral normativity that the face-to-face brings to all of our daily lives, all of ordinary experience, is always already in place, prior to anything that we do or anything that happens to us. It has a kind of a priori character; Levinas calls it "anarchic," in the sense that it is there always prior to any *archai* (principles, origins) or foundations. Our responsibilities to others, as we might put it, are always already in play at any moment, independent of any choices we make or acts we perform. In this way, it is possible to say that the relationship between the Saying and the Said is never unequivocal, never asynchronous. There can be no assimilation of the Saying to the Said; it would be like treating the bank of a river and JP Morgan Chase synonymously and grouping them into a common class. In the case of skepticism, if the claim to knowledge and the denial of knowledge were synchronous and thereby unambiguous, then once the philosopher had pointed out to the skeptic that his claims against knowledge were self-refuting, that would be the end of skepticism. But they are not and have not been so; skepticism always returns. Throughout the history of Western philosophy, skepticism and philosophy have never ceased to be partners, an unholy marriage, so to speak. Or, as Levinas puts it, no matter how often the philosopher refutes skepticism, it always returns. It is philosophy's constant and ever-present associate. It is the philosopher's other.

Not only *can* the Saying and the Said occur together, they *must* occur together. There is no utterly particular engagement with the face of the other by the self without that relationship occurring in the context of myriad other everyday relations and relationships, ones that are structured and can be described generically. On the other hand, there can be no generic relations and relationships that do not already have as their transcendental condition the normative and primary relation between the subject and the other person who are so related. Without this being so there would be no point or significance for the generic relations to have occurred. And indeed, without it being so there would be no such thing as morality and the normativity of conscience. There would be no goodness, as Levinas likes to put it.

It is against this background, then, that Levinas describes, in his own way, how the introduction of the third party brings with it the structuring and generalizing mechanisms of everyday experience and ultimately with it the institutions of society and the state. In *Totality and Infinity* Levinas says that "the pluralism of society [is] possible" only "starting from this secrecy."[3] It is to this account that we now turn.

EARLY PERIOD

It is well-known that for Levinas, society and the political arise in his thinking with the idea of the third party.[4] The first important mention of this idea occurs in *Totality and Infinity*. As I read him, the third party is the image or figure that Levinas uses to pick out the fact of social existence at the ordinary, everyday level. That is, the face-to-face in which the particular other person confronts and calls into question the individual self or subject is bi-polar and structural. It involves two and only two persons who relate to one another as petitionary-commander and respondent. When a third party or third person is present, then that person is an other for the self's other and also an additional other to the self itself, and more, that is, the self is the other's other, and the self becomes the third party's other. In short, the presence of third parties creates a network of interpersonal, relational nexuses. But this complexity is no longer at the level of the face-to-face, the transcendental level; it is at the ordinary, everyday level. In other words, the third party is the condition that precipitates the factuality of social life in everyday affairs. With multiple third parties, that factuality is constituted. When, therefore, Levinas says that the third party is always with us, what he means is that we are never in everyday experience face-to-face with one particular other person alone; rather we are always one among many persons in which there is a complex network of self-other relations. Politics is the set of strategic practices, institutions, and norms that we construct to organize that social reality.

What does Levinas say about these subjects in *Totality and Infinity*? Here Levinas calls this social reality the "public order," and he associates it with language and justice. "Justice" is the face-to-face. But Levinas warns that both justice and the public order come together; they are coordinated with one another. "It is not that there first would be the face, and then the being it manifests or expresses would concern himself with justice; the epiphany of the face qua face opens humanity."[5] What does this mean? If the face-to-face occurs as the infinite lines of relation between the self and each and every particular other, then in what sense does it already "open" humanity? In what sense is the collective, the species, the whole of humanity present in the face-to-face?

In these pages, Levinas distinguishes humanity, with which he associates the face and the emergence of a *we*, as he calls it, and fraternity, and, in contrast, the "human race as a biological genus." He also calls the *we* "the human community instituted by language" or "a kinship of men" and distinguishes it from "the unity of genus." This is Levinas's version of the older distinction between *Gemeinschaft* and *Gesellschaft*, genuine community and society, or, more specifically, it is his way of distinguishing between the biological or scientific category of humankind as a genus or species and the collectivity of all human beings tied together by bonds of mutual responsibility.[6] And his point, I believe, is that the identification of the face-to-face as a structural and ethical relation between every two persons, insofar as it occurs between every two persons, ties together all of humanity as a network, as a kind of kinship, as he calls it. Once there is a third party, each of us becomes a petitioner and a commander; we join one another. We become a *we*, as he puts it. And this is our equality, he says, so that the fundamental asymmetry or inequality of each face-to-face registers in an equality of all as petitioners and as commanders. We are all responsible and we are all members of the "poor, the widow, and the stranger." "In this welcoming of the face," he says, "equality is founded." Levinas also calls this "fraternity." We are brothers, as others and as subjects, as petitioners and as responsible selves. And this, Levinas underscores, is what makes equality more than a mere formal notion, "but an abstract idea and a word." Finally, Levinas surprises us; the name for this "fraternal community" or "human kinship" is "monotheism."[7] In one sense, this is no surprise. The term comes from Hermann Cohen, who had taken the idea of the one God to mean that there is one moral law for one humanity, and it also is an allusion to a passage from Martin Buber's *I and Thou*, where Buber defines a "true community" as one in which all people "stand in a living, reciprocal relationship to a single living center, and . . . stand in a living, reciprocal relationship to one another."[8] For Levinas, there is no common center; what there is is the fact that each relational pair of persons is tied by the same responsibility, in a sense. In religious terms, this is what monotheism signifies: the oneness of humanity is a function of the sameness of ethical responsibility.

What applies to humanity itself also applies to each separate human community, each society and each polity. In every case, the whole is—and ought to be—as unified, as harnessed to genuine equality and fraternity, as it is responsive to the needs of its members. Political communities respect equality to the degree that they act out mutual responsibility to people both within and without.

THE ARGUMENT

As early as 1970 Levinas presented in a lecture the material that became "Essence and Disinterestedness," the initial chapter of *Otherwise Than Being*. In it, in the section entitled "Being and Beyond Being," Levinas explains how the face-to-face—what is called in this later work "proximity" and the "otherwise than being" (and much else, as we shall see)—is related to the domain of being, that is, the ordinary, everyday world, and what is also the political.[9] This is what Levinas means when he says that "everywhere proximity is conceived ontologically, that is, as a limit or complement to the accomplishment of the adventure of essence."[10] Unbounded responsibility is always present as a person-to-person relationship within all our everyday relations and in such a way that how our lives go in ordinary life is "limited" or "enhanced" by the responsibility one person acts out with respect to others. In *Otherwise Than Being* Levinas also calls the face-to-face "saying." It is prior to the "said" or "language," insofar as language and speech are ultimately grounded in and find their point in being a way in which one person encounters another responsibly. Looked at from this perspective, "the saying" is that "without which no language, as a transmission of messages, would be possible."[11]

Here we have a clue about how the primary ethical relation is related to ordinary, everyday life and thereby to politics. This is what Levinas says:

> The act of consciousness is motivated by the presence of a third party alongside of the neighbor approached. A third party is also approached; and the rela-

> tionship between the neighbor and the third party cannot be indifferent to me when I approach. There must be a justice among incomparable ones. There must then be a comparison between incomparables and a synopsis, a togetherness and contemporaneousness; there must be thematization, thought, history, and inscription. But being must be understood on the basis of *being's other*. To be on the ground of the signification of an approach is to be *with another* for or against a third party, with the other and the third party against oneself, in justice. . . . Reason, to which the virtue of arresting violence is ascribed, issuing in the order of peace, presupposes disinterestedness, passivity or patience. In this disinterestedness, when, as a responsibility for the other, it is also a responsibility for the third party, the justice that compares, assembles and conceives, the synchrony of being and peace, take form.[12]

As I have argued, as Levinas sees it, being and beyond being occur together; or, in other words, ethics and politics are coordinated. Ethics is the condition for and the measure of how politics is conducted, how everyday life ought to be lived. Furthermore, since ordinary life involves large pluralities of persons in relation one to the other, the process of rational comparison, grouping of responsibilities, and discriminations and weighing of priorities, all this is necessary. In other words, the foundational significance of consciousness and rational deliberation about how to respond to the challenges one faces is to serve the purposes of justice and peace. This account is not about how psychologically these cognitive and rational processes arise. It is rather an account of what ultimate goals make them worthwhile and significant for human life as ethical life.[13]

What follows from this, moreover, is that when consciousness, conceptualization, discrimination, comparison, and weighing of alternatives do not serve this ultimate purpose, when these processes do not facilitate justice and peace among persons, then they are ill-performed or performed in some truncated or defective way.[14] The values represented in the face-to-face, the primacy of responsibility for others, are the standard by which—by extension—all everyday activities are judged. This is what Levinas ought to say. To see if this is what he does say, we need to turn to that passage, later in *Otherwise Than Being*, where the above text is elaborated and developed.

The crucial passage is section 3 of chapter 5, entitled "From Saying to the Said, or the Wisdom of Desire."[15] It is the single most important strictly philosophical text in Levinas's writings that deals with our question, the relation between ethics and politics. The title of the section by itself already indicates that for Levinas, there is some kind of path from the face-to-face to everyday language and life, and this means from responsibility to politics. There is, as he says, not only desire, which is the self's unlimited aspiration to care for and answer to the other person, but also a "wisdom" of desire, that is, the understanding of what responsibility requires and rational reflection concerning what justice demands. Let me, then, clarify the main themes of this central text.

Levinas does not raise the question as one about ethics and politics. Rather he announces the problem as one about knowledge and philosophy. In the language of *Otherwise Than Being*, it is about "the saying and the said," about the ethical relation as primordial and originary, and the world of everyday language, consciousness, thought, and more. He asks: what is the "latent birth" of "cognition and essence" in proximity and responsibility?[16] Surely, he does not mean the literal birth, as if human life first of all is pure relation and only later becomes thought, speech, judgment, and more. He cannot mean, when he says that knowledge and the problem of knowing only arise when the third party enters, that the third party—another other, alongside the other—literally enters or comes on the scene. Minimally, the entrance of the third party refers to the condition of there being more than one other person, a collectivity or plurality. When there is such a plurality of persons, how is responsibility realized? How does responsibility become justice, as he now calls it?

What is the "third party," and where does the third party stand in relation to my neighbor, my other, and to me? This is where Levinas begins. He asks us to take a plurality of persons seriously and to ask what happens to responsibility when there is such a plurality. And his account is that the number of relations is multiplied, and my relation to others ramified. I am responsible to the other person as a neighbor, but I am also distant from the other, for every relation I stand in is both one of responsibility for the other and also mediated by reflection, comparison, and evaluation. That is, with the acknowledgment of the plurality of others, the subject's relation to each and every other becomes one of justice and the limit of responsibility, as Levinas calls it. Conceptually, if before there is a third party my relation to the other person is unmediated and direct, one of unlimited responsibility, then after there is a third party my relation to the other person is mediated and one of limited responsibility. What does this mean? In practice, what it means is this: At the everyday level of ordinary relations, my resources are limited, and the needs of the plurality of others are far more demanding than I can meet. Once there is a second other, I have to evaluate who needs my time and resources with greater urgency, whose dependency is more telling, more compelling. When I am faced with one person, I am called upon to acknowledge her or not; when I am faced with two or three or more, then I am called upon to choose, to discriminate, to weigh needs, resources, and more, all the considerations that play such important roles in what we would take to be everyday normative deliberation and decision making.[17] That is, as Levinas says, it makes justice necessary, "that is, comparison, coexistence, contemporaneousness, assembling, order, thematization, the visability of faces, and thus intentionality and the intellect, the intelligibility of a system, and thence also a copresence on an equal footing as before a court of justice."[18]

This is a central passage. Here Levinas makes clear that the presence of the third party, or what we might call the fact of plurality—which makes it necessary to organize or domesticate or orchestrate the responsibilities of the various parties—does not "generate" or cause justice to come into being, and hence it does not cause the preconditions for justice, that is, the cognitive resources for classification and comparison, discrimination and judgment, and so forth. Nor does the face-to-face or responsibility "give birth" to these cognitive resources and capacities, such as conceptual skills and language. This is what I was referring to when I said that the "latent birth" of justice in responsibility or proximity is not a literal birth. Their relationship is a different one. Justice is a ramification of responsibility; it is what results when one organizes and orchestrates the responsibilities of all involved parties. Therefore, the conditions that make justice possible, the cognitive resources and capacities, are justified in terms of their relationship to the responsibilities involved. It is only because each and every self is responsible for every other that justice, as the result of every responsibility becoming both unlimited and yet limited, becomes necessary and hence that thought and language, as justice's prerequisites, also become necessary. That is, thought and language are necessary for justice, and justice, given the plurality of social existence, is necessary as the coordination and organization of individual responsibilities. In other words, the tools of everyday human life are justified by their role in ethical life.[19]

Levinas describes this arrangement by saying that proximity or saying or responsibility is the "reason for the intelligibility of systems."[20] Moreover, this line of reasoning is not an "empirical" matter. It is as much a transcendental "fact" as the face-to-face itself. The third party is always with us, as Levinas says elsewhere; it is not an accidental matter. Here Levinas puts it this way: "The other is from the first the brother of all the other men. The neighbor that obsesses me is already a face, both comparable and incomparable, a unique face and in relationship with faces, which are visible in the concern for justice."[21] From another point of view, the human condition is one of original plurality and multiplicity; human beings are always already engaged in numerous (perhaps infinite) interpersonal encounters. "The incomparable subject" is always "a member of society."[22]

Indeed, this is the foundation of political society, of the state. "Justice, society, the State and its institutions, exchanges and work are comprehensible out of proximity."[23] Totality, politics, and all dimensions of normativity and collective organization in our lives derive their meaning—their justification—through their relationship with proximity, the face-to-face, the ethical character of all social existence. Moreover, these structures, insofar as they aspire to justice to the highest degree, are not a distortion or corruption of responsibility one for the other.[24] Justice may seek equality, but it is based on a fundamental "inequality" or asymmetry. This claim is at the core of Levinas's political sensibilities: duties, so to speak, are prior to rights. In Pufendorf and in Kant and other Enlightenment moral and political philosophy, there is a distinction between perfect and imperfect rights and duties. Onora O'Neill develops a contemporary moral philosophy that seeks to incorporate both, for the one is a matter of protections and obligations, while the other is about needs and generosity.[25] Levinas's claim, in one sense, is that ethics is foundationally both obligatory and yet also a matter of care and concern for others. It is not originally or fundamentally about protections and limits but rather about kindnesses and unlimited demands for it. Levinas calls this a "surplus of my duties over my rights."[26] This is the starting point, the center around which moral systems and political normativity are constructed.

Hence, "it is then not without importance to know if the egalitarian and just State in which man is fulfilled (and which is to be set up, and especially to be maintained) proceeds from a war of all against all, or from the irreducible responsibility of the one for all, and if it can do without friendships and faces." And what applies to the egalitarian and just state also applies to philosophy itself and the "rational necessity that coherent discourse transforms into sciences, and whose principle philosophy wishes to grasp."[27] In short, it makes a difference, Levinas claims, that politics, the just state, sciences, and philosophy are all grounded in responsibility for others.[28] He calls this "the very rationality of reason" and a "rationality of peace."[29]

What is a rationality of peace? What makes it rational and what makes it a rationality in the service of peace? What Levinas has in mind, I think, is that all these everyday orders or institutions or domains are rational, organized to serve their purposes best and in the most ethical way, when they are organized to maximize concern for the needs and dependencies of others. "Peace" refers to the relationship the self has with the other to whom and for whom it is responsible. This is a deep peace, the peace of human relatedness. Social and political institutions involve rational deliberation and decision in behalf of peace, serving the purposes of egalitarian and just institutions and society and acting in behalf of science and philosophy that serve the needs of others. Rationality is classification, comparison, and judgment, and when we realize that rationality has its point by serving others as an obligation and duty, we know it to be a rationality of peace, "a rational order, the ancillary or angelic order of justice."[30]

Furthermore, rationality and consciousness are ultimately ethical matters; what justifies them and gives them their significance or weight is that they ultimately serve ethical purposes. "The foundation of consciousness is justice."[31] And what is the foundation of consciousness is also the foundation of language, of everyday life, and of the political. All ultimately serve ethical purposes, which is why it makes a difference whether our modes of political organization and our institutions are grounded in a Hobbesian conception of human nature and in a social

contract theory of one kind or another or in Levinas's understanding
of caring interpersonal relatedness, what he calls the face-to-face. All
daily life and all political institutions and practices can be evaluated
against this standard; all express to one degree or another justice and
equality. And the test is not whether a regime respects rational agency or
maximizes the satisfaction of desires; it is whether and to what degree it
minimizes suffering and poverty for others and cares for those in need,
such as orphans, widows, the elderly, and the ill and infirm. How does
the state care for its citizens and all those under its jurisdiction? Levinas's
conception of the political does indeed confirm the claim that societies
and governments must be evaluated by how they treat and care for those
least well off, the poor and the hungry and the homeless.

Even though, then, society and the state are organized in terms of
the needs of others and hence aspire to egalitarian and just institutions
and practices, this order is not "anonymous." Its laws and policies are
rooted in care and concern for others; they do not express a "view from
nowhere" and do not legislate generic conduct. Justice and society are
not "an anonymous law of the 'human forces' governing an impersonal
totality."[32] Just as true community is not a biological genus or a collection
of rational beings but rather a network of the *we* constituted by responsible relations between each person and every other person, so the society or state is not governed by laws and regulations that express some
generic sense of human nature. They are not impersonal; rather they are
deeply personal and interpersonal. The moral norms of a moral community and the laws and policies of a civil society are both affirmations
of how members should respond with care and concern for others both
within the society and external to it.

Levinas ends the section with the sentence "Philosophy is the wisdom of love at the service of love,"[33] and what is true of philosophy is
also true of politics. It is an understanding of love—of human responsibility, concern for the other, and justice—in the service of that human
responsibility and justice. And beyond this, politics is the institutional
implementation, the policies and regulations, of justice in the service
of shaping a just and humane life for all its members. In *Otherwise Than
Being* this is as far as Levinas goes toward characterizing the political and
its relation to ethics.[34] With this account in hand, then, we can ask with

more clarity and precision what Levinas's philosophy contributes to understanding everyday morality and political life. Can we derive precise principles of political life? Does Levinas's conception of justice and the face-to-face provide a standard for judging political regimes and practices? Does it recommend some forms of constitution and reject others? Does it help us to make particular normative proposals?

CLARIFICATION

One way to begin to answer these questions and to bring into sharper focus Levinas's account would be to see him apply it—in the political domain, narrowly speaking, or in a domain similar in character and purpose to the political domain, such as cultural institutions, language, law, religion, or art. For that purpose, in subsequent chapters, I will turn to his comments on Zionism and the Jewish state. But before I do, let us turn to some of Levinas's interviews, where he responds to questions about just these matters. Because he is responding directly to an interlocutor or interlocutors sitting in front him, he not only draws upon his written accounts but also allows himself some flexibility in trying to clarify what he means.

In an earlier chapter I discussed Levinas's comments in "The Paradox of Morality," an interview given in 1986 to three graduate students from the University of Warwick. There, as I pointed out, Levinas says that justice, which involves calculation, is "inseparable from the political." It will be helpful, however, to supplement those remarks with others, now that we have had an opportunity to describe Levinas's systematic, philosophical exposition of how the Saying makes possible and necessary the Said, that is, how the ground of moral normativity in our second-person relations with others is the condition for our daily social and political lives and also cannot exist without them.

In order to understand the problem of the relation between the ethical, the face-to-face or responsibility, and the political, we must underscore and understand the fact that the two occur in two dimensions of human existence. I have called these the transcendental and the ordinary dimensions. Levinas pictures the former as oblique to the latter, as entering into it from the outside, as it were, or as interrupting it. By the time he wrote *Otherwise Than Being* his conception of this responsibility for others was extreme. It is infinite and extends to everyone and everything about everyone. Hence, he says in *Ethics and Infinity*, "These are extreme formulas which must not be detached from their context. In the concrete, many other considerations intervene and require justice even for me. Practically, the laws set certain consequences out of the way. But justice only has meaning if it retains the spirit of dis-interestedness which animates the idea of responsibility for the other man."[35] Infinite responsibility does not occur except in a context, the everyday context in which other considerations affect how I act, and these considerations are generic, involve general practices, rules, and law. Acting justly, according to such norms or laws, only has meaning insofar as it is ultimately grounded in my infinite responsibilities, but these can only occur in concrete circumstances where the infinity of the responsibility is mitigated or qualified. In short, the Saying and the Said must occur together; each one limits the other.

This is just what Levinas says in an important passage in the interview, a passage that I cited earlier and that occurs, in similar form, also in *Otherwise Than Being* and in the essay "Peace and Proximity":

> It is extremely important to know if society in the current sense of the term is a result of the limitation of the principle that men are predators of one another, or if to the contrary it results from the limitation of the principle that men are *for* one another. Does the social, with its institutions, universal forms and laws, result from limiting the consequences of the war between men, or from limiting the infinity which opens in the ethical relationship of man to man?[36]

In other words, Levinas here tells us that it is important to know whether society—ordinary life, social institutions, and the state—arises from limiting our individualism, with its emphasis on human liberties and property, or from limiting the infinite responsibilities we have to others. This intriguing passage will be central to our discussion of ethical critique, but for the moment what I want to focus on is another point, that our everyday relationships, norms, and institutions are limitations—and indeed necessary ones—of our fundamental responsibilities to other persons, which are infinite, "extreme," and in fact impossible to live. Moreover, just as this regime of justice, as Levinas calls it, is a limitation on our fundamental responsibilities, so our fundamental responsibilities are a limit on the regime of justice. To put this in other terms, once we appreciate that our everyday lives are populated by a vast plurality of other persons, each one a particular other to us and to everyone and each to one another, we realize that all of our lives are filled with "negotiated" and "qualified" responsibilities and never with infinite and pure ones. At the same time, although all of our lives are lived with generic relationships, norms, and so forth, we realize that all of these are grounded—formally and substantively—in the normativity of our particular face-to-face or second-person engagements with each other person. In human life neither the Saying nor the Said can exist independently of the other.[37]

When Levinas speaks, in his later writings, of justice or a regime of justice, he does not mean the face-to-face or responsibility for the other person. Rather he uses these expressions to refer to our relationships and experiences at the ordinary or everyday level, where our very particular second-person encounters with others are embedded in the vast network of relationships and experiences that I described earlier and which are generic. Unlike the face-to-face, which is asymmetrical and in which the self is passive, ordinary relations with other persons are frequently "reciprocal," and the selves involved are equal.

> Here, starting from the third, is a proximity of a human plurality. Between the second and third men, there can be relations in which the one is guilty toward the other. I pass from the relation in which I am obligated and responsible to a relation where I ask myself who is the first. I pose the question of justice: within this plurality, which one is the other par excellence? How to judge?

This situation, then, where this is evaluation and judgment, leads to equality:

> I pass from the relation without reciprocity to a relation wherein, among the members of society, there is a reciprocity, an equality. My search for justice supposes precisely this new relation in which every excess of generosity that I should have in regard to the other is submitted to justice. In justice there is comparison, and the other has no privilege in relation to me. Between the men who enter into that relation, there must be established a *rapport* that presupposes the comparison among them, that is, that presupposes a justice and a citizenship.[38]

In short, when it comes to determining who should receive what, and when, each and every person is evaluated in terms of a variety of considerations—their needs, the availability of resources, the likelihood of the assistance being effective, any practical or conventional relations between the self and the other, and much else. In the face-to-face, the other's rights come before my own, but in society, as Levinas calls it, all of our rights count equally. As citizens, each one counts and no one counts more.

The introduction of the third, as Levinas describes it, applies both to each of us as a particular self and to the society as a whole. That is, in everyday life, there are situations where I have to ask myself to whom I am most obligated, what my resources are to meet my responsibilities to others, who deserves prior attention and who might have to wait, and so forth. There are personal decisions to be made, and while I am fundamentally obligated to all, in fact I can and must distribute my time and resources based on contextual factors that play a role in my deliberations and decisions about what to do. In addition, there are situations where society as a whole, the governing institutions or agencies of a society, must decide how to organize itself to deal with the needs and interests of its members. All citizens are to be treated equally, and their needs must be considered and weighed against the available resources. Here the state or some civil institution or agency is the subject. Citizens will be treated equally according to the law and according to policies for distributing resources and services, although different programs will target different needs and hence different populations.

Levinas's notion of the third party has several outcomes. Two are the following: It introduces a plurality of face-to-face relations, beyond the one between the self and a single particular other person. This means that each of us is responsible for each and every other person, but it also means that each and every other has an infinite number of selves responsible for it. Both outcomes will be factors that contribute to the actions taken both by individuals and by the state. In addition, the third party introduces generality or universality by calling for generic relations and relationships. Once we have to take into consideration a plurality of other persons who need our acknowledgment and assistance, both individually and politically, we will be required to group others in various ways, discriminate levels of need, compare the needs of some against the needs of others, and so forth. Whatever decisions we make or policies or programs or rules we put in place will generalize for groups of recipients and for groups of agents.

Levinas's systematic account of the domain of ordinary life and in particular its political dimension does not begin with a founding principle, claim, or value and then derive a range of rules or norms and the institutional framework for implementing and protecting these rules or norms. In this respect, Levinas's account is not like that of Hobbes or Locke, Rawls or even Habermas. Instead, as we have seen, Levinas begins with his insight into the second-person ground of moral normativity for human existence, and he then adds the fact of plurality to it, identifying in broad strokes the devices and tactics human beings employ to implement that ethical core within complex pluralities and social settings. In effect, then, the ethical core becomes the basic presupposition without which these various devices and tactics are justified, and at the same time, these devices and tactics become the means of realization for the ethical core in everyday social and political life. Neither one can occur without the other; they are interdependent.

FOUR

ETHICS AS CRITIQUE

In chapters 1 and 2 I have argued that for Levinas one role of the ethical is to serve as a ground of critique of political conduct, policies, norms, and institutions. Levinas himself says that politics is subject to ethical critique. Since the ethical is a dimension of every relation and every relationship and insofar as it is constituted by our responsibilities and obligations toward other persons, Levinas must mean that politics is subject to evaluation by the standard of such obligations and responsibilities. Levinas calls the latter charity or love, and as we have seen, he says that it makes a difference whether society and the state are founded on a kind of individualism and personal competitiveness or on charity and justice. How well or how poorly do our political conduct and programs meet the standard of the ethical?

I have also, in chapter 1, compared Levinas's conception of ethical critique with Avishai Margalit's arguments in behalf of a decent society, one that seeks to avoid humiliating its citizens and others or degrading them. What is especially interesting about Margalit's argument for a decent society is that it is similar formally to Levinas's account of how justice is not sufficient for the best society or form of state. Justice is one thing, and we may feel strongly that a good society must be just. But justice may not be sufficient to make a society a good one; for that we need also an attention to our care and responsibilities for the other person. But what exactly does Levinas mean? If Margalit is concerned especially about respect and self-esteem, Levinas is not in the same sense. Nor is fairness or equal treatment sufficient. Levinas argues that as human beings we want and need more. He is concerned with charity, kindness, and generosity.

What is critique—social and political critique—insofar as the concept might be helpful in understanding how Levinas takes the ethical to be a standard for judging society and the state? The type of critical evaluation and judgment that I am associating with Levinas has a long lineage.[1] To engage in critique, in the sense I have in mind, is to consider social, cultural, and political institutions and practices in terms of the degree to which they meet the demands of standards that are related to them and apply to them but are external to them in some sense. The natural law or natural rights traditions, for example, have regularly subjected legal and political systems to their standards in order to determine how just and how right they are. Civil law and the political system are distinct from the laws of nature and natural rights. But the former can be and often have been evaluated in terms of the latter. One strand of these traditions of critique goes back to the Bible and the biblical prophets, as someone like Michael Walzer suggests, where the critics are what he calls "connected" or engaged critics, who address those currently in power as members of the society in question, the society being subjected to critique.[2] As we have seen, Levinas presumes that some critics will be wholly outside a given society, some will be private citizens, and some will represent the political system itself. Of these, the latter two are "connected critics," in something like Walzer's sense. The society or state is of concern to them because they are members or representatives of it, and they wish to correct its flaws. It is their home, and its character and ethical commitments are their concern.

Critique, then, has three dimensions. It has a subject or agent, an object, and a ground. The subject or agent is the critic, who can come from any number of different venues and perspectives. The object is the target of the criticism, a government in power, a social structure, an ideology or power structure, or any number of things. Finally, the ground is the standard or ideal or value that gives content to the critique; it is that in terms of which the critique is conducted.[3] In the case of the biblical prophets, for example, the prophets themselves are the agents of critique, the object is the kingship and priesthood of Israel or Judah—that is, the political institutions par excellence and their conduct and policies—and the ground is the Torah, broadly speaking, or the values of the Hebraic tradition, especially the desert and Mosaic traditions, the values of justice (*tzedek*) and righteous concern (*gemilut hasadim*). In several cases, the biblical prophets challenge the priestly practices of sacrifice, taxation, and privilege and call for a return to the desert faith, the concern for the disadvantaged in society—the orphan, the widow, and the stranger. Moreover, while there are questions that arise regarding the agent of critique (e.g., Walzer's claim that the social critic ought to be engaged and connected), the real core of critique is its ground and questions regarding that ground, such as whether there is a single ground in terms of which all societies and states should be criticized or whether there are various standards or grounds that critique employs to challenge social and political practices, institutions, and conduct.

Of special interest, perhaps, is whether Levinasian critique is anything like what the Frankfurt school might have called immanent critique. In certain ways, it clearly is not. Levinasian critique is not primarily about exploitation or power, although it does distinguish between good and bad violence.[4] Nor is it exclusively or primarily a critique of one's knowledge or understanding of how society and government work, registered in order to liberate those who are oppressed. Nor is it like a Freudian critique, which involves arriving at knowledge that is intended to free one from illusions, confusions, and errors.[5] Levinasian critique has two major foci: One is a call or reminder to all citizens, individually and collectively, to attend to the particular individual, his or her concerns and needs.[6] The other is to remind us of our responsibilities to others for everything from basic acceptance and acknowledgment to substantial aid, protection, and security. In order to clarify the specific features of this Levinasian critique, it will be helpful to call upon the work of several people who have focused on social and political critique, including Walzer, Seyla Benhabib, Raymond Geuss, and James Tully. Levinasian critique may share certain features identified by such thinkers, but in other respects it will turn out to be distinctive.

Walzer, in *Interpretation and Social Criticism*, distinguishes three modes of moral philosophy and ultimately defends what he calls the "interpretive" mode. This interpretive mode provides us with an "account of the actually existing morality . . . that is authoritative for us because it is only by virtue of its existence that we exist as the moral beings we are. Our categories, relationships, commitments, and aspirations are all shaped by, expressed in terms of, the existing morality. . . . The critique of existence begins, or can begin, from principles internal to existence itself."[7] I am not sure that Levinas's insight into the primacy of our responsibilities to others is a product of interpretation as Walzer goes on to describe it; nor am I certain that it would count as the constituent of such an interpretation. But this point does seem to be true of Levinas's conception of what the ethical is and how it is related to human existence overall. It is a framework, as it were, for existing morality; it is also that which determines us as the moral beings we are; it is furthermore the grounds for a critique of existence that begins from within existence itself.

The criticism that arises from such a ground Walzer calls "social criticism." It is the product of social critics, who are "individuals . . . [who are] most of the time, members, speaking in public to other members who join in the speaking and whose speech constitutes a collective reflection upon the conditions of collective life." The people who fit this description, moreover, are characterized by a certain status—more marginal, he says, than detached—and can be called "connected critics."[8] Surely wholly detached or impersonal criticism is possible, but, for Walzer, it is not a kind that is serious or that counts for much in the critic's life. Real social criticism is conducted by citizens who are invested in the life of their society and whose social problems and policies mean something to the critic.[9] About such critics, moreover, Walzer asks a telling question: "Are standards available to him that are internal to the practices and understandings of his own society, and at the same time properly critical?"[10] Walzer takes societies and cultures to be interpretive wholes (communities) within which we live and acquire our identities and character. Our values and interests are all understood within such societies and cultures. Outside of them, there are others, but there are no independent, neutral, or wholly objective standards for judging and criticizing what occurs within them. Hence, his question is about how, on such a view, there can be any grip for critical leverage. Are not all the values, principles, and interests within such a worldview parts of the coherent whole and hence compromised or domesticated, as it were? What could count as a standard for judging conduct within the whole?

Walzer calls upon Marx to illuminate how and why the ideals or standards that come to be the stock and trade of social critics arise (at least for one way in which this is so). He begins with the intellectual work of "cultural elaboration and affirmation," carried out by prophets, sages, and many others. These figures do the work of the ruling class by presenting its task as a universal one. In such a picture, rulers are portrayed as standing "above the struggle, guardians of the common interest, their goal not victory but transcendence." The work is apologetic but in such a way that it provides the materials for later social critics. "It sets standards that the rulers will not live up to, cannot live up to, given their particularist ambitions. One might say that these standards themselves embody ruling class interests, but they do so only within a universalist disguise."[11] In short, the ideals and standards that become the stock and trade of social critics are provided by the very same ruling classes that do not and will not bring them to realization. They project aims, ends, and interests with which others can identify but that the rulers themselves do not serve.

But not all ideals and standards emerge this way. Walzer argues that moral ideals are often conceived as coming from outside of a society and not from within it, as if they are brought by foreigners and must first be appropriated before they can become the implements of an internal critique. This point can be made in Levinas's terms: ethical demands arise out of our relation to transcendence. But, of course, for him transcendence is something we always meet in our everyday lives and not in extraordinary or eccentric experience. In effect, what Levinas does is to argue that ethical standards for the critique of everyday social and political practice are already present in human existence from the beginning. They are external and internal at once, and hence become the tools of social and political critique not because they are projected by duplicitous rulers or their intellectual spokespersons or because they are conveyed from external sources, but rather because they are present, even if ignored, in all social experience. Levinasian critique, that is, always presents itself as corrective, as returning our social and political lives to a course from which they have strayed. It is a critique of recovery.

At the same time, however, since the face-to-face, while always present even if occluded, is impossible to live fully or to accomplish without compromise, critique that directs us to greater attention to it and to our responsibilities is always utopian or at least has a utopian element. Perhaps it is more correct to say that instead of looking toward an impossible distant future, Levinasian critique looks to a reasonable proximate one. It does not aim unequivocally at recovery; it points toward an as-yet unaccomplished future.

Walzer has his own reasons for acknowledging the shift from God to other people, a shift that one might see too in Levinas's interpretation of the relationship between religious language about God and divine command, on the one hand, and the ethical primacy of the face of the other person, on the other. Walzer says, "In a secular age God is replaced by other people." Drawing on Thomas Scanlon, he observes that "each of us wants to be justified in the eyes of all the others" not only in response to our moral beliefs but also in order to "trigger" moral beliefs. As he puts it, "We try to justify ourselves, but we cannot justify ourselves by ourselves, and so morality takes shape as a speculation with particular other people, our relatives, friends and neighbors; or it takes shape as a speculation on what arguments might, or should, persuade such people of our righteousness."[12] The moral principles that result become the resources for social critique. If for Walzer and Scanlon these moral principles arise out of the process of justifying ourselves to others, for Levinas they are already built into or are already present in all of our second-person relations with others, prior to all our ordinary encounters, including those that involve justification and conversation.

Levinas is more Kantian than Walzer is; the standards employed by social critics for Walzer arise within historically and culturally local communities and hence are constantly undergoing interpretation and reinterpretation. For Levinas, there is a morally normative dimension to all of our experience, which is fundamentally social, second-person, and particular. All societies and practices are responsive to this normative dimension to some degree or other, and in this respect we are all alike. The ground of social and political critique, as in Kant, is something universal—for Kant, autonomy and rational agency; for Levinas, the pre-experiential responsibility present in all second-person relations.

In distinguishing connected criticism from "immanent critique," familiar from the Marxist tradition and the Frankfurt school, Walzer makes an interesting point relevant to Levinasian critique. Although immanent critique is a critique of the power structures of society aimed at a kind of liberation or freedom from oppression, Walzer also calls it, strangely enough, "disconnected criticism." It lends itself to "manipulation and compulsion" and "one or another version of an unattractive politics." Why is this so? Walzer answers: the immanent critic's critique "is a kind of asocial criticism, an external intervention, a coercive act, intellectual in form but pointing toward its physical counterpart."[13] No doubt Walzer, like Levinas, has in mind Soviet totalitarianism, which began as Marxist social criticism and ended as Stalinism, an oppressive political regime founded on rigidity and coercion. Levinas is concerned with fascism and totalitarianism for many reasons, but I do not think that they are exactly the same reasons that Walzer has in mind. Walzer's thought is that although immanent critique is aimed at relieving a kind of self-imposed oppression, it can itself become oppressive. Walzer, like Marxism and the Frankfurt school, is concerned primarily with freedom. Levinas advocates a humanism as well, but it is a humanism oriented around the needs of others and our obligations to take responsibility for them and to meet them. It is less about our agency than our passivity, as he puts it. Moreover, it is not at all "disconnected." It never becomes "an external intervention." Levinasian critique is always internal and "connected."

This is not the only way that Levinasian critique differs from the "immanent critique" that is associated with Marxism and the critical school. One might describe Levinas's type of social criticism as a change of perspective, a revised orientation that gives rise to an altered attitude toward others and toward one's responsibilities to them. Most frequently, Levinas presents this change or transformation as a product of education and training. It is an education about what is primary and how it binds and moves us, and training in responding from this new point of view. But, and this is important, Levinasian critique is by and large *not* a matter of knowledge or theory. It does not involve a better understanding of ourselves and society that liberates us from self-imposed confusions and errors. Its classic image can be found in book 7 of Plato's *Republic* where he describes *paideia* as a form of *periagoge,* or a turning around of the soul toward its proper objects. Plato's image, of course, is a paradigm of cognitive achievement as a form of vision; Levinas's revision is not cognitive but practical, and its object is a turn from the self to the other person and not from the ordinary empirical world to the world of Forms. But it is still a turn toward transcendence, albeit under a different description from Plato's of what transcendence means.

The centrality of knowledge to social criticism forms part of the basis of Raymond Geuss's important analysis of the idea of a critical theory. In the introduction to *The Idea of a Critical Theory: Habermas and the Frankfurt School,* Geuss lists three theses that distinguish such theories:

1. Critical theories have special standing as guides for human action in that: (a) they are aimed at producing enlightenment in the agents who hold them, i.e., at enabling those agents to determine what their true interests are; (b) they are inherently emancipatory, i.e., they free agents from a kind of coercion which is at least partly self-imposed, from self-frustration of conscious human action.
2. Critical theories have cognitive content, i.e., they are forms of knowledge.
3. Critical theories differ epistemologically in essential ways from theories in the natural sciences. Theories in natural science are "objectifying"; critical theories are "reflective."[14]

Here I want to focus attention on the cognitive aspect of Geuss's profile. As he describes them, critical theories are just that, theories, and ones that criticize or disclose the hidden contents of ideologies. They produce knowledge about society that enables the agents in those societies to understand themselves in such a way that they become aware of their "true interests" and thereby free themselves from illusions that may largely be a matter of self-deception or delusion. Such criticism, then, is engaged and connected, in Walzer's sense, and it is aimed at power and coercion, as Tully suggests. Moreover, it facilitates a change in citizens by providing them with a better understanding of themselves than they previously had. It operates through theory or knowledge and the unraveling of the threads of binding ideologies.

Levinasian ethical critique does not operate by means of theory or knowledge. It does not propose a better or deeper self-understanding, although, in a sense, it does seek to correct errors on the part of citizens and on the part of the state. But these errors are ones of ignorance or forgetfulness or blindness, as it were, whereby for one reason or another and in one way or another, a society's members fail to appreciate the primacy of their responsibility to others, the priority of attending to the needs of particular others, and the various ways that generality and universality obscure or occlude the real human and ethical obligations we have to others. For Levinas, it is crucial that our failures are ones of action and in particular of responding to others. As I have suggested, social and ethical revision is a matter of training and education—regarding what such responsibilities and obligations mean and what it means to respond to other persons as fully and as thoughtfully as one can. It is not, as in critical theory, a matter of developing social and political theories, exposing ideological illusion, and reducing through the mechanism of more illuminated understanding the degree of self-imposed coercion the society and its members suffer. Levinasian critique is a matter of reorientation and not rethinking and re-understanding.

One feature that distinguishes Levinas from critical theory and also from someone like Foucault might be called his aversion to history and his affection for metaphysics. What I mean is this: both the Frankfurt school and Foucault, albeit in different ways, take human existence to be historical through and through; they take contemporary worldviews, ideologies, and conceptual schemes to be historical. Such views and schemes have grown historically, constantly undergoing change and alteration, and their meaning and even their truth is historically determined. The purpose of critique is ultimately to uncover the historical stories that have resulted in these ideologies and worldviews and thereby to provide contemporaries with the means for exposing domination, violence, and oppression, for accomplishing self-liberation. Levinas, on the other hand, takes human existence to incorporate more than what is historical or natural, in a broad sense, and that supplement is primary and determinative of what makes human existence worthwhile and meaningful. That supplement he calls "transcendence," and he takes our relationship with it to be fundamental for us as the kind of beings we are. Moreover, that relationship is present in every second-person relation we experience as a normative dimension, as an ever-present responsibility for others that is infinite and in itself unbounded. That dimension of normativity, which he takes to be the ground of the ethical in our lives, does not require understanding, but it does require attentiveness and responsiveness, not to an abstract property or feature but rather to other persons as dependent upon our concern and care, as claimants against our self-interest and self-indulgence. For Levinas, then, ethical responsiveness does require disclosure of a kind, but it is not an intellectual or theoretical disclosure based on historical and social scientific analysis and explanation. What it involves instead is a kind of attunement to the moral salience of situations, decisions, institutions, and such. There is, then, an Aristotelian element in this conception, one that perhaps draws Levinas closer to contemporary philosophers like John McDowell, David Wiggins, and others than it does to figures like Habermas and Foucault.[15]

INFINITE RESPONSIBILITY AND THE DECENT SOCIETY

A striking comparison worth our attention, as I indicated in chapter 1, is between Levinasian critique and the social and political criticism described by Avishai Margalit in his book *The Decent Society*. Margalit appreciates that good societies ought to be just, but he argues in the book that this is insufficient. Their institutions must, more importantly, cultivate respect for people and seek to avoid humiliating or degrading them. More precisely, using Margalit's own distinction, "a decent society is one whose institutions do not humiliate people," while "a civilized society is one whose members do not humiliate one another." Moreover, Margalit is interested in these institutions not as abstract, legal institutions, but rather as agents of concrete behavior.[16]

For Levinas, the regime of justice, as he sometimes calls it, is distinct from but related to the responsibility for others that is central to the face-to-face or second-person dimension of all our interpersonal relations. Similarly, for Margalit, non-humiliation or respect is distinct from but related to justice. While respect is a positive characteristic, however, non-humiliation is a negative one; it is about not harming others in a certain way, and the avoidance of this negative conduct is what Margalit has primarily in mind. Levinas is concerned with harm as well, but only in the sense that failures of attention to the needs of others and such can involve injury or harm. His primary interest is in what we do for others and ought to do for others and less in protecting others from us. This is not a minor difference, as we shall see. Institutions and policies that protect against harm will be different in character and orientation from those that enhance or facilitate responsibilities toward and for others.

One aspect of Margalit's analysis we can set aside. He treats humiliation not psychologically as a *feeling* of being degraded or being shamed but rather normatively as conduct or conditions that give the recipient *reason* to take their self-respect to be injured.[17] It may be that Levinas's understanding of responsibility is also a normative notion or at least can be, but for the moment I want to defer that matter and focus instead on the role of self-respect in Margalit's account. What is it that institutions ought to avoid? It is the violation of self-respect, which Margalit takes to be "the honor a person grants herself solely on the basis of the awareness that she is human."[18] Margalit has a lengthy discussion of what exactly this violation of self-respect involves or what it is to humiliate someone, and his conclusions are that "the key concept for humiliation is rejection from the human commonwealth," and "the rejection consists in behaving *as if* the person were an object or an animal . . . in treating humans as subhuman."[19] Given this outcome, it is not surprising that Margalit calls upon the *Musselman* in the death camps as a paradigm of such humiliation and of the shame that accompanies it.[20] In a society that humiliates, people are made to take themselves to be less than human. But, Margalit goes on to argue, this is highly abstract and needs to be refined in order to deal with the restricted or mediated rejections and degrading conduct that occurs within specific groups and especially within particular states. He uses the expression "encompassing groups" and claims that what makes humiliation "more concrete and more applicable to societies familiar to us" is "the rejection of an encompassing group or the rejection from such a group of a person with a legitimate right to belong to it."[21]

I am ignoring a great deal that Margalit provides in his rich and detailed account, but at this point I want to notice an important concrete implication of the move from the "Family of Man" to "encompassing groups" like societies or states. With regard to the concern with humiliation, a central worry is the treatment of those who are members but not majority or dominant members, that is, minorities. Margalit discusses this issue under the social ideal of "fraternity." As he puts it, "The idea of encompassing groups assumes that there is a human possibility of feeling a sense of fraternity even toward unfamiliar people, if they can be identified as belonging to the encompassing group." Specifically, he criticizes initiation rites that target those who are liminal, not yet but about to become members, and he also mentions marginal groups, but what he says—that humiliation is incompatible with a decent society—applies to minorities as well.[22] Degrading policies and practices give minorities a sense of being non-members of a society and furthermore of being non-members of the human family.

Margalit considers what kinds of bureaucracy are compatible with a decent society and in particular whether a welfare society is compatible with it. Both issues are intrinsically interesting and also very relevant to clarifying how Levinasian critique might be conducted. With regard to bureaucracies, Margalit says that to the question what kind is compatible with a decent society, the answer is obvious: "the sort of bureaucracy that does not systematically humiliate those dependent on it."[23] Most such systems are inefficient and irritating, as Margalit notes. In social democracies, he remarks, they are necessary but problematic. They harbor a number of trite defects, such as the fact that they typically "shrink" in areas where they matter most and dismiss people based on longevity and not efficiency. But irritation is one thing, humiliation another, and here the issue is what people often call its "mechanistic" quality. One can easily imagine how Levinas would respond to Margalit's description: "Bureaucracies are based on impersonal relations, and so they are indifferent to individuals and their suffering and remote from their individuality and uniqueness. This impersonal attitude often becomes an inhuman attitude. . . . That is, bureaucracies are accused of seeing human beings as nonhuman—as numbers, or forms, or 'cases.' This attitude of seeing persons in a machinelike manner is humiliating in its very essence."[24] This remark is certainly Levinasian in spirit, but, as Margalit goes on to point out, there can be advantages to impersonal treatment, and I think that Levinas would agree. If you do not fit the paradigm, one wants attention to the individual but only if there are good results; at times such attention makes the action less rather than more favorable. And if you fit the rules, you do not want any discretion or particular attention but simply the fair application of the procedures in force. Second-person particular encounters have a privileged place for Levinas, but he realizes that impersonal procedures, required for fair and just treatment, are necessary limitations on the infinite responsibilities we all have to and for one another.[25]

To clarify more fully how bureaucracies can be humiliating, Margalit turns to the way they function in a welfare state.[26] Here, he says, we have an especially difficult case, where the government seeks to collect taxes and redistribute funds and services, outside the market system, and to do so efficiently and fairly. But this requires an elaborate and extensive bureaucracy that often functions, as he puts it, in irritating and even degrading ways. One might call this the "paradox" of welfare systems, that they aim to help the poor and those in need and yet often cultivate procedures and programs that are humiliating and degrading to just those people whom they serve. Indeed, there is something fundamentally degrading about welfare distributions if they are received in the spirit of receiving charity. They should not be, for while charity may be an expression of pity, "welfare state was created to eradicate poverty or at least to eliminate some of its humiliating features" but "to do this differently than the charity society, which relies on pity as the emotion motivating people to give to the poor."[27] Levinas might put this difference in this way: other persons have rights against each and every one of us to act responsibly toward them; welfare distributions are not charity but rather a kind of obligation, and for Levinas not an imperfect one. Failing to act on such fundamental responsibilities or obligations is a serious matter for which one is culpable—not legally perhaps but certainly morally. If this is the case, then the way to dissolve the paradox of welfare systems is in part to provide funds and services with dignity and in part to be sure that the recipients realize that there is no indignity in receiving them. As human beings, we are naturally dependent on the acceptance and assistance of others, and yet, at the same time, we are ourselves obligated to accept and assist others. As long as we do our best to do the latter as well as to receive the former, we can and should do so with dignity.[28]

Margalit, however, describes a feature of the historical background to the welfare idea that shows how an awareness of assisting the needy was historically associated with degrading conduct. The English Poor Laws, he says, since the time of Elizabeth I, "played a part in the use of humiliation as a deterrent against the exploitation of welfare by people looking for a free meal. The idea was that providing people with the bread of charity would encourage laziness and undesired dependence on society. The way to deter lazy people from asking for support was by offering such support under particularly humiliating circumstances. Anyone who could accept these debasing conditions would thus be someone without any choice." Margalit refers to the "deep suspicion" of the poor, the sense that they were often "swindlers" and cheats and that a procedure was needed to separate out the "swindling poor" from the "deserving poor." The assumptions here were that people by nature cannot be trusted, that poverty is a result of bad choices, and hence that the poor are at fault for their condition. Poorhouses in nineteenth-century England were organized as tests to determine who was authentic and who not, and the vehicle of such tests was humiliating and degrading treatment. Moreover, Margalit emphasizes, these assumptions and practices continue to be present in our own society and so are still relevant to understanding and evaluating debates about welfare services today, in the early twenty-first century.[29] Too often, instead of distributing funds and services to those in need with dignity and respect, we do so with the attitude that they themselves are culpable in their own poverty and that many who are in need would and do exploit the system to their advantage.

For Margalit's purposes, welfare is valuable for a decent society only if it aims at reducing humiliating and degrading conduct. Since historically the assumptions of the welfare system are that poverty is an outcome of an individual's choices, in a certain sense, and also that people cannot be trusted but will, if given the opportunity, exploit the system, it might seem that one way to avoid humiliation is to abandon welfare altogether. This of course Margalit does not want to encourage. The challenge, then, is to endorse a state that is responsive to people's needs and yet to reform the system that provides for the impoverished and destitute so that it does so in a dignified way.[30] Ultimately, for Margalit, the welfare state seeks "to eliminate the degrading life conditions of poverty, or at least to mitigate them substantially" and to do so "without making use of the insulting and perhaps also humiliating motive of pity, the emotion which motivates the charity society."[31] Levinas would not see the motive behind the organization of welfare procedures as decency; rather, for him, it is a matter of responding to others' needs and to act on one's responsibilities for them and to others. Moreover, for him, to do so in a dignified way is to do so with respect, for after all the other not only needs us but also makes a claim against us and calls us into question. Caring for the destitute and vulnerable is an obligation and not wholly voluntary or discretionary.

The final section of Margalit's analysis of the welfare society is entitled "The Charity Paradox," and to clarify what that paradox is and how to solve it, he turns to the famous account of welfare systems by Richard Titmuss and his comparison of the blood bank.[32] Welfare originates in resources got by taxation, whereas charity, in its purest form, is an expression of generosity. As Margalit notes, this would seem to give the edge of nobility to the charity society. And Titmuss's use of the blood bank might be taken as an endorsement of this judgment, since receiving blood is not like receiving funds got under a kind of duress, by taxation; rather it looks like benefaction by generosity pure and simple. Hence, "if accepting donations of blood is not humiliating, then we must see to it that accepting donations of money should be considered equally respectable by the needy."[33] But, Margalit argues, the analogy is not a perfect one. Because receiving blood can be done without humiliation does not mean that receiving money or services as welfare can also be done in a similar way. Giving blood is a way of saving lives. Not giving blood cannot be viewed as selfish or as hoarding a scarce resource, and the recipient cannot accept the donation in a devious or manipulative way. If someone donates blood (outside of the situation in which one sells blood), we presume a good motive, and when someone receives it, we assume they do so out of need and for good reasons. That is, there is the potential for humiliation and degradation in the case of welfare distributions that there is not in the case of blood donation.[34]

In the end, however, Margalit takes blood donation to be a rather good "model of pure charity in a fine spirit of voluntarism and generosity, without humiliation." But having such a model gives rise, Margalit explains, to what he calls the "charity paradox." He asks: is it better for charity to be given out of good or bad motives? Our intuition, certainly from the point of view of the agent or giver, is the obvious one—that it is preferable for charity to be given for good motives, out of generosity and with sincere regard for the other person in need. But we should not be so hasty. What may seem preferable from the agent's point of view may not seem so pleasing from the recipient's perspective. As Margalit puts it, when the giver's motives are selfish, the recipient can be thankful but need not be grateful, but when the giver acts out of generosity, the charity or generosity invites gratitude, and the recipient who feels compelled to feel grateful and yet cannot compensate the giver in any way is put in an inferior position. "The problem [for the recipients of altruistic charity] is admitting that they are in such an inferior position that they are unable to return the kindness shown them. . . . Selfish donors can be compensated, but altruistic donors cannot be." That is, selfish donors can be thanked, which is sufficient, whereas with altruistic donors more is required, and the recipient cannot provide it.[35]

What can we conclude from this analysis? Margalit compares a charity society and a welfare society. The latter requires bureaucratic means that frequently enough belittle or demean the recipients of welfare. It is tempting to think that the ideal is to convert a welfare system into a charity society. But there is a puzzle or paradox at the heart of a charity society that pivots on just that humiliation or disrespect that Margalit wants to reduce or eliminate. There is no clear and convincing case for one over the other. As he puts it, "If the welfare society wins this competition, it is a decision on points rather than a knockout." A welfare society could be decent or non-humiliating, but so could a charity society. Both are possible; neither is necessarily decent or non-decent, but there may be reasons to prefer a welfare society.[36]

In his concluding chapter, Margalit turns to the question we raised earlier when we first introduced his account, the relationship between a just society and a decent society. We might be inclined to take a just society to be one that treats people fairly and hence that has respect for people as citizens; it is tempting, for this reason, to think that a just society will always be a decent society, one that avoids degrading and humiliating conduct and practices. But, as Margalit shows, this temptation should be resisted. Even a just society or one that aspires to justice can engage in humiliating conduct and practices.[37] First, Margalit argues that self-respect, on the Rawlsian scheme, is the most basic good and is prior to all the other primary goods, so in principle the "spirit of a just society [in Rawls's sense] cannot tolerate systematic humiliation by its basic institutions."[38] But this claim concerns members of the society and not non-members, and these non-members can be resident others or others outside the society in question. For example, in many countries where there are migrant workers who are not citizens, the treatment of these workers is demeaning and degrading. This is true in the United States and in Israel, as well as in other places. Second, it also concerns basic institutions and not derivative or non-basic institutions. Even if a society's basic institutions treat people fairly, it may be that subordinate institutions and groups, such as religious communities, do not; I am thinking of the treatment of women in Islam and in other religious groups. Finally, the issue is not only how institutions are organized but also the precise ways in which those who distribute goods and services act toward their clientele. Margalit calls to mind the distributing of food to victims of a famine when it is done by throwing the food off the back of the "truck as if the recipients were dogs, while still making sure that all the recipients get their just portion in an efficient manner." As he says, "the distribution may be both efficient and just, yet still humiliating."[39] I recall, in the same spirit, an Israeli film in which the searching of Palestinian women and children at a checkpoint is conducted according to proper procedures without prejudice, yet it is nonetheless carried out without sensitivity, indifferently, and in a degrading manner.[40]

Margalit makes a compelling case that in practice a society that aspires to be just may not, in these several ways, also avoid humiliation and degrading treatment of others. Since justice and decency can occur independently, he then turns to the question how both might be worthwhile social ideals. One question that Margalit raises—and it is very relevant to understanding how infinite responsibility for others might be an ideal or standard for Levinas—is whether decency and justice are ideals toward which we should aspire according to the "approximationist strategy" or according to the "second-best strategy." Both justice and decency cannot be achieved perfectly, but should we aim at them and try to accomplish them as best we can? Are they like the top of a mountain or a goal like making one hundred free throws? Is the strategy to get as close as one can to the goal one has in mind, to ignore the obstacles one will face, and to attain as close an approximation as possible? Or should one face up to the obstacles and aim for a "second best" goal, rather than the ideal one? Margalit gives an example of vacationing in Hawaii. Suppose you are piloting your own plane and want to vacation in Hawaii, but you calculate that you do not have sufficient fuel. Surely it is better to change your destination, say, to San Diego, rather than to try to fly to Hawaii but to come up short and crash into the ocean. It is better, that is, not to ignore the lack of fuel but to take it into consideration and alter your vacation destination.

While Margalit uses this distinction to consider whether the decent society is an ideal on the way to realizing the ultimate ideal of justice, I would like to use it for a different purpose. Margalit makes the point that the decent society is not a step along the way to the ideal of a just society. They are distinct ideals, albeit related ones, insofar as a perfectly just society would be decent. What I would like to ask is whether for Levinas justice and responsibility for others are related in the same way. Are they distinct ideals? Would a just society be one in which all its members were responsible for all others?

Levinas's conception of our lives in society differs from Margalit's in a number of ways. One is that for Levinas the infinite responsibility each of us has for all others is prior to justice as a kind of metaphysical or transcendental condition. It cannot be realized, neither individually nor collectively. No one of us could ever act fully on our responsibilities to and for any particular other, nor could we act on our responsibilities to infinite others. Nor, therefore, could all others act on their responsibilities to me. Hence, no society of perfect responsibility could ever occur. But if responsibility to others is impossible in certain ways, justice is impossible in others. Justice, in Levinas's mature vocabulary, is what

occurs between persons in a complex, plural society, when our responsibilities are acted on in the most reasonable and justifiable way; it is the
arrangements we have with one another, the institutions we put in place,
the rules and policies we develop, and the actions we perform. All of
this is the domain of justice. Hence, at any given moment, in any given
situation, the justice of our actions, our policies and rules, our institutions, and so forth, all occurs to some degree or other, approximating
as best we can the ideal—the unreachable goal—of perfect justice, the
maximal acting on our obligations to others to serve their needs, to care
for them, and to acknowledge their particularity. What kind of ideal or
standard, then, is justice for Levinas, and what kind of ideal or standard
is infinite responsibility? One possibility is this: justice is a second best
with respect to infinite responsibility, and justice is a goal that we approximate to the best of our abilities. That is, infinite responsibility to
others is the ultimate justification for all our life's experiences, including
all we do in the domain of justice. Justice is the best we can aim at, but it is
always a second best, and approximating to just conduct and practices is
the best we can do, given the natural and historical limits on our infinite
responsibilities.

Unlike Margalit, then, justice and infinite responsibility for others
have a closer relationship than decency and justice, but like Margalit,
they are not the same ideal. Justice is a lived, everyday ideal, while infinite responsibility is a regulative ideal of a special kind. It is unattainable,
and yet it is the ultimate justification of what is worth our seeking and
what we can accomplish. It always functions as a check or measure by
which whatever justice we do achieve is to be measured. As Margalit has
argued, a just society can for various reasons fail to be decent; it can conduct itself toward certain persons and in certain contexts in humiliating
and degrading ways. For Levinas, a just society can fail to be responsible
to others in every way. It can fail to be attentive to others in all their
particularity and singularity, and it can fail in its efforts to organize and
regulate its attention to the needs of others, to regulate generosity and
kindness in the most efficient and beneficial ways. In a sense, then, for
Levinas justice is a second best, but given our condition as natural beings
responsible to one another, that justice is all we can hope to achieve, and

even then, we can only approximate perfect justice. A social critique or a political critique will consider how and in what ways that justice has been accomplished—in the light of our infinite responsibilities one to another. The latter is not an ideal wholly independent of justice, nor is justice an ideal wholly independent of infinite responsibilities to others. They are, on the contrary, both ideals of different sorts and yet intertwined ones. Earlier I noticed that Margalit portrays his project as a story of a cluster of concepts—including decency, humiliation, and respect—which results in a picture of a utopia through which reality is criticized. Somewhat similarly, Levinas provides us with a story about how infinite responsibility and justice are interrelated in our everyday lives; the result is a picture of an ideal and what it will take to approximate that ideal in the best way possible. Critique is the evaluation, in a given situation, of how poorly or how well individuals and institutions are doing in meeting these obligations.

EVALUATING LEVINASIAN CRITIQUE

How might this conception of Levinasian social and political critique be itself evaluated? What are its strengths and weaknesses as a conception of critique? In papers on Habermas and Foucault, James Tully addresses several problems that can usefully be discussed with regard to Levinas.[41] Tully compares Habermas and Foucault with the goal of defending Foucault and his historical and genealogical method of critique. Although they differ in important ways, Habermas and Levinas do share certain strategic features; Tully's defense of Foucault is a useful way of approaching Levinas in a critical spirit. The first thing that I would like to consider is whether the relation between infinite responsibility as a transcendental structure of all of our relationships and our ordinary lives—and hence between the ideal of charity, so to speak, and the ideal of justice—is like the difference between understanding and interpretation as Tully discusses them, that is, in terms of a Wittgensteinian critique of modes of critical reflection. Or is infinite responsibility the justification for justice and an ideal that qualifies how justice should be organized and conducted? That is, if we distinguish understanding as a practical activity and interpretation as reflective articulation that arises only at critical moments, is this distinction useful as a way of understanding how infinite responsibility for others and ordinary life are distinguishable and yet related in Levinas?

One reason for Tully's use of this Wittgensteinian distinction in his critique of Habermas is that he takes Habermas to employ a traditional notion of explanation or justification and a quasi-foundationalist conception of how an account of human experience, for Habermas the basic communication situation, is ultimately grounded and explained. Tully argues, following Wittgenstein's famous account of rule-following, that contexts of meaning and other normative domains cannot be explained or justified by identifying an ultimate ground for their possibility, even a transcendental ground; they should be understood as embedded in forms of life or customary practices. For all their differences, Levinas's account of the face-to-face relationship as one concrete manifestation of how the self and transcendence are related can be read as such a transcendental grounding of everyday life and everyday interpersonal relations. My question, therefore, is whether we can object to Levinas in the same spirit that Tully objects to Habermas and others like Rawls, Kant, and Hobbes. Or, alternatively, is the face-to-face or infinite responsibility itself a form of life or a way of living interpersonally in which our everyday interpersonal relations are embedded and that provides the framework in which that everyday life is understood and lived?

One way of answering these questions is to notice that for Levinas ordinary or everyday experience is the starting point, in a sense, just as the communication situation is the starting point for Habermas. What the face-to-face provides is a "hidden" or "occluded" horizon of meaning, or a dimension or aspect of our everyday relations and experiences that is, in a sense, manifest in everyday life but only in a way inaccessible unambiguously or in a non-figurative way to everyday conceptual and linguistic tools. Thus, for Levinas, what is a lived activity or a form of life is ordinary, everyday experience. The face-to-face or infinite responsibility is a condition that makes such experience meaningful and provides its point or purpose. This relationship is most fully worked out in *Otherwise Than Being*, where ordinary experience is represented by the expression "the Said," and the face-to-face is called "the Saying."

Tully might very well register his Wittgensteinian objection against Levinas. To be sure, Levinas's identification of the primordial face-to-face that underlies and justifies, in a sense, all of our everyday experience and all of our ordinary relations is not a matter of discovering the most basic reason for such experience and relations. But this quasi-transcendental disclosure or discovery does arrive at a foundation of a sort—a pre-experiential foundation—that provides the framework in which everyday experience and life take on meaning and significance. It is not an origin or starting point, nor a fundamental agency or conceptual order, but it does carry within it an ethical normative influence on our lives as lived in ordinary experience, and with that normative influence it carries a profile for what the self is as the subject of interpersonal relations and what constitutes the other person's impact on the self.

Tully says, in clarifying how Foucault's genealogical and historical method works, that its purpose is to provide a different way of seeing the world and our lives in it. This is what makes the method a method of critique. By exploring how our current view or experience arises out of earlier ones and setting alongside that present view various alternatives, the method of articulating different points of view or perspectives gives us the opportunity to see the world and our lives in different ways.[42] In contrast, Habermas and Levinas seem to install our present experience and our present lives as givens and to proceed to explore what makes them the way they are. Tully calls this objection Habermas's "presentism." One might elaborate it in the direction of a kind of conservatism. Habermas—and Levinas—seems to privilege the present and then proceed to explain and justify it—but not to alter it. Foucault, on the other hand, seeks to call upon history to register a range of different possibilities regarding our subjectivity and concerning the relation between power and knowledge, alongside the present one, and to encourage the reader to take up some alternative to the subjectivity that holds us in the present. The notion of critique seems to have a firmer grip in Foucault's work than in Habermas's.

But this criticism of Habermas seems to be ungenerous and narrow; it certainly is so when applied to Levinas. The face-to-face, when extended to all persons as infinite responsibility to all others in every

respect, is an impossible ideal, but it is an ideal, a corrective to the complicated, qualified ways in which we actually live our responsibilities to
others in the everyday world. This is what it means to say that the regime
of charity or kindness, as Levinas calls it, is a utopia. Habermas's vision
may or may not have this utopian dimension, but Levinas's conception
surely does.[43] Some take Levinas's focus on responsibility to be revolutionary, and there are situations in which that may be true. But at least,
in more pedestrian settings, it is corrective and revisionary. What it calls
for is a different perspective on society and politics, as well as on our daily
lives, and a reorientation toward what Levinas calls "disinterestedness"
and "self-sacrifice." Such a reorientation need not be ascetic; it does not
demand self-denial all the time. What it does require, however, is taking
one's obligations to others into consideration at all times in some way or
other and to appreciate that such obligations need no further justification than the very existence of our social existence itself. Living in conversation with others brings with it concern and attention toward those
others; nothing more is needed to introduce such concern and attention.

Unlike Foucault and Tully, then, Levinas does encourage us to take
up an alternative perspective on our lives and our subjectivity, our selfhood, but it is not simply some different perspective. It is a very important
and distinctive one, without which morality itself would lack any normative force for us. The perspective is, in a sense, a frequently occluded
or forgotten one. It is the point of view of an abiding and demanding
responsibility toward others. In a sense, like Foucault, Levinas seeks to
disclose domination and the way in which power shapes our lives and our
decisions, but the domination is not political or concrete domination. It
is the domination of a picture, a naturalism and egoism, and the power
is the power of our own interests, appetites, and drives. But in contrast
to Nietzsche and Foucault, Levinas is not self-critical regarding the fact
of infinite responsibility. It is not a theory for him and hence cannot be
exposed as an ideology; rather this primordial responsibility is exhib-
ited in our conduct and a phenomenology of it, as it were, and whatever
transcendental status it has is not the result of a metaphysical or transcendental deduction. It discloses itself in our experience, relationships,
and conduct when we look at and describe them in a certain way. For
Levinas, infinite responsibility for others is indeed limited, but it cannot

be subject to critique. It can never, in our ordinary lives, occur by itself or perfectly, but it must always determine our conduct and experience. For this reason, the ways in which we regulate and organize our ordinary experience—and this includes our political lives—are always subject to critique in terms of how well or how poorly we accept others, acknowledge them, respect them and their needs, and act in humane and just ways. In short, the regime of justice can be subject to critique by ethics but not vice versa. The ethical character of our social lives is a kind of a priori. Neither Tully nor Foucault would be happy with this, but Levinas denies that it is a prejudice or a bias. Without it the very notion of morality and its normative force dissolves, and these are ubiquitous features of all human experience.[44]

There is one interpretation of Levinas's critique that must be avoided, and it is similar to an objection that is often made of someone like Foucault. In the case of Foucault, the objection is that his nominalism prevents him from calling upon any general or universal standard when judging that a culture or regime is more or less violent, oppressive, or dangerous than another.[45] Foucault's descriptions and judgments are all historical and contingent. There can be no comparison of events or cases or conduct from a detached point of view; hence, there can be no real critique. Or, as Bernstein puts it, for Foucault "all effective criticism must be *local*." In the same spirit, with regard to Levinas, the objection would be that since the face-to-face and therefore our infinite responsibilities to the other person are always utterly particular, all forms of justice are always oppressive or violent; all justice fails to be just. Levinasian critique must be particular and singular; it cannot be comparative without itself becoming totalitarian, in a sense. And since ordinary experience always takes place within the domain of justice, it is always a failure. This means, however, that Levinasian critique either always applies or never applies, and a critique of this kind is vacuous or empty, for a critique that always applies is no less vacuous than one that never applies.

But this kind of objection makes the mistake of failing to appreciate how, for Levinas, the particular and the universal or general do not come apart; they always occur together. To be sure, there are times when Levinas seems to exaggerate or emphasize his objections to totality and to generality. He frequently says that Stalinism and Hitlerism are paradigms of oppressive ideologies. Such comments appear to be a criticism of generality from the perspective of the particular individual and the particular case. Moreover, from this perspective, his critique of a society, policy, or institution as failing to be sufficiently responsive to individuals may itself seem to be a general criticism and a lapse into totality. But such reactions are based on the failure to appreciate how ethics and politics, the Saying and the Said, infinite responsibility and efforts at accomplishing justice, are all are interrelated and interdependent. To clarify how and why this is so and rather than simply repeat what I have already said, let me turn to Levinas's essay "Useless Suffering" to exhibit the kind of reorientation that Levinasian critique has in mind.

THE UNIVERSALITY AND PARTICULARITY
OF ETHICAL CRITIQUE

A central theme of the essay is the way in which the historical conditions of the late twentieth century ought to have provoked in us a reorientation in our social and political lives. It is this reorientation that Levinas calls the "end of theodicy." As Levinas puts it, "Perhaps the most revolutionary fact of our twentieth-century consciousness—but it is also an event in Sacred History—is that of the destruction of all balance between the explicit and implicit theodicy of Western thought and the forms which suffering and its evil take in the very unfolding of this century."[46] This "destruction of balance" he later refers to as "the disproportion between suffering and every theodicy." Sensitive interpreters ought to appreciate that after all the horrors of the century—"two world wars, the totalitarianisms of right and left, Hitlerism and Stalinism, Hiroshima, the Gulag, and the genocides of Auschwitz and Cambodia"—we live in a new epoch that is marked by the extremity and character of assaults on human dignity and worth, on the one hand, and the avoidance that characterizes our attempts to explain and understand this suffering and evil, on the other. That is, such interpreters ought to appreciate that cognitive efforts to cope with suffering have been discredited; they have contributed to too much suffering or been complicit in permitting it to take place. It may be that Levinas takes such theodices—explanatory schemes—to be inadequate as explanations of the century's atrocities, but whether or not they fail as explanations, they surely fail as responses, that is, as ways of dealing with such suffering. This "avoidance," as I have called it—using Stanley Cavell's term—applies to social scientific explanations and accounts as much as it does to religious ones. All cognitive attempts to comprehend and thereby to "domesticate" or "accommodate" such suffering and atrocity have been shown to be acts of wrongful self-deception, moral failures.

Levinas does not say what about these twentieth century atrocities and this suffering discredits such cognitive responses. I take it that he is referring both to the ways in which bureaucratic and administrative programs were central instruments for carrying out these atrocities and to the ways in which social scientific thinking—for example, political decisions based on considerations of security and self-interest—were central to arguments for non-intervention or for standing by when direct intervention might have reduced the atrocities. Levinas also is thinking about the ways in which theological explanations immobilized the victims and led them to accept what was being done to them rather than resist. All of this might have been in Levinas's mind when he argues for the "imbalance" or "disproportion" between the atrocities of the century and theodicy. But his central point is clear. Levinas's criticism is leveled at cultures, societies, and ways of life in which the sufferings of others provoke not assistance and aid but rather indifference, caution, and avoidance, especially when such responses are facilitated by "too much thought." For Levinas, in general, responsibility to and for others requires acting in their behalf—everything from saying "hello" to providing food for the hungry, aid to victims of famine or natural disasters, and welfare to the poor. Explanations of why the poor are impoverished, what groups are particularly susceptible, and more may be informative and even helpful for the purposes of deliberating about possible policies and programs. But they may very well—and often do—delay or impede providing actual help and support. Moreover, they can be manipulated to do so. It is this collection of tactics, I think, that Levinas is calling to our attention and warning us against. It is, to put it otherwise, one way of expressing the impotence of thought in the face of the demands of the other person to be acknowledged and supported.

Against this background, this judgment against avoiding facing up to the suffering of others and to responding to their needs, Levinas asks:

what "meaning [can] religiosity and the human morality of goodness
... still retain after the end of theodicy"?[47] His answer is that our lives
take on meaning insofar as we transform our own effort—and suffering—into work in behalf of the suffering of others, into love and care for
others. There is, he says, no "consoling theodicy" in our world, no way
to comfort ourselves with the thought that the horrors and atrocities of
wars, genocides, and atrocities can be explained or understood in some
way or other. It may be that Levinas believes, as others do, that there
are no explanations that can adequately and satisfactorily comprehend
and understand the evil of this century, and hence relying upon such accounts to provide peace of mind and a kind of satisfaction or comfort is
impossible, even cognitively. But even if he is unsure about the epistemic
issue, Levinas seems confident about the moral one, that one ought not
rely upon explanation when what is needed are efforts in behalf of reducing suffering and indignities.[48]

Societies and polities, therefore, can be criticized for failing to grasp
and follow this warning. A society that is attentive to our interpersonal
responsibilities Levinas calls, in this essay, "the inter-human order." To
see our lives with an attunement to these responsibilities and their priority for our lives he calls "the inter-human perspective." It is, he says,
"to envisage suffering ... as meaningful in me, useless in the Other."[49]
Furthermore, he says that to seek to comprehend suffering in thought,
in explanatory systems or accounts, is to make suffering into an "abstraction" and to fail to engage it in all its concreteness, both in oneself and in
the other person. Reflection and explanation create a distance between
us and suffering and most importantly between us and others in need.

It is this distance that the twentieth century exposes as a critical
failure in political life, for reciprocity and generality can lead to imper-
sonality and the risk of losing altruism altogether. In Levinas's words:

> The inter-human perspective can subsist, but can also be lost, in the political
> order of the City where the Law establishes mutual obligations between citizens.
> Properly speaking, the inter-human lies in a non-indifference of one to another,
> in a responsibility of one for another. The inter-human is prior to the reciprocity
> of this responsibility, which inscribes itself in impersonal laws, and becomes
> superimposed on the pure altruism of this responsibility inscribed in the ethical
> position of the self as self. It is prior to every contact which would signify pre-
> cisely the moment of reciprocity where it can, to be sure, continue, but where it

can also attenuate or extinguish altruism and distinterestedness. The order of
politics—post-ethical or pre-ethical—which inaugurates the "social contract"
is neither the sufficient condition nor the necessary outcome of ethics. In its
ethical position, the self is distinct from the citizen born of the City, and from
the individual who precedes all order in his natural egoism, from whom political
philosophy, since Hobbes, tries to derive—or succeeds in deriving—the social
or political order of the City.[50]

Graphically, that is, the domain of the ethical—of infinite responsibility
one for the other—lies between the "natural egoism" of the state of nature and the "reciprocity" and "mutual obligations between citizens." Alternatively, the political order arises out of selves who need it to protect
and ensure their interests and rights, but it also is what it is only insofar
as those selves are related ethically, by ties of responsibility that need
to be enacted and enhanced in order for "the marvelous alterity of the
Other" to be manifest in the help or assistance the other needs from the
self, in my responsibility "to help [the other person] gratuitously, without
concern for reciprocity."[51]

In this essay, then, Levinas registers a warning for and a critique
of modern, post-Holocaust politics and society. The warning is about
abstraction and avoidance and the risks attendant to excessive reflection
and efforts at explanation—social scientific, historical, and religious.
The critique is about failing to be attuned to the unilateral and utterly
particular responsibilities that each of us has to those in need and those
who suffer, when their cries and sighs call out to us and indeed even more
fundamentally when we acknowledge the claim of their very existence.
This warning and this critique are utterly particular, made in a post-
Holocaust world, but they are completely general as well, for they apply
to all and at all times. In this sense, the ethical critique of the social and
political, as Levinas sees it, is both particular and general.[52]

FIVE

RESPONSIBILITY FOR OTHERS
AND THE DISCOURSE OF RIGHTS

As I have shown, one of the roles played by the quasi-transcendental or structural relationship that Levinas calls the face-to-face and later calls the self's infinite responsibility to and for each and every other person is the role of the ground of social and political critique. That is, societies, institutions, political policies, and legal systems can (and should) all be judged in terms of how adequately or how inadequately they promote and permit this responsibility (generosity toward and care) for others. Moreover, since infinite responsibility is characteristic of all human social relationships and relations and since "substitution" is the core of our selfhood, critique can be understood to be the evaluation of all of our experience in terms of what is fundamental and normatively salient about the human condition itself. Critique is about being true to oneself. In the language of Foucault, care for the other and care of oneself go hand in hand.[1]

Levinas emphasizes throughout his career that for him subjectivity is characterized by its initial and primary passivity, and our social relationships are grounded in heteronomy or an other-determined asymmetry. All of this is intended to distinguish Levinas's understanding of our existence from those like Descartes to Kant, Fichte, Nietzsche, Heidegger, and beyond, on the one hand, and others such as Spinoza, Hegel, Foucault, and the French structuralists, on the other. This is one way of setting out the background for Levinas's very unusual approach to ethics, morality, and politics. Another would be to contrast him with any form of materialism or naturalism, in which human agency is interpreted as a complex form of natural responsiveness to physical and basically causal conditions. In any case, the result of Levinas's conviction that his conception of selfhood or agency is distinctive as normative and founded on an external demand is that his conception of how our lives are socially and politically organized must differ as well. And this difference will have implications for the precise way in which his ethical critique of politics will be realized.

In chapter 1 I noted that on several occasions Levinas makes this very point and virtually in the same words. He puts it this way: "It is then not without importance to know if the egalitarian and just State in which man is fulfilled . . . proceeds from a war of all against all, or from the irreducible responsibility of the one for all, and if it can do without friendships and faces."[2] In *Ethics and Infinity* he repeats this sentiment: "Does the social, with its institutions, universal forms and laws, result from limiting the consequences of the war between men, or from limiting the infinity which opens in the ethical relationship of man to man?" And he goes on to describe this limitation as politics being "checked and criticized starting from the ethical."[3]

For Levinas, our social and political arrangements—their structure, institutions, purposes, policies, rules and norms, and practices—are mechanisms for organizing and implementing within pluralities, especially large groups of people, our infinite responsibilities, each one to all others. To put it more succinctly and in other terms, these arrangements institutionalize and organize imperfect duties or what Simon Caney calls "positive duties."[4] But this must be understood to mean that they orchestrate infinite particular responsibilities into rules for regularized general ones. And since politics—if we use this term for all that I have just enumerated, our social and political lives—is always aimed at creating or organizing general patterns of distribution, it runs the risk of "forgetting" or compromising particular persons with their needs and dependencies. Hence, the limits on our infinite responsibilities that become institutionalized themselves need to be "checked and criticized"—or limited—by a constant attention to the responsibilities in behalf of which it is the purpose of political and social life to respond. In short, an ethically sensitive political life is mutually limiting and mutually interdependent.

If this account of what Levinas has in mind is correct, then it means that he believed that social and political life conceived this way should differ in some important ways from social and political life conceived in a different way—a traditional liberal way, we might call it.[5] That is the core of the statement I just repeated and which Levinas himself repeated so frequently. More specifically, he says that "it is not without importance to know," which means that knowing the ground of our social and political lives will make a difference in how we carry out the ethical critique of our society and our state. And furthermore what it is not without importance to know is something about the "egalitarian and just state" and what its grounds are. Societies and states are structures in which persons live, the former a general collective structure and the latter a structure in which a group with a shared geographical location is governed. Levinas tells us that it is important to know—for outsiders with an interest in how a given society conducts itself and for insiders or citizens concerned with how their own society is organized—what conception of selfhood underlies its institutions, norms, and practices. There is benefit in this knowing, and it is a practical benefit. Moreover, even if that society is "egalitarian and just," which Levinas advocates, it is still important to know this about this society. But why, we might ask? Because, I would think, as a historical and changing entity, called upon to modify, act, adapt, and respond in changing circumstances, the society and the state that governs it ought to do all this in terms of some conception of human selfhood that it advocates and seeks to facilitate, to realize. In short, critical reflection both from inside and from outside the society in question and its political agencies needs to know what end guides it, what conception of human existence and selfhood it seeks to realize. This is true both because of the kind of society and state it wants to be—egalitarian and just—and because of the kind of enterprise or activity it is, human and social and itself oriented to the responsibilities one has to others.

RIGHTS DISCOURSE AND THE DISCOURSE OF RESPONSIBILITY

In these passages, Levinas contrasts two discourses, as I shall call them. One is the discourse of infinite responsibility, or the language of the regime of charity, as he sometimes calls it. The other I will for now call the discourse of rights, which he designates with an allusion to Thomas Hobbes's famous characterization of human existence in the state of nature, a war of all against all.[6] This is not to say that Levinas thinks narrowly of all modern liberal political theories as grounded on the same conception of human nature. Nor does he think that all such theories—from Locke to Rousseau, Kant, and beyond (we would include Rawls, Scanlon, and a host of more recent neo-Kantians and contract theorists)—are grounded on the Hobbesian conception of atomized, competing, mutually threatening, power-seeking individuals. Rather I take Levinas to be distinguishing two discourses in terms of two differing conceptions of individual agency or selfhood. One is primarily concerned with us as natural beings, broadly speaking, and hence as grounded on what Grotius, Hobbes, Spinoza, and others would have taken to be the individual's desire for self-preservation—what Spinoza called the *conatus*. The other is primarily concerned with what others need us to do for them and what others call upon us to do for them. For our purposes, let me call one the "responsibility discourse" and the other the "rights discourse." In one discourse moral normativity is internal, in a sense, and in the other it is external or derived. Hence, in one discourse, moral normativity is introduced into our social and political lives intrinsically, insofar as those lives are social and always involve infinite second-person responsibilities; in the other discourse, moral normativity is introduced into our social and political lives extrinsically, by means of the mechanisms by which natural beings construct the social and political orders in which they live. Levinas claims that it is important for those interested in or invested in a given society to know which is true.[7] We now must ask why it is important to know which discourse one's critique employs.[8]

To begin, notice that for both there is a process of limitation. Within the rights discourse, political authority and political institutions require limiting individual desires and individual freedom. To establish a sovereign and to fix and articulate laws, a collection of individuals must agree to limit what they want and what they are free to do in order to create stability and order and to maximize the possibility of satisfying those desires. On such a view, the political and legal mechanisms of the state identify which rights and obligations are necessary in order to maximize security and peace for its citizens. Within the responsibility discourse, on the other hand, it is the infinite responsibilities each individual has to and for each and every other person that are limited or restricted. Such limitation or restriction occurs in all of everyday life, once there is a plurality of individuals with whom one lives and engages. What social and political organization and institutions add, above and beyond what individuals must do whenever they choose to act and then do act, is regularity, generality, and patterns of limitation and restriction. For example, I must limit the responsibilities I act upon whenever I am faced with the option of meeting a friend for lunch or taking the time to console another friend for a recent death in the family. That is, given a finite amount of available time and the necessity of choosing to spend time with one person or another, we limit what responsibilities we act upon. What government programs, policies, or regulations add is a normative pattern for distributing time and resources. Taxing citizens and then subsidizing a homeless shelter with some of the funds compels everyone in a society to contribute some resources for a specific but general clientele. This political and legal process generalizes both those who act on their responsibilities and those who receive their beneficence; the funds come from someone or other (or from everyone) and then provide services for someone or other.

There is a good deal more that we might say about the differences between a rights discourse and a responsibility discourse. But although Levinas certainly takes them to be different, he also does not want to reject the rights discourse entirely in favor of the discourse of responsibility. If we take the rights discourse to focus on human rights, then both express what Samuel Moyn calls the shift to a moralization of the political that he takes to be characteristic of the postwar period and becomes especially salient in the late 1970s.[9] While Moyn argues that it is the discourse of human rights that emerges as an alternative utopia during this period, we can see Levinas as proposing a different but related approach to ethical critique. Part of the difference is that the rights discourse assumes that the most important thing that a state can do is to protect people from one another and from outsiders; it does so by regarding our contesting needs and desires and by setting out what rights and obligations are required to secure tranquility and maximum opportunity for personal freedom. Levinas's responsibility discourse, on the other hand, suggests that the most important thing a state can do is to regulate and organize our innate sense that we ought to help and care for others, presumably because it assumes that others need us and because we recognize that we ought to meet those needs to the degree that we can. One discourse assumes that our deepest interpersonal attitudes are ones of threat and mistrust; the other assumes that our deepest interpersonal attitudes are concern and love. One worries that without regulation we might be tempted to care primarily and largely for those closest to us; the other worries that without regulation we might fear primarily and largely those who are stronger and more powerful than we are. That is, one discourse notes that we need most of all to be protected against those who are more powerful and more violent, while the other notes that we need most of all to be made to appreciate how much everyone else depends on us, no matter who they are.[10] I could go on and on, then, about how the two discourses differ, but instead let me move directly to the central questions: Why is it important for those interested or invested in a particular state to know what discourse best characterizes the state's central purpose and role? What difference would it in fact make to how citizens or critics approached a particular state and its policies and conduct? And yet how does Levinas's discourse of responsibility not exclude the notion of rights but rather incorporates it in its own distinctive way?

Critics of states who share the rights discourse are primarily concerned about the ways in which a state or government defines and then respects the rights of its citizens and of others, whether and how it protects them or fails to respect and protect them, and to what degree it is implicated in rights violations. Of special importance are not only the rights that the state defines through laws and statutes, so-called "civil rights," but also those rights that are common to all human agents, what have come to be called "human rights." A rights-based critique of a particular government or society might focus on one or both such rights, and the critique would be aimed to show that the very purposes for which the society came into being were being subverted. In a very real sense, a society or a government might be charged with failing to be true to itself, or it might be charged with failing to be true to its nature as a state and true to itself as a set of human institutions that respect the human beings for which they were created and constructed.

To ask what difference it would make to appreciate that a society or state was founded on our infinite responsibilities to all others does not mean that an ethical critique would dismiss or ignore the transgressions of citizens' rights, both civil and human rights. It might mean that the critique of the political and social character and conduct of a state, even if formulated as a critique of its respect for and promotion of rights, would have different content if the idea of rights was somehow itself grounded in our interpersonal, social existence and our infinite responsibilities to each and every other person. That is, when Levinas says that it is not unimportant for a social or political critic to know that the ground of the state is "charity" or "love" rather than mistrust and conflict, he might mean that genuine ethical critique of the state could be conducted either directly as a critique of how a state organizes and conducts the responsible treatment of citizens and others or indirectly as a critique of how citizens' and individuals' rights are not respected or dealt with within a given society and state. Ethical critique might be responsibility-based directly or rights-based albeit insofar as rights are themselves to be understood as an expression of infinite responsibility.

Levinas's insight that ethics is fundamentally a matter of how individuals are related in terms of claim and responsibility can be seen to express a number of developments that Moyn has described regarding the relationship between morality and politics and utopian thought.[11] One development is the disenchantment with a conception of international relations as a matter of realpolitik, of power and self-interest. Increasingly this kind of realist view has been challenged by individuals, movements, groups, and agencies that call for policies and conduct based on humane concern for the victims of persecution, neglect, and suffering of all kinds.[12] Another development that Moyn notices is the shift from a de facto statism and commitment to the inviolability of the nation-state to a concern for individuals within a global and international setting. After World War II and more recently in the wake of various genocides and civil wars, the status of refugees and stateless peoples, among others, has compelled a reorientation from civil rights as primary to rights that apply to everyone, whether or not they are citizens of a particular state and are protected by a state. Furthermore, there is the movement to make all of our lives—socially, economically, and politically—subject to moral considerations that apply everywhere, even when specific determinations may result in various differences. That is, this priority of the moral and ethical has a universality about it, but one that is attentive and responsive to the particular differences of context, culture, locale, and such. Finally, Moyn has called attention to the failure of various utopian visions and the need to replace them with some ground of hope, especially when global pictures no long have the effect they once did. In their place, the movement for human rights has come to be an individualized and piecemeal replacement—what Moyn calls the "last utopia." I would call what he has in mind an "episodic messianism," and this is a term I have used not only to characterize our contemporary discourse of redemption but also Levinas's conception of the ethical.[13]

Against this background and these changes, Levinas's use of the discourse of infinite responsibility to assess political conduct can be viewed at least as *structurally similar* to the use of the human rights discourse that Moyn and others have begun to investigate and evaluate in recent years.[14] That is, on the one hand, to use Levinas's terms, it is important to know that political institutions and practices are founded on responsibility rather than rights, and on the other hand, it is important to know that the critique of the state should be conducted in terms of responsibility and not narrowly in terms of human rights. The former issue concerns the ultimate purposes for which political institutions are established and organized; the latter issue concerns the duties that all of us have toward one another, either directly through personal conduct or indirectly through the conduct of both political and non-governmental agencies and institutions. The former conception of the state and its foundations is individualist; the latter is particular but based on the demands and claims others make on the individual and hence is relational in a direct and fundamental way. Moreover—and this may be the most important feature of the difference—the former view, as Levinas sees it, does not account for the normative force of the rights in question, not even if they are human rights that apply to everyone, while the latter view provides the normative structure in which rights, duties, and ethical critique have their compelling character.

In his helpful book *Making Sense of Human Rights*, James Nickel
points out that the post–World War II political developments that are
associated with the international concern for human well-being and dignity, as a series of historical events, have taken the form of a discourse
about human rights. This discourse is in some ways indebted to an Enlightenment vocabulary of natural rights, a vocabulary that has its roots
in antiquity, in both the philosophical and the biblical traditions, and in
the tradition of natural law. But while it does have a lengthy prehistory,
this recent political movement has distinctive features. Nickel asks why
this movement to hold states accountable for how they treat their own
citizens as well as others has taken the form of a discourse about rights.
Along with other philosophers such as James Griffin and Charles Beitz
and with historians from Lynn Hunt to Moyn, Nickel realizes that this
feature of the movement is contingent and requires some explanation.
Historians might give a variety of answers, largely seeking to provide a
causal account of what factors led to the coalescing of an international
eagerness and willingness to find a shareable set of common interests
about how governments should treat people. Philosophers, on the other
hand, might turn to what the very concept of a right provides that other
concepts would not. To answer the question, Nickel considers the special
contribution that a rights vocabulary makes to the movement and how
different it would be if, instead of rights, one called those central considerations "high-priority goals." The outcome of his remarks is that by calling these considerations rights—freedom, privacy, life, minimum sustenance, self-determination, and so forth—journalists, political leaders,
and humanitarian activists confer a certain status upon them. They call
attention to the fact that these considerations have a significant weight
or importance, that they specify who will benefit and who is responsible with some definiteness, and finally that they come with "mandatory
force." Goals or ideals are one thing; rights are another.[15]

Since Levinas's point about the primacy of infinite responsibility
and the way in which it grounds a critique of modern society is analogous
to the way the modern international movement in behalf of human rights
forms the core of a critique of modern states and governments, Nickel's
question about the human rights movement might serve as a further clue
for understanding Levinas's remark about the discourse of rights and

its difference from the discourse of infinite responsibility. If a political movement in behalf of concern for human matters were to employ the vocabulary of infinite responsibility, what would be the significance of the fact that it preferred the Levinasian vocabulary to that of rights?

If the laws and institutions of the state should be grounded in a desire to organize and ensure our unlimited responsibilities for others, then in a sense the direction of such an aspiration is from the point of the view of the agent and of the obligation to assist, provide for, and help others. But, from another perspective, such organization is about how the needs, interests, and goods that people require are met and how they are protected from harm and suffering. Like the talk of rights, then, the talk of responsibility is about both the persons in need and those who provide for those needs. It is about both rights and duties, about protections and interests and freedom, and also about responsibilities, ways of meeting them, and programs for organizing them and caring for others.[16]

If we are going to be able to clarify Levinas's rhetorical question, that it is important to know whether a just and egalitarian society or state is founded on the "war of all against all" or whether it is founded on the infinite responsibility of each and every person to and for every other person, we will need to explore how these two discourses differ but also how they are related. I have made note of three ways in which they can be distinguished—in terms of (a) the role of the particular individual, (b) the difference between negative and positive duties, and (c) the possibility of accounting for the normative force of the notions of rights and duties.[17] But even if distinctive, Levinas's orientation based on interpersonal responsibility cannot ignore the complexity of social and political norms and institutions and the various kinds of roles that they play.

It is undeniable that a host of laws and governmental agencies are devoted to protecting citizens from injuries of various kinds and to regulating interactions to guarantee fair treatment. Caring for others often will mean preventing harm from coming to them, reducing pain and suffering, and protecting them—from the government, from other persons, and from organizations. There are also laws and institutions that provide for people and regulate benefits—how much to be received, of what kinds, in what ways, and so forth. In his account of how to justify specific human rights, Nickel argues for six tests that must be satisfied for the justification to be satisfactory. These are empirical tests and include, for example, "showing that people today regularly experience problems or abuses in the area protected by the proposed right," explaining how the norm is important or has a high priority and protects something that is central to living a decent life, and showing how the burdens the right imposes are not unfair or extremely demanding and are regularly provided by countries around the world.[18] One dimension of this process of justification, that is, involves showing why the kind of norms that are needed in various cases are rights and not some other kind of norm. The importance of this, as we have seen, is that a right is a weighty or powerful protection against injury or mistreatment by one's government and others. Moreover, it is, in the case of human rights, a claim against one's own government to support individuals and to protect them. Furthermore, it goes some way toward justifying others—other states, individuals, and organizations—to intervene in the affairs of a government that fails to provide this protection or this assistance when it is needed.

Levinas's point is that while we cannot ignore these functions and roles, it is unsatisfactory to take the just and humane conduct of a state and society to be grounded in the Hobbesian view of the state of nature.[19] This means a number of things. It means, for example, that for Levinas the assistance to and protection of individuals in a state are not being provided by the state primarily to protect individuals from one another, from others, and from the state itself. It is otherwise for advocates of human rights. Rights discourse, as Nickel suggests, is founded on the likelihood and even the actuality of injuries and mistreatment. It presumes that by nature human beings are competitive and aggressive; they are threats to one another. The state is primarily an institutional organization for preventing interpersonal harm and injury; it formulates norms that express limits on individual liberty that threatens others. The state publicizes those norms, polices conduct in terms of them, and adjudicates transgressions. Among the most serious of such transgressions and injuries are those associated with what we today call "human rights." They are a set of strong norms, negative and positive, aimed at freeing individuals from threats to their living decent lives. Griffin, for example, focuses on rights to life, liberty, and basic sustenance, because these are the basic rights that protect our personhood, our basic status as normative agents.[20] Nickel is more empirical and less inclined to ground human rights in some conception of basic personhood.[21] But the assumption that both share—and they are not alone—is the assumption that we are by nature competitive beings who threaten one another and that governments too are by nature inclined toward oppression and domination and manipulation. What needs acknowledging and protecting, most fundamentally, is something we might call human dignity. The practice of human rights and indeed the very status of rights as minimal and weighty protections and regulations or norms are one way of respecting this aggressive nature and recognizing what is necessary to mitigate its effects. In the end, then, the Hobbesian view begins with interpersonal threat and mistrust and also with the assumption that each individual is the basic locus of authority and power regarding his or her own decisions, actions, and policies. What authority and power the state comes to have is had by transference or delegation from the individuals who submit to it. Hobbes calls this natural liberty or freedom and identifies it with natural power and natural right. But this view is precisely what Levinas does not encourage.

What is unsatisfactory about taking society and the state to be founded on such a view of individuals and rights? Surely Levinas would not deny that individuals do in fact suffer at the hands of others—of other persons, agencies, and the government itself. He is aware, as we all are, that there are those in need of health care and treatment who cannot afford it, that there are citizens who cannot adequately feed themselves or their families or provide shelter and a home for themselves and their families. Levinas knows that some are prevented from receiving an adequate education and some do not have jobs and work. In fact, not only is Levinas aware of all these and other ways in which people have needs and interests or are subject to degrading and harmful treatment by others or by the government itself, he is in fact very attentive to these facts. One might even say that they are at the center of his account of moral experience and of human social or interpersonal experience. We harm others, and we fail to come to their assistance. We need to do better, personally and collectively. Indeed, that is the very purpose of our lives—to do better toward others. Civil and social institutions and practices ultimately are ways by which we, collectively, seek to do better at just these things.

In a sense, then, these institutions and practices are organized to do as much as can be done and what should be done to assist others, to help them to live full and decent lives. Levinas's way of putting this, however, is that it is not ultimately a matter of respecting the rights of individuals; it is rather a matter of organizing and deploying responsibilities.

It would be a mistake, then, to think that Levinas rejects the vocabulary of rights and would have nothing to say about natural rights or "human rights," as they have come to be called. Moreover, it would be a mistake to think that Levinas is interested not in negative duties but rather solely in positive ones. In the 1980s, in several essays, Levinas discusses natural and human rights and shows a great deal of respect for them. But, he argues, these rights are not grounded on a Hobbesian view, the kind of conception of the state of nature as one of mutual aggression and threat that I have just described. Rather natural and human rights should be understood as grounded in the infinite responsibility each of us has to and for each and every other person.[22] Moreover, while such a view shows what is authoritative and justified about positive duties toward others, it also enables us to understand what is authoritative and normative about negative duties with regard to others. Both are ways of treating other persons, and ethics is the framework for all of our interpersonal relationships, whether they involve avoiding certain forms of behavior or accomplishing certain forms of help or assistance. The negativity or the positivity is not the central issue. What is central is that the normative force, direction, and scope of our personhood are always aimed outward first, toward others—indeed all others. In our everyday lives, in society and in the domain of moral and political life, our infinite "rays" of unbounded responsibilities require orchestration, determination, and qualification. The norms of morality and law and social, political life are ways of accomplishing these organizational tasks, or at least they are ways of providing these tasks with order and direction. The authority of rights, that is, as much as the authority of social and moral obligations, all rests in the "face" of the other person as it targets me, in all its singularity and concreteness, addressing me as it does with the trace of a common forcefulness, the force of the morally normative, that it shares with each and every face that confronts me, near or far.

Elsewhere, I have depicted Levinas's vision in contrast to the Hobbesian picture as follows. Naturalists like Hobbes—and not they alone—begin with an array of individual agents each with infinite liberty and infinite power. To be sure, these agents and their power or might are constrained by natural conditions, but they have no intrinsic constraints or limitations. Morality and the norms of civic life identify types of actions or conduct that individuals should not perform, and they have force, if they do, because the rationality of the individuals inform them that their interests are best served if they follow these rules or norms. They organize conduct in a way that the individual takes to be the most rational way for him or her to act. In short, moral and then legal norms are self-imposed limitations on an originally unbounded freedom. Levinas has a different picture of human motivation and conduct. For him, we do not begin with unlimited liberty and power and then identify ways in which that liberty and power ought rationally to be structured and organized. Rather we begin with infinite or unlimited responsibility to others; this arises for us in the relationships we have with each and every other person. These relations all exist prior to our doing anything and prior to the other person's doing anything; moreover, internal to these relationships is a structure of plea and demand, initiated in the other person and aimed or targeted at each other individual, and a responsiveness of infinite responsibility, oriented from each person to each and every other person. This is the form and content of interpersonal relationship that Levinas calls by numerous names—transcendence, the face of the other, enigma, proximity, persecution, hostage, accusation, substitution, and more. To the complex, multidimensional relations we have with one another, this dimension or framework brings the form of normative claim or force and the content of needs and interests. At the deepest level of our personality or character as socially engaged human beings, each of us is called upon to be for each and every other person, to be responsive and responsible, and to act therefore out of a sense of generosity, beneficence, charity, love, concern, or whatever one wants to call it. Social and political institutions and policies are ways of organizing—that is, limiting and orchestrating—this infinite responsibility for all members of a society or state. Without seeing things this way, there is no hope, Levinas thinks, of understanding what gives our social and political lives the normative force or authority that they have. Nor will we see our social and political lives in the right light. We will be tempted to see them as limitations or as "chains" rather than as expressions and recipes or programs. Normative ethics and political life are ways of maximizing and organizing our concern for others; they are not primarily sacrifices of our freedom and our desires and interests and acts of self-abandonment. They are instead modes of the deepest and most true self-expression or self-affirmation. Insofar as we are most deeply responsible to and for others, we are most true to ourselves when we are as well organized to help and support others as we can possibly be, given the differences in distance and familiarity between ourselves and others, and given the plurality of our social lives, the complexity of our lives with others in the world, and the limited resources available to us.

In one respect, then, the reason that we are better off knowing that our social and political institutions are grounded in our infinite interpersonal responsibilities is that knowing this provides us with the confidence that our social and political norms and practices are as authoritative as we take them to be. They really do carry the normative force that we take them to carry. And this means, in part, that human rights are in fact authoritative and justified, because they are constitutive of our normative agency, as Griffin argues, but also because that agency is itself a function of the other person's claim upon us. Normative agency is not a function of autonomy, liberty, and basic human capabilities; rather it arises out of the infinite claim that our social relationships bring to us.

Furthermore, the Levinasian picture suggests that social and political norms and institutions are established to enhance our opportunities for fulfilling our responsibilities to others, our duties to assist, rescue, and care for others. Only if they in fact do channel or organize our efforts to do these things, attentively and to a significant degree, are they successful. Security and increased economic and social freedom are not the most indicative measures of how a state is doing; rather how a society deals with poverty and destitution, how it provides health care, jobs, education, and social services, all these are better indications of a society's accomplishment. Therefore, in general, while there is nothing wrong with greater freedoms, the true measure of a community's humanity is its treatment of those most in need—the marginal, the vulnerable, and the unprotected. For reasons like this, Annabel Herzog, for example, focuses on Levinas's concern for the widow, the stranger, and the orphan. It is at this point that Levinas seems closest to someone like Hannah Arendt and to those like Judith Butler and Seyla Benhabib who follow in her footsteps and privilege the treatment of the disenfranchised—refugees, minorities, and the stateless. How a society and a state deal with refugees or aliens, on the one hand, and minorities, on the other, becomes the crucial indication of how well it is serving those ethical responsibilities on which all social and political life is founded. These become the litmus test for political responsibility and decency, so to speak.

Moreover, as I have pointed out, Levinas's picture reminds us that all of our dealings with others, even when they are organized according to regular practices and are institutionalized, should be understood as meeting the claims of individuals on individuals. For organizational or tactical purposes, administering health care may involve relationships between the government, health providers, and classes of patients or clients. But ethically speaking, providing health care is always a matter of single, particular persons—social workers, insurance evaluators, patients, doctors, nurses, and more. Ultimately, each case involves several one-on-one relationships, and the distinctiveness of the agents and the recipients of concern, care, assistance, and attention introduces all the special features that determine how the needs of others are met, in what ways, and to what degree. Every relationship and every relation are unique, even when they share some features and are like one another; the duty that must be met is that of a particular agent, and the need that must be fulfilled is that of a particular person. This singularity and particularity emerge again and again in the implementation of governmental programs, especially when the particular case and the particular aid recipient call for an exception to be made to normal procedures or when special consideration is called for or special needs must be met. When a specific health plan does not cover a particular drug but the patient cannot tolerate the generic version and requires an exception to be made, one is reminded vividly that the goal of a drug plan is to meet the needs of the patient and to do so with sensitivity and concern for the individual's situation and available resources. Levinas's caution about the primacy of our responsibilities to others in part reminds us never to forget the other person and to do what we can to prevent general procedures and rules of practice from being an obstacle to the successful attention and assistance to the person in need, rather than being a means of accomplishing just that attention and assistance.

Nickel underscores how the discourse of rights is introduced precisely in order to call attention to the dangers of social and political institutions.[23] It is in cases where these institutions break down and fail to provide for but rather act in opposition to the interests of the state's citizens that the language of rights is appropriate. When the injuries or failures are great and the particular needs and interests are of high priority, Nickel argues, then we need rights and often human rights to articulate the level of importance and the seriousness or urgency of the obligations. Levinas would not agree that only with the most serious needs and at the most dangerous of times is it necessary to underscore the normative duties of the government and its officials. Rather he would say that rights, in addition to presuming that moral and political authority ultimately resides in the subject or agent, only mark off one dimension of the ethical claims upon us. To understand the limitations of the language of rights, one must realize that whatever normative force they have comes from the other's claim upon us and that that claim and our corresponding responsibility to the other person is in and of itself unlimited and uncircumscribed. It is also primordial and prior to any action or conduct. Appreciating this helps us to understand what role social and political institutions and norms play in our lives and what their limits truly are.

LEVINAS ON RIGHTS AND HUMAN RIGHTS

As I indicated above, Levinas wrote several essays in the 1980s in which he discusses the concept of human rights or the "rights of man" from the point of view of his own ethical understanding of human existence and the primacy of the face of the other person. There are four essays, and I will take them up in their order of publication.[24] It is during this same period that Levinas raises the question I have discussed earlier, whether it is not unimportant to know whether a just and humane society and state are founded on the conception of man that we associate with Hobbes and the contract tradition or on Levinas's conception of charity and love. If this question suggests that Levinas rejects the discourse of rights, the central theme of the four essays we are about to examine shows clearly that this is not so. The central question he raises is how we ought to understand the foundation of the concept of human rights if we are to remain committed to it. In short, Levinas does not reject the language of rights; rather he shows that its foundation is not in human freedom and individuality but rather in the claim of the other person and responsibility. If we are concerned, as we should be, about human rights, it is because each of us has such rights as other persons and insofar as our rights correspond to the responsibilities that each and every person to whom we are related has to and for us. This account builds on Levinas's concept of the third person, the relation between ethics and politics, and his account of objectivity that are developed most fully in *Otherwise Than Being*.

My interest in the essay "The Prohibition against Representation and the 'Rights of Man'" is primarily in the latter half of the title. Levinas frames the piece around the biblical prohibition against images and physical representations, which he takes more broadly to be a criticism of the status of representation of all kinds, including language and thought in the broadest terms. For Levinas, of course, this criticism does not entail a rejection of representation or a dismissal of it; rather it involves appreciating how its significance and function derive from the broader, ethical context—social existence—in which it occurs and that provides all representation with its purpose and framework. The few passages that introduce and propose the role of rights in this scheme seem almost digressive and gratuitous, but as I read them, they do express a line of thinking about how the role that rights and talk about rights figure into his primary claim about the primacy of the social-ethical fact that underlies all human existence.[25] This same line of thinking is developed more fully in the later essays from 1985 and 1989, but it will be helpful to see how it is presented here, in the first text in which it finds a place.

Once Levinas introduces the concrete manifestation of transcendence as the face of the other person, a relation to the other that is "frozen in art itself," a "defenseless nakedness" and "precariousness," he goes on to point out that the content of the face is the ethical claim with which the other targets the self. As an explication of this ethical claim, Levinas

then makes his first point: the other person makes his or her vulnerability and life my business, as he puts it, and this is a "proclamation of a
right that peremptorily calls upon my responsibility for the other man."
That is, the self is responsible for and to the other, and the other person
has a right to the self's support and assistance. Already at this quasi-
transcendental level, there is a correspondence similar to that between
rights and duties. Moreover, as he points out, this responsibility does
not derive from guilt. That is, it is not based on anything I have done to
the other.[26] Rather it is a "gratuitous responsibility responding to a commandment not to leave the other alone in his or her last extremity, as if
the death of the other, before being my death, concerned me." The "Thou
shalt not kill," which is a way of expressing this claim, "means then 'Thou
shalt cause thy neighbor to live.'"[27] The other person has a right not to be
killed—or harmed or injured, and the self has a duty to provide for and
sustain the other's life.

We might put Levinas's point this way: if each of us is infinitely responsible, each one for each and every other, then the claim on the self to
be responsible for the other's life can be understood as the other's right
to whatever I can do to contribute to their living. It is a right to my concern for the other's life and sustenance, to my effort to provide for her,
to care for her, to protect her, and more. In short, the language of infinite
responsibility may be prior to and the basis of our everyday talk of duties
and responsibilities toward others, and it is also prior to and the basis of
our talk of the right to life that the other person possesses and therefore
that each of us possesses vis-á-vis each other.

Levinas now takes his second step to appropriating the language of
rights by showing that this primary or foundational right of the other
person with respect to each and every self, each interpersonal relation
being utterly particular and unique, is itself the foundation of the concept of human rights, the rights of man. Here are Levinas's own words:
"Event of sociality prior to all association in the name of an abstract and
common 'humanity.' *The right of man, absolutely and originally*, takes
on meaning only in the other, as the right of the other man. A right
with respect to which I am never released! Hence infinite responsibility
for the other. . . . An affinity that 'comes to mind' in the silent command of the face."[28] What exactly does Levinas mean? Here we must

recall that the essay overall is about representation—narrowly in art and more broadly in all consciousness, thought, conceptualization, and so forth. Biblically, the prohibition against representation is specifically a prohibition against representing God in concrete images. But Levinas reads the biblical prohibition as a figure for the primacy of the ethical in human relations. It is, in Levinas's terms, to acknowledge that divine transcendence, primary and foundational, cannot be manifest in concrete terms—in images, concepts, thoughts, and consciousness. To try to represent divine transcendence in concrete terms is to distort one's understanding of the divine. In the terms of rights, to treat the right of the other person as the "rights of man," as an abstraction and a generic classification, would be to distort the notion of rights in its primordial or basic sense. Hence, as Levinas says in the last sentence I just quoted, "the silent command of the face"—the infinite responsibility each self has uniquely to and for each and every other person—calls to mind what he calls here an "affinity." An affinity between what? Between the right of the other person aimed at me and the concept of human rights? Between the concrete and the abstract? Between the unique and the general? Perhaps all of these, but at least the unique right of the other person aimed at me in all its particularity and the "rights of man" as an abstract concept, a representation.

Is this primordial responsibility to and for the other the "word of God"? For if the divine command against making concrete images of God is a literary or imaginative figure for transcendence as the ethical relation, the rights I have toward you, then the affirmation of that infinite responsibility and the concept of universal human rights ought to be the "word of God." In a sense, Levinas argues, it is. That is, if we consider the face-to-face as it is embedded in our everyday lives, once it is expressed in ordinary experience and is present in ordinary relations, we realize that the basic or primordial responsibility for the other—or the right of the other person—is realized as responsibility of one sort or another, to one degree or another, and as a case of human rights. Moreover, it could be said that an everyday case of addressing the other person's rights is a matter of responding to him or her in the light of God's command to enhance the divine image, to respect their human rights, to protect and provide for them. This is the meaning of this third step in Levinas's reasoning:

> In this scheme of things, the other man, the neighbor, will already have compro-
> mised or enervated the radical alterity of his uniqueness itself, facilitating the
> administration and statistics necessary for the economic, military and technical
> equilibrium of totally represented being. And indeed to the extent that that
> equilibrium makes it possible to respond better, with responsibility for the other,
> to the right of man (which is originally the right of the *other man*), that universal
> representation cannot be forbidden. But it is the epiphany of the face that, before
> any particular expression, uniqueness or alterity is expressed, which is refractory
> to the image, to the consciousness of . . . and its "transcendental synthesis." It is
> there that an "unheard of command," or "the word of God" is heard.[29]

The command of God, then, that prohibits making concrete images of
God, of transcendence, is ambiguous. In one sense, the right of the other
person is beyond or other than ordinary life and thought; in another
sense, the generalizing of that right, the *concept* of human rights, is necessary—and productive. It facilitates the "economic, military and technical equilibrium" of everyday life; it makes possible the political. And
arguably, the central doctrine of the political is that of the universality
of human rights. We all face death and have a right to the aid of others
to protect us from it—and from the dangers and the injuries that might
lead to it.

In 1985, in "The Rights of Man and Good Will" and "The Rights of
Man and the Rights of the Other," Levinas adds a number of features
to this account and this line of reasoning.[30] The first essay sets his view
against a Kantian account of the justification of human rights.

First, Levinas acknowledges the special historical significance of
the recognition of the "rights of man" and associates them with rights
that human beings have, independent of social, physical, and personal
qualities. He notes that these human rights, as we shall call them, have
been elevated to legal principles and play a role in social and political
order. Second, Levinas privileges the right that distinguishes human
beings among natural beings—a right to freedom or free will and to
the special human status among natural beings that we associate with
being free, the right that corresponds to an "obligation to spare man the
constraints and humiliations of poverty, vagrancy, and even the sorrow
and torture" inherent in natural existence and "the violence and cruelty
of the evil intentions of living beings." The core of human rights is the
right to be free. Third, the rights of man, in the plural, are all grounded in

this primary right to be free, but they are determined in particular ways depending on the features of the concrete situations in which we live. These determinations—the conceptions we have of particular human rights and how they function—are the product of reflection based on our understanding of society, "technical procedures opened up by science."[31] Levinas describes this as a process: "the further refinement of a human order of freedom by the elimination of many material obstacles of the contingent and social structures that encumber and pervert the application and exercise of the rights of man."[32]

The most recent accounts of human rights by philosophers—in the work of Charles Beitz, James Nickel, and James Griffin, for example—distinguish between the conceptual and the empirical aspects of such accounts. Moreover, they distinguish between conceptual justifications of rights and empirical or functional justifications. Levinas seems to believe that human rights are plural, but they are all in some way or other derived from or manifestations of a fundamental or core right, the right to be free, to act freely. Furthermore, although this right has been known in the West since antiquity, Levinas claims that its justification, what gives it its normative force, has not been known. "The question of the justification of this right, the question of its very *'should be,'* remains open."[33] As we have seen, in the essay of 1981 Levinas had argued that human rights are themselves grounded in the right of the other person, which is a way of describing, from the other person's point of view, the duty each of us has to provide for, protect, and assist every particular other person with whom we are related. Here, in 1985, he locates the core of all human rights in the right to be free, and he asks what gives *that* right its normative force. What justifies *it*?

Levinas proposes that what justifies the right to be free is its rationality and that on Kant's reading this means its necessity and universality—hence the second part of the essay's title. That is, on the Kantian reading, what grounds the right to be free is human autonomy itself; the right to be free is the right to be respected as a free will, a good will, and it is a right shared by all rational human beings. To be free is to be worthy of respect; it is to have the right to that respect. Indeed, to have a human right is to be worthy of respect by others. "The categorical imperative would be the ultimate principle of the rights of man," as Levinas puts it.[34] The principle of practical rationality justifies human rights, or, in other terms, human rights are expressions of the respect owed to human beings as human beings, as normative agents or rational agents. Levinas ascribes such a view to Kant, and it is also present in the account of James Griffin, at least to a degree.

To this Kantian account, Levinas makes his alternative proposal. Human rights are grounded not in the categorical imperative, the good will, the right to respect; rather they are grounded in "charity and mercy and responsibility for the other, and already the possibility of sacrifice in which the humanity of man bursts forth." This is the "dis-inter-estedness of goodness: the other in his demand which is an order, the other as face, the other who 'regards me' even when he doesn't have anything to do with me, the other as fellow man and always stranger—goodness as transcendence." In contrast to Kant, Levinas refers here to Descartes and a passage from his *Passions of the Soul*, where Descartes speaks of generosity as the "free disposition of [a man's] soul" and of generous persons as not holding "anything more important than to do good to other men and to disdain their [own] individual interests."[35]

These are the main points that Levinas makes in this essay.[36] They are elaborated in Levinas's second essay in the volume, also from 1985, the much longer "The Rights of Man and the Rights of the Other." To be more precise, each one of the points that Levinas has made in the essay we have just discussed is developed and explored more fully in the longer essay. The line of reasoning about rights is the same as what we have seen. The core of human rights is the right to be free, and that right is itself justified by its relation to the fact of infinite responsibility that structures every social relationship we have, and that face-to-face or responsibility can itself be reformulated as a right, the rights of the other person. Although this is the logic of Levinas's argument, he takes up the argument's key points in a different order in this essay. Let me take them up in the order that they occur.

The first section in the essay is entitled "The Original Right," and it begins with Levinas acknowledging that the rights called "human rights," including the rights to life, liberty, and equality, and the right to respect are all "based on . . . the sense of an original right." These rights, which are a standard for law and morality, in the eyes of many, are, he says, *a priori*, independent of historical and social conditions, from natural power and capacities, and so forth. They are also *a priori* in another sense, Levinas suggests, in their *authority*, which he calls "ineluctable" or inescapable and which he describes as "older and higher than the one already split into will and reason and that imposes itself by an alternance of violence and truth." By "authority" here, I take Levinas to be referring to the normative force he had mentioned in an earlier essay, and by the "original right" he means the responsibility that occurs in the face-to-face relation as we have come to understand it. It is this that he now here calls "the original right" and that accounts for why human rights are norms at all. Levinas goes on to say that these human rights, which themselves are "irrevocable and inalienable," *express* and *manifest* "an alterity of the *unique* and the incomparable," which "remains concrete, precisely in the form of the various rights of man, claimed unconditionally . . . as various modes of freedom."[37] That is, human rights express the universality of rights that people have as human beings and the utter particularity or uniqueness of the person, both at once, "the paradox, or mystery, or novelty of the human in being."[38] They occur at a crucial nexus, the point where our general humanity and particular humanity are manifest together, and he quotes a marvelous Talmudic image, cited from Tractate Sanhedrin 37a, to portray this conjunction, the image of human beings as innumerable coins cast from a single original die, Adam, all the same but each uniquely different, both at once.

Moreover, as the Talmudic passage indicates, this moment—when the human species is said to occur only in infinite unique beings—is also the moment when the concept of human rights brings to mind the idea of God. This is a point we have seen Levinas stress in both of the other essays we have discussed. Here he puts it this way:

> The fact that the identity of species can include the absolutely dissimilar, a multiplicity of non-additive, unique beings—that the unity of Adam marks the individuals of incomparable uniqueness in which the common species disappears and in which the individuals cease being interchangeable like coins—that they affirm themselves to be, each one, the sole purpose of the world (or the sole one responsible for the real): surely this is the trace of God in man, or, more precisely, the point in reality at which the idea of God comes to man. This is a possible meaning of that [Talmudic] apologue, which . . . means . . . the coming of the idea of God on the basis of a patency of the rights of man.[39]

As the passage from Sanhedrin puts it, it is because God mints infinite persons from a single model, each a copy of a single paradigm but each unique and distinct, that each person should say, "The world was created for me." That is, each of us is wholly responsible for everything, and it is this realization that brings with it the idea of God; it is the "trace of God in man" or "the point in reality at which the idea of God comes to man." The recognition of human rights as universal norms and yet as authoritative only because they express the infinite responsibilities of each unique person marks the nexus when the word "God" comes to mind. The objective universality of humanity present in each unique person is what Levinas calls "the trace of God in man."

In the second section of the essay Levinas turns to the broad notion of human rights. He makes three interesting points. The first concerns the role of science and technology in the emergence of our understanding of these rights; the second is the particular list of human rights that he describes as having developed since the Renaissance and especially in the period after the Enlightenment and during the twentieth century; and the third are the risks that come with scientific and technological advances.

To begin, Levinas notices that "the possibility of ensuring the enjoyment of these rights" is something that needs to be created; we have to produce the "conditions for the respect of these rights" by being aware of the responsibility that grounds them and gives them normative force, by appreciating the social forces and natural conditions that influence our choices and conduct, and by becoming aware of "the practical procedures, issuing from that *knowledge* [of those social and natural forces], capable of freeing the person from these pressures and of subordinating them to the exercise of his rights."[40] I know of few passages in Levinas that speak so directly to the practical process of realizing one's moral goals in everyday life. To do this—to show the proper respect for rights and to come to enjoy them—we have to become attuned to our sense of responsibility to others, to come to understand what drives us as natural beings, and to free ourselves sufficiently from those drives and appetites so that we can come to respect and respond to the deficiencies and concerns and frailties of those who need us.

But being able to do this is not, as Levinas puts it, "inevitable." When it occurs, to the degree that it has, it is an accomplishment. He even calls it a "revolutionary act" and associates it first of all with "science and technology" as they have developed since the Renaissance in Western civilization. The history of the emergence of the language of natural rights, as a standard for law and society, is the history of a process of liberation. Levinas credits this history with bringing with it the possibility of social, political, and legal life organized by such *a priori* principles, so-called natural law. That is, Levinas takes the emergence of the rights of man "to be inseparable from . . . their requirement of transcendence . . . of the inhuman that may be contained in pure nature, and of blind necessity in the social body."[41] In other words, as natural beings, we are bound by causal chains and driven by forces beyond our control; recognizing the human rights of others involves understanding these natural and social forces for what they are and then liberating ourselves from them by responding to the uniqueness and irreducibility of other persons to whom we are related and by respecting the claims they make upon us.

To this picture, Levinas adds two features: an elaboration of the human rights that follow from our core right to be free, and a brief account of the risks attendant upon our advanced scientific knowledge and technological accomplishments. First, Levinas elaborates briefly a list of human rights. All recent philosophical accounts do the same, and all rely on documents such as the Universal Declaration of Human Rights to provide models for what such lists should contain. Furthermore, they tailor their justifications to those lists, since recent philosophical accounts all appreciate that elevating certain norms to special status and then conferring upon them the title of rights are not purely *a priori* matters. The starting point of such endeavors are the lists of human rights widely accepted, especially since 1948, by nations, regions, and internationally.[42] Levinas does not provide a full-scale articulation of the contents of the primary human rights and explication of how further rights are derived from this core, but he does distinguish between a core right and others that he suggests provide conditions for that core right.

As we have seen, Levinas takes the core right to be the right to freedom, and he seems to take that freedom to be a freedom from the determinism of natural forces, social and physical. For him, being free in this way is what constitutes our capacity to be normative agents, to use James Griffin's term. We might say, then, that for Levinas the core right is the right to be a normative agent. All the other natural rights are rights to those considerations without which such freedom or normative agency is not possible. Here, in this essay, he takes them to be articulated in legal rules, the content of which identify "the necessary conditions" without which human rights cannot be respected, provided, and protected. This is what Levinas says about these rights:

> Behind the rights to life and security, to the free disposal of one's goods and the equality of all men before the law, to freedom of thought and its expression, to education and participation in political power—there are all the other rights that extend these, or make them concretely possible: the right to health, happiness, work, rest, a place to live, freedom of movement, and so on. But also, beyond all that, the right to oppose exploitation by capital (the right to unionize) and even the right to social advancement; the right (utopian or Messianic) to the refinement of the human condition, the right to ideology as well as the right to fight for the full rights of man, and the right to ensure the necessary political conditions for the struggle. The modern conception of the rights of man surely extends that far![43]

Although Levinas gives no precise indication of the sources for this list, there seems little doubt that he takes them from documents like the Universal Declaration of Human Rights, which begins with articles that announce the conviction that all human beings are born free and equal in dignity and rights; goes on first to proclaim the rights to life, liberty, and security; then proceeds to prohibit slavery and cruel and degrading treatment; and eventually arrives at freedom of movement and various political, social, and economic rights.[44] Levinas's list, as we have it, does have its idiosyncrasies—for example, what he calls the "right to the refinement of the human condition" and the Marxist-inspired "right to oppose exploitation by capital."[45] But overall, what Levinas provides in this passage is evidence that in discussing the ultimate ground of human rights and declarations of the "rights of man"—French and otherwise—in the infinite responsibility of the face-to-face relations of social existence, what he has specifically in mind is a justification of the various human rights documents that have been produced since the Enlightenment, and then since 1948—among the latter the Universal Declaration of Human Rights, the European Convention for the Protection of Human Rights and Fundamental Freedoms, the International Covenant on Civil and Political Rights, the International Covenant on Economic, Social and Cultural Rights, and the Helsinki Final Act.[46]

Levinas realizes that to put these norms into practice, to respond to these rights in concrete situations, one will have to weigh various considerations. "It is also," he says, "necessary to ascertain the urgency, order, and hierarchy of these various rights, and to enquire as to whether they may not compromise the fundamental rights."[47] But he cautions that such practical evaluation and consideration do not mean that one opposes these rights but rather that balancing and limiting them are a practical necessity. The structure of human rights, with the core right to freedom, and the ultimate ground in our ethical relations with others—all this is, he says, "unquestionable." But implementation requires compromise and coordination and even mutual limitation. That is undeniable and necessary. As we will see, the practical deliberations that Levinas does attend to—largely in the context of reading Talmudic passages where concrete situations arise in which ethical norms and considerations bear on one another—do involve such accommodations and compromises, but Levinas says no more about that here.

The second point that Levinas makes is that advances we have made in science and technology, valuable as they are for arriving at an understanding of what rights are of high priority and play vital roles for us, have also had serious shortcomings. They can have and have had terrible consequences. Levinas has in mind Hitler's Germany, Stalin's Soviet Union, and other fascist, totalitarian regimes that have utilized new technologies and have been facilitated by technology and scientific developments to create dominating and violent societies in which rights are denied and people oppressed. Levinas refers to these as "inhuman requirements that make up a new determinism" and elaborates, "In a totally industrialized society or in a totalitarian society—which are precisely the results of supposedly perfected social techniques—the rights of man are compromised by the very practices for which they supplied the motivation. Mechanization and enslavement! And this is the case even before adducing the banal theme of the necessary connection between technical advances, the development of destructive armaments, and the abusive manipulation of societies and souls." One should not, of course, be too quick to criticize science and technology, for the very notion of the rights of man is occasioned by these advances. The same Enlightenment that was produced by the new science and its quest for knowledge also produced an understanding of what all human beings shared as rational and free beings and not only in the civilized West but also in "the 'third' and 'fourth' worlds, threatened by disease and hunger."[48] Levinas is not alone both in tracing our sense of human dignity and common humanity to our better understanding of nature and human nature and in attributing much of the horrific decline of the twentieth century to the barrenness of a mechanistic worldview and its determinism. This part of his story he shares with Adorno, Horkheimer, and other members of the Frankfurt school, with Hannah Arendt, Heidegger in a way, and a host of others, among them numerous theologians and religious thinkers who call attention to the incompleteness of creation and nature and the need for redemption through the human response to revelation and the fact that all of this—creation, revelation, and redemption—comes under the auspices of one and the same God. And there is a serious need to be met—in Western societies and especially, as he notes, in third world countries, often under military and despotic regimes, and locales in which famine, poverty, and disease are rife.

The last section of the essay is called "The Rights of the Other Man." Here Levinas explores more fully the role that the face-to-face and what he calls the ethical plays as the ground of those human rights that he had earlier elaborated. What distinguishes his account of what justifies the normative priority of these rights? What does it mean to claim that human rights are grounded on the rights of the other person?

Rights are norms or rules of a certain kind, and hence they need to be justified; reasons must be given for why they have the special normative force and features that they have. Legal rights have their authority as part of a system of legal rules; moral rights have their authority in virtue of being a part of a moral system. Human rights are moral rights that have an especially high priority and are shared by all or at least most human beings. Hence, human rights are grounded in fundamental moral considerations. This sketch is very rough, of course, but it helps us to appreciate what Levinas sets out to do in this section. As we have seen, he takes human rights, or the "rights of man," to be grounded in the ethical character of all our social relations, what he calls the face-to-face, enigma, and much else. Griffin, as I mentioned, takes human rights to be defined conceptually and in terms of various practical considerations. Conceptually, human rights specify by their content conditions for our normative agency as persons; something like that is going on in Levinas. The face-to-face is the nexus in which such normative agency arises for us as persons, and human rights are those matters that the self needs in order to be such an agent. Moreover, as rights, they have what Wayne Sumner calls both a subject and an object; that is, they are someone's rights and they call upon others to comply with them, respect them, and so forth.[49] These others have duties or obligations toward the bearer of the right. Levinas says that fundamentally each of us is the object of such rights for each and every other person; each of us is infinitely responsible for everyone, in every way, all the time. In ordinary, everyday life, this infinite responsibility is restricted, limited, focused, determined, and organized; the precise content of our duties to the rights bearer are worked out this way, but the normativity of the rights and the duties is grounded in the relation of subject to object itself.

Having spelled out this response in general terms, we can better understand what Levinas says in this essay about the rights of the other person. The first point he makes is that since each of us, both you and I, are rights bearers, with regard to human rights, we bear these rights vis-á-vis one another. This means that in everyday circumstances rights will come into conflict. Levinas calls this a "war between multiple freedoms" and "a conflict between reasonable wills." But in legal space, these conflicts of rights can be adjudicated and regulated, which is what Levinas calls "justice" or a "just legality," "the resolution of a plurality of opposing wills." This is a Hobbesian or Kantian picture. On it, for all we gain, "justice represents nonetheless a certain limitation of rights and free will." Furthermore, "the limitation of rights by justice is . . . already a way of treating the person as an object by submitting him or her (the unique, the incomparable) to comparison, to thought, to being placed on the famous scales of justice, and thus to calculation." On the one hand, this brings a kind of peace, of reconciliation, but on the other, it comes at a cost. There is a respect for the rights of each person but at the same time a limitation of those rights. Levinas puts this by suggesting in his somewhat elusive terms that by acting according to the categorical imperative, the will becomes good but not totally good; this always involves some limitation, some negation, some self-denial.[50] This is what we meant in an earlier chapter when we claimed that for Levinas, while justice and politics are necessary, they do involve limiting the self's infinite responsibility and freedom; ethics and politics are mutually supporting but also mutually limiting. Here he focuses on the way that politics or justice limits the ethical.

This structure tells us that justice limits the rights of man or human rights; the peace that results from this compromising of conflicting rights and freedoms is "uncertain and precarious." It is better than a good war, but it is only a bad peace, "yet an abstract peace, seeking stability in the powers of the state, in politics, which ensures obedience to the law by force." Levinas goes on to call this a domain of necessities—those of the law, of politics and political life—that constitute "a determinism as rigorous as that of nature indifferent to man, even though justice—the right of man's free will and its agreement with the free will of the other—may have, at the start, served as an end or pretext for the political necessities." In other words, the result is a form of fixity and stability, akin to the determinism of natural law, even if it started out as a way of reconciling the conflict between the rights of two persons. What began as a noble enterprise has a grim outcome. In practice, he warns, these political strategies regularly lead to oppression and could very well result in totalitarianism, a political situation in which human rights become a "mockery."[51]

I have argued that for Levinas politics and the state are necessary, and I do not believe that anything in this essay on human rights suggests otherwise. But this means that if one is going to advocate in behalf of human rights, which must be compromised in civil society and in the state, one must somehow speak from outside the political, even if that "outside" is located "within" the very society put in question. Levinas makes this crucial point about the ethical critique of the political in the current essay:

> The defense of the rights of man corresponds to a vocation *outside* the state, disposing, in a political society, of a kind of extra-territoriality, like that of prophecy in the face of the political powers of the Old Testament, a vigilance totally different from political intelligence, a lucidity not limited to yielding before the

formalism of universality, but upholding justice itself in its limitations. The capacity to guarantee that extra-territoriality and that independence defines the
liberal state and describes the modality according to which the conjunction of
politics and ethics is intrinsically possible.[52]

The biblical prophets speak in behalf of God from within ancient Israel
but also, in a sense, from outside it. They speak to the kings of Israel,
to the elite and the aristocracy, but they speak from another place, so
to speak.[53] This is the "extra-territoriality" to which Levinas refers. To
those who are satisfied with compromising rights or denying them in
favor of the interests of the powerful or of the state, the prophet speaks
with a sensitivity to the needs and the suffering of the individual, especially minorities, the weak, the impoverished, and the abandoned.
He speaks with a "lucidity" that does not accommodate itself to the
"formalism of universality." The prophet will not sacrifice the one to
the many, nor will he ignore the utterly unique claim that each citizen
makes upon those who rule. Nathan will not abandon Uriah the Hittite
and allow David to live with himself.[54] But only some social and political
regimes permit this kind of extra-territoriality, protect it, and guarantee
it.[55] Later we shall return to this theme, Levinas's views on the liberal
state. For the moment it is sufficient to note that the liberal (democratic)
state's capacity to promote this kind of extra-territorial ethical critique
of political practice is one fact that speaks in its behalf.

But if human rights can be viewed from the political point of view—
that is, in terms of how such rights are in everyday affairs reconciled,
accommodated, and coordinated—they should also be viewed from this
other, ethical point of view, in terms of what normative foundation they
express or manifest, and this brings Levinas to his discussion of the
"authority" that grounds the rights of man and the face-to-face relation.
Human rights and justice are founded not on the universality of the
class of human beings; their authority does not come from generality.
Instead "one and the other is one *facing* the other. It is myself *for* the
other," or what he elsewhere calls the infinite responsibility of the one
for the other.[56]

The crucial feature of this relation, this self being for the other
person, is that its priority to generalization and universality, its utter concreteness, is expressed in what Levinas calls the self's "non-indifference."
That is, in ordinary, everyday life, when we approach other persons as

members of the species, as human beings or as subsumed within some class or other, we aspire to a kind of indifference or detachment from them. Sometimes this is because in treating the other person generically we want to facilitate our conduct—as an employer we treat the other as an employee; as a salesperson, we treat her as a customer. But at other times, we aspire to impartiality; we want to avoid preference or bias—for example, as a member of a jury listening to and evaluating a witness's testimony. But, Levinas claims, in every relation to the other, our initial, default stance is not one of detachment and indifference; rather it is one of non-indifference or involvement of a special kind, the involvement of one who is called upon and claimed by the other to acknowledge, accept, and assist her, to care for her—simpliciter. This relation, Levinas tells us, is the face; it is "original sociality—goodness; peace, or the wish for peace, benediction; 'shalom'—the initial event of meeting. Difference— a non-in-difference in which the other—though absolutely other, 'more other,' so to speak, than are the individuals with respect to one another within the 'same species' from which the I has freed itself—in which the other 'regards' me, not in order to 'perceive' me, but in 'concerning me,' in 'mattering to me as someone for whom I am answerable.'"[57] That is, primordially and prior to our everyday encounters with others, near or far, our relationship with each of them is one of their "being of concern to me" or "mattering to me." Before anything else, any other relationship or conduct or category, I am answerable to the other person as a particular individual, for everything about her prevails upon me, claims me, calls me into question. All human rights have the normative force that they do because they express this primordial or foundational relationship.

Moreover, this primordial responsibility to and for the other person is "also the exercise of a freedom . . . in which the I frees itself from its 'return to self,' from its auto-affirmation, from its egotism of a being persevering in its being." It is free from self-involvement and the natural desire, the overwhelming desire, for self-preservation, and it is free "to answer for the other, precisely to defend the rights of the other man."[58] We recall that for Levinas the right to be free is the core human right, and now we can see that it is the expression of that primordial freedom from the chains of self-interest and self-involvement; it is the sense of being given over first and ultimately to the concerns of the other person. It is one thing for the other to matter to me; it is another for me to be free to answer to that claim, that mattering of the other which is aimed at me. The latter is the core of human rights, the content of which elaborate the conditions without which that freedom cannot express itself and without which the call or claim of the other person cannot be responded to in social and political life.

For Levinas, then, responsibility and fraternity, this relation the other has to the self, are the basis of the authority and the content of human rights. They are normatively binding, because the other's claim on me is binding, and they have the content they do—rights to life, liberty, sustenance, and so forth—because they express what this primordial responsibility means in the domain of justice, that is, in ordinary, everyday matters.

WHAT IT IS IMPORTANT TO KNOW ABOUT
THE FOUNDATIONS OF SOCIETY

Why, then, is it important to know whether a society or state is founded on a Hobbesian conception of competing individuals or on Levinas's conception of "charity and love"? I think that we can now see precisely what Levinas has in mind. First, if Levinas is right, then only if we approach social and political life with his understanding of their foundation in interpersonal relations that are normative and ethical will we understand what makes them just and humane and what does not. Second, on the Hobbesian view, the state is one outcome of rational self-interested individuals, fearful of one another, who seek peace and security and hope to avoid conflict, risk, and danger; on Levinas's view, the state is one framework in which we extend ourselves in behalf of others and live not only for ourselves, but also for others. The function of political institutions and practices is to facilitate responsible conduct in the service of others, both our fellow citizens and others who live elsewhere. Third, instead of regularly sacrificing or being willing to sacrifice individuals in order to secure generic goals or to follow generic rules and principles, Levinas reminds us that all of our conduct—institutional and collective as well as individual—involves how each of us does what we can to serve the unique other persons with whom we interact. Everyday actions are always ultimately about how we act toward particular other persons.

Finally, Levinas can be taken to be warning us against preferring political to moral considerations and ways of acting. If we think of political
conduct as often instrumental, frequently self-interested or concerned
with power and control, and largely generic, then he is encouraging us to
prefer ethical and moral action—responsive to the needs and concerns
of others, responsible and accountable in terms of moral considerations,
and willing to forgo our own interests for what others need of us.

SIX

LIBERALISM AND DEMOCRACY

When Levinas was a child, his family had to leave their home in Kovno, Lithuania, during the First World War, and after their return, he lived under the young Soviet government until he left for Strasbourg in 1924. In France he came into contact with a generation of philosophers whose political views had been shaped in the wake of the Dreyfus Affair, and he adopted in his own way the ideals of the French Revolution as they were recovered during that period. In the 1930s he was brought face-to-face with fascism and totalitarianism and the question of where philosophy stood in the encounter between Hitler's fascism and Enlightenment liberalism. In the 1930s, he experienced the impotence of liberalism in the struggle with the forces of fascism, and yet by the 1970s and '80s he appears to have changed his mind about liberalism and come to endorse the virtues of democracy. He experienced the struggles of French parliamentary democracy after the war and the turmoil of the 1960s, particularly 1968, and while he lived to see the fragmentation of the Soviet empire, it is clear that the horrors of Stalinism had already alienated him from any sympathy with Cold War communism. He had an ongoing dislike for American capitalism. To be sure, throughout his career, he had a complicated relationship with Marxism, at the same time appreciating its strengths and its weaknesses, and he showed strong signs of favoring some form of socialism or at least a welfare state of some kind. One of the perspectives one might take on Levinas's ethical critique of the political is to place it in the context of his views about these various types of political system and political doctrine, and in this chapter I want to begin to provide such an account.

The classical model for an account and evaluation of various types of state or political rule is Plato's *Republic*.[1] There Plato portrays life within four types of state in terms of the personalities characteristic of each, he organizes his evaluation as an account of decline, and he focuses on those features that lead each type of state or *politeia* to undergo change and ultimately disappear. In the end, of course, he defends the benefits of a kind of benevolent aristocracy of philosophical rulers, the so-called Kallipolis, or beautiful city-state. Levinas provides nothing like this account or that of Aristotle and their classical descendants. Nor does he target one or another form of government and subject it to systematic evaluation. What we find instead are indications in his writings about what he finds attractive and defective about various forms of government, political ideologies, and types of state that play a particularly important role in the world in which he lives, especially in the world of twentieth-century Europe.

Levinas's nemesis is fascism, especially fascism as a form of totalitarianism. At the same time, he continually returns to liberalism as a political ideology and later in his career to liberal democracy. Fascism and totalitarianism he despises and fears; liberal democracy he admires and endorses but not unequivocally.[2] Annabel Herzog has raised the question, in an oft-cited paper, whether Levinas thinks that liberalism is enough, and Robert Bernasconi has defended what he takes to be Levinas's changing views about liberalism. As a way of entering this arena, I suggest that we explore Levinas's reflections on liberalism by considering these two interpretations.

LEVINAS AND PROPHETIC LIBERALISM

Robert Bernasconi has written an outstanding essay on these issues in Levinas.[3] I want to use Bernasconi's formulation of the issue and his examination of it to set the stage for understanding Levinas's engagement with liberalism. Bernasconi's account is clear, rich, and largely correct, but often it stays with Levinas's own terminology and suffers from failing to make clear exactly what is at issue. Moreover, his discussion of Levinas's reading of Mendelssohn's *Jerusalem* is not sufficiently detailed to appreciate the meaning of Levinas's response. This is what I shall try to contribute.

Bernasconi begins by citing Levinas's discussion of the rights of man in terms of the rights of the other in the essays from the early 1980s that we have discussed in a previous chapter. It is clear that by then Levinas had developed a positive view of liberalism. As Bernasconi points out, Levinas explicitly endorses the liberal state in "The Rights of Man and the Rights of the Other" in 1985; he also does so, I believe, when he refers, in "Peace and Proximity" in 1984, to the "egalitarian and just State in which the European realizes himself."[4] At the same time, Levinas's endorsement of liberalism in the 1980s occurs alongside claims that there is something incomplete or unfinished about the liberal state and the justice of that state.[5] It seems clear that Levinas, by the 1980s, admits to advocating democracy and especially a liberal democracy, although it is not wholly clear what kind of liberal state that is.

This later endorsement—not wholly clear and also qualified—might appear to conflict with the very explicit evidence in Levinas's earlier writings, from the 1930s through the 1960s and perhaps even later, that he was critical of liberalism and the liberal state. Given the almost uniform way in which European intellectuals of this period responded to liberalism, Levinas's opposition and critique are hardly surprising. Like so many others, he took liberalism to be too weak to oppose fascism and totalitarianism. As Bernasconi notes, Levinas understood liberalism to have such an inadequate appreciation of the body and the forces of nature that it could not oppose them effectively. Rather it expressed itself in a kind of freedom that either fled history and nature and became a form of intellectualized spiritualism or sought to transform history—economics and politics—into an idealism. In slightly different terms, liberalism either was overwhelmed by nature or could only deal with it by reducing it to ideality. In neither case could it challenge the forces of nature as expressed in Nazism and totalitarianism.

These views are expressed in several places in Levinas's early work but nowhere so sharply and critically as in his well-known paper "Reflections on the Philosophy of Hitlerism," published in *Esprit* in 1934. Bernasconi quotes a passage from Levinas's paper in which he expresses this kind of Platonism in a powerful way: "Man in the liberal world does not choose his destiny under the weight of history. He does not know his possibilities as troubled forces churning within that already orient

him on a determined track. He sees them simply as logical possibilities offered to serene reason that chooses while eternally keeping its
distance."[6] Levinas shows that he has in mind the liberalism of the Enlightenment and nineteenth centuries and its elevation of the "sovereign
liberty of reason." Real freedom is the freedom of reason to liberate the
human from its natural, corporeal situation. As he puts it, "All philosophical and political thought of modern times tends to place the human
mind on a plane higher than the real, creating an abyss between man
and the world." This is true, I believe, of Descartes and Kant, less so of
Hobbes and Spinoza, but the crucial point for Levinas is that liberalism,
as he understands it, elevates freedom and reason beyond the natural
world. "It substitutes for the blind world of common sense a world re-
constructed by idealistic philosophy, bathed in reason and subject to
reason." In short, Levinas's liberalism is the liberalism of Kant, Fichte,
Hegel, and their legacy, and what it harbors, on his reading, is a human
being so "free and alone before the world" that "he may not even be able
to bridge this distance, to make the choice." And even if he overcomes
skepticism and does bridge it, he does so without any security. "Thought
becomes a game. . . . He transforms his capacity for doubt into a lack of
conviction. . . . Sincerity becomes impossible. . . . Civilization is invaded
by everything that is not authentic, by cheap substitutes subservient to
special interests and passing fashion." It is no wonder, Levinas goes on to
argue, that the "Germanic ideal of man comes as a promise of sincerity
and authenticity." He is "bound to certain truths . . . [for] ideas . . . come
from his concrete being, anchored in his flesh and blood and shar[ing]
their gravity."[7]

How should we characterize this liberalism that Levinas subjects
to withering criticism? According to Geuss, as I indicated above, classical liberalism is committed to toleration, to freedom as a preeminent
value, to individualism, and to the eradication of absolute power and
oppression. Levinas does focus on freedom but primarily because of its
association with reason and with liberation from the world, from nature.
That is, Marxism and racist despotism share a foundation in the concrete world, in a kind of biological determinism. Liberalism opposes or
fears the world, and insofar as we as individuals are unavoidably bound
to the world, liberalism cannot compete with either. We shall return to

Levinas's understanding of Marxism later, but for now it is sufficient to appreciate that the kind of freedom that liberalism eulogizes is incapable of confronting and challenging biological or physical determinism of any kind. Hence, liberalism cannot oppose cruelty and oppression; it cannot prevent toleration from sliding into relativism and even skepticism; it cannot protect the individual or prevent suffering and humiliation.

Given this picture, one might expect that Bernasconi would seek to uncover evidence in Levinas's writings that Levinas's later endorsement of liberalism and liberal democracy is facilitated by a new view of liberalism, but it should be one that attends fully to the concreteness of human existence. Ought he not to show that Levinas came to view liberalism not as tied to rationalism and to Platonism at all but rather as somehow engaged with the world and hence able to transform our way of living in it? That is, ought Bernasconi not to find a form of liberalism grounded in a different conception of what is central to human existence, a liberalism not focused on reason and freedom but on something about our concrete existence and yet not reducible to our natural, deterministic character? Is there reason to think that this is what Bernasconi in fact does?

Bernasconi claims that the "historical record" shows that what led Levinas to become more open to liberalism was his "study of the eighteenth century Jewish thinker, Moses Mendelssohn."[8] What exactly does Bernasconi find in this study of Mendelssohn? Is he right that it is this encounter that educated Levinas to be more open to liberalism? Has Bernasconi understood correctly what Levinas found in Mendelssohn?[9]

According to Bernasconi, what Levinas discovered in Mendelssohn were "radically different conceptions of freedom and of the relation between religion and the state."[10] Let me begin with Bernasconi's reading of Mendelssohn on freedom. He notes that in a rare reference to recent scholarship, Levinas turns for assistance to the most important expositor of Mendelssohn of the twentieth century, Alexander Altmann, and in particular to a paper entitled "The Quest for Liberty in Moses Mendelssohn's Political Philosophy."[11] Bernasconi points out that to Levinas Mendelssohn's liberalism is still relevant, but it requires a "philosophical elaboration" unavailable to an Enlightenment thinker. We have already seen that Levinas reformulates the notion of the "rights of man" in terms of "rights of the other," but only once he introduces the notion of rights to explicate the ethical relation between the subject and the other person. As Bernasconi puts it, rights only appear as rights—that is, as normative claims—when they appear as the rights of the other; if all rights are my rights, they would appear to me as my interests, my self-interests. But this cannot be so; rights would lose all their normativity.[12] Here too Levinas must see how to interpret Mendelssohn's political philosophy so that he can see its relation to his own account of the ethical. In particular, he must find a way to interpret Mendelssohn's social contract theory so that he can supplement it by showing how it is ultimately grounded in his conception of the ethical character of the face-to-face.

Bernasconi uses Altmann as the bridge between Levinas's comments and the text of *Jerusalem*, but I think that we learn more by considering what Levinas says about part 1 of *Jerusalem* in the light of Mendelssohn's work itself. After all, although Levinas does cite Altmann as his guide, we can presume that he had read and took himself to be commenting on these pages, in which Mendelssohn develops his distinctive natural law version of a contract theory.[13] Mendelssohn, drawing on Grotius and Pufendorf, employs the distinctions between perfect and imperfect rights and duties to show how the state and political authority are grounded in a pre-political agreement, conducted in the state of nature. As Bernasconi suggests, Mendelssohn's originality can best be appreciated by comparing his account of the contractual process that results in the establishment and authority of political institutions with the accounts we find in Hobbes especially but also in John Locke. In fact, in *Jerusalem*, Mendelssohn refers primarily to Locke, although the comparison with Hobbes is perhaps more revealing. For Locke, the purposes for establishing the various institutions of government are to authorize, clarify, publicize, and police those laws that are required to protect the property of the citizens of the state. That is, for Locke, moral and political personhood are described in terms of rights and protections, which are defined by a set of norms or laws. These latter, in order to be applied uniformly, to be publicized and familiar, and for violations to be identified, judged, and punished without prejudice and fairly, require an array of institutions—legislative, executive, and judicial. All of this is the outcome and justification for the Lockean social contract theory. As Mendelssohn sees clearly, there are moral laws—articulated in terms of perfect and imperfect rights and duties—that apply to everyone in the state of nature. The purpose of the state is to put them into practice; politics is necessary for morality to be publicized to everyone in a canonical way and for violators to be identified, captured, tried, and punished.

For Hobbes, the social contract differs in crucial ways. First, there are no moral norms in the state of nature for Hobbes. There may be tendencies or dispositions, even rational ones, but they are not norms or laws. Secondly, what moves individuals in the state of nature is the desire for self-preservation, power, and security, and hence the distrust and fear of others. What drives individuals to seek cooperative agreements and the establishment of institutions capable of formulating laws and enforcing them through the use of power and violence is that desire for security and hence for peace. Therefore, if Locke takes civil authority to guarantee the protection of citizens or, to put it differently, the preservation of the individuality of each citizen, what Hobbes takes the state to provide is a guarantee of security, that is, of life itself.

Mendelssohn shares with Locke the natural law conviction that there is rationality, freedom, and morality in the state of nature. The social contract does not subtract from them as it does for Hobbes, who has no notion of positive freedom—he is a materialist and a naturalist for whom the only freedom we have is the liberation from external force or compulsion—and no notion of natural morality. In Hobbes's social contract theory, individuals transfer almost all of their freedom, in the sense of control over their desires and actions, to the state, in trade for security and the reduction of fear and anxiety. But while Mendelssohn shares a good deal with Locke, he differs with him and dramatically differs with Hobbes in his understanding of what the establishment of civil institutions provides the citizens of the state.

As Bernasconi sees—following Altmann—the crucial issue is the natural beneficence that persons feel toward one another. That is, if perfect rights are the individual's claims not to be harmed or injured, not to have his goods or his substance taken from him without permission and without compensation, and so forth, and if perfect duties are therefore the obligations not to steal, to do physical harm, to kill, to trespass, to malign or defame, and so forth, then imperfect duties are our dispositions or tendencies to share with others, to rescue those in need, to provide help and assistance, and more. All of these duties, rights, and dispositions are characteristic of persons in the state of nature, for Mendelssohn, and just as perfect duties correspond to perfect rights, so there are imperfect rights that correspond with imperfect duties. Our natural dispositions toward providing food for the hungry correspond to the interests of the hungry for food to eat; the disposition to benefit others is correlated with the interests of the needy to be treated well by others. In short, there are imperfect rights, just as there are imperfect duties, and like perfect rights and duties or obligations, they are reciprocal. It may be, as Mendelssohn sees, that some civil institutions have as their justification the regularizing of the implementation of perfect rights and duties, but the real purpose, the central aim, of government is to guarantee that imperfect rights are respected and that imperfect duties are met. Without civil institutions, there would be no guarantee that those who are destitute or hungry are housed, clothed, and fed; nor is there a guarantee that a surplus of goods is distributed fairly and responsibly to those in need. In somewhat different terms, if for Locke government is paradigmatically a legislature, a police force, and a court, then for Mendelssohn it is a process of taxation and a set of welfare agencies. Bernasconi, using Altmann, frames all of this primarily in the vocabulary of freedom—that moral freedom is natural, cannot be diminished or abandoned in order to create political institutions, and is expressed as beneficence. Mendelssohn himself says that the central purpose of political institutions is to convert imperfect duties into perfect ones; it is to organize and enforce the distribution of surplus wealth to those in need. It is to convert a disposition to beneficence into an obligation to provide for the needy and to convert the interest in or need for food and shelter into the right to basic provisions.

I think that Bernasconi appreciates much of this, but it is only when it is laid out clearly and fully that one can see how and why Levinas takes this form of liberal state to express in its own way his insight into the ethical character of our social existence. One way to put this would be to say that the very notions of imperfect rights and imperfect duties disclose dimensions of the face-to-face, albeit as rules or norms or at least normative dispositions or attitudes, and by privileging them as the very core of political establishment Mendelssohn already hints at the kind of foundation that Levinas takes himself to have identified and clarified. As Bernasconi sees, Mendelssohn's Enlightenment turn is to understand the foundation of his natural law and contract theories as human freedom and rationality. Levinas could be seen to have reformulated what that freedom and rationality mean, or alternatively, he could be seen to have reinterpreted how the relationship between imperfect and perfect rights should be understood, as one powerful way of expressing the ethical claim of the face-to-face and the infinite responsibility that corresponds to it.

Mendelssohn's account leads to a view about how religion and the state are related. He distinguishes between actions, on the one hand, and beliefs or opinions, on the other. And he argues that while neither the state nor ecclesiastical institutions can compel one to believe anything, insofar as all beliefs and opinions are grounded in rationality and cannot be the outcome of force, the two differ regarding conduct or action. Only the state is given the authority, by its citizens, to dictate and then enforce actions; the purpose of religion, on the other hand, is to teach, exhort, persuade, and endorse but not to compel. Religion and the state, then, are for Mendelssohn to be distinguished solely with regard to human conduct, to actions, and for Levinas, this distinction corresponds to the distinction that he makes between ethics and politics, between generosity as infinite responsibility and explicit norms and actual institutions. This, then, is what Bernasconi means when he takes Levinas's revision of Mendelssohn to be associated with a kind of "extra-territoriality." Indeed, Levinas himself is explicit about this point; the normative foundation of the liberal state lies in a "territory" outside of its own actual domain. It is outside of the political altogether, in the ethical.[14] This extra-territoriality of the state, of politics, is not the "outside" that classical liberalism endorses, that is, the private realm. Nor is it the "outside" of the social contract tradition, the state of nature. Rather it is the religious, or in Levinas's vocabulary, it is ethics.[15] Moreover, this separation is both an otherness and a relation, the otherness of religion and the state, of ethics and politics, and the relation that is the connectedness of the face-to-face with all our other relationships. This separation shows that what lies outside of the concrete, historical world of political affairs is not a private domain, isolated and detached.

If it were, then this "Mendelssohnian liberalism" that Levinas finds here would simply collapse into the vacuousness and impotence of the classical liberalism that he had once severely criticized in "Reflections on the Philosophy of Hitlerism." Rather the "outside" is intimately tied to the political—as the real content of what religion is—and this connection helps Levinas to understand the implications of Mendelssohn's political philosophy for his understanding of Judaism—of Jewish life in modernity, the risks of assimilation, the viability of Jewish peoplehood, and indeed of Zionism.

It also helps Bernasconi to show that "extra-territoriality" refers not only to the separateness of the ethical but also to the way in which it "speaks" to the political and opposes totalitarianism. This refers to what Levinas calls "prophecy."[16] One feature of this revised conception of liberalism is that religion or the ethical can, and perhaps should, serve as the ground of a critique of the political. Bernasconi has some very helpful things to say about this in his essay.

Recall that for Mendelssohn the function of religion in the state is to evoke, admonish, teach, comfort, and support, among other things.[17] But these are the characteristic activities of the prophet, who invokes the teachings of the past and calls monarchs to task, as Nathan did David. Bernasconi brilliantly illuminates this connection between the function of religion, as Mendelssohn portrays it, and Levinas's reinterpretation of the notion of human rights: "Just as justice needs to be always put in question from elsewhere so that conformity to its abstract rule does not become a new tyranny, so one cannot rely on the politicians for protection and implementation of the 'rights of man.' Hence the need for voices from outside, like those of the Old Testament prophets."[18] The "rights of man" is a vocabulary that comes out of the Enlightenment and natural law tradition, the same tradition that Mendelssohn invokes. In a sense, then, Levinas compares—and more than compares—the role that Mendelssohn gives to religion and the biblical prophets, the role that invoking human rights has as a critique of sovereign states that fail to protect and care for their citizens, and his own role for ethics as the ground of social and political critique.[19] Bernasconi goes on to cite an essay that we discussed in an earlier chapter: "This also means (and it is important that this be emphasized) that the defense of the rights of man corresponds to a vocation outside the state, disposing, in a political society, of a kind of extra-territoriality, like that of prophecy in the face of the political powers of the Old Testament, a vigilance totally different from political intelligence, a lucidity not limited to yielding before the formalism of universality, but upholding justice itself in its limitations."[20] An ethical, non-political attention to the claims of the other person is the core of prophecy. And such a figure is characteristic of Mendelssohnian liberalism. After suggesting that Levinas valorizes Sadat's visit to Jerusalem in 1977 as such an act of vigilance, Bernasconi goes on to cite the next sentence: "The capacity to guarantee that extra-territoriality and that independence defines the liberal state." It is this, Levinas says, that makes the conjunction of ethics and politics possible. It is, in Levinas's words, a "universalist singularity" that is "the Hebrew genius itself," which is expressed in various ways—in the Diaspora, in the State of Israel, in a Jewish distinctiveness of various kinds—and is indeed characteristic of all liberal societies.

If Bernasconi is correct, and I believe that he is, Levinas came to endorse, in the 1980s at least, a kind of liberalism—what might be called a Mendelssohnian or prophetic liberalism—unlike the classical liberalism that he had earlier criticized and rejected. To Levinas, classical liberalism was insufficiently engaged with the concrete world in which we live; Mendelssohnian or prophetic liberalism rectifies that flaw. It is intimately and deeply engaged with the world and with nature. It is attentive to our needs and to our responsibilities, and it takes normativity to be originally intertwined with nature and not something reducible to it or detached from it. In a sense, one might say that this mode of liberalism—of welfare liberalism and of liberal democracy—was a normative necessity, but if Annabel Herzog is right, it is not enough for Levinas. She has argued that more is needed. It might be that what she thinks is insufficient is the classical liberalism that Levinas had always rejected and that it is the relation to his new conception of rights and the relation between ethics and politics that Herzog thinks must be added to it. Or there might be other considerations that make liberalism inadequate, even a kind of welfare liberalism. I want now to consider what Herzog has to say and to evaluate her proposals.

In her valuable paper, "Is Liberalism 'All We Need'? Levinas's Politics of Surplus," Herzog points out that Levinas himself, in 1990, commenting on his earlier essay "Reflections on the Philosophy of Hitlerism," remarks, "We must ask ourselves if liberalism is all we need to achieve an authentic dignity for the human subject."[21] The ambiguity of Levinas's formulation aside, if we take this comment to say that he himself in 1990 was somehow reticent about liberalism, that he was then—after the essays of the 1980s and his endorsement of it—nonetheless not completely happy with what it had to offer, we might ask if the liberalism he here has in mind is the classical liberalism that in the 1934 essay he had criticized and rejected or if his reticence is meant to extend even to that form of prophetic liberalism that Bernasconi has found in the essays of the 1980s. What, in short, is the point of Levinas's caution in this remark? In the end, is liberalism not enough?

In one sense, of course, there is no regime for Levinas that is sufficient as it is. For him, politics or the regime in which justice is played out to one degree or other is always incomplete; it is always "interrupted" by the ethical, which is to say that the institutional and regulated lives we live are always responsive to others to some degree or other and never perfectly so. In part this is because our responsibilities to others are infinite and hence can never be realized fully, and in part this is because politics always involves some level of generalization, categorization, and abstraction, so that one is always being reminded that our dealings with others are encounters with utterly particular individuals in all their uniqueness. Hence, when Levinas endorses democracy precisely because of its openness to revision, to its responsiveness to change, and to adaptation, and to the degree that this kind of democracy is a liberal one, he is not saying that liberal democracy *as it now exists* is sufficient and complete or perfect. Rather what he is saying is that this form of polity is the most attractive precisely because it does not take itself at any moment to be complete or perfect. What Levinas endorses is the ideal of the liberal democracy, and to the degree that any given state seeks to exemplify that ideal, he advocates for particular liberal states. But he does not praise them for what they have accomplished as much as he praises them for their flexibility and receptivity to modification and their inclination to become better and better states.[22]

One-half of Herzog's reading, then, is that Levinas himself suggests that there is something defective about liberalism; it has inherent weaknesses. The other half of her reading is her contention that what liberalism lacks, it does because it is a form of conceptualization, and there are those—indeed just those about whom Levinas says we must care most of all—who are so weak and poor that they evade any such conceptualization. Her point, that is, is that the other is so weak and so poor that he avoids all conceptualization and his presence becomes demand. On Herzog's reading, the ones whom we face, the other persons, are "the stateless, the oppressed, the poor and the homeless, hungry widows and orphans."[23] Her question, then, is that if these are others who cannot be represented—in two senses of the notion of representation—then what is a politics that deals with them and does not exclude them? She calls this a "politics of *surplus*, a politics of nonrepresentation that is open to the irreducibility of the undefeated and the dead."[24]

Herzog's diagnosis and her solution are very attractive, or at least they would be attractive to commentators like Butler and Benhabib (and perhaps to Caygill) who would measure the success of a moral or political way of thinking by how well or how poorly it deals precisely with those who are neglected or excluded—the stateless, refugees, non-citizens, and those who live on the margins of society, the poor and minorities, for example. Doubtless, this is a compelling reading of Levinas, for it enlists Levinas as a serious philosophical advocate-critic of the limitations of modern forms of statism and especially with critics of the nation-state and its hegemony. Moreover, it is an interpretation that privileges the violence and injury done to those most marginalized in modern society and to those who are the most abandoned among the victims of war, civil war, and political oppression of all kinds. All this and more makes Herzog's type of reading quite appealing, and this appeal is supported by the attention she gives to Levinas's own words and to texts that require careful reading.

Nonetheless, Herzog's reading of Levinas is seriously confused and mistaken, and the confusions and mistakes are deep ones indeed. She takes the notion of the face to be associated with persons who are experienced as other particularly insofar as they are weak, poor, disenfranchised, excluded, exiled, rejected, oppressed, and victimized. Only insofar as a person suffers in one or more of these ways is he or she a person with a face. But this means, as one can readily see, that for Levinas not all others have faces, so to speak, or to put it differently, not all others are we individually responsible to and for. This implication, however, is wholly false for Levinas. For him, the face-to-face is not a relation that one has with some persons but not with others. Rather, as I have argued for elsewhere, each of us has the face-to-face relation with each and every other person. This is what it means to say that the ethical underlies all of our everyday, ordinary relations with other persons; all of our relations occur together with this fundamental one; all everyday relations supervene upon this one. It is the transcendental relation in which normativity and especially moral normativity enters our lives. All that we do is, to one degree or another, in one way or another, done for others, to others, both in behalf of and on behalf of others. To put this in terms of Herzog's reading, the "poor" and "hungry" are not expressions that refer to particular other persons; they are ways of signifying the dimension of vulnerability and dependence that is present within all of our relations with all others.

Herzog's confusion can also be clarified by noticing the ambiguity in the word "representation" that she employs as a central device for reading Levinas as she does. On the one hand, she says that the poor, the stateless, and the excluded are just those who cannot be represented. But this means that the face of the other cannot be described conceptually or grasped in terms of categories or thoughts; it is beyond thematization. On the other hand, she argues that it is precisely refugees and the stateless who are not represented politically within states in which they are not members or of which they are not citizens. They are beyond representation, thus, in two senses: epistemologically, so to speak, and politically. Even in a liberal democracy, then, these groups are not represented; they have no voice. No one listens to them, deals with them, cares about or for them. Now presumably what we need is a politics that appreciates the impossibility of representing these individuals while at the same time it seeks to do something for them, to acknowledge and respond to them.

The problems with this reading are evident, given what I have already said. There is much about those who are homeless, the poor, and the stateless that can be and has been discussed, understood, clarified, and addressed. We have, in states with a sense of benevolence and concern, laws that deal with some issues relevant to caring for refugees, for the poor and the homeless, and for others on the margin of society. It is rather that dimension of vulnerability, of claim and response, that

Levinas calls the face-to-face that cannot be articulated in language, that cannot be expressed. Moreover, even if that dimension cannot be expressed or described, one can and indeed ought to respond to vulnerable and suffering others by seeking to assist them, to reduce their suffering and support them in various ways. And in doing this, one might very well be giving them a voice in political decisions; one might, that is, be representing them and their needs, their distinctive claims for acceptance, acknowledgment, and support. Political representation is not conceptual or epistemological representation. There is nothing in Levinas's writings or in his thinking that excludes minorities from adequate representation or that prohibits the refugees from conflict and violence who seek shelter within one's borders from receiving attention and concern—in policies, programs, and even in laws—as well as in discrete acts of kindness and concern. The face cannot be represented, thematized, or conceptualized; the other person can. And in political settings the other person can be represented, while the subject is substitution for the face of the other. Substitution is a primal form of identification that is deeper than advocacy and representation, but which can be realized in political, legal, or social representation—acting in behalf of the other to act on her behalf. In short, while substitution is more fundamental than being a proxy, it can be expressed by various forms of going proxy.[25]

Herzog, then, takes Levinas to have distinguished between two classes of people, those who cannot be represented and those who can and are represented. Hobbes, she argues, formulates a contract theory that applies only to those who can be and are represented by the sovereign whom they authorize. It is in the light of this distinction, then, that she interprets the important claim that I have discussed earlier: "It is then not without importance to know if the egalitarian and just State in which man is fulfilled (and which is to be set up, and especially to be maintained) proceeds from a war of all against all, or from the irreducible responsibility of the one for all."[26] But she takes this to mean not that even a just and liberal state must be founded on the right understanding of what we are as social and moral beings rather than on a naturalism that cannot account for moral normativity and is not oriented to the concern for others but to our own self-preservation. Rather she takes it to mean that "the legitimacy of politics should not consist in its relation to its participants but, on the contrary, in its responsibility for its *interruption*, its *holes*, its *absentees*." The limit to the state, even the liberal one, Herzog argues, is that it "does not represent everyone." Even in the just state, there are "unrepresented people."[27] Moreover, Herzog claims that this is not a matter of the state caring for the poor, of it becoming a welfare state; rather it is a matter of it being a state that is for the unrepresented; it would exist for them.

To be sure, I think that Herzog is right to caution that for Levinas the state should not treat charity as one among its many functions, and she is right to think this because concern for others should be not just one among many functions but in a sense the ultimate goal of all that the state does. In Mendelssohn's terms, the central purpose of political authority is to organize a society so that our responsibilities to others and our care for them is facilitated in the best way possible; in short, beneficence is the spirit of all the state does and is. In practice, this means that a liberal state will be judged by how it treats its own minorities and also all those refugees or stateless persons who are its responsibility. But, contra Herzog, this is not a state that is beyond liberalism the goal of which is to care for all those who have no status in the state but are outsiders; it is a state whose purpose is to facilitate the infinite responsibilities of all its citizens in ways that reduce suffering, feed the hungry, provide shelter to the homeless, and so forth.[28]

ON DEMOCRACY

Throughout his career Levinas took totalitarianism to be the nemesis of all forms of political regime. Hitler's fascism and Stalin's Soviet tyranny are its classic forms. They were driven by their naturalism, determinism, and monism. Both dominated and oppressed their own citizens and all others whom they could assimilate to themselves. As we have shown, early in his career Levinas took classic liberalism, as I have called it, to be incapable of confronting and overcoming totalitarianism. Nor was Marxism capable of such a victory. Like totalitarianism, from Levinas's point of view, it was a form of naturalism and thus was fully capable of appreciating the importance of our concrete, natural lives. And Marxism was also a form of determinism and of monism. Later Levinas would commend it for its humanism, but its weaknesses and deficiencies were exposed by its failure to prevent it from declining into Stalinism. The best form of government, as we have seen, and the only one that had the resources to engage with totalitarianism and oppose it successfully, is liberal democracy. Thus far I have focused on the liberal side of this form of government; I want now to turn to its democratic side. What are Levinas's reasons for promoting democracy, and how do his reasons suit recent discussion of the nature of democracy, its strengths, and its weaknesses?

Democracy is rule by the people, and in principle that means equally by each and every member of the state. Although in antiquity that rule was taken to be direct, through popular assemblies, such as the Athenian *ecclesia*, in the modern period it is normally associated with representative government and parliamentary rule. This indirect rule of the people through elected representatives means that democracies are characterized by popular elections, the existence of more than one political party, universal suffrage or its approximation, the rule of law, and an extensive judicial system. They also feature, as a result of regular elections and term limits, constantly changing legislative bodies and elected officials, public discussion as part of the electoral process, and popular debate about legislative matters and policy decisions as well as extensive debate within the legislative bodies as part of the lawmaking process. Thus, democratic regimes are also marked by a free press, independent of the government, largely unrestricted access to information, and so forth. The advantages and weaknesses of democratic rule are well-known, and nowhere does Levinas explore them in a systematic way or to any great extent. The central issue for us is to clarify Levinas's reasons for taking democracy to be the most suitable form of government for a state that seeks to be as just and humane as possible.

In an earlier chapter, I pointed out that Levinas's commitment to democracy is grounded in his belief that justice in the state is always imperfect and in need of further accomplishment and fulfillment. No state is ever just enough, and democracy is best suited to this incompleteness. It is the most flexible political regime, the one most suited to change and variability.[29] Democracy has built into it a sense of dissatisfaction, a permanent sense of inadequacy. In an interview in 1992, Levinas helps us to see just this. In the spirit of the Talmudic discussion we examined in chapter 1, Levinas considers a judicial proceeding in which the sentence to be handed down is being determined. But here he goes beyond the earlier point, that "in order to determine this sentence, one finds oneself again face to face with the other, and one must look only at the face." In this interview he goes on to point out, "But once the sentence is pronounced, once it is made public, one must be able to discuss, contest, approve, or combat it. Public opinion—other citizens and the press— can intervene and state, for example, that this sentence ought to be reviewed. Therein lies the very foundation of democracy. One can debate decisions; there is no human decree that cannot be revised. Charity is thus put to the test of public verification."[30] Hence, if human existence is grounded in the ethical character of all social relationships, and if the state and political institutions are necessary to cope with the complexity of human sociality insofar as it seeks to be responsive to the demands of infinite responsibility, then the most suitable form of political institutions is the most flexible, the most "humble" and variable, the democratic form. Levinas calls this a "Greek contribution to European culture."[31] It is the form of government most receptive to change, to adjusting its practices and policies to greater and greater justice and more effective ways of caring for all its citizens and for others, to expressing and then responding to varying dissatisfaction with current practices and conduct, and so forth.[32]

Moreover, if Levinas's conception of human existence is grounded in utterly particular person-to-person relations, then the most suitable form for governing and ordering human collectivities ought to be the one that is most attentive to the particularity of individuals, and one might argue that that form is democracy. It is the form of government that ideally includes each and every individual in the process of legislating and organizing the state and locates the authority of government in the decisions and commitments of each and every citizen. Furthermore, although it must operate by voting and hence by accepting the role that each person plays in a collection of voters, in the majority or in one or another minority, still democracy does take each citizen to be no more powerful or less powerful than any other, in principle. As is often said, the principle "one person, one vote" applies equally to all.

Finally, this equality of each and every person in the state, at least in principle, ought to be important to Levinas. His "ethical metaphysics" holds that each and every person is infinitely responsible to and for each and every other person. To be sure, as I have emphasized, in everyday life we are always mitigating, limiting, and distributing that responsibility, so to speak, so that while everyone ought in principle to have an equal right to my time and resources, I do not and cannot provide and employ those resources and give that time equally to everyone. Of all the forms of government, democracy most of all aspires to pay equal attention to every citizen and to consider its authority to be equally founded on the endorsement of all. In short, equality is a value built into Levinas's conception of the ethical character of all relations; inequality is always a result of concrete, historical, particular circumstances. Inequality follows context and compromise.

Raymond Geuss, in *History and Illusion in Politics*, sets out to explore the very notion of a democratic liberal state with a capitalist economy and with a commitment to human rights for its citizens; it is an ideal model that is taken for granted in Western Europe, and yet it is a model whose parts and the whole of which are more complicated and perhaps even suspicious than one might think.[33] Except for the commitment to capitalism, it is also a model that one might attribute to Levinas, and so a look at what Geuss says about it might help us to understand the advantages and disadvantages of Levinas's support for it. Moreover, for Geuss, the way to study democracy is not by abstract analysis; rather it is to study its history, genealogically to use Nietzsche's term, since "concepts . . . which refer to human phenomena are usually historically accumulated constellations of rather heterogeneous elements."[34] In order to understand what Levinas meant by democracy and what his endorsement of democracy or liberal democracy means, then, we need to understand what that constellation meant in the 1980s, to Levinas, in the French conversation about political matters at the time. I cannot carry out such a project here, but by noting some of the highlights in Geuss's account, we can begin to see what Levinas's praise of democracy means.

Geuss helpfully points out that while democracy is present in antiquity and recurs at various moments in the history of the West, its history has no continuous development. Once it becomes a central feature of political discourse at the end of the nineteenth century, advocates and students of democracy create a history for it that originates in ancient Athens, but this history—from the Athenian experiment, through popular assemblies during the Roman period, various medieval forms of self-government, and so on—is "grossly inaccurate," Geuss notes. The relevant notion of democracy, for all practical purposes, is really a modern invention.[35] Furthermore, the term comes to have both empirical and normative uses. Empirically it describes political situations in which the people engage in deliberation about what to do, make decisions, and execute those decisions—sometimes directly, sometimes indirectly, and to varying degrees and with various complications or ramifications. I have listed above some of these possibilities, all of which can be called democratic to one degree or other.[36] Against this background, Geuss turns to considering different approaches to evaluating the strengths and weaknesses of democracy. Levinas favors it as a form of government for certain reasons. Geuss helps us to see that his estimate of democracy's strengths is not always seen that way.

Basically, Levinas endorses democracy because it seeks a just polity and because it is flexible and recognizes its own imperfection or incompleteness. I take these to mean that democracies are grounded in the well-being of all citizens without any special attention to rank or privilege; justice is the fair distribution of resources to as many as need them and to the degree that it is possible. In addition, for Levinas, justice is always compromised; no given distribution is completely fair and flawlessly attentive to each and every person's needs and concerns. Every program can be improved upon and made better, more productive of fair distribution and more attentive to individuals and their special circumstances. When it comes to positive evaluation, neither of these issues arise in Geuss's account. He notes that a multi-party democracy with regular elections "maximis[es] the likelihood of smooth transitions in the transfer of power from one group to another." Parties that lose power are less likely to resort to violence if they appreciate that elections will occur regularly and they will have another opportunity to gain power. This is a political advantage of democracies. Furthermore, the role of public discussion and deliberation of possible policies increases the chances that the greatest amount of information and relevant knowledge will be introduced into the process, and also the deliberations encourage that the parties to the discussion will be tolerant of one another's views. I do not think that Levinas gives any weight to these considerations. For Levinas, making deliberations more informed is not a freestanding value, nor is tolerance. Moreover, I am not sure Levinas would find either possibility particularly realistic. As for the political gain for political stability, while Levinas might agree with it as a legitimate prediction, surely he would realize that the stability gained in this one sense must be balanced against the overall instability that comes with democracies.[37]

Geuss points out that one line of criticism comes from Max Weber. "Democracy, he thinks, is incompatible with one of the basic requirements of modern social life. . . . In a large modern society with a capitalist economy all organisations will have a tendency to become bureaucratic." But bureaucracies function best when they are strictly organized by rules, are hierarchical, and promote regularity and stability. Democracies, on the other hand, are "inherently anti-hierarchical and egalitarian," and even if they employ rules and patterns, they emphasize flexibility and change rather than fixity and regularity.[38] According to Geuss's reading of Weber, then, democracies are intrinsically opposed to the virtues of bureaucracies, and modern society is unavoidably bureaucratic. But if Geuss draws the conclusion that democracy might not then be the most suitable or most functional regime, Levinas would surely opt for the other alternative, advocating democracy precisely because it is the form of government that mitigates and even opposes some of the worst by-products of bureaucratic society. Moreover, it is important to remember that Levinas's choice would not be a social or functional one in some narrow sense. Rather it would involve choosing democracy for moral reasons, because it offers the fullest possible expression of our interpersonal responsibilities and our attentiveness to the individuality of each and every person. Democracy shows that even if we have to take rules or norms for granted as necessary for complex social life, we need constantly to be aware of the limitation of rules; they are always set for classes of persons and mitigate against taking particular individuals seriously one by one. Alongside welfare programs, we might say, democracy makes a good deal of room for personal acts of kindness and charity.

Indeed, democracy makes room for them within the political (in both narrow and wide senses) and not only outside of it.

It is instructive too that Levinas never admires democracy for a reason that has seemed to many to be associated with its most important feature, that is, the fact that in it people rule themselves and hence are free. Self-rule or a kind of autonomy is often taken to be good in itself, which elevates democracy as also good in itself, but not for Levinas. For him, goodness is achieved when one extends oneself to acknowledge, accept, care for, and assist others, and regularly this is accomplished when one chooses—freely—to do so. But there is no privileging of freedom in Levinas's view of human existence, as we have seen. Hence, for Levinas, democracy is superior not because of all forms of government, it expresses that freedom best.[39] As I have pointed out, it is rather its appreciation of the incompleteness and inadequacies of any given political regime, of any system of rules and programs, when it comes to organizing and accomplishing one's responsibilities to others, that is the central feature of a democracy of which Levinas makes note.

Surprisingly, this reasoning brings Levinas close to what Geuss calls a third approach to evaluating democracy positively, one that he associates with John Dewey. As Geuss puts it:

> Democracy for Dewey is a good form of political organization because it is the appropriate political modelling of a more general form of human interaction which has both epistemological and valuative advantages, and which finds its best realization in a free scientific community devoted to experimental research. Just as such a research community is trying to invent theories that will allow us to deal with our environment in a satisfactory way, so a good human society would be one that was a kind of experimental community devoted to trying to discover worthwhile and satisfying ways of living.[40]

As Geuss clarifies, the crucial point here is that science not only comes to new and different results, it also devises new and different methods of experimentation and for testing theories. Similarly, for Dewey, societies or communities seek new and different ways of testing ways of life. Nothing Levinas says is precise enough or detailed enough for us to draw a close comparison, but one can see how Levinas's evaluation of democracy as a form of social organization is in the spirit of Dewey's analogy. A democratic society constantly rethinks its policies and programs and the ways these are applied in order to make such programs and policies more just and also more caring, more humane, and attentive to others' needs. For Dewey, in the domain of science, we seek better and better theories; for Levinas, in our lives, we seek more effective and caring programs for acting responsibly to and for others, which is what we mean by better and better just practices. To be sure, this is not an exact comparison, but it is a helpful way of understanding what Levinas's endorsement means and what kind of an endorsement it is.[41] Recall the interview from 1992 where Levinas gives, as an example of a democratic moment, the public discussion—among people and in the press—of a sentence pronounced by the court in a trial. Here the interplay between the law and its application in a particular case is debated and discussed in public opinion, and in one way or another the judgment of the people is expressed. One can imagine that Levinas could very well be recalling the situation ten years earlier, after the horrific events in West Beirut, when the Israeli people called upon the government to establish a board of inquiry. Before any evidence was presented and evaluated, the people had made it clear that they wanted such an inquiry conducted, and then, after the report was made public, there was widespread discussion of its findings, and then too, in the press and elsewhere, the people expressed their views about the commission's results. Democracy is the form of society and state in which such a process can go on. Tyrannies and oligarchies do not permit it, or they do not acknowledge it responsibly. Rather they crush it. One need only recall events such as Tiananmen Square in 1989.

In short, Levinas's endorsement of democracy arises from within his conception of the ethical critique of the political.[42] Insofar as ethics provides the grounds for social and political critique, Levinas takes the best form of government to be that in which such critique is possible. It is the form of state and government in which there can occur most productively the interplay of the ethical character of human existence and its sociality, on the one hand, and the everyday, political life in which that ethical normativity expresses itself, on the other. Hence, democracy—the liberal democratic state—is the most suitable political form for human life to take. If "Europe is the Bible and the Greeks," democracy is the form of Europe.[43]

PART THREE

Ethics, Politics, and Zionism

SEVEN

TEACHING PROPHETIC POLITICS

Ethics and Politics in Levinas's Talmudic Lessons

Levinas's published writings include books, collections of essays and articles, interviews, and Talmudic lessons. Generally speaking, the best places to look for Levinas's comments on concrete and particular situations in which ethics and politics encounter one another are his many published interviews and his twenty-four published Talmudic lessons.[1] In the interviews Levinas speaks directly to an interviewer and responds to his or her questions; the informality of the setting often elicits from him examples, illustrations, and textual references and comments that are very helpful for understanding the themes of his thinking. In the Talmudic lessons Levinas selected texts to discuss that were chosen precisely because they expressed themes that Levinas associated with the announced topic of the colloquium for that given year. Often—although not always—in the course of the lesson, he refers to contemporary events or widely publicized incidents that contributed to the choice of that year's topic. Also, the texts themselves typically include stories or legal discussions concerning particular types of conduct. Hence, both the setting for these lessons and their Talmudic focus move Levinas to make comments that, relative to the bulk of his writings, are quite concrete and particular.

In this chapter I will turn to several of these lessons to examine Levinas's ethical politics in action, so to speak. The lessons also dramatize the relation between ethics and politics and portray it in vivid language and evocative images. There are two contributions that such an examination can make to our project. First, it will help to illustrate and possibly even to confirm the conception of ethical critique of the political that we have discussed in earlier chapters. Second, studying selected passages from these lessons will exemplify how Levinas thinks these texts—as the core of the Jewish literary tradition—help us to understand the primacy of the ethical for human existence, social and political, and thereby it will provide a paradigmatic example of how Judaism's educational role is carried out. And insofar as education is a primary feature of political training and development in general, the role of the Talmud in educating Jews and others regarding the centrality of ethics to human existence becomes a model for how civic education should work in any liberal democratic state.

In other chapters I have referred to Levinas's Talmudic lessons at times in order to clarify the issues we have been discussing. As I have said, they supplement the abstract account that Levinas provides elsewhere with detail and concreteness. In this chapter my goal is both to add to what we have already accomplished and to show how the resources for ethical critique can be found in the Jewish literary tradition. I will discuss a selected number of the lessons to show how rhetorically and conceptually Levinas's ethical critique appears in action.

JUSTICE, ETHICS, AND THE COURTS

At a metaphysical level, so to speak, human existence contains two dimensions, the ethical and the political, or, in other terms, the conceptually articulated and linguistically expressible features of everyday human experience are accompanied, at a deep level, by an ethical or normative dimension that is present in all second-person interpersonal encounters. At a historical level, Levinas refers to this coordination of two dimensions as the fact that European civilization is a blending of the Bible and the Greeks, of the biblical tradition and the tradition of science and philosophy. In October 1966, at the colloquium the theme of which was "Is Judaism Necessary to the World?," Levinas gave a lesson entitled "As Old as the World?" In the terms we just mentioned, the question for the colloquium might be paraphrased in two ways: does European civilization need the Bible, and do the political and our everyday lives need ethics? Levinas of course believes that the answer to these questions is yes, and hence he believes that Judaism is necessary to the world. Or, more precisely, the world needs whatever Judaism has to contribute; the world needs normativity as well as the natural order. Ethical critique is necessary for the political.

What is especially interesting about this Talmudic lesson, which is a commentary on Sanhedrin 36b–37a, is not only the central theme but also the subject of the Mishnaic text, the seating arrangements in the ancient court, the Sanhedrin.[2] Here the Talmud refers explicitly to the foundation and order of the judicial institution of the Jewish community. And the Gemara examines the biblical text from Song of Songs 7:3 on which the arrangement is based, and its theme of course is love. Hence, Levinas's theme: judicial institutions aimed at just decisions are not sufficient without love. At one level, the central lesson of the text could not be clearer: justice without love is unsatisfactory. Politics requires ethical critique, which is a Levinasian modulation on the traditional rabbinic view that God must have alongside the standard of justice that God applies (*middat ha-din*) also the standard of mercy or compassion (*middat ha-rahamim*). But here the focus is not on a divine duality of attributes; rather it is on a duality of dimensions in the single institution of the court.

The first thing that Levinas notes is that the court was arranged in a semicircle "so that its members could see each other," and he elaborates this, as one might expect, to mean that the court was arranged with face-to-face relations, in dialogue, each person facing the other or presenting a profile to the other. No one saw only the other person's back or spoke impersonally. Of course there are three rows of "students of the law"—"those who study the Torah but are not yet invested as judges"— seated in front of the judges, but Levinas's point is that what the Mishnah emphasizes is that the arrangement is not in linear rows but in curved ones that place speakers and listeners in such a way that they face one another, to one degree or another.[3] Moreover, with the students present, it is clear, Levinas underscores the point that the court is also a school. The purpose of the judicial proceedings is both legal and educational.

Levinas turns to the Gemara, which begins with a question about the "basis for the structure of the Sanhedrin," and he notes that the response indicates a "narrow, dishonest, or bizarre mind." Why? Because the respondent offers a literal reading of a piece of ancient Hebrew writing to provide that basis rather than considering the possibility of his-

torical borrowing, in particular rather than introducing a borrowed tradition from ancient Greece. After all, the Sanhedrin is an institution in
ancient Judaism that dates from the Hellenistic and Roman periods and
not earlier. And we have very clear evidence in Greek literature from
the fifth century BCE about the Hellenic antiquity of the establishment
of courts in ancient Greece. In short, does not the Talmud's response
show a rather bizarre kind of parochialism? Why not just admit the fact
that the organization and structure of the Sanhedrin is modeled on an
already existing judicial institution? Is this an expression of historical
ignorance or just parochialism?

Levinas offers a nice explanation: the crucial point he takes the text
to be making is not about the historical origin of the court and its structure; rather it is about the spirit in which the institution was appropriated
and modified. "Whatever the historical causality and the antecedents of
ideas and institutions might be . . . what matters is the discovery of the
convergence of the spiritual efforts of mankind or . . . what matters is to
know *in what spirit something is borrowed*." As a general point, this is a
thoughtful and worthwhile one to keep in mind. And in this case, it is especially salient. As Levinas clarifies the issue, "Whatever the channel of
history through which the Sanhedrin was established in Israel, whatever
the forms of its historical existence in pre-exilic society, it is interesting
to know what meaning Jewish thought and sensibility attributed to it.
For it is around this institution that, for twenty centuries, the notion of
justice and truth have been reflected upon and experienced."[4] We can
take for granted that the basic functions and structure of the court were
drawn from Greek antecedents, but the crucial point is not what was
appropriated, but rather the meaning that Jewish sensibility gave to the
institution insofar as it was the central locus of justice in Jewish society.
How was that justice understood?

Here Levinas takes what he claims is his central step. The textual citation that is used to reveal that meaning and that spirit is from an erotic
text and from perhaps the most erotic text in the whole of the Bible, the
Song of Songs. This textual reference is what is so surprising: "an erotic
text founding a court of law and a system of justice."[5] The association of
this erotic text with mysticism is one thing; its association with law and
justice is a wholly different matter. Given what we know of Levinas's

thinking, of course, the connection is suggestive and provocative, but Levinas wants his listeners and readers to be stunned by the oddity, the strangeness of the juxtaposition, and not to respond complacently.

Song of Songs 7:3 begins by comparing the beloved's navel to a round goblet, and Levinas admits to reflecting on the image of the Sanhedrin functioning at the "navel of the universe," justice arising at the place where creation has left its trace. A friend reminded him that this image of the "navel of the universe" occurs in Aeschylus's *Eumenides*, in which Delphi, the home of the Delphic Oracle, is called the navel of the world. Levinas rereads the play and finds in it the "struggle [between] Zeus's justice and the justice of the Eumenides, the justice with forgiveness to the justice of unrelenting vengeance." That is, the play portrays the establishment of the Areopagus in Athens as a court of justice, to replace the rule of vengeance represented by the Furies, and, as Levinas notes, with this he is moving closer to the theme of his lesson. As he puts it, "Isn't Aeschylus enough?" He notes that in the play the Eumenides and "vengeance-justice" are not simply expelled from Athens; they remain and must remain, for they represent the criticism of overindulgence and forgiveness in the face of strict justice. "In her great wisdom, Athena keeps the Eumenides and finds a function for them in her city." Both the old gods and the new have a vote, each having an equal voice, and then human beings decide between them. What arises from Delphi, the navel of the world, is an interpretation of what Zeus wills—the decision made by a human court between the old justice and the new. Moreover, Levinas takes this image of the navel of the world to mean that the "Jewish contribution to the world is therefore in this world as old as the world itself." On the face of it, then, Levinas might have wondered whether the role of justice, of the courts, in Judaism might have already been present in the *Eumenides*, which was written by Aeschylus in 458 BCE, shortly after the Persian Wars, and predates the Mishnah by more than five centuries, indeed probably by more than six. But, as he then says, he is consoled by the thought that the "*Eumenides* is nonetheless three centuries later than the prophets of the Bible."[6]

Levinas, however, is sensitive and cautious enough to warn us and himself against any simple judgment about priority. Every nation, he says, conceives of itself as "dwell[ing] at the navel of the world." Every nation takes itself to be original and central to the world and the career of history. Indeed, Levinas points out that it is this commitment to pre-eminence and originality that supports the claim—now enshrined in the United Nations Universal Declaration of Human Rights—to sovereignty.[7] We must not indulge in "facile and rhetorical antitheses: we are justice, they are charity; we love God, they love the world."[8] But even though Levinas admits therefore that ancient Greek culture incorporated an "authentic spirituality," still he does think that one can distinguish between what one finds in the Mishnah and what one finds in the *Eumenides*. Levinas's commentary on Song of Songs 7:3, however, begins by pointing to features that both cultures share. But, as he goes on, he turns to what the text, and the Gemara overall, presents as the portrayal of something distinctive. It is not the institution of the court that is the Jewish contribution; it is not justice. Rather it concerns the character of the judges, first of all, and then all those whom the court serves, the members of the community, the people. What does Levinas say about them?

Basically, in the form of a commentary on the Talmudic text, Levinas presents a sketch of his central insight about the responsibility for others and takes it to be a distinctive contribution of the text that it underscores this ethical responsibility as characteristic of the Jewish people and of Jews. In short, it is not the institution of a court that seeks justice that is the special Jewish contribution to European civilization; it is the insight that to function that court must occur within a population of people who are oriented to one another as infinitely responsible, as obligated to acknowledge, accept, and care for others.

To arrive at this insight about the text, Levinas focuses his attention on the Gemara's comments on the final expression in Song of Songs 7:3, "hedged with roses." What does the Talmud's enigmatic claim "Even if the separation is a hedge of roses, they will make no breach in it" mean? Levinas explains. The "they" are judges, who are separated from their own sin by the thinnest of barriers and yet will not "breach" that barrier. The Sanhedrin, he says, "is possible only with such a human breed. Otherwise, justice is a mockery."[9] Here, Levinas sketches a bit of moral psychology. The roses are tempting and yet have thorns that warn the judges away. They resist and must resist if justice is to prevail in the courts of law. "There is no justice if the judges do not have virtue in the flatly moral sense of the term. There cannot be a separation between the private life and the public life of the judge. It is in the most intimate area of his private life, in the secret garden—or hell—of his soul that his universal life either blossoms or fades."[10]

The text goes on, Levinas claims, to expand the judgment from judges to "the entire Jewish people." "The excellence demanded earlier of the members of the Sanhedrin is extended to the Jewish people in its entirety,"[11] for in response to an objection Rav Kahana says that "the Torah has testified to us through a hedge of roses." "To us" refers to all the people, and the culture grounded in the Torah "preserves" us from evil and sin only by the slimmest of barriers. And yet the Jews make no "breach" in that barrier. They do not sin. Morality, moreover, begins within the person and within institutions. Or, in terms we used earlier, ethics originally is not articulated in rights and duties; they come later. Foundationally, ethics has a different origin, one that is prior to institutions.[12] But we still have not been told about the ethical content of this moral psychology, so to speak.

The Gemara includes a third response to the objection. Rav Zera calls attention to Genesis 27:27, which reports Isaac's remark when he smells Esau's clothes that are worn by Jacob; he says that his son's clothes smell like a lush field. Rav Zera tells us to read not "his clothes" but rather "his rebels," and Levinas explains that these are all those who will rebel against the Law but who will be "incense to Isaac's nostrils." Even the least worthy are "full of merit." Moreover, as Levinas goes on to comment, the theme of disguise and taking upon oneself responsibility for the other person adds an important feature to the Gemara's understanding of who the Jew is:

> How to preserve oneself from evil? By each taking upon himself the responsibility of the others. Men are not only and in their ultimate essence "for self" but "for others." ... Nothing is more foreign to me than the other; nothing is more intimate to me than myself. Israel would teach that the greatest intimacy of me to myself consists in being at every moment responsible for the others, the hostage of others. *I can be responsible for that which I did not do and take upon myself a distress which is not mine.*[13]

The Gemara uses the wordplay, asking us to replace "his clothes," or *begedav*, with "his rebels," or *bogedav*. Levinas continues, "Isaac had a premonition of all the rebels that would come out of Jacob. But Jacob already bore the weight of all that rebellion.... For the human world to be possible—justice, Sanhedrin—at each moment there must be someone who can be responsible for the others. Responsible! The famous finite liberty of the philosophers is responsibility for that which I have not done. Condition of the creature.... Responsibility for the sins you did not commit, responsibility for the others." It is this that Levinas later says "may be something that we would not find in Aeschylus."[14]

What, then, does Judaism add to the Greek teaching about the institutionalization of justice? It adds what we might call its normativity or normative force: "the man who is hostage to all others is needed by men, for without him morality would have no place to start."[15] Or, alternatively, the courts can function only in a world in which there is already a ground for acting toward others with kindness and charity. "The little bit of generosity that occurs in the world requires no less."[16]

ECONOMIC PRACTICES, REVOLUTION, AND COLLABORATION WITH THE GOVERNMENT

All of this, however, is still rather abstract. The text we have been discussing focuses on the courts and hence on the broad question of how ethics provides the context in which judgment takes place and in which the system of courts is established. Elsewhere, Levinas's Talmudic lessons provide a much more concrete and engaged picture of ongoing political life and the way in which ethics provides a vehicle by which political activism takes place and how it is justified. An excellent example is the extremely important and timely lesson "Judaism and Revolution," which Levinas conducted at the tenth colloquium in March 1969, the year after the transformative events of May 1968. The topic of the colloquium was "Youth and Revolution in Jewish Consciousness," which shows, if there are any doubts, that the events of 1968 were the precise context and subject of the colloquium and hence of Levinas's Talmudic reading. The text is from Baba Metzia 83a–83b; it includes discussion of economic and political issues, especially the role of religious leaders in helping to police crime and the nature of revolution.

The passage from the Mishnah that Levinas selected deals with employers and employees and the contractual arrangements for employment, in particular the daily starting and ending time of work and, if meals are customary, what they should include. The Mishnah emphasizes that in both matters the determining factor is "custom." Whatever the local custom is, that is what the employment contract or arrangement should require. Levinas makes several important points about the Mishnah.

First, the worker for hire is in a precarious position. He or she is free and seeks employment willingly, but needing to work puts the person in a weak position, where his or her freedom is at risk. Levinas says that "commerce is at the borderline of alienation, and freedom easily turns into non-freedom." What the Mishnah introduces into this risky situation are limits on the worker's freedom in the form of rights, what Levinas calls "rights of the other *person*" and which he characterizes as "limits imposed on freedom for the greater glory of freedom." We can appreciate what Levinas has in mind: the worker needs to be protected from exploitation precisely because his weak or inferior position puts him or her at a disadvantage; the employer's responsibilities need to be regulated, because the worker is susceptible to being manipulated. And since this is a matter of custom, it is in place prior to the law and prior to the actual employment contract. It is a "resistance against the arbitrary and against violence." Second, these limits are fundamental; they "concern the material conditions of life, sleep and food. Sublime materialism!" Levinas calls this an "authentic humanism, materialistic humanism." It is one thing to be concerned about the workers, another thing to donate money to support them, but another thing still to "open . . . the doors of our own homes." And here Levinas associates this very concrete responsibility to the other person, the worker, with Judaism and also with Marxism or "Marxist humanism."[17] Third, it is important to appreciate that these rights are not those of the subject but rather those of the other person, and hence they are aimed at each of us as potential "employers," so to speak. Levinas says this is "typical of Jewish humanism." "The man whose rights must be defended is in the first place the other man; it is not initially myself. It is not the concept 'man' which is at the basis of this humanism; it is the other man."[18] That is, this Jewish humanism is grounded in the claim the other person makes on me and not either on my freedom and selfhood or on being an example of the abstract category humanity. The person who needs to be protected, cared for, and provided for is the person whom I encounter and who addresses me out of his weakness and vulnerability. The core of the employer-worker relationship is the responsibility of the employer.

Furthermore, and this is Levinas's fourth point, this right is infinite, or, as he puts it, our obligations or duties to the other person are without limit. In the Mishnah this is expressed by saying that even if the employer provides a meal like the one King Solomon would have served, it would not have fulfilled his obligation to the worker. "The extent of the obligation toward men who are fully men has no limits." Fifth, these workers, the Mishnah says, are "descendants of Abraham, Isaac, and Jacob." Here Levinas recalls that his teacher—Chouchani, I take it[19]—has taught him that a reference like this to the people of Israel in fact can be understood to refer to "a particular ethnic group which is probably fulfilling an incomparable destiny." This means here that the workers are "human beings who are no longer childlike," "a perfected humanity." They know what responsibilities they have and what each of us owes one another. Or, as Levinas also explains, the workers are people who know "how to receive and feed men," for that is Abraham's bequest, the awareness of limitless hospitality to others. "The heirs of Abraham [have received from him] . . . a difficult tradition of duties toward the other man, which one is never done with, an order in which one is never free."[20]

Finally, Levinas notes that this infinite obligation or responsibility that each person has for the other must also be limited. In fact, this is precisely what the content of the employment contract does. It fixes the terms, and in this case, for example, it dictates exactly what the meals owed the workers will contain. Levinas puts this by saying, "There is more in the family of Abraham than in the promises of the State." On the one hand, just giving is not sufficient; one must give in such a way that the other person's *dignity* is respected; on the other hand, the extent and scope of the giving must be fixed by rules or norms: "It is not through the State and through the political advances of humanity that the person shall be fulfilled—which, of course, does not free the State from instituting the conditions necessary to this fulfillment."[21] That is, "everything begins with the right of the other man and with my infinite obligations toward him," but then society—in this case the employ-ment contract—is the "limitation of this right and this obligation toward him." Both are necessary, the infinite responsibility that reaches out to the other person's dignity and respects it, responds to it, and also the contractual limits that fix how employers must deal with those whom they hire. "It is possible, when the other man is in principle infinite for me, to limit the extent of my duties to a degree but only to a degree. The contract is more concerned with limiting my duties than with defending my rights."[22] In the Mishnah, the father tells his son to fix the conditions of employment with the workers before they start work.[23]

The Mishnah ends, Levinas points out, with a reaffirmation that the determining factor in arriving at the details of the employment arrange-ment is custom, and while it is not yet law, custom or the way things are regularly done is already a limitation on the infinity of interpersonal obligation. Unless, he points out, the notion of custom carries with it a kind of conservatism, and with this, Levinas points ahead to the main theme of the lesson, which has yet to emerge, the theme of revolution. The Mishnah, then, in terms of that theme, simply sets the stage; it does not yet reach the real drama. For this we need to turn to the Gemara.

But on its own, even without any direct link to the main theme of revolution, the Mishnah and Levinas's reading of it explore some very important themes concerning economic and social relationships and the way in which they are grounded in the ethical character of social exis-tence. Of course, we have heard this before. But here Levinas's account emerges from a reading of a Talmudic passage that deals with a very spe-cific type of relationship, that between employers and workers; this adds concreteness to Levinas's views and also shows how his views can in fact make a real difference in how our economic relationships are arranged. How Levinas arrives at some of his characteristic doctrines—about the infinity of interpersonal rights and duties, for example—is a real tour de force, and I am sure many will take the exegesis to be strained or exagger-ated. But for our purposes, the importance of the reading comes in the way in which the mutual limitation of ethics and politics is framed. The regime of norms or contractual arrangements is a limitation not only on the employer's freedom but more importantly on his responsibilities. The contract must specify when daily work begins and when it ends, and it must specify what meals are to be provided and what they must contain. Even if custom ultimately determines how these factors are determined, they must be specified, and when they do, they limit what is ultimately a limitless responsibility the employer has to and for the employee. At the same time, the contract as a normative agreement is itself limited or determined by the rights and responsibilities that underlie it. It is a contract aimed not merely at the employee's material needs and interests, important as they are. It is also aimed at his or her dignity, as Levinas puts it.

The need for the explicit presence of provisions in the contract is the first point taken up in the Gemara. If custom already determines when the workday begins and when it ends, why must it be stipulated explicitly? The reason, the Gemara says, is that if the employer overpays the worker, he cannot later say that he expects the worker to start earlier or to work later. The contract allows the worker to claim that the extra compensation is about the quality of his work and not for extra hours. It is a protection for the worker; it secures his leisure time from the bargain, as Levinas puts it.[24]

What does the text have to do with revolution? To begin, Levinas says, revolution is not "a purely formal matter, . . . violence or . . . the overthrow of a given order." "Revolution must be defined by its content, its values; revolution takes place when one frees man; that is, revolution takes place when one tears man away from economic determinism."[25] These remarks are an interlude, and a preface, as it were. We cannot know what they mean fully until we read the Gemara and Levinas's interpretation of it. Still, these brief comments are puzzling. For Levinas, all we do should be aimed at accepting and caring for others. What has this to do with freedom from economic determinism? One thought suggests itself—that the freedom as negative is a relief from naturalism or materialism. It is being free to express one's essential normative interests, and since our daily lives are increasingly driven by natural interests, new technologies, and self-interest, a revolution would be any movement or alteration that enhances the normative dimension of our lives. But this is all rather formal itself; we will learn more as the reading continues.

Resh Lakish asks who is responsible for traveling time—the time it takes the worker to get to work from home in the morning and to get home after work in the evening. He tells us that the morning time is the employee's responsibility, while the evening return time is to be paid for by the employer. Why? Levinas, drawing on Psalm 104:22–23, provides the reasoning: "A workday is measured by the length of the day." So if the worker awakes at sunrise, the time it takes for him to get to work is excluded from the workday; that is, the employer is responsible for the daylight hours. Since the worker works until sundown and the return home is during the night, it is the worker's own responsibility. Levinas apologizes for the precise calculation, which may seem erroneous; the issue is that there are limits to who pays for what and that these limits express "the inalienable rights of the worker."[26]

The next stretch of the Gemara includes a dialogue or debate about why Resh Lakish felt that the conclusion required a textual demonstration if the Mishnah had already said that the question of when the workday began and ended was determined by custom. Levinas wonders whether this is not just an example of the "sterility" of the Talmudic method; he asks what could be gained by such a reference and in particular what the Psalms and its poetry could possibly have to do with the rigorous issues of economic relations. Nonetheless, a literal reading of Psalm 104:22–23 does tell us that the workday begins at sunrise and ends with evening, when the sun goes down. But there is more to be learned, Levinas says, if one follows Chouchani's advice and looks at the whole of Psalm 104 to understand the context in which the verse occurs and hence the spirit in which this precise determination of the workday is introduced.

Psalm 104 is praise of God as creator by a creature that conceives of itself as fulfilled or perfected. It is about the "profound harmony" within all creatures if taken to be perfected and fully accomplished.[27] Verses 22–23 occur near the end. What do they mean, this association of the wild beasts returning to their lairs and the beginning of work? "As soon as the day begins, nothing savage remains. Integrally human life is possible: work begins. In this psalm, work is not associated with misfortune, a curse, meaninglessness. The psalm seems to place the work of men amid the successes of creation."[28] In other words, Levinas here reads Psalm 104 as providing a positive evaluation of work as part of what perfects creation. In *Time and the Other* Levinas introduces work or labor as the means by which human beings expend effort to cultivate and then appropriate the natural world for their enjoyment and nourishment. The same theme is elaborated in *Totality and Infinity*.[29] His comment here is in that spirit. Work is not a punishment; it is not a curse. Rather it is part of the perfection of the created world in which humankind lives. In other words, by citing Psalm 104, not only does Resh Lakish identify the length of the workday; he also underscores "the meaning of human work and thus [provides] a reason for the dignity of the worker."[30] As he puts it, "The rights of the worker are due to his function in the general economy of creation, to his ontological role."[31]

All of this suggests a very positive view of creation, however, what Levinas calls a "beatific reading of Psalm 104" that obscures "how evil can enter the world through work." He asks: Does the psalm have "no feeling for dialectic?" Does it "affirm, in short, that this is the best possible world?"[32] Levinas thinks that the Talmud has this same worry, but before it turns to the issue of evil, the text sets out a debate between a defender of Resh Lakish, who tries to support his use of the biblical citation, and an opponent, who wonders why it is necessary if the Mishnah has already grounded the details of the employment contract on custom. In defending the use of the psalm, Levinas suggests, "[Resh Lakish] at least thinks that the natural law attached to the person of the worker and consecrated by the Torah guarantees better than custom the rights of the person. Perhaps Resh Lakish is a revolutionary because he denounces custom" in this manner.[33] What lies behind the account of a perfected creation and the role of work in it, of course, is Levinas's conception of the ethical character of human existence and the infinity of our responsibilities to another. His suggestion here, then, is that the Talmud may already realize here that justice in employment contracts and other institutions depends ultimately not on custom but rather on the rights of the other person and the infinite responsibilities to him or her.

The objector raises the specter of custom, and Resh Lakish's defender then says cryptically "in question is a new city."[34] That is, the biblical proof-text is needed because what is in question are cities without traditions, or what Levinas calls "the mushroom cities of our industrial world" and "American cities." Levinas does not avoid the long-standing anti-Americanism of French intellectual life.[35] But the critical point is that Levinas takes Resh Lakish to realize that employment contracts must rely upon deep foundations in human existence and not merely on a legacy of practices or the authority of tradition, and this is the point of his reference to Psalm 104. And the text underscores this point by suggesting that even if we admit that such "industrial societies" come from nowhere and have no traditions of substance, still their population does come from other places, but with such people being "mixed together" and yet highly "dispersed," the result is that "all traditions are lost." Such individuals no longer "belong to a human community conscious of its history, organized and structured." We should abandon efforts to "save [such a city or society] through patriarchal virtues of the group." What is needed is for its institutions and norms to be grounded on a conception of human existence, of human dignity and worth. As Levinas puts it, "Away with customs and myths, all of Spinoza's knowledge of the first kind, all those instruments of enslavement."[36] The Talmud makes this point in its own way, by suggesting that the hiring could be done according to the laws of the Torah. The legal length of a workday is determined not by custom or tradition, but it is written in the laws of the Torah, which is another way of saying that it is a feature of our understanding of human existence as ethical and social.

Insofar as this interpretation of Psalm 104:22–23 places the employment contract under a kind of natural law that assumes a perfected creation, it seems to "do away with revolution" because it presumes that the world is the best of possible worlds, as Levinas puts it.[37] But another reading of Psalm 104 leads in another direction—to the possibility of evil and of revolution. According to Rav Zera, the reference to night in verse 22 must be understood in the context of Psalm 104:20, "You bring on darkness and it is night." This world is like the night, and the night in which the beasts stir (v. 22) refers to the "evil-doers in this world, who are comparable to the beasts of the forest."[38] As Levinas notes, "The night of wild beasts would be a mode of human existence. Evil is within the human. Creation is not already in order. Night must come to an end so that order can take the place of night. Evil must be eliminated, . . . and the just must receive his reward."[39] In other words, Rav Zera reads the text metaphorically. The beasts returning to their lairs are the wicked withdrawing to hell, and the workers leaving for work are the just receiving their rewards.

At first Levinas reads this in abstract terms. On Rav Zera's interpretation, evil serves the good and hence somehow the two are confused; the night is this confusion. Something is needed to remove this confusion, and this is the purpose of revolution, "to dissipate this confusion" so that "Good [will] be Good and Evil Evil."[40] Then, using the notions of home and work, Levinas interprets the "night" to be a time of isolation, in which persons are "strangers" to one another and to themselves, and work is involvement in the divine order, that is, by reaching out to others and acting out of concern and responsibility. The crucial idea, however, remains the same, that the night is a time of evil and estrangement, alienation, that requires a revolutionary act to free oneself from it. And this is the direction in which the Talmud now moves.

The Talmud now narrates a long story about Rabbi Eleazar ben Rabbi Simeon. Levinas tells us that the Rabbi Simeon mentioned here is the famous Rabbi Simeon bar Yochai, the Tanna (first-generation rabbinic sage) to whom tradition attributes the authorship of the *Zohar* and who is known for having hid from the Romans in a cave for thirteen years. But, as Levinas points out, if Rabbi Simeon bar Yochai is renowned for his mysticism, his son Rabbi Eleazar reveals himself to have been "a man very gifted in police work or politics." Indeed, it will turn out that the overall context for the narrative and the Talmudic discussion of it is the struggle with Rome and collaboration with the Romans. But, as Levinas notes, such Talmudic texts, even if they arise out of a very specific historical context, have a much more general meaning. "The text, even if it did arise as a result of cases of collaboration, opens up the entire problem of the relation between politics and Evil, the problem of the relationship of political struggle and Evil. That is, the text opens up an essential aspect of the problem of revolution. For a revolution does not destroy the State: it is for another political regime, but for a political regime nonetheless."[41] As we have argued, for Levinas, the political is necessary, but its purpose must be to express most fully the ethical. Revolution is an effort to advance the ethical dimension of all political life; it seeks to replace one regime with another that is more just and more humane.[42]

A central purpose of the story of Rabbi Eleazar is to clarify the sources of evil. The rabbi interrogates a Roman official responsible for catching thieves, a police detective, asking him how he determines who is a genuine thief. Perhaps they are the same as brutes. Rabbi Eleazar cites Psalm 104:20, the very verse just cited by Rav Zera, to prove this identity, reading the verse to mean "in it [i.e., the night] all the beasts of the night stir." Levinas takes this to mean that "evil—or bestiality—is non-communication."[43] It is hiding from others and from oneself. The evil are beasts who hide during the day and only expose themselves at night, that is, in doing evil. Others, however, take Rabbi Eleazar to support his claim with Psalm 10:9: "He waits in a covert like a lion in his lair; waits to seize the lowly."

This alternative suggestion about what verse Rabbi Eleazar had used to support his identification (or comparison) of the wicked with beasts sets Levinas on an interpretive exploration of this other psalm, Psalm 10, which, he points out, is the "opposite of Psalm 104," insofar as Psalm 10 is "about the absence of God," while Psalm 104 is about God's perfect presence, so to speak.[44] Psalm 104 praises God for His presence in all creation; Psalm 10 chastises God for His absence or neglect of all those who need Him, abandoning the weak to the wicked. Psalm 10:9 then refers to the wicked who seek to ambush the poor man. Wickedness is the outcome of the assault on the powerless, on all manner of harm or neglect aimed at them. And hence, if there is to be real revolution, it will be to take action against such victimization.

Rabbi Eleazar continues by asking the police detective what he would do if he caught a just man and let an evil-doer go, and the detective answers, "What can I do? It's the order of the king."[45] This is the dialogue that follows Rabbi Eleazar's claim that the wicked are like beasts or brutes. The rabbi's question about the possibility of capturing a just person while letting an evil one go clarifies the point of the earlier question about how the detective determines who is the guilty party. How does he know who is evil? Levinas takes this to be the point of this exchange. "Unquestionably," he says, "violent action against Evil is necessary. And we shall soon see that this violence takes on all the appearances of political action." "But," he continues, "it is no less evident that this action must seek the nature and cause of Evil."[46] And this project requires more than just identifying the outward signs of evil conduct; it requires identifying what evil is, where it comes from, how it corrupts society, and more. Levinas raises all these questions and calls them "the metaphysical and spiritual reason" for evil.[47] All of this is suggestive, of course, and we will only be able to see the kind of solutions or answers he thinks are appropriate and helpful as we go on. For the moment, it is sufficient to realize that Levinas takes the exchange between Rabbi Eleazar and the detective to be about doing what is necessary to guarantee that one does not mistakenly capture and convict innocent people and allow guilty ones to go free. Levinas takes the Talmud to be exploring what kind of understanding would be required.

Moreover, it is not sufficient simply to rely upon civil or legal norms to avoid this error. In short, the official can do something; simply saying that the king has ordered it is not sufficient. Levinas calls this "the difference between a police action at the service of the established State and revolutionary action." "It is not," he says, "enough to be against a cause, one must be in the service of one." As he goes on, Levinas becomes rather dramatic: "Revolutionary action is first of all the action of the isolated man who plans revolution not only in danger but also in the agony of conscience—in the double clandestinity of the catacombs and of conscience. In the agony of conscience that risks making revolution impossible: for it is not only a question of seizing the evil-doer but also of not making the innocent suffer. In this also is to be found the difference in Jewish thought between the police and revolutionary politics."[48] This is the point of the detective's response. As Levinas puts it, "The police official does not have time to ask himself where the Good is and where the Evil; he belongs to the established power. He belongs to the State, which has entrusted him with duties. He does not engage in metaphysics; he engages in police work."[49]

The meaning of this outcome, for Levinas, is clear: within the regime of politics—of laws, norms, duties, procedures, policies, and such—there is the convenience of firmness and precision. There is a protocol. But the precision may not bring accuracy. Within this domain one cannot ask for explanations and justifications; they require us to go beyond the norms and rules, seeking what might give the reasons that provide these norms and rules with legitimacy, not simply procedural legitimacy but a legitimacy grounded in something deeper—our understanding of ourselves, of our existence, of what it means to be a person. What we have elsewhere called the ethical or Levinas's ethical politics, in this essay

Levinas calls or at least associates with "revolution" and "revolutionary action." Here Levinas also calls it the relation between "the State and the Absolute," and he asks whether the two can be reconciled in "non-Jewish political thought" and in Judaism. Can either or both think a "revolutionary action thought in terms of politics?"[50] To avoid punishing the innocent, one must know who they are, and, Levinas argues, this requires a deeper understanding of evil than can be found at the level of politics alone.

Rabbi Eleazar proceeds to explain to the police officer how to identify the evil-doer. He advises that the detective go to the tavern and look for someone with a glass of wine in his hand, dozing. If he is not an intellectual, a day laborer, or a night-shift worker, then he is a thief, and he should be arrested. When the king hears, he is pleased, and Rabbi Eleazar does police-work for him. This is the story. What does Levinas make of it? What in the narrative tells us how to identify thieves? What helps us to understand the roots of evil? He makes two suggestions. One is that it is the occupations that are crucial: "Man must build the universe; the universe is built through work and study. Everything else is distraction. Distraction is Evil." The second is that the venue is the central feature of the story. The tavern represents a place in society in which people do not engage one another seriously and responsibly; it is a venue for casual interaction, where people go without any serious needs, drink without being thirsty, eat without being hungry. "The café is not a place. It is a non-place for a non-society, for a society without solidarity, without tomorrow, without commitment, without common interests, a game society . . . without responsibility, without seriousness—distraction, dissolution."[51] Levinas contrasts the tavern or café with movies and theaters, where people go for a purpose and the performance or film has a theme, a lesson, a point. Taverns are not like this; when there, a person is released from worldly concerns; it is a place of forgetfulness and ultimately "of the forgetfulness of the other." Levinas apologizes if the listener might think he is criticizing taverns; rather he is pointing out how this venue characterizes a "form of life" and that it is this that the Talmud is warning against.[52]

It is not hard to dismiss these fanciful readings and to worry that Levinas is asking too much of the Talmudic text, more than it contains.

But I think that we can see what Levinas has in mind. The text distinguishes between the police officer and Rabbi Eleazar and their roles. One represents for him the norms, rules, and procedures of the state, of political bureaucracies; the other represents a special kind of wisdom about good and evil, right and wrong. The rabbi's advice is informed by an understanding that ought to found the state's police procedures, and for Levinas that understanding concerns the good and this means the interpersonal responsibility that pervades our social relations. It may be fanciful to find evidence of that wisdom in this story, but we can see why it is important for Levinas to propose that it is there. Let us move on, however, for what follows is very important. After all, Rabbi Eleazar not only gave the advice; he ultimately becomes a political official, a detective, himself. He does not remain outside the state and deliver his ethical critique of its practices from the outside; he becomes part of the state's bureaucracy. The ethical becomes political itself. He becomes a collaborator with the Romans.[53]

Levinas tells us that the crucial point for contemporary Jewish life in France and elsewhere is already present in the story and emerges vividly at this point. The issue is "either to serve the ideal through action concerned with preserving the framework of Judaism or to place oneself deliberately on the political level common to the men around us." That is, what is already present at this moment in the story of Rabbi Eleazar is "the inner conflict arising from the contradictions of an action which, in order to fight against Evil, adopts the path of politics, the king's service." But Levinas does not want us to take this "inner conflict" and these "contradictions" to express an irresolvable dilemma. The question is not which alternative to take; it is how to do both at once, for this is "revolutionary action." The "revolutionary action, which can go so far as to overthrow the king, belongs to the service of the king." Levinas says that "no one doubts this."[54] Presumably he means "no one among us." In other words, revolutionary action must be political action, even if its ultimate outcome replaces one regime with another. The only way to act in behalf of our obligations to others and to defend their rights is to act politically and publicly. What this means we have discussed elsewhere. Here Levinas finds the conjunction of ethics and politics expressed in the paradigmatic traditional Jewish text.

It is because this problematic is so serious that the Talmud continues with a criticism of Rabbi Eleazar leveled by Rabbi Joshua bar Karhah: what he has done is a betrayal of his father's purity—the son of wine has become vinegar; he has given up the Jewish people to the authorities. At least this is Rabbi Joshua's judgment; to collaborate, no matter what the reason, is to betray what Judaism stands for and the Jewish people—to which Rabbi Eleazar, defending himself, says: I am simply removing the thorns from the vineyard. But Rabbi Joshua will have none of Rabbi Eleazar's self-righteousness; he insists, "Let the owner of the vineyard come and remove the thorns himself."[55] That is, Rabbi Joshua underscores his criticism: let God root out evil in the people of Israel Himself; it is not for you to do.

We learn here, if we had not realized it before, that the police officer was hunting for Jews. One might think that he is simply doing his job and looking for thieves, but the text makes it clear that he is looking for them among Jews, and for this reason one might doubt his intentions. Perhaps the state and the police have other purposes in mind. Might the Roman police be looking for thieves among Jews just as the Nazis were hunting for Jews? Rabbi Eleazar's proposed procedure might have very well been an attempt to protect some at the expense of others; seeing this, the king compelled him to employ it himself, not out of respect but in order to implicate Rabbi Eleazar in the king's own policies. Levinas does not suggest this line of interpretation, but it is a very natural one and one that some French readers—against the background of Vichy—might very well have had in mind.[56]

But Levinas moves in a different direction. How does he understand this important conclusion to the narrative of Rabbi Eleazar? He worries that we might think that the issue here is one of parochialism and chauvinism, that Rabbi Joshua is simply reducing morality to a "petit-bourgeois racism and particularism" and that his criticism of Rabbi Eleazar is his way of saying that "Good and Evil" is determined by whether or not an action is "good or bad for the Jews." But this is to misunderstand who this people is and what its existence means. The Jewish people is a persecuted people, the "most fragile and most persecuted in the world. More persecuted than the proletariat itself, which is exploited but not persecuted. A race cursed . . . through its destiny of misfortune, and probably through its books." In other words, what cannot be betrayed is the teaching of responsibility that the existence of the Jewish people exemplifies through its abandonment and through their suffering. It is this people that Rabbi Joshua seeks to protect and this people who were the victims of Nazism. Moreover, as Levinas remarks, it is this people with which so many student activists and other demonstrators, in 1968, came to identify when they called out in the streets, "We are all German Jews," in response to the French government's refusal to allow Daniel Cohn-Bendit to return to France from Germany. It is in this spirit and with this conception of the Jewish people that Rabbi Joshua objected to Rabbi Eleazar's collaboration. Levinas interprets that criticism this way: "Doesn't political action, be it revolutionary, turn against the people of God, against the persecuted, against the non-violence which it wishes for and for which a revolution is attempted? Doesn't political action turn against the non-violence which alone can end all persecution?"[57] In short, when Rabbi Eleazar becomes an official of the state, does he not abandon the very possibility of genuine ethical critique? How can one serve the purposes of peace by engaging in war? How can ethics remain pure if it is contaminated by politics? It is an old and problematic conundrum that beleaguers Levinasian ethics in a special way.

What, then, does Rabbi Joshua's final response mean? What does it mean to leave it to God to tend His own vineyard, the Jewish people? The issue concerns the role of human action in the connection between ethics and politics. Rabbi Joshua's point is that "the concordance between Jewish destiny and the destiny of the world does not depend on human plans."[58] The Jew, the person genuinely attuned to ethical relations with others, should concern himself with that and not with politics. "Let the Eternal One resolve the conflict between morality and politics." Levinas calls this a "non-revolutionary interpretation, the interpretation of religious resignation,"[59] and he notes how the ultimate conclusion of such a line of thinking is that one should not seek to bring the Messiah but rather only to wait for the messianic coming. This, then, is one way of reading Rabbi Joshua's final response; it is the response of quietism and of what Gershom Scholem called "deferment."[60]

But Levinas offers another reading and one that speaks more directly to the question of violence and the "inner tension" in revolutionary action. On this reading, when Rabbi Joshua calls Rabbi Eleazar "vinegar son of wine," he is arguing that the latter's becoming a government official is itself the wine's becoming vinegar, its corruption. "You have betrayed," he is saying to Rabbi Eleazar, "the vine of the Lord that is Israel by associating it with the political activity of the Roman." Therefore, when Rabbi Eleazar responds that he is removing the thorns from the vineyard, he is saying that the "vine is not as excellent as we think it is." His own actions are meant to remove the brambles or thorns. "The vine's corruption has produced violence which, through violence, Rabbi Eleazar will bring to a halt." In the end, he sees that only violence can remove violence so that in the end, society will be purified and only produce goodness. It is unavoidable that revolutionary action be action, that ethical critique take the shape of revolutionary action. In terms I have suggested, ethical critique is unavoidably ethical, but it is also unavoidably responsive in everyday conduct and hence political; there is no other possibility.[61]

But there is a risk, and Rabbi Joshua's final response, according to Levinas, expresses that risk. "While we recognize in Judaism, as in certain aspirations of the left, a defender of the human person . . . we cannot identify the destiny of Judaism with the destiny of the proletariat."[62] Judaism is not simply another oppressed or marginalized people; it speaks out of a very distinctive "persecution," one that calls for infinite responsibility and that deeper care and concern for others we have associated with the face-to-face. In the terms we have been using, Judaism is not another social or political category; it designates a responsiveness that is shared by all and yet that is the central teaching of the Jewish tradition. In the current story, then, the Jewish people is "a vineyard more complicated than a plot of land that is cultivated." And for that reason, Rabbi Joshua claims, only the owner is capable of removing the thorns. In short, while Rabbi Eleazar saw the possibility of revolutionary action as political activism as the only way for Judaism to be true to itself, Rabbi Joshua saw the danger in it: "the death of Judaism in revolutionary man." One risks becoming the violence one seeks to eradicate. Hence, Levinas finds in this confrontation between the two sages a formulation of the deepest theme of the lesson: "To what degree will revolution be fatal to Judaism, not because Judaism is a survival but because it is at the ser-

vice of older, more delicate values than those at the disposal of socialism
... ?" These values are, of course, the preeminence of infinite responsibility of which we have spoken from the outset. Here he calls them an
"obscurely perceived ideal" and also an alienation beyond social and
economic alienation; he also calls it a special "Jewish particularism" but
one, he goes on to show, that can also be felt by non-Jews. Indeed, it is a
sensibility that lies deep within all human beings.[63]

Let me turn, finally, to a letter from which Levinas quotes at this
point in his lesson to illuminate how this tension within Judaism, how to
be both ethical and political at once, manifested itself for him and for at
least one of his friends in the wake of the events of May 1968.[64] The letter
is by Maurice Blanchot, and it explains how Blanchot had changed his
mind about the activists of May 1968 and why he had come to be critical
of them. As Levinas says, his friend had been involved in the events and
then suddenly withdrew; "he separated from his revolutionary friends
when they opted against Israel."[65] Levinas quotes the end of the letter
where Blanchot explains why.

Blanchot gives two reasons. The first is that the choice to stand
against Israel was made with empty concepts (imperialism and colonialism) and in terms of a mistaken judgment about weakness and vulnerability. But it is the second that I think is more important to Levinas.
"The meaning of Israel itself, in its most obvious aspect, escapes them.
... As though Israel were put in peril by ignorance—yes, an innocent
ignorance perhaps, but from now on gravely responsible and deprived
of innocence." The result, Blanchot points out, is that there are two enemies to Israel—"those who want to exterminate the Jew because he is
a Jew and those who are completely ignorant of what it is to be Jewish."
And this means that allied with anti-Semitism will be "those who are
as if deprived of anti-Semitism."[66] Blanchot seems to mean that by and
large these student activists, his former friends, had now turned on Israel without any sense of anti-Semitism, which is why, he says, "it is not
true that anti-Zionism is the anti-Semitism of today." But while their
antipathy was not aimed at Jews but rather at Israel, they had no understanding of "what anti-Semitism was." That is, Blanchot charges his former associates with ignorance about what role anti-Semitism has played
in Jewish life and Jewish history and hence what the State of Israel means

for the Jewish people as a persecuted people. They fail to appreciate this and hence have no understanding of what it is to be Jewish and what the Jewish state means. But he does; even though he is a non-Jew, he can identify with "Jewish particularism," with the persecution of the Jewish people and the role the state plays in responding to that persecution. In Levinas's terms, the Jewish people is a "vineyard more complicated than a plot of land that is cultivated," and the State of Israel is more than another state. It speaks out of a distinctive "persecution," an "absolute persecution" that speaks in behalf of everyone, the rights of all others.[67] To be sure, this is 1969, and Blanchot is referring to the student activists in France in those years and their abandonment of Israel. Much has happened since then, and much is known now in ways it was not then. Nonetheless, we can, in Blanchot's letter, see an expression of the spirit of revolutionary activism that Levinas has characterized through his Talmudic lesson and also a witness to the dangers that face such political engagement, what he calls the "acute tension between political action and Jewish existence."[68] Through Blanchot's eyes, we see both those dangers and the possibility of a real accomplishment.

"Judaism and Revolution" shows how Levinas is able, using his method of Talmudic exegesis, to explore the nature of revolutionary action, which is a form of political activism grounded in ethical critique, and its relation to Judaism. Along the way, he helps us to see what these Talmudic texts from Baba Metzia, beginning with the Mishnah, have to say about certain economic issues, in particular employment contracts, and the political issues connected with collaboration with a ruling power or with the state. The large issue, of course, is really the very relation between ethics and politics and the role of political action in behalf of a cause or of a critique of the government or a governmental policy. This same structure can be found in several of the lessons, where Levinas's primary concern is the relation between ethics and politics, while other, more concrete themes arise along the way.

HUMANIST URBANISM:
LIBERAL SOCIETY AND ITS DISCONTENTS

Revolution is political activism in behalf of ethical purposes; it is an effort to change the state and to realize greater justice. Variations on these same themes appear in the colloquium in November 1978 whose topic was "Jerusalem." Thirty years after the reestablishment of the Jewish state, the meeting took place in the years following the Yom Kippur War and during the early years of Gush Emunim and the settlement movement in Israel. It also occurred at the time when the Labor Party, for the first time, would lose its grip on Israeli politics and Likud, under the leadership of Menachem Begin, would come to power. It was a critical time to reflect on politics, the state, and the city. Levinas selected a Talmudic text (Makot 10a) that deals with the cities of refuge.[69] The central theme of his commentary is the relation between an earthly and a heavenly Jerusalem and "the impossibility for Israel of religious salvation without justice in the earthly city," what he calls a "humanist urbanism."[70]

Levinas begins his commentary by turning to the end of the Talmudic text, which refers to Psalm 122:1–2, and especially to the reference to Jerusalem in Psalm 122:3, the verse after the two referred to, as a city built as a "harmonious unity" or a "city that is compact together."[71] This Jerusalem he identifies as an ideal, as an image of the "heavenly Jerusalem," and he notes that the earthly Jerusalem is conceived in the Talmud—he shows this by reading Ta'anit 5a—as "the unavoidable antechamber" to the heavenly Jerusalem. Although Levinas then gives three interpretations of this relationship, it is the third that points in the direction of what Levinas says is the "theme of the rest of [his] commentary." Levinas goes on to paraphrase this central theme in various ways: "No vertical dimension without a horizontal dimension. An unavoidable stage-of-justice for all elevation.... There is no other access to salvation than that which passes through the dwelling place of men. That is the fundamental symbolism attached to this city."[72] Oblique as these terms are—"vertical dimension," "elevation," and "salvation"—they clearly refer to the accomplishment of the teachings of the Torah or justice. The notion of a heavenly Jerusalem is of this ideal, but the gist of the text from Ta'anit 5a, in which Rabbi Johanan says that God must enter the earthly Jerusalem before He enters the heavenly one, points toward the text from Makot on the cities of refuge and hence to a "real city," as Levinas says, "where men dwell, and where they are faced with concrete questions relating to their relations with their neighbors, with other men."[73] Levinas could not be any more explicit that his commentary is intended to help us understand what an ethical politics will look like. To pass through a real city on the way to an ideal one is to accomplish ethical life—a life of responsibility toward other persons—only within a political regime; there is no other way, as we have seen. Moreover, given that this particular city is Jerusalem, this political task is the core of Zionism, as Levinas sees it.

This introduction leads us to the substance of the Talmudic text from Makot, the constitution of real cities, a "humanist urbanism."[74] Levinas begins by describing the biblical law regarding manslaughter or unintentional killing, the rights of the avenging relative of the victim, and the cities of refuge to which the killer can flee and seek asylum as all of this is set out in Numbers 35. He notes how these cities are both a refuge and an exile or punishment for the unintentional killer: "In the city of refuge . . . there is the protection of the innocent which is also a punishment for the objectively guilty party." In order to flee vengeance, the guilty party must leave his home and seek asylum.[75] Moreover, this teaching is not anachronistic.

First, in our own societies, the disparity of wealth between rich and poor has resulted in various kinds of agony and suffering on the part of the poor, without any specific intention on the part of the wealthy to harm the poor. Second, are there not in societies like ours expressions akin to vengeance—"people's anger" and the "spirit of revolt and even of delinquency in our suburbs, the result of the social imbalance in which we are placed"? And, finally, are not the protections we find in our liberal societies against these forms of vengeance—these forms of anger, revolt, and delinquency—like vehicles of asylum? Are they not like "the protection of a half-innocence or a half-guilt"? In short, our liberal cities and states are safe havens that are also prisons; they are "cities of refuge" that are also "cities of exiles," "a necessary defense against the barbarity of heated blood, dangerous states of mind, and threatening disorder." All of this, Levinas claims, makes the institution of "cities of refuge" relevant to our own day and a teaching worthy of serious attention.[76]

We might summarize Levinas's clever analogy this way: Inequality of wealth and other inequalities lead to negligence and injury to the disadvantaged, failures of responsibility and obligations to assist and help those in need. One outcome of these disparities and this suffering or injury is the presence of resentment, frustration, and the spirit of rebellion, at least one way of reading the social explosions of the sixties and early seventies. But, at the same time, the guilty—even if unintentionally—construct institutions and develop practices to protect themselves from these expressions of social frustration and resentment. In the end these institutions and programs are both asylums for the innocent and prisons for the guilty. The perpetrators of injustice and neglect live safe and secure lives in the suburbs of blighted cities.[77]

Levinas goes on to read the Talmudic text as a description of these cities, that is, of the political and social solutions employed to protect the guilty and innocent parties. The first set of restrictions or conditions that the Talmud requires has as its ultimate goal the real security of the unintentional killer; the size of the city, its population, its location, and so forth, all these features are tailored to the need for safety and security from the forces of vengeance, that is, from the resentment, frustration, and rebellion of the poor and suffering classes.[78]

Next, Levinas asks, "On what Scriptural facts is it founded?" What tells us about "the spirit of the institutions" to be found in these cities? And here the crucial point is ascribed to Rabbi Isaac, who cites Deuteronomy 4:42 and takes it to mean that the cities must "provide him [the unintentional killer] with whatever he needs so that he may live." Levinas calls this the "humanitarianism of the cities of refuge." They must provide means of sustenance and the study of the Torah—for cultural needs and for more, a sense of ethical purpose and the aspiration for a "complete justice which goes beyond the ambiguous situations of the cities of refuge . . . a call for absolute vigilance," as Levinas puts it.[79]

What, then, does the city of refuge and the Talmudic reflections on it tell us about our society and our situation? "The city of refuge is the city of a civilization or of a humanity which protects subjective innocence and forgives objective guilt and all the denials that acts inflict on intentions." In other words, the city of refuge is a metaphor for an aspect of our social and political lives that allows us to live with inequalities and with the shortcomings of real, concrete conscience. Levinas also calls this a "political civilization" and tells us that it is not perfect by any means, but it is better than a civilization based on passion and free desire, "where, according to an expression from the Pirqe Aboth, 'men are ready to swallow each other alive.'" That is, it is better than a Hobbesian, naturalist society. It is "a civilization of law, admittedly, but a political civilization whose justice is hypocritical and where, with an undeniable right, the avenger of blood prowls."[80] The kind of political society that Levinas here envisions, then, is one that is founded on a qualified, conditioned desire to help and care for others, one that fails often enough and in enough ways to generate conflict and to try to protect those who innocently harm or abandon others. In such a society, a political one, justice is hypocritical; it is the foundation of critique—it underwrites ethical critique and yet must deal with the anger and frustration of those who are abandoned by neglect or unintentional oppression. Even in such a society, a liberal one, protections are required as well as long-term efforts to achieve more—to transform the earthly Jerusalem into the heavenly one.

At the end of Levinas's commentary he claims that this "humanist urbanism" incorporates an aspiration central to Zionism. "The longing for Zion, that Zionism, is not one more nationalism or particularism; nor is it a simple search for a place of refuge. It is the hope of a science of society, and of a society, which are wholly human. And this hope is to be found in Jerusalem, in the earthly Jerusalem, and not outside all places, in pious thoughts."[81] What Levinas here means by a society that is wholly human is of course a society whose institutions, policies, laws, and practices are oriented to the concern for people's needs and interests by individuals and by the public at large. It is a human society and a humane one, as just as it can be and also decent, to use Margalit's expression. Jerusalem, Zion, is the image for that hope.

FORMS OF NATIONAL LIFE

The Talmudic lesson "Cities of Refuge" tells us something about our cities and states, our political civilization, and the ways in which it fails and seeks to accommodate some of its failures. In a much later lesson, from December 1986, Levinas tells us more about the various kinds of political situations we find in our world, many of them highly defective. The theme of the meeting that year was "The Sixty-Nine Nations," and the Talmudic texts Levinas selected to examine are from Pesachim 118b.[82] He titled his lesson "The Nations and the Presence of Israel."

The text includes a series of interpretations, reported by Rabbi Ish-mael and ascribed to his father, Rabbi Yosi, of the beginning of Psalm 117, where "all the nations" are called upon to praise God for His kindnesses toward the people of Israel. I want to focus on the second of Rabbi Yosi's teachings, the claim that in the future Egypt will bring gifts to the Mes-siah, and what Levinas takes to be the relation between the nations of the world and messianism. Levinas begins by introducing Deuteronomy 23:8, where Israel is called upon not to abhor or hate the Egyptian, since the Israelites themselves were once strangers in the land of Egypt; the accomplishments of Israel are "assessed by the degree to which their na-tional solidarity is open to the other, the stranger."[83] If the figure of the coming of a personal Messiah refers to this openness to other nations and peoples, then the image of Egypt bringing gifts to the Messiah calls to mind the response of the other person to kindnesses done for him or her. In his commentary, Levinas calls this accomplishment "fraternity," "humanity," and "hospitality." We are in familiar territory here; the mes-sianic and the ethical are very close. I will return to the political role of the messianic idea in Levinas in the next chapter. For now, I want to look at Levinas's next comment, which concerns the way in which the three nations mentioned in the text—Egypt, Cush, and Rome—form a "ty-pology of national life, in which, through the forms of existence that are pure history, there can be seen the inhuman or the human," or, in other words, a typology of various forms of just and unjust societies and states. This theme takes up the bulk of Levinas's commentary.[84]

Levinas first discusses Egypt and picks out its essential features. "It is the country of servitude, but also the place where Abraham and Jacob found refuge in time of famine; where Joseph was able to assume univer-sal political and economic responsibilities at the very core of Holy His-tory; and where, at the hour of exterminating cruelty, Pharaoh's daughter saved Moses from the waters." To be sure, ultimately Egypt became a "place of slavery," but initially it was "a place offered to the stranger." And it is this offer that stands out as characteristic of the state's generosity, its openness and hospitality to those in need: "To shelter the other in one's own land or home, to tolerate the presence of the landless and homeless on the 'ancestral soil'" is "the criterion of humanness."[85] The Talmudic text has Egypt offer a gift to the Messiah, which is at first rejected and only received at God's behest. Or, as Levinas puts it, "no peace without superhuman pardon!" which means, I take it, that Israel and Egypt can be reconciled only when there is sufficient generosity and humanity in Egypt to warrant being weighed against her failures. In short, Egypt represents a conflicted state, capable of humanity but also an oppressor; in such a state, refugees can be welcomed but may also be degraded and even impoverished.

Next, Levinas turns to Cush (Ethiopia), which realizes that it should be treated more positively, since unlike Egypt, it never enslaved the people of Israel. Levinas's portrait is not flattering to him: "A country of black men with nothing to reproach itself for, nor anything to congratulate itself for. According to the Bible, at least, it is never the theater of important events." He refers to it as "a bit marginal. Neither friendly nor hostile to the message of Israel."[86] That is, Ethiopia stands for all those nations whose role in a philosophy of history is nonessential or who play no active role, no primary one. Levinas's Eurocentrism is not attractive; in other—well-known and unflattering—references, he is dismissive or barely more than dismissive of the rest of the world. All of this is unfortunate, but it does not discredit Levinas's central insight. What we can say is that here, trying to say something substantive about how just or unjust various societies and states are, the reference to Cush or Ethiopia really does not add anything other than the suggestion that the relationship to others as the ethical core of all human existence is the lever of critique for all societies, even those whose contribution to the development of humane and generous societies has not been appreciated—not by ancient Judaism and its texts and not, apparently, by Levinas.

Finally, Levinas turns to Rome, "the third order or political category, or the third possible destiny of the human." It is, he says, "a criminal empire . . . Rome the villain . . . but also the Rome of universal history—violent, warlike, imperialistic."[87] Here it is the reference to Edom in Deuteronomy 23:8—"Do not hate the Edomite, for he is your brother"—that Levinas takes to introduce Rome, who claims to be Israel's brother and demands her due, to be received by the Messiah, Edom the heritage of Esau, Jacob's brother. Rome, Levinas suggests, is the forebearer of the "distant West, a future America. Enough to feed mankind from all quarters!" And he asks, "Did Rome fully grasp the word of the Lord, consecrating fraternal bonds of love between beings?" When he asks whether Rome's share in the messianic future is "compromised by the inhuman tenor of ethics and politics in actual everyday Roman life,"[88] his puzzlement is genuine; surely the highly affluent, consumer-driven society annuls any possibility of acting out of humanity and concern for others. If Egypt is a society that aspires to justice but fails too often, then Rome is a failed society and even one that inclines toward totalitarianism, an empire of self-interest and material desire. And to these passions or desires, Levinas takes the Talmud to add "the idea of financial abuses—the rich humiliating the poor."[89] He summarizes all that he takes to be signaled by the reference to Rome and its Talmudic elaboration: "In all this the reader should see . . . the impressions of an entire unsettling aspect of our Western world, its so often bloody history, with its cult of heroism and military nobility, its nationalistic exclusionism, its racial, social and economic injustice."[90] Hence, "the struggle against Rome is the preservation of Israel, the chance of a regenerate humanity!"[91] There is here an anti-Americanism that we have already seen in Levinas, but also an indictment of the Western civilization that brought ruin to Russia, Germany, France, and so much of Europe.

In the final section of his commentary Levinas extends this indictment of Rome and of the modern West, the European civilization that resulted in Soviet Russia, Nazi Germany, fascist Italy, and Vichy France. The Talmudic passage tells us in picturesque terms that in Rome there are such vast quantities of food that it is enough to sustain the world tens of thousands of times over—affluence and plenty to solve the problems of famine and poverty worldwide, what Levinas calls the "indubitable and irresistible greatness of a colossus." Here we have "Rome suffocating beneath what humans need! . . . An economy of the wealth of pure accumulation." Humanity requires serving others, while here we have self-indulgence run rampant. Rabbi Shimon asks for whom all this material prosperity provides, and Levinas says, "For there is no longer anyone. There are no more men."[92] At some point, with so much prosperity and so many resources, is there any longer anyone who is being provided for? Rabbi answers that it is "for you and your fellows and acquaintances,"[93] and he cites in support Isaiah 23:18, which remarks of the evil city that even "her ill-gotten profit will eventually be consecrated to the Eternal." In other words, ultimately the vast holdings of the worst of societies and states will be used to satisfy and serve the needs of the suffering, the outsider, and the destitute. In Rome there is "a forgetting, a failure to recognize the other," but in the end the "piling up, amassing, unending totalization of the objects and money that mark the rhythm and essential structure of the perseverance of being in its being" all will serve humane and caring purposes. The scientistic, naturalist world will produce beyond our imagination and our needs, but ultimately, there is a humane and responsible ground that will win out. Goods will be consecrated to God, as Levinas reminds the reader, and God is, throughout the Bible, the "Father of orphans and defender of widows."[94]

HOPE FOR THE FUTURE

This is the possibility and therefore the hope that we should live with. It is why, I think, the Talmudic passage is framed as a series of comments on how the nations or societies of the world will respond to the coming of the Messiah and what God will do to make possible their ultimate association with him. That is, Levinas's comments are framed as reflections on the future, on what we might aim for or aspire to, but we must keep in mind that their meaning applies to societies and states as they are, ethical-political entities. Before we conclude discussing these few Talmudic lessons and as a transition to our subsequent treatment of politics and messianism in Levinas's thinking, I want to turn to one or two Talmudic readings that further develop this theme that the ethical critique of the political provides the substance of what Levinas takes the messianic idea to mean. There are two lessons that I want to discuss briefly, one from the middle of Levinas's career and the other from late.

The first lesson was delivered at the colloquium in the fall of 1965, the theme of which was "Israel." Levinas selected the Talmudic text from Sotah 34b–35a and titled it "Promised Land or Permitted Land." Much of the text is about Numbers 13 and the spies sent into the land to scout it, what they said, how they were understood, and more. Levinas raises the question of the legitimacy of conquest and the issue of a land's current occupants and what one's responsibilities are to them. And of course these matters are not merely abstract. In the case of the Land of Israel and the conquest of it, the issues are concrete and highly charged, especially in today's world.

Reflecting on the fears of the spies, Levinas asks, "Perhaps the explorers had moral qualms. They may have asked themselves whether they had the right to conquer what had been so magnificently built by others."[95] And after a fanciful analysis of the text, he answers, "The children of Israel will go into an already inhabited country; but in this country, the tombs of the ancestors Abraham, Isaac, and Jacob are to be found."[96] This fact provides a kind of "moral superiority," he says, although it is a debatable and contested point. Even, he says, the Talmudists doubt it. Levinas finally concludes that having the Bible and a kind of originality provides no justification; the Israelites are no less morally compromised than the land's inhabitants. Israel has no "moral advantage."[97] Jewish sovereignty over the land is grounded in no right or privilege.

But does this mean that it is not grounded at all? That it has no justification? Hardly. Levinas reads the Talmudic comments on Caleb, who finds a way to defend Moses even while he appears to be attacking him. Caleb's testimony and his speech belie an understanding of Moses and the divine teaching that is profound. He is "aware of the disproportion that exists between messianic politics and all other politics"—between "our history" and an "ordinary history." Levinas goes on to clarify why Caleb refers to the events of the Exodus and the wandering in the desert and especially the provision of manna. It is "miraculous food," for "the real miracle is not that manna falls from heaven but that it corresponds exactly to our needs. To be nourished by manna [is] not to need to stock up." It is a figure for "messianic times," and providing it—a state that provides for its citizens, especially those in great need—is "messianic politics." To be at the "end of time" is to be in a situation where "one need no longer think about tomorrow." And what this account of Mosaic leadership implies is that the real conquest is not the conquest of the land per se; it is the conquest of poverty, inequality, and injustice. Levinas paraphrases Caleb's homily: "If Moses brought us out of Egypt, split the red sea, and fed us manna, do you think, then, that under his leadership we are going to conquer a country the way one conquers a colony? Do you think that our act of conquest can be an imperialistic act? Do you think that we will appropriate a plot of land for ourselves so that we can use and abuse it?" Not at all, Caleb implies. The text says that entering the land is "to ascend to heaven," which Levinas takes to mean: "We will not possess the land as it is usually possessed; we will found a just community in this land. . . . That is what it means to sacralize the earth."[98]

This reading of Caleb's comments at Numbers 13:30 should be read against the background of our earlier discussion of Levinas's social ethics and his conception of an ethical critique of the political. What he here calls a "just community" is a society and a state founded on the realization that everyday life, communal life, and politics are all grounded in our unlimited responsibilities to one another to provide for our needs, reduce our suffering, prevent harm and injury, and enhance our lives together. This he here calls "messianic times," and the effort in its behalf he calls "messianic politics." Later he will call it "prophetic politics." It is politics open and responsive to ethical critique.

Levinas is aware that this kind of self-understanding can easily—all too easily—slide into unbridled justification for self-righteousness and conquest. We have seen it all too often—in Germany, Russia, France, England, and America. In this commentary, one witnesses his awareness of this risk, of the self-delusions that promote colonialism conceived as elevating and benevolent, when in fact it is a camouflage for conquest and domination. All he can say here is that such an attitude regularly rests on a form of relativism, and the view he is endorsing about Israel and its conquest of the land is not that. He puts it this way:

> You will say that everyone can imagine that he is founding a just society and that he is sacralizing the earth, and will that encourage conquerors and colonialists? But here one must answer: to accept the Torah is to accept the norms of a universal justice. The first teaching of Judaism is the following: a moral teaching exists and certain things are more just than others. A society in which man is not exploited, a society in which men are equal, a society such as the first founders of kibbutzes wanted it—because they too built ladders to ascend to heaven despite the repugnance most of them felt for heaven—is the very contestation of moral relativism. What we call the Torah provides norms for human justice. And it is in the name of this universal justice and not in the name of some national justice or other that the Israelites lay claim to the land of Israel.[99]

Levinas is rarely as clear and definitive as he is here about his commitment to moral realism and the objectivity and universality that it brings with it. Living in France—a decade after Algeria and with its own history of colonialism—and delivering this lesson at a meeting devoted to thinking about the State of Israel and her issues with her Arab citizens and neighbors, Levinas may sound like an apologist interested in defending colonial aspirations rather than a critic of them. But if he is being honest, and I am inclined to think that he is, what we have here is a sentiment not all that far from someone like Martin Buber. There is something distinctive and yet universal about the refounding and establishment of a Jewish state in Palestine. It aspires to "just community" as an example of universal justice. And the obligation to create such communities is built into our social existence at the most foundational level. The Jewish people have no right to enter and conquer the land and to found its state if all it desires is to dominate and control and even to protect itself. But it does have such a right, because it has such an obligation, if it takes seriously its historic, messianic purpose. For Buber, the paradigm of the social democratic state can be found in the kibbutzim; in *Paths to Utopia* he called them "the experiment that did not fail." So it is for Levinas, as he says here. In 1965, at any rate, in their heyday, the kibbutzim—flourishing agricultural and manufacturing collectives—were an ideal. They may no longer be, as they are today, nor may they be characteristic of Israel—its economy, its social and political ideals, and more. But they once were, and they represented a concrete effort to accomplish in relatively small communal settings what Israel and other nations should seek to accomplish on a larger scale.

But Levinas is not finished. As he continues his commentary, he takes the Talmud to ask: perhaps even Israel's messianic purposes and "moral reality," as he calls it, is insufficiently strong to win a victory over "historical reality." Or, alternatively, perhaps "the right of the native population to live is stronger than the moral right of the universal God. . . . One cannot take away from them the land on which they live, even if they are immoral, violent, and unworthy and even if this land were meant for a better destiny." He takes this to be an extremely "radical thought. . . . Even an absolutely moral people would have no right to conquest."[100] The Talmud puts this in a very picturesque way: "Even the Boss, so to speak, cannot remove the tools from there." That is, regarding the current inhabitants, "as long as the tools correspond to their needs, there would be no right on earth that could deprive them of them." And Levinas makes the point that this radical thought accompanies the earlier one to the end, and this, I would contend, makes for tragedy or at least complication. The people have a right to create just community in the land, but its commitments and purposes give it no right to deprive the current inhabitants of their right to satisfy their needs in the land. To be sure, this says nothing explicit about sovereignty and rule, but it does point toward challenges that have shown themselves to be all but intractable.

At the conclusion of his commentary, Levinas points to the underlying assumption of all his comments. The Torah and the Talmud have us wonder about the motives of the spies or explorers who came back with warnings about entering the land. "Did the crime of the explorers consist of being too pure and of having thought that they did not even have rights to this land? Or did these people back off from a project which seemed to them utopian, unrealizable? Did they think that their right lacked might or that they had no rights, that the Promised Land was not permitted to them?"[101] They were wrong, in both cases, but possibly for various different reasons. I have focused on what Levinas says about Caleb, who by and large did not shy away from the Mosaic project. The majority of the spies did. Caleb knew that they had rights, but he also saw that the current inhabitants did as well.[102]

As we have seen, there are indications in some of these lessons that "prophetic" or ethical politics, for Levinas, is also "messianic politics." This connection is apparent as well in the Talmudic lesson entitled "Beyond the State in the State," which was delivered at the twenty-ninth meeting of the colloquium on December 5, 1988. The theme of the meeting was "Question of the State," and the texts on which Levinas commented are Tamid 31b–32b. The text records a fictitious interrogation; Alexander the Great addresses ten questions to the "elders of the Negev," the Jewish leaders. The eighth question is "What should one do to be popular?" The elders answer, "Hate power and authority." But Alexander responds, "I have a better answer than yours. One must love power and authority and take advantage of them to do favors for people." Levinas takes Alexander at his word: "Political authority harbors by essence a nucleus of irreducibly arbitrary tyranny, like that denounced by the prophet in Samuel I, 8:11–17." It is allegiance to power and political authority that is "irreducible to the attractions of the Good in itself" or "ethical dynamism." Levinas refers to this as "perhaps the central moment of our entire dialogue," the moment when the rabbis express their "hatred of this irreducible tyranny and the State that appeals to it."[103] Furthermore, Levinas goes on to claim, this rejection should not be taken to mean that the rabbis reject the state as "equivalent to anarchy." Rather "it would mean that the acceptable political order can only come to humanity by way of the Torah, its justice, its judges, and its learned teachers." He then calls it, in terms we have seen him use already in 1965, "messianic politics. Yearning—extreme and historical attention as a vigil."[104]

In addition, Levinas takes the expression "hatred of tyranny" to mean more than an attitude or emotional response. It is "a high degree of criticism and control regarding a political power unjustifiable in itself, but to which a human collectivity, through its very multiplicity—while yearning for better—is pragmatically obligated." Levinas describes this criticism as "merciless" and says that this power, which is inevitable even if unjustifiable, can be reformed or modified. And he underscores that in this way "the outlines of democracy take form," within a civil society that permits "this refusal of the politics of pure tyranny" and that is "open to what is better, always on the alert, always renovating, always in the process of returning to the free persons who delegated to it their freedom subject to reason without losing their freedom." In other words, to the degree that the state permits such opposition to tyranny within it, the state is democratic and open to revision in behalf of providing for its citizens and more. He calls this democracy, for it opposes tyranny and oppression, favors freedom, and aspires to greater and greater justice for its citizens. We ought not to reject all politics but only bad politics; anarchy is not the answer; democracy and ultimately a messianic democratic socialism is.[105]

This answer, then, to the eighth question is the centerpiece of this lesson; in it Levinas returns to old themes—his opposition to tyranny and the misuse of power to cultivate special favors. Later in the lesson, he underscores the central dichotomy represented by Alexander and the teachers of Torah: the "radical difference between everything that can have validity in a reasonable politics, on the one hand, and authentic justice, on the other. That is to say, mercy, charity, *chesid* [kindness], which are the fiery furnace of justice, the Torah which is the source of its flames, and the study by which this source shoots forth. Justice is opposed to this political desire, born of the insatiable look toward distant horizons, to this infinite taste of politics, this horizontality which was in question from the start, taken for the essential of existing." This latter is the "hard realities of political violence" as opposed to the "reconciliation of men. Torah—presence of God in the face-to-face, vision of the invisible, peace, thought together."[106] These formulations or this cascade of expressions all point in the same direction, of Levinas's conception of the conflict and also the complementarity of ethics and politics, what he earlier calls a "messianic politics" that is opposed to raw power and the extremity of political violence, tyranny and empire, totalitarianism, and underscores the virtues of liberal democracy. In several Talmudic readings, as it happens, this "messianic politics" is his central theme. The relation in his work of the messianic and the political is the theme of chapter 9.

EIGHT

ZIONISM AND THE JUSTIFICATION
OF A JEWISH STATE

There are places in Levinas's writings where he attends to politics and political values and ideas. Some of these occur in his Talmudic readings, as we have seen. In this chapter, however, I choose a different route. From the early 1950s to the end of his life, Levinas turned and returned to the State of Israel and Zionism, often in terms of its role and place in Judaism and also for other reasons. Since he came to associate the appreciation for the centrality of ethics, responsibility, and the face-to-face with Judaism, any thoughts about how Judaism is related to the State of Israel are thoughts about ethics and politics. It is these writings that I would like to consider, in part to see if what he sees here, in this concrete case, confirms his theoretical account as we have outlined it and in part to determine if he provides any guidance or clues concerning how ethical responsibility has implications for political conduct and political life.

Let me start with a piece from 1951, "The State of Israel and the Religion of Israel."[1] This is the same year in which he wrote "Is Ontology Fundamental?" It is an early essay, a review of a collection of articles by Israeli authors on religion and the state. In it Levinas makes note of a conflict between Judaism, concerned as it is with justice, and the modern state, with its emphasis on human freedom, leisure, and security. Furthermore, modern states, with their universality of purpose and function, have contributed to the decline of the tension between particular religions as particular and clerical and the state as universal and humanistic. Given this situation, what is the special role of the State of Israel for Judaism? Levinas's answer has two parts. First, he views Judaism in his own particular way: in Judaism the "belief in God [does not] incite one to justice—it *is* the institution of that justice." Moreover, this justice is not an "abstract principle" but rather "the possibility for a man to see the face of an other." In short, Levinas interprets religious language so that it in fact points to the face-to-face as human responsibility and the justice that issues from it. Second, the State of Israel "finally offers the opportunity to carry out the social law of Judaism.... [Until now] it was horrible to be both the only people to define itself with a doctrine of justice, and to be the meaning incapable of applying it." After centuries of statelessness, without the opportunity to realize its special purpose, to apply its sensibility for justice, politically, now, in the twentieth century, there is the opportunity to do so. Levinas summarizes this role and this justification for what Zionism means when he says that "the contrast is between those who seek to have a State in order to have justice and those who seek justice in order to ensure the survival of the State."[2] That is, "justice is the *raison d'être* of the State: that is religion."[3]

From this early date, then, Levinas believes that ethics and politics are related as a founding ideal of justice and the reality in which that ideal needs to be implemented. This conception, as he realizes, is a form of Platonism, with its aspiration to realize goodness, but it is a realistic Platonism, realistic both because he thinks that it can be realized and also because he thinks that the ideal of justice is not an abstract or otherworldly ideal. Rather it is a dimension of our social lives that is always present and yet must be cultivated, disclosed, and become operative, as it were, as the guiding standard for political life. This is the very precise task of Zionism, to put the laws of justice into practice, to construct a just state. There is no other reason for Zionism, no other justification. All the rest is mythology. Hence, to the degree that Zionism addresses this task, it is genuine and serious; to the degree that it ignores that task or fails at it, Zionism is a distortion and irresponsible. Levinas seems serious about such judgments. Zionism receives no blanket endorsement from him; like any political regime, it can succeed or fail to one degree or another. And Zionism has not always succeeded.[4]

LEVINAS'S ZIONISM AND LIBERAL DEMOCRACY

The final section of the collection *Beyond the Verse*, entitled "Zionisms," includes three essays that deal with this task and this challenge.[5] In the foreword to the volume Levinas describes the subtle and intimate connection he sees between ancient themes and current, modern realities. He makes the following points. First:

> The three studies grouped together under the title "Zionisms" aim merely to show how the historical work of the State, which it is not possible to do without in the extremely politicized world of our time, a work of courage and labour which claims to be secular, is impregnated in Israel, from the beginning, and progressively, with young thoughts, but thoughts which issue from the Bible; how the continuation and development of this biblical culture showed itself to be inseparable from the temporal ends of the State, and extended beyond those ends.[6]

Levinas takes this connection between the central teaching of biblical culture—responsibility and justice—and the institutions and policies of the modern state as unbreakable. The State of Israel is about the humanity of man, as he puts it. He calls this "Israel's unrepentant eschatology," an expression that surely would strike some as odd, so unabashedly religious and messianic. That is, the historical work of the Jewish state is to be Jewish, which is to be just and humane, and this is what it means to feel and be responsible for the future one hopes to exist for others, all others.

Second, this aspiration, this central justifying commitment, is sorely threatened by "the conflict between Israel and the Palestinians or Israel and the Arabs."[7] "It is," he admonishes, "time to take the heat out of such adversity." Could Levinas be any clearer or more explicit that the conflict that has and continues to be so enflamed and so horrific is incompatible with the heart of Zionism and the heart of Judaism? Could he be more specific that the goal of Israel must be peace and that peace is "inseparable from the recognition of the other in the love of one's neighbor taught by the Scriptures"? And here he points at the Jews who utterly confuse the election of the Jewish people with pride and misplaced self-righteousness: "Is being chosen a scandal of pride and of the will to power, or is it moral conscience itself which, made up of responsibilities that are always urgent and non-transferable, is the first to respond, as if it were the only one to be called?"[8] The Palestinians are indeed the responsibility of Israel; similarly all that has befallen the Jewish people is an Arab responsibility. Both sides must acknowledge this and each other. In 1981, when this foreword was written, Levinas affirms what he had written in 1963, prior to the Six-Day War and the Yom Kippur War: a call for the Arab peoples to recognize Israel and a conviction that Israel would—because it should—respond with "brotherly zeal" toward the Palestinian people. Israel needs the recognition of the Arab world, and the fundamental idea of "political Zionism . . . is the necessity for the Jewish people, in peace with its neighbours, not to continue being a minority in its political structure." This, he says, is a "historical necessity" to prevent the "attack and murder of Jews in the world."[9] He implies, but does not say, that other nations, the Arab nations included, must respect that necessity and the reasons for it, but at the same time Israel must recognize the needs of its Palestinian neighbors. Still, he ends on this note about what the Arab world must recognize as Israel's responsibility to her own citizens and people, and he defends this concern against those who might argue that his view of responsibility to and for the other might make no room for such a thing:

> I think of the last words of the verse from Genesis 30:30: "Now when shall I provide for my own household also?" In the biblical context they can mean neither that a self vowed, of itself, to others, is making a simple and sharp claim for its own interests, nor that the essential structure of the self is being denied. I think that in the responsibility for others prescribed by a non-archaic monotheism it reminds us that it should not be forgotten that *my* family and *my* people, despite the possessive pronouns, are my "others," like strangers, and demand justice and protection. The love of the other—the love of one's neighbour. Those near to me are also my neighbours.[10]

Responsibility, the face-to-face, is who I am; it is my selfhood toward each and every other. This responsibility must be as aware of the needs and vulnerabilities of those close to the self as of the needs and vulnerabilities of those who are not, indeed of one's enemies. Simply because someone is a friend or a spouse or a cousin does not mean that they are not an other person. This is not self-interest, Levinas says; it is acknowledging need when the need is urgent, when help is deserved, and when protection and care are required.

As we move on to the essays of "Zionisms," we have shown that Levinas takes ethics and politics to be partners. Ethics cannot do without politics, and politics cannot—should not—do without ethics. But how is the connection to be made out? We have seen that politics is justified in terms of its attunement to ethical concern; Zionism is justified only as the opportunity of the Jewish people to realize institutionally and legislatively an ethical sensibility, a concern for justice and peace. But how? In what way does that sensibility for justice and peace influence political practice and decisions? Is there detail that Levinas fills in or are there clues he gives regarding how to add that detail? Are there features of the face-to-face relation that become the "devices for moral critique," as it were, the precise characteristics that can be called upon to assess political policies and practices when they are judged to be mistaken or unjust?

Let me look at the three essays on Zionism in chronological order. The first, "The State of Caesar and State of David," was published in 1971, during the years between the Six-Day War and the Yom Kippur War. On the face of it, the essay appears to be about the problem of church and state.

Levinas begins by reviewing the biblical, rabbinic, and medieval discussion about how Judaism views the state and its eventual accommodation to political necessities. After commenting on Deuteronomy 17:14–20 and 1 Samuel 8, for example, the one a text that endorses the state as "a power that safeguards Israel's moral principles and particularism," and the other "an impassioned indictment" of "power [that] eventually becomes tyranny," Levinas concludes that "it is impossible to escape the state."[11] Rabbinic texts go on to underscore the fact that "the State . . . is possible only if the divine word enters into it," which means, he says, that "not only does the essence of the State not contradict the absolute order, but it is called by it." This dependency, this infusion of the holy and moral order into the political, is underscored by the idea of the Messiah, a king who "institutes a just society" whereby "the divine invests History and State rather than doing away with them."[12] Levinas then notes that Maimonides's famous account of the Messiah and the messianic kingdom in very realistic and natural terms is itself a reaffirmation of this same idea of the unity of the religious and ethical with the political: "As a non-apocalyptic Messianism . . . it does allow us to measure the importance that Jewish thought attaches to going beyond beautiful dreams in order to fulfill the ideal in events promised by the State."[13] Levinas's point is that when the rabbis and then Maimonides conceive of the ultimate end of history, they conceive it as a state that realizes religious and moral ideals. Neither is the Messianic City beyond politics, nor the worldly City beneath the religious or moral.[14] Judaism and its central themes—justice and humanity—cannot do without the state, but just as importantly, the state cannot do without them. Judaism is grounded, he says, in "an irreducible fraternity," that is, in the responsibility to others that is expressed in every face-to-face relation we have, and the state needs to remember that, for without it, there is a risk of falling back into the war of all against all. The allusion to Hobbes and the temptations of naturalism is obvious.[15]

One cannot, however, forget those temptations and the fact that the state "is also the place of corruption *par excellence* and, perhaps, the ultimate refuge of idolatry."[16] That is, although Judaism needs the state and politics, and ideally the state will become just and humane and this is what the messianic ideal represents, there is no false optimism on Judaism's part. Levinas is clear about this realism. "The State [is] in search of hegemony, the conquering, imperialist, totalitarian, oppressive State, attached to realist egoism. . . . It is idolatry itself."[17] And Talmudic wisdom, Levinas shows, is fully aware of this vulnerability or weakness or even tendentiousness on the part of the political domain. Levinas realizes that everyday life and its structures are necessary for life, but they bear within them a proneness to defect and distortion. Once again, there is a kind of Platonism in this side of Levinas. It is not Gnosticism, but it is realism and carries with it a sense of aspiration and not simply of accomplishment.[18] Indeed, Levinas points out that there are rabbinic texts that support the idea that politics is eventually to be superseded, ultimately by the "world to come." In short, if there are texts that seem to endorse the necessity of politics, there are others that support the idea that it is disposable and to be transcended and set aside, outmoded. In the end, deliverance or redemption is redemption from history and from politics.[19]

The structure of Levinas's argument, then, is that there are arguments in behalf of the political and those that qualify its ultimate importance. What then does he make of this apparent tension in Judaism? How can we understand this fraught relationship between ethics and politics, between religion and history? Levinas ends the essay with a section entitled "Towards a Monotheistic Politics." What is this "monotheistic politics"? How does it "solve" this problematic relationship?

First, the question of how to formulate "the political philosophy of monotheism" or a "political doctrine suitable for monotheists" is raised specifically regarding Zionism, which seeks to realize a Jewish reality in the ancient land but in the form of a modern state. Second, in order to explain what such a monotheistic politics would look like, Levinas turns to a lecture by Dan Avni-Segré, a professor of law in Haifa, delivered in Paris.[20] As Levinas describes Segré's conception of the modern Jewish state, he takes it to open up opportunities and possibilities unlike any that were present in antiquity. To put it in terms used in recent debates, is the notion of a Jewish state a contradiction in terms or is it the ultimate fulfillment of Zionism? "Beyond the concern to ensure a refuge for those who are persecuted, is this not the main task?"[21] The reestablishment of the Jewish state has given birth to a new set of possibilities and new challenges, ones that were not available during the long history of exile and statelessness. Segré refers to "daily conflicts" that address the initiatives of "political invention" in new ways.[22] The challenge of Zionism, for him and presumably for Levinas, is to implement policies, laws, and programs that take seriously the reduction of suffering, poverty, and more and also the enhancement of human possibilities, the attention to the needs of others. This is what in recent discussion might be called the special challenges of ethnic or particularized democracies, if we take the heart of democracy to be respect for the needs of all citizens and a policy of equal treatment.[23]

Moreover, while in this essay Levinas sets up the problem as a problem for Zionism and for a Jewishly engaged politics in a Jewish state, it is in effect a problem for every state. How can a state be organized such that it serves the purposes of fraternity, that is, justice and humane treatment of others? This applies to all states and not exclusively to Israel. For the face-to-face and the responsibility for others involves a demand given to all persons and hence to all collectivities, all societies.

The litmus test—certainly one litmus test—for a just and humane society and state with a religious or ethnic majority that is organized around the priority of that majority is how it deals with minorities within.

There are many varieties of democratic states currently in existence in the world, and only one aims at being impartial in its constitutional and legal rights and privileges; that is the United States. All the others have a place for a privileged group or collectivity, a state religion or ethnic group; Israel is one of those. And in Israel's case, the status of women, non-Haredi Jews, migrant workers, Mizrahi Jews, and Arab citizens is problematic, as is the relation between Israel itself and its Arab neighbors. The conflicts between Israel and the Palestinians were well-known to Levinas, if not in detail at least in general. And the same holds for conflicts between Israel and certain of her Arab neighbors—Iran, Syria, Lebanon, Jordan, and Egypt among them. This is the general theme that Levinas addresses in "Politics After!," which appeared in *Les Temps modernes* in 1979. The specific event that stimulated Levinas's reflections was the visit of Anwar Sadat of Egypt to Jerusalem on November 19, 1977, an event that Levinas takes to be of momentous significance and that he considers heroic and courageous. It gives him an opportunity to comment on a decisive political action and to evaluate it in terms of its importance for the prospects of peace, in this case for peace between Israel and her Arab neighbors.

Levinas begins by commenting that the Jewish-Arab question has always been treated in sociological and political terms; commentators and others have neglected what he calls their "moral particulars."[24] His belief, in contrast, is that there are matters that pertain to human beings regardless of their ethnic or religious associations. "The meaning of the human, between peoples as between persons, is exhausted neither in the political necessities which hold it bound nor in the sentiments which release that hold."[25] This meaning is the ethical character of social existence as manifest in the face-to-face, which is "without recourse," he says, "to any supernatural or miraculous factor." In short, the real issues underlying the Jewish-Arab question concern justice and peace, and these are neither political nor traditionally religious in nature. Levinas calls this goal, this hope, a "fraternal community" between the two groups.[26]

A heroic first step, he says, is the peace between Israel and Egypt, an outcome of Sadat's trip to Jerusalem in November 1977. It provides the possibility of reconciliation. Why? Because it originated, for all the political machinations no doubt involved, in profoundly ethical and moral sources. Levinas may be too generous in identifying one of these sources as the central message of the Jewish people, its literature and its experience, but he does have an ethical conception of the central teaching of Zionism. The deepest impulses of Zionism, he contends, are to realize Judaism's "difficult freedom," the innermost demands placed on it to care for others, the stranger, the widow, and the orphan—and indeed for all others. Israel can only be a Jewish state if it takes upon itself "the whole ethical heritage of Israel," whereby "self-assertion is responsibility for everyone."[27] That is, from the Jewish side, it should be ethical and not merely political considerations that speak in behalf of peace. This is the true essence of the Zionist movement, Levinas claims. It was not a mere refuge or an attempt at normalization; rather Zionism, to all those who really understood, was the "identification between *Judenstaat* and the Promised Land and the reopening of the eschatological, forever planetary perspectives of holy History."[28]

What Levinas means, of course, is that the religious impulses in behalf of the establishment of a Jewish state were really in essence an effort to realize politically and socially the responsibility to everyone that is the heart of Jewish spirituality. His strategy in the essay is to show that there are genuinely moral resources on both sides of the conflict, and for this reason, there is hope for a serious reconciliation or peace, one based not on political—that is, practical and prudential considerations—but rather on ethical impulses to take responsibility for one another. Indeed, Levinas even remarks on how the refusal of Zionism after the Dreyfus Affair and before the rise of Hitler was grounded in the confidence about the "triumph of justice" in France based on the ideas of 1789 and 1848. That is, until the rise of Nazism, Jews tended to think that "Zionism seemed inadequate to the prophetic ideal whose achievements the Western Jew thought he could perceive at the heart of the great democratic nations."[29] A nationalist and pragmatic Zionism hardly seemed worth sacrificing participation in these democratic societies. It was only the failures of these states, especially during the Nazi years and thereafter, that would encourage Jews to transfer their loyalties and their hopes. Still, as Levinas points out, there were some people of insight who saw clearly early on, even prior to Nazism and Stalinism, what the essence of Zionism was all about. In this spirit, he refers to (but does not quote) Gershom Scholem's autobiographical narrative about his journey from Weimar Germany to Jerusalem, which "analyzes quite remarkably the spiritual dimension (which is not just a religious dimension) of Zionism."[30]

This, then, is the background to the current situation of Israel among her neighbors. It is a situation in which Israel is criticized as "an armed and dominating State, one of the great military powers of the Mediterranean basin, against the unarmed Palestinian people whose existence Israel does not recognize!" But to this claim Levinas responds, "Is that the real state of affairs? In its very real strength, is not Israel also the most fragile, the most vulnerable thing in the world, in the midst of its neighbours, undisputed nations, rich in natural allies, and surrounded by their lands?"[31] These are claims and counterclaims, oft heard, that Israel is a belligerent power that dominates the oppressed Palestinian people and that Israel herself is the embattled, fragile victim of threat and whose very existence is at risk.

What, then, is the significance of Sadat's trip? Levinas is unrestrained in his praise: "His trip has probably been the exceptional transhistorical event that one neither makes nor is contemporaneous with twice in a lifetime." Why? What did Sadat's trip make possible? What kind of an act was it? Levinas says, "For a moment, political standards and clichés were forgotten, along with all the deceitful motives that a certain wisdom attributes even to the gesture of a man who transcends himself and raises himself above his cautiousness and precautions."[32] He then asks what Sadat understood about Zionism; did he see behind the imputed imperialism and the apparent militarism? And did he understand "the opportunities opened up through friendship with Israel—or simply through already recognizing its existence and entering into talks—and all the prophetic promises that are hidden behind the Zionist claim to historical rights and its contortions under the political yoke?"[33] What should we make of these passages? They could mean that Levinas takes Sadat's gesture, his trip, to have defied personal wariness and political judgments about its negative political repercussions. That is, he could mean that Sadat himself acted on ethical and moral motives, reaching out to Israel in friendship, in defiance of his Arab colleagues. He does, after all, ask what Sadat understood about Israel and what opportunities presented themselves. On the other hand, Levinas could mean that whatever Sadat's own motives, it is possible—easy?—to forget or set aside political principles and questions about whether Sadat acted honestly or not and to interpret his action as grand and important, as an audacious and bold act. With regard to Sadat's state of mind, Levinas is not wholly clear or committal. Cynically, he could be claiming only that we can understand his action morally; generously, he could be saying that Sadat himself saw in Israel "a State which will have to incarnate the prophetic moral code and the idea of its peace" and sought to reach out to her.[34] On either reading, however, Levinas makes the point that the trip, as a gesture toward Israel and reconciliation with her, "opened up the unique path for peace in the Near East, if this peace is to be possible at all." In other words, the gesture expresses the claim that "peace is a concept which goes beyond purely political thought."[35] There is political peace, the cessation of war and conflict, and there is a deeper, ethical peace, a fraternal sense of community, of mutual recognition, concern, and generosity.

What does Levinas's assessment of the importance of Sadat's trip tell us about the relation between ethics and politics? On the one hand, Levinas emphasizes that Zionism makes possible political opportunities for Judaism, and these must be to implement her sense of prophetic morality—understood in terms of Levinas's conception of Judaism as an austere humanism—and hence to create institutions and laws whose purpose is the just and humane treatment of everyone. On the other hand, Levinas does distinguish between ethical or spiritual motives and political or prudential ones. There are political acts and ethical ones. Sadat's action can be understood as a political error, or it can be seen as a bold moral gesture. That is, the evaluation of Sadat is ambivalent about how to treat the ethics-politics relationship. Politics can be viewed as a deficient mode of conduct; it can also be viewed as necessary and unavoidable. If deficient, one ought to aspire to transcend it; if necessary, one ought to aim at the most humane and just political practices possible.

If my reading of Levinas's essay is correct, then on either reading of ethics and politics, ethics must be implemented and acted upon to the greatest degree possible. Either ethics should replace politics or correct it. In either case, ethics is relevant and significant; ethical responsibility is normatively primary. One ought always to seek to determine what responsibilities to others are most compelling and require the greatest attention one can provide, and this applies personally and collectively, to one's society as a whole. Justice in a social setting, justice in the state requires attention to the needs of those least well off; Levinas's conception of human existence leads to a welfare state and to equality of treatment and of well-being, to the degree that such equality is possible and desirable.

In the third essay on Zionism (1980) Levinas turns to the problem of assimilation, for Jews both in the Diaspora and in Israel. Assimilation, especially to modern European culture, can be viewed as an attraction or a threat, and of course Jews have taken it to be both. Moreover, its virtues—Levinas mentions "the spiritual excellence of universality, the norm of feeling and thinking, and the source of science, art, and modern technology, but also the thought of democracy and the foundation of the institutions linked to the ideal of freedom and the rights of man"—must wrestle free of the dark weight of the twentieth century's wars, fascism, and the Holocaust in order to retain their appeal. But they do. Even in a century of such horrors, "we continue to admire universal principles and whatever sound logic deduces from them."[36] The problem of assimilation, Levinas claims, is still with us, this story of atrocity and human suffering notwithstanding. The risk is still with us, "of the traditional side of our existence descending . . . to the level of folklore."[37]

Levinas characterizes this problem as a tension between the universal, which is the primary figure of modern culture, and the particular, in this case the Jewish people and its life. Moreover, he distinguishes between two ways in which modern civilization is universal, first because it presents itself as the "common patrimony of humanity," of all peoples, and second because its content is universal—"sciences, letters, plastic arts" and its ethics and philosophy itself, which expresses "all lived experience." On the one hand, there are local cultures with their languages, and, on the other, there is philosophy, "a type of Greek that is generously widespread in Europe." The degree to which these cultures and nations "belong to humanity" is measured by "the possibility . . . of being translated into and expressed in this language of philosophy." "Everything else is local colour."[38]

But there is something distinctive about Judaism, what he calls its "congenital universality . . . deposited in the riches of Scripture and rabbinical literature." This is what we have seen as his fundamental insight, that the human condition is characterized by an "awareness of a surplus of responsibility toward humanity," as he here calls it, by the face-to-face and responsibility for all others. It is, he says, a "strange and uncomfortable privilege" and a "peculiar inequality."[39] We can appreciate what these expressions mean. Responsibility to and for others grounds human dignity and is hence a kind of privilege, but the privilege does not arise from what we do or create ourselves, nor is it a form of satisfaction or fulfillment. Rather it is "uncomfortable" because it is the ground of deontic normativity and burdens us, and it is "strange" because it is grounded in what is alien to us, the other's standing and dependencies. Nor is the face-to-face an equal encounter; rather the other speaks from beneath and from above, out of a "peculiar inequality," as he calls it. This is, he says, what "chosenness" or "election" means. Hence, it is a universal teaching at the heart of Jewish particularity.

Assimilation, then, is at once a threat, as I have said, but it is also an attraction. Jews "enjoy the enlightened ideas [assimilation] has brought." The Jewish spirit is particular, but it is attracted to the universality of modern culture. Levinas calls this "the paradox of Israel"— "particularism or excellence . . . The excellence of an exceptional message, even though it is addressed to all." That is, the paradox of Judaism is not that it is particular and risks assimilation to what is universal; it is rather that Judaism itself is in a sense both particular and universal at once. Or, as Levinas wants to put it, how can Judaism be a "peculiarity beyond universality?" How can Judaism "contain those Western values that cannot be repudiated, but also lead beyond them?" Let me put this in slightly different terms. Platonism affirms a Good beyond Being; Levinas acknowledges and points to a responsibility, an ethics, that is beyond the ontic-ontological domain of everyday life, because it is more fundamental than that domain. At that everyday level, Judaism is both particular and universal, but it is so because it points to and advocates for the primacy of that ethical responsibility for all people and for all peoples. Moreover, it expresses this advocacy in its own way, in

Hebrew. It has "never formulated the meaning of this beyond in Western language," that is, in the language of philosophy, Greek.[40]

What is the relation between this "beyond" and the universalism of the West, of modern Western civilization? This universalism is the ethics of Kant and Mill, as well as the science of Newton and Bohr and Einstein. It is the politics of democracy and human rights. How is the "beyond," "the peculiarity beyond universality," related to these systems and programs for all humankind? As I read him, Levinas appreciates how appealing this universalism of Western culture can be, how "arrogant" it appears, and how tempting assimilation is.[41] But he warns how this universalism, this rationalism perhaps, is insufficient. It has been co-opted by fascism and totalitarianism. The face-to-face as a permanent relational normativity and responsibility is a constraint on such distortion and excess. This is how Levinas puts it: "One would have every right to ask if this apparent limitation of universalism is not what protects it from totalitarianism; if it does not arouse our attention to the murmurs of inner voices; if it does not open our eyes to the faces which illuminate and permit the control of social anonymity, and to the vanquished of humanity's rational history where it is not just the proud who succumb."[42] Somehow, that is, the ethical ground of our social lives is a safeguard against the risk of universalism falling into totalitarianism, of rationality becoming domination. It is what secures the voice of conscience within us, the sense of being called into question from outside ourselves and being aware of that summons from within. It refuses to allow us to ignore the utter particularity of those who need our help, our support, our acceptance, and of those who have been victims of policies, programs, and pogroms.

In sum, Jews should appreciate all that Judaism shares with Western culture and yet realize too what it bears as its distinctive destiny, its special message. Assimilation shows us the one, but we need to beware of being drawn into it fully. Judaism is a humanism, but, as Levinas says elsewhere, it is an austere humanism; it bespeaks freedom but a difficult freedom. The "beyond of universalism," which Judaism teaches and is aware of, "is what completes or perfects human fraternity."[43] Rules, laws, institutions, and policies are necessary—as we have seen—and they endorse worthy ideals, but they are insufficient by themselves. They are at risk of totalitarian excess, what Arendt called falling into "total domination," without a fence, a boundary, a limit, and that limit is the original, foundational responsibilities to others that always make a claim on us. This is the central teaching of Judaism. It is not a "relapse into an antiquated provincialism." To be sure, Jewish particularity has been clouded by folklore and has seemed an appeal to "sentiment and faith." Instead, this core teaching "needs to be made explicit to thought.... It still needs to be translated into the Greek language which, thanks to assimilation, we have learnt in the West. Our great task is to express in Greek those principles about which Greece knew nothing. Jewish peculiarity awaits its philosophy."[44]

Levinas ends the essay, which he delivered as a talk, by making special note of its venue, to an audience at the State Presidential Palace in Jerusalem, and the propriety of his theme to that venue. The lesson of his talk is that there is something beyond simple assimilation and simple isolation or opposition. There is something "beyond" assimilation. This lesson calls, he says, for a "new life in Israel" that will promote the development of a new Jewish culture. To this end, "the state of Israel will be the end of assimilation," which is a task "full of practical, concrete and immediate consequences."[45] Can there be any doubt that what Levinas has in mind is that the Jewish state's special task is the concrete, practical realization of a just political and legal system? Out of such a system will arise a new form of life and a new culture, Hebrew and Greek at once. It will be the particular expression of a universal justice and generosity.

Zionism is a very specific historical movement and political ideology, and the modern state of Israel is a particular political entity. But, when it comes to the relation between ethics and politics, what applies to Zionism and Israel applies as well to any and all political systems and institutional frameworks. The State of Israel is an opportunity for the Jewish people to establish and organize a just social and political life. Other states provide similar opportunities for other groups—ethnic, religious, and national. Moreover, Judaism is not the only literary and cultural tradition that teaches the centrality of interpersonal responsibility, justice, and benevolence. There may be other similar traditions, and there certainly are other literary expressions of these themes—from

Shakespeare to Dostoyevsky and others. Indeed, there is reason to think that for Levinas, the Jew and Judaism are figures for the human being and all cultural traditions, while Zionism and the State of Israel are figures for all institutional life and reform movements aimed at organizing just and humane ways of life.

LEVINAS, GAVISON, AND ISRAELI REALITIES

The view of Judaism, the people and state of Israel, and Zionism that Levinas suggests in these essays is an ideal, of course. Even when he turns to concrete events, as in the case of his reflection on the challenges to peace between Israel and her Arab neighbors and Sadat's visit, his depiction of the situation avoids political analysis and remains with his highly idealized views. Insofar as his intention is to remain attentive to the ethical obligations that ought to elevate and also constrain political actions, however, he does remain true to his conception of the essential teachings of Judaism and the prophetic tradition. Can we nonetheless speculate on how he would respond to the complicated realities of contemporary Israel?

One way to respond to such a question would be to ask how Levinas's understanding of Zionism and democracy, admittedly idealizations, would shape his commitments to the real, historical Israel as a Jewish state. We have seen that for Levinas, the best form of state is a liberal democracy. This ideal ought to be the political ideal of every society and hence of every nationality. We can easily see why. Such a state would protect rights and hence would acknowledge individual needs and the importance of addressing them; it would encourage taking responsibility for the lives and well-being of its citizens, treat others in a humane and sensitive way, insofar as that is possible, and do what it could to acknowledge the particular needs and suffering of its citizens. Moreover, such a state would be open to revision and change and would recognize its own "imperfection," its perfectability. This means several things: that a liberal democracy would always seek to revise laws and policies so that they are more and more just; that it would always be attentive to the particular needs and suffering of its citizens even when they are being treated fairly according to the laws of the state; and that it would recognize that even the best laws and policies treat citizens generically and not individually and hence that the state must make room for and even encourage acting in response to individual suffering and pain. It would seek to have just laws and aim at impartiality and fair treatment for all, even if it only approximated such a goal, and also appreciate its intrinsic limitations regarding responding to individual need.

But Levinas takes Judaism as the ideology of the Jewish people to be specially attuned to recognizing all people's infinite responsibilities to one another and therefore to acting in humane and caring ways. It is in Judaism's best interest to cultivate such an attitude on everyone's part, to encourage such conduct, and to create—when it has the opportunity—institutions and policies that are as considerate, humane, and benevolent as they can be. In short, it is in the interest of Judaism, when given the opportunity for territorial and political self-determination, to create a democratic and Jewish state. That is what Levinas takes Zionism ideally to be, the movement to create that opportunity and hence to realize such a state to the greatest degree possible.[46]

How does such an argument and such a justification differ, if at all, from that which we find in figures like Alexander Yakobson, Amnon Rubinstein, Sammy Smooha, Ruth Gavison, and Chaim Gans? As an example, let me focus on Ruth Gavison and Chaim Gans.[47] For both, the test for Israel's status as a democracy is how it deals with and treats minorities, especially its Arab minority. They consider, for example, a number of concrete problems: Can Israel's immigration policies be defended as just and humane? Is her citizenship law a fair and just one? Does she treat her minorities fairly with regard to education and political representation? As we have seen, Levinas has a distinctive foundational view about the human condition and its ethical character, and hence he has his own reasons for a commitment to human rights and to democracy. Does such a view align Levinas with liberal political critics like Gavison and Gans?

Ruth Gavison has been actively involved in Israeli debates both intellectually as a philosopher and legal theorist and politically as a prominent defender of Israel's dual character. In books and a host of articles, she has defended a liberal position regarding Israel's character and responsibilities in which Israel is justified both as the nation-state of the Jewish people and as a democratic state with responsibilities vis-à-vis its

Arab minority, religious Jewish communities within Israel, and all other groups outside the secular-Jewish majority. Gavison's argument is a fairly straightforward one, for all its details and sensible engagement with the realities of the Israeli situation and its past. She begins by examining three concepts: Jewishness, a Jewish state, and democracy. She then argues that a Jewish and democratic state is possible and finally that Israel as a Jewish and democratic state is justified. She excludes conceptions of Jewishness and democracy that make their combination impossible and then shows how the rather lean and minimal conceptions remaining are justified, that is, not merely possible and compatible but desirable and normatively worthwhile.

In his writings about Zionism and Israel Levinas does not discuss in any detail particular issues that face and have faced Israelis during the last decades of the twentieth century and into the twenty-first century: the treatment of Arab Israelis—legally, economically, socially, and more; the Law of Return and issues connected with immigration; the features of Israel's public culture—its anthem, flag, official language, and so forth; the role that Orthodoxy plays with regard to marriage, divorce, and questions of personal status; the rights of non-Jewish religious organizations and the place of non-Jewish religious practices and events in Israeli civic culture; and, above all, the debates between one-state and two-state solutions to the Israeli-Palestinian conflict and the central issues connected with the conflict concerning land, refugees, immigration, and so forth.[48] But, as we have seen, there are attractive reasons for asking how he would respond to Gavison's defense of Israel as both a Jewish and democratic state. He discusses Zionism and Israel often. He takes Zionism to be a genuine expression of Judaism, with its ethical core, and to be a unique opportunity for the Jewish people to define and organize a polity in view of the primacy of the ethical and interpersonal responsibility. In short, insofar as Levinas is deeply interested in Judaism and in its ethical implications for politics and everyday life, he ought to be concerned with Zionism and Israel and Israel's overall character as both Jewish and a liberal democracy.

Moreover, this question—what kind of a state Israel is and ought to be—has been a subject of discussion at least since the United Nations partition plan ratified in 1947, and legally speaking, it has been a matter of public debate in Israel and elsewhere since the basic laws of 1992 and also in more recent years. In 2011 and again in 2013 bills were written and submitted to the Knesset regarding the question of whether Israel is a Jewish and a democratic state, and in 2013 then minister of justice Tzipi Livni, who had refused to bring these bills to the floor, commissioned Gavison to prepare a report on how Israel's Jewish and democratic nature could be most appropriately, realistically, and helpfully given constitutional or legal status. Gavison's work on the issue since the 1990s can best be viewed in terms of this most recent effort of hers to clarify the issues and then to ask if and how they might be given what she calls "constitutional anchoring." Once we provide an overview of what Gavison claims and argues, we can look at how Levinas might respond both to Gavison's conception of Israel as democratic and Jewish and to Gavison's cautious conclusions about providing even such a liberal and lean conception of Israel as a Jewish state with "constitutional" or legal anchoring.

Gavison's account is conducted with an appealing combination of conceptual nuance and practical or empirical realism.[49] It is helpful to begin by noting that those who challenge the possibility of Israel being both a Jewish and a democratic state can come from the right or the left, but their strategies are parallel. Either they characterize democracy in such a strong or extreme way that no democracy could possibly privilege one national, ethnic, or religious identity, or they portray Judaism similarly in such a radical way that no Jewish state could possibly be democratic in any serious sense. Substantively, these alternatives involve, on the one hand, arguing that democracies must, with regard to their institutions and legal principles, be unconditionally neutral toward all the groups or subcommunities with which their citizens are associated, while, on the other hand, arguing that a genuinely Jewish state must be a theocracy or one whose policies and practices are governed by halakhic standards, which are determined by the decisions of authoritative religious interpreters and legal scholars. In the one case, it follows that no democracy can be ethnic or nationalist, while in the other, it follows that a Jewish state could never be democratic in any responsible way. Gavison argues often that the two positions are unacceptable; a Jewish state need not be a theocracy to be Jewish, nor need a democracy be neutral to be democratic.[50] There are perfectly reasonable and plausible other conceptions of both categories in virtue of which they can be compatible.[51]

A Jewish state could be the state of the Jews who are a majority of those who live in a single, particular locale, but while it is ultimately important to Gavison's conception that the Jews in Israel be a majority, this is not what is central to the state's Jewishness. If it were, the state would lack its important relationships with Diaspora Jewry, and its Jewishness would in the end be no more than an accident of the fact that it is the majority in a democratic state. Another way of putting this objection is to say that a majority is not an absolute classification. It is relative to some way of grouping those who constitute the majority, and it is that feature or characterization that would constitute the group's Jewishness, not the mere fact that those counted as Jews are in the majority. These concerns, then, lead us to a conception of Jewishness as an identity, akin to an ethnic or national identity and which we associate with a common culture, festivals and celebrations, practices and conduct, a shared history, and so forth. For Gavison, it is important that such an identity or national grouping be secular and not religious, not because such a grouping or identity would not be exclusive and substantial, but rather because the members will be conceived as citizens whose participation in a democratic state and culture will be vital and whose rights derive from their role as participants in such a society. For her, then, a Jewish state is a state whose civic culture is that of the Jewish people or nation and whose goals include protecting and securing that culture and that national existence.[52]

Moreover, if a democracy need not—and perhaps cannot—be unqualifiedly neutral among various conceptions of the good life and among various peoples, ethnic or national groups, and religious communities, it nonetheless can be a state that privileges one identity or group, while at the same time requiring that others be treated, both individually and collectively, with respect, fairly, and without causing harm or injury or without making it difficult or impossible to express their membership or association in their lives, personal and public. There can be a democratic nation-state. In fact, except for states like France and the United States, all democracies are such nation-states. Israel and her situation may have distinctive features, but she is anything but sui generis.[53]

Ultimately, then, Gavison argues that being a Jewish state, an outcome of the Jewish people's right to self-determination at the level of state government, and a democratic state, with institutions, policies, and laws that seek to be fair and respectful toward various interpretations of Jewish life and toward non-Jewish citizens of the state, especially Arab Israelis, is both conceptually possible and factually accurate to the reality of Israel and its history. To be sure, especially with regard to her Arab Israeli citizens, Israel's treatment and attention to their interests and even to their rights has not been without flaws and deficiencies. But, she argues, there are imperfections in all historical democracies; none have been or are perfect, and in this respect Israel is no different from other national democracies. There may be no analogies that are without their flaws, but the treatment of blacks, Latinos, and other groups in the United States; of Indians, Pakistanis, and others in England; and of North Africans in France belies any claim that the Israeli mistreatment of Arab Israelis is unique or that it disqualifies Israel from being a democracy. Gavison argues that there are good reasons to take democracy to require a narrow rules-of-the-game conception of rule by the consent of the governed and to exclude fairness, just treatment, and so forth from its definition—in short, to distinguish between what makes a polity a democracy and what makes it a liberal or fair or good democracy. Hence, while there is much to be done and much to criticize about Israel's policies and conduct, these matters do not prevent Israel as a Jewish state from being democratic.

As a factual or empirical matter, however, Gavison is not unaware of the many ways in which Israel has failed to give her non-Jewish citizens fair and equal treatment. She rejects the objection that no nation-state with a dominant cultural, national, ethnic, or religious character can do so and that in such states others are always "second-class citizens." She denies that the only alternatives are to privatize one's cultural, national, or religious identity or to treat all fairly and equally by abandoning the dominance of one over all others. On the one hand, as a historical fact, this is not what most of Israel's critics desire for themselves. Arab Israelis, Palestinians in particular, and those who support them do not oppose the very idea of a nation-state; what they oppose is a Jewish one on land that they take to be Palestinian. On the other hand, since matters of fair and responsible treatment of others are a matter of degree, the objection takes them to be "all or nothing." In a nation-state, the dominant nationality seeks to promote itself, to enhance and protect itself, and to cultivate an environment in which it will thrive and continue. As long as these tasks can be performed without crushing other groups or causing them serious injury or damage or suffering, they can be pursued and ought to be. Gavison uses the language of rights: a particular national identity can and should flourish as long as it does not trample on the rights of others, to the degree that this is possible given the facts on the ground and the circumstances in which the relevant peoples find themselves.[54]

Gavison is fully aware of and does not shy away from the facts of the situation regarding Israel and her Arab citizens. Many—probably most—feel deeply alienated from the Israeli state. They are descendants of an Arab population that rejected the Zionist project from the beginning, that never recognized the United Nations partition plan or the legitimacy of the state, and that either remained in Israel under duress or fled and became a nation of refugees. In short, Arab Israelis rarely feel part of Israel; the Jewish people is not their people, and the government is not their government. As Gavison puts it, "The challenge here, despite appearances, is contingent and not conceptual." The "intensity of the conflict" and the feelings of "alienation" are not the result of some abstract or conceptual issue about Jewishness and democracy; they are "the result of the past and the present of the conflict in the region."[55] Nonetheless, while this rift and the passions that underlie it exist and will no doubt persist, this does not, Gavison claims, mean that Israel is not or cannot be a democratic Jewish state. Conceptually, nothing prevents a nation-state from treating minorities within it fairly and respectfully and equally; factually and concretely, the State of Israel can do more than it currently does to meet these challenges. It can deal with membership issues and the rules of immigration differently; it can modify the way in which Arab Israelis are treated economically, socially, and administratively; it can alter its views about education, about public and civic symbols and culture; and so forth. In short, even in a situation of intense animosity, frustration, and anger, more can be done than is being done, Gavison argues.[56]

To be precise, Gavison argues first that Israel *could* be both Jewish and democratic insofar as the two conditions are compatible, both conceptually and concretely or factually. She then argues that Israel *should* be both. That is, the combination is justified; it is the right political shape for Israel to take. Or, more helpfully, since it is desirable and right for every state to be democratic, the real issue for Israel is whether it should be a Jewish state. Should it be a nation-state? Or, on some portion of land between the Mediterranean Sea and the Jordan River, should there be a nation-state of the Jewish people?[57] To provide such a justification, Gavison must explain what gives the Jewish people a right to establish and maintain a Jewish state, and she must also show that the costs to others, most notably to the Arab populations displaced by the state's establishment, are not unjust and do not outweigh the considerations that count in favor of the Jewish nation-state.[58]

Gavison calls upon a general consensus that nations have the right to self-determination, since membership in rich and ongoing national and cultural communities is a valuable or even necessary feature of individual well-being. This is as true for Palestinians as it is for Jews in Israel. This general right, however, does not entail that national communities have the right to political self-determination at the state level; there are other possible ways in which such self-determination can be expressed at the sub-state level. But various historical reasons, regarding both the history of the Jews as a persecuted people, the particular developments of anti-Semitism in the nineteenth century, the attractions of assimilation that attended increased emancipation, and later the catastrophic level of destruction to the Jewish people suffered during the Holocaust, while they do not entail the need for a state, do encourage the conclusion that self-determination for the Jewish people should take the form of the establishment and ongoing direction of the government of a state in some specific location.[59] Moreover, although in the early twentieth century and for some decades that right did not entail that Palestine ought to be the location of that state, the development of the Yishuv and ultimately a Jewish majority in portions of Palestine provide a secure reason why that state should be in Palestine as the state of the Jewish majority in that land. Arab resistance to the goals of Zionism in Palestine was historically coupled with the Arab failure to prevent the establishment of that majority. Gavison wisely avoids claiming that the Jewish people was always justified in establishing a state in Palestine, but by giving a historical argument based on an account of the changing circumstances over the years, she argues that by the time of the United Nations partition plan in 1947, there did exist conditions sufficient to warrant such a right and to justify the state's establishment—alongside an Arab state of course.[60] By then, in parts of the Palestinian region, Jews were a majority and hence had the right to establish a state whose goal was the welfare and flourishing of Judaism as a culture and way of life, albeit a right the implementation of which depended upon the costs to be paid by other peoples in the region.[61]

Just as the question whether the Jewish people came to have a right to self-determination in some portion of the region has a historical character, so the question of whether the costs or burden upon the Arab peoples who occupied that land was too great to warrant acting on that right is also a historical matter.[62] The dialectic between the peoples that led to war in 1947 and has continued thereafter is neither surprising nor unjustified, in a sense, Gavison argues. There is right on both sides. And the most justified and realistic response, if one considers the Palestinian people as well as the Jewish people, is the establishment of two nations, alongside one another, even if the option of a single bi-national state is theoretically possible and perhaps more desirable in principle. Gavison is explicit that while historical conditions have led to Israeli hegemony in the region, "the present situation, however, of political self-determination for Jews and no self-determination for Palestinians, cannot be justified."[63] On the one hand, then, Israeli's Palestinian citizens must be treated fairly and respectfully as members of the state, and on the other, the Palestinian people in general must be understood to have the same right to political self-determination as is had by the Jewish people.

Gavison had worked out this conception of Israel's Jewish and democratic character and her obligations to her Arab citizens and to the non-secular Jewish positions within Israel long before she was approached by Tzipi Livni in August 2013 to prepare a report on these issues and on the question of how best to formulate legislation to express a vision of Israel's character. In her report, once she has set out a position by and large derived from her earlier work, Gavison turns to the problem of how to provide such a vision with "constitutional anchoring," as she calls it. And here we are in for a surprise. In earlier writings Gavison had advocated a constitutional setting for such a conception, but in her report to the minister of justice she does not. Rather she argues, largely on practical grounds, that there should be no constitutional or legislative formulation of Israel's status as a Jewish and democratic state. The issue should arise politically in public debates concerning specific policies and conduct and not be brought to the Knesset and become subject to adjudication by the courts. The three central themes in her vision of Israel—Jewishness, democracy, and human rights—should remain vague and flexible, subject to moral, social, and political debate and not given over to attempts at legal or legislative precision. The vagueness and flexibility are virtues in a situation that is tense and conflicted, in which there is a good deal of mistrust and animosity and in which what is needed is compromise and negotiated cooperation. In the spirit of Arendt and others, advocates of deliberative democracy, Gavison argues that the divisive issues—education, civic symbols, language, immigration, and so forth—should not be legislated once and for all as laws or as constitutional components; they must again and again become the setting for vested interests to engage one another in face-to-face conversations, debates, and negotiations. In her report Gavison says, "Questions of vision are not legal questions, and should not be decided by law or in courts. A separate anchoring of the vision would transfer the locus of discussion about disagreements on interpretations of the vision from the public and political arenas to the courts. Against the background of Israeli reality, this process will enhance uncertainty and disagreement. Debate and discussions concerning interpretations of the shared vision are desirable and contribute to the betterment of society. A move to anchor the vision will put the vision itself as the focus of disagreement."[64] As Gavison puts it, the vision of Israel as Jewish and democratic should function as a "compass" that can serve Israeli society as a whole and that can appeal to various groups of citizens to interpret its components as they will, as part of an ongoing conversation and debate about how to implement its features.[65]

As a preface to her objections to a constitutional or legal formulation of the vision of a Jewish and democratic state, Gavison reviews the arguments of those who support such a formulation and those who reject it. Overall, her fear is that legislative deliberations will be "polarizing and conflictual" and will "increase adversity and will not encourage cohesion and solidarity." In short, the overall practical goals of such a process

ought to be unifying and not divisive. But enacting the vision constitutionally or legislatively would encourage a resolution or firm conclusion
rather than ongoing conversation. And "legislation invites judicial determination, based on the interpretation of the law and a human rights
discourse, instead of dynamic resolutions based on ongoing negotiations
among social, cultural and political forces."[66] Moreover, if the process
is undesirable, so for several reasons would the outcome be. First, where
there are disagreements, what is needed is a flexible environment in
which to work out differences and not a fixed standard that threatens to
polarize. Second, even if one enacts as law such a vision, it will have to be
at a level of generality and abstraction that will only make disagreements
and differences more rigid. Third, there is a widely held impression that
the components of the vision, Israel's democratic character and its Jewishness, are, as universal norm and particular allegiances, contradictory
and internally inconsistent. Enacting a law to encapsulate the vision will
promote internal tensions and this belief that the vision is riddled with
contradiction. Fourth, campaigning in behalf of or against the vision
may encourage partisanship; "it may weaken both civic cohesion and
Jewish solidarity, instead of strengthening them."[67] Fifth, continued di-
vision over the state's vision may support those who argue that Israel as
a Jewish state is not justified. Sixth, such legislation might in fact have an
effect on educational, cultural, and academic realities opposite to what is
desired. In order to counter the vocal rejection of Israel as a Jewish state,
both by Arabs and by some Jews, what is needed is a "political culture in
which these matters are discussed in an informed way and without slo-
ganeering. . . . Against the background of a broad consensus, a basic law
would indeed be an anchor to such educational activity. In the absence
of such a consensus, however, the enactment of a basic law could lead to
the opposite result."[68] In other words, the serious and intense divisions
within the Israeli citizenry regarding these foundational issues and the
particular social and political arrangements that they involve make it all
the more essential that there be ongoing discussion of particular situations and proposals and practices in an informed way, without focusing
attention on large-scale differences that are ideologically based and less
subject to open-minded discussion and debate. As a result of considerations like these, Gavison concludes that "strengthening the vision of the

state [as both Jewish and democratic], including the emphasis on the importance and centrality of its Jewish character, will be better achieved through other varied and focused activities" rather than by legislative enactment.[69] To summarize, then, Gavison argues that the vision of Israel as a democratic and Jewish state ought not to be enacted as law or constitutionally; not the courts but rather public and political discussion and debate are the most valuable venues for consideration of its features.

How might Levinas respond to Gavison's conception of Israel as Jewish and democratic and to her argument that it remain a feature of public debate and not be "anchored constitutionally" or enacted as law? What might Levinas think about Gavison's recommendations for the treatment of Israel's Arab citizens concerning educational and economic subsidies, immigration law, and aspects of Israel's public culture? How would he respond to the role of halakhah and Orthodoxy in Israeli policies and practices? Would Levinas endorse her defense of a Jewish nation-state?

In earlier chapters I have examined Levinas's understanding and assessment of liberalism, in particular his support for human rights and the rights of the other person, and of democracy, especially the possibilities it provides for public discussion and deliberation, flexibility, and change. At the same time, Levinas takes Zionism to represent the project of realizing Jewish life, as a life of responsibility to and for others, in a political context. Clearly, then, Levinas takes the State of Israel to be a Jewish state in this sense; it is the institutional and political context in which Judaism's commitment to ethics is being and should be realized. And just as clearly Levinas would support Gavison's claims that Israel ought to respect the human rights of its citizens and of others and that it ought to deal humanely and fairly with its own citizens, with particular attention to the treatment of Mizrahi Jews and Israel's non-Jewish citizens, especially her Arab citizens, simply because in a nation-state minorities are most vulnerable. In a sense, whereas Gavison, as a legal and political philosopher and as a public intellectual, seeks to characterize both democracy and Jewishness in terms that permit their compatibility and hence argues strongly against the theocratic interpretation of Jewishness and the neutralist reading of democracy, Levinas would find it easier to argue for their compatibility. His purpose is to locate and understand the ethical teaching central to Judaism and its role in an understanding of the human condition and social existence generally. The upshot is that for Levinas, what Judaism means and what democracy—or liberal democracy—requires converge. For him, it is not surprising that Israel ought to be both Jewish and democratic. In this respect, Israel is no different from any state. It would be the ideal for any state to be politically democratic, in that it ought to be attentive to the needs and concerns of all her citizens, ought to treat all fairly and humanely, and ought to seek justice and peace, and hence, speaking metaphorically, the ideal for any state ought to be that it be "Jewish" in the sense that it be as ethical as possible in its social, economic, and political programs, policies, and practices.

There are reasons, of course, why Gavison is more realistic than Levinas and hence more attentive to the possible tensions between the Jewish majority in Israel and her minorities. Levinas recognizes that states will be more or less just, more or less humane and caring, and so forth. But he expects a good deal from Israel as the Jewish state and as the expression of Zionist aspirations. Levinas is not trying to persuade any particular constituency; his overall position about Judaism and Zionism has no particular political agenda. He has a philosophical conception of the human condition; he associates that conception with Jewish culture and literature and with Judaism; he therefore takes it to be the core of Zionism as an ethical-political and even "messianic" project, in his sense of the word. In a sense, when Levinas speaks and writes about these matters, he seeks to speak and write what he takes to be the truth about them, independently of any rhetorical context. He is not involved in public debate or political discussion; unlike Gavison, he plays no political role.

Gavison, on the other hand, is always playing the role of what Michael Walzer calls an "engaged critic." Hence, her arguments draw upon presuppositions or assumptions that are to be sure distinctive, but they are also widely held and are part of the tradition of discussion about law, rights, and such matters. Gavison is seeking to articulate a responsible position on Israel's character and to do so in such a way that what she says could persuade the greatest number of readers. Certainly she herself is committed to these "liberal" and "democratic" principles or assumptions and to the ways in which she employs them to formulate a responsible, seriously Jewish but also humane and fair portrait of what kind of state Israel should be. But she is also keenly aware of those to whom she is speaking. Especially in her latest writings on the subject, the report to the minister of justice and recent papers, she emphasizes that the proper venue for discussion of the subject of Israel's character is public and political debate in an open forum. All along, the balance, judgment, and good sense that characterize her writings on the subject suit well this appreciation of its place in the public arena. Gavison realizes that she will not persuade everyone; in fact, she may never reach those who are polarized by the conflicts and divisions in Israeli society. But her arguments are generally moderate in design. She rejects extreme positions and regularly seeks a moderate view that respects various sides and various interests. She will not abandon a commitment to Israel's Jewishness, but she always rejects a conception of Jewishness that would not appeal to many Israeli Jews and that would be utterly unacceptable to Israeli's non-Jewish minorities. The Jewishness she seeks is a conception of an identity, a cultural or way of life of a people, that would suit secular Jews and would least offend others. Moreover, she is willing to acknowledge all the ways in which Israeli institutions, practices, and policies offend Arab Israelis, do them indignities, or harm them. She argues that there is now a Palestinian people and a Palestinian identity. The people have as much a right to national self-determination as the Jewish people does, albeit in lands where Palestinians are in a majority and in ways that are compatible with the security and integrity of Israel. But what applies in one direction also applies in the other. One can imagine that she would take all her strictures about what it means for Israel to be Jewish to apply as well to what it would mean for a Palestinian state to be Palestinian—and of course, what would make one democratic, liberal, humane, and just would also apply to the other.

Where, then, might Levinas differ with Gavison? I do not think that the issue here concerns large-scale differences, as if Levinas would deny that Israel should be Jewish or that it should be democratic and respect human rights. For him, as we have indicated, Israel should be both, even if they are characterized in his terms. Moreover, when it comes to specific issues—subsidies to schools and the design of curricula; statutes and regulations concerning marriage, divorce, and other matters of personal status; laws regarding political parties and voting; public practices regarding employment, economic opportunities, and so forth; and immigration practices and the Law of Return—Levinas might very well agree with Gavison in general. In all of these areas, with regard sometimes to Israel's non-Jewish citizens and sometimes to her Jewish citizens, Israel should alter laws and practices that are unfair or insensitive to local needs and sensitivities.

Even with so much agreement, however, he might underscore certain features of Israel's policies and conduct. He might very well emphasize the importance of dealing with all citizens with scrupulous attention to the needs and circumstances of individuals and with concern and sensitivity. As we have shown, his conception of our social nature as ethical and responsible beings never abandons the idea of the ineliminable particularity and concreteness of our relations to others. Responsibility to the other person always involves acknowledging and accepting each person in all his or her particularity, showing them respect both for having a kind of authority over us and for being so utterly dependent upon us. In the spirit of Margalit, as I have suggested, Levinas would be deeply disturbed by how Arab and particularly Palestinian citizens of Israel are treated insofar as they are degraded and shamed by those who deal with them.[70]

In an earlier chapter, I have referred to Levinas's attentiveness to the particularity of how one person treats another, in occasional encounters and in typical ones, as a formal feature of the normative element in his ethical account of our interpersonal relations. When we turn to the way in which general rules or norms are applied in particular situations, there are substantive issues that arise alongside this formal one about treating the particular other person with respect and dignity. In the case of the Law of Return, for example, Levinas would surely agree with Gavison that the law is justified and not racist; the Jewish state has an interest in and need to control immigration in order to "preserve a national majority."[71] But, at the same time, I also think that Levinas would agree with Gavison's objections to the present formulation of the law, which was modified by the Knesset after the Shalit decision by the court, and in which a Jew is defined as "a person born to a Jewish mother, or one who had converted to Judaism, and is not a member of another faith." Gavison opposes extending the right of citizenship in Israel automatically to many who might have no connection with Judaism, and she finds the use of a halakhic standard confining and inflexible in ways that the old formulation was not.[72] On the one hand, Gavison—like Levinas—worries about categories that fail to deal with the particularity of the other person's needs and interests, in this case the kind of commitment found in a Jew who seeks citizenship in Israel under the Law of Return. What should be the critical feature of the person's application is his or her willingness "to integrate fully into modern Jewish life" and hence his or her commitment to "building a democratic Jewish nation-state." In this regard, birth and genealogy are not the crucial factor. On the other hand, Gavison reminds us that fixed and inflexible categories often are unfair to some and do not serve the purposes that are essential. They risk being both "over-inclusive" and "under-inclusive." Levinas ought to agree. The centrality of responsibility to others tells us that citizenship—which involves a variety of opportunities, rights, and capacities—is appropriate for individuals who recognize and will serve the rights and needs of others; it ought not to be bestowed simply on the basis of one's birth status. Like Gavison, I think, Levinas would take the current law to be unfair and dysfunctional. But it is not unfair because it grants a right to many who ought not to have it and because it does not give a right to many who do. Rather it is unfair because it does not appreciate in any apparent way that the purpose of citizenship in Israel is a way of acknowledging the applicant's needs, responding to his or her claim for acceptance and hospitality, and a way of providing care and assistance where it is needed. Moreover, insofar as Israel is a political project whose aim is to create a society in which persons join with and assist one another, the law does not recognize that purpose in any way. It replaces both of these types of considerations with the brute fact of having genetic roots within the Jewish people according to a halakhic standard.

This reasoning suggests how a Levinasian interpretation of Gavison's position on the Law of Return and immigration to Israel might be seen to be even more compelling than Gavison herself argued. She argued in effect that citizenship in Israel ought to be extended to those who are committed to shaping Israeli society as democratic and humane; Levinas helps us to understand what that means and how the Law of Return ought to be an enactment of being responsible to and for those

Jews who seek to join the state and also how the person's becoming a citizen ought to express his or her willingness to care for and support others, members of the majority and of the various minorities within the Jewish state.

As a final point, what would Levinas say about Gavison's argument that the vision of Israel as both Jewish and democratic should not be given "constitutional anchoring" or a legal form—that is, that discussion of the vision should be a matter of public and political debate and not a matter for the courts and legal interpretation? We should recall that Gavison's argument is based on her conviction that vagueness and flexibility are virtues of the vision's central terms and expressions and that anchoring it constitutionally or legislatively would promote polarization and disagreement rather than provide opportunities for overcoming them. Can there be any doubt that Levinas would agree with Gavison's position? I hardly think so, and in fact Levinas would surely endorse Gavison's belief that the issue of what kind of state Israel should be and in particular how it can be and should be both Jewish and democratic should arise as part of the engagements and conversations between citizens as part of public debate over policies, programs, and practices. Such debate itself ought to express mutual respect and concern for one another on the part of a state's citizens, and in Israel it ought to provide a setting in which Jews and Israeli Arabs come to greater respect for one another. At least this is something one might hope for, and practically speaking, as Gavison argues, to entrench fixed and sharply defined conceptions of Jewishness and democracy in law would only maintain disagreements and petrify animosities. Allowing the question of Israel's character to arise naturally, as part of political debate about particular subjects such as the cultural symbols of the state, its official language and the role of Arabic, immigration policies, and so forth, may lead to greater mutual understanding and a greater sense of unity and solidarity with one another and with the state than currently exists. Levinas takes flexibility and the capacity to shift and change to be virtues of a democracy, and if Gavison is right, encouraging ongoing discussion and debate about Israel's Jewish character and how it can be compatible with her liberal and democratic commitments may in fact make Israel more democratic. It may do something to reduce tensions and mitigate the spirit of animosity that is so serious a social and political problem for Israel. Of course, there are no guarantees that such discussion and debate will have this effect, but Levinas would surely oppose solidifying the separations and the conflict and foreclosing on active conversation.

In conclusion, then, I am confident that Levinas would find much of Gavison's position on the character of Israel, her Jewishness, her sensitivity to human rights, and her democratic form and practices to be congenial and worthy of support. At the deepest level, of course, he would frame his agreement by emphasizing that the reasons for Israel to be Jewish and to be democratic concern the fact that it ought to be a setting in which people acknowledge, respect, care for, and assist one another; it ought to be, in short, a state and a society in which people take responsibility for one another and act in behalf of one another. It ought to be a state and a society in which people are sensitive to how they depend upon one another, need one another, and are willing to sacrifice for one another in a variety of ways and to various degrees simply because they are called upon by each other to do so. Israel, like all states, ought to want to become a network of mutual support and concern, in which people come to each other's aid and support one another to the degree and in ways that they determine to be the most effective and best.

LEVINAS, GAVISON, AND GANS ON ISRAEL AND NATIONALISM

It is not difficult to see how Levinas would differ from extreme religious Zionists, on the one hand, and post-Zionist critics of Israel, on the other. Locating him within the broader middle ground of liberal views is less easy to do. My discussion of Gavison has been intended to begin such a process. Originally, I had planned to follow this discussion of a Levinasian response to Gavison with a similar account of how Levinas might react to the arguments of Chaim Gans, both in *A Just Zionism* and in his more recent *A Political Theory for the Jewish People*. As interesting and valuable as such an account might be, however, it would require much more space than I can now allot. In its place, I want to limit myself to asking one question, what Levinas would say about the central difference between Gavison's Zionism and that of Gans, at least as Gans portrays it. In his more recent work, Gans distinguishes among three Zionisms. He calls one "mainstream" or "proprietary" Zionism, a second "hierarchical"

Zionism, and a third, his own position, "egalitarian" Zionism."[73] Gans rejects the historical-propriety position, which justifies the Zionist return to the Land of Israel on the grounds that the land and its political institutions are the property of the Jewish people and have been since antiquity. He also rejects unqualifiedly the post-Zionist denial that the Jewish people collectively has any right to hegemony over the land and any right to control its political institutions. Dismissing these opposing extremes, however, he realizes that there is greater affinity between his own view and that of the "hierarchical" Zionists. He associates Gavison with this second position, "hierarchical" Zionism or the Zionism of academics and legal scholars, and he distinguishes it from his own position, which also relies on a right to self-determination but which strives for equality for all the citizens of the state.

Gans argues that Gavison's position, which is based on a right of peoples or nations to self-determination, cannot account by itself for the territorial feature of Zionism, the location of the Jewish state and its particular boundaries. He points out that Gavison claims that in the period of the earlier Yishuv, both the Arabs who resided in the land and the Zionist settlers had the liberty to inhabit the land, but neither had the right to do so and to exclude the other. Gans believes that the Arabs had more than a liberty, but the core of his objection or worry about Gavison's view is that he doubts that the Jewish people had any liberty at all to occupy the land. Without calling upon some historical considerations, there is no reason to think that it did. There is, after all, no blanket liberty to occupy lands, even within the constraint that there is no violence against the inhabitants, even for individuals and certainly not for collectivities or peoples. To admit that there were would, would be to condone colonialism everywhere, without any further justification.[74]

In the light of these considerations and objections, Gans proposes a third form of Zionism, which he calls "egalitarian" Zionism. According to it, the Jewish people collectively does have a right to national self-determination. Furthermore, historical considerations and the persecutions suffered by the Jewish people justify the claim that that self-determination should occur in the Land of Israel, that this should be the case even though it had been inhabited by Arabs, but that there is no argument that would justify a Jewish state in the whole of the land or indeed in more of the land than was defined by borders at the time of the emergency, that is, in 1947.[75] Rather, the Palestinian people also have a right to national self-determination, and they also are justified in establishing that state in the same land. This provides a framework in which a form of equality is achieved; each people is dominant in its own country and state. Moreover, there are limits to how extensive should be the control or "monopoly" over the public culture in each state by the dominant people.[76]

The crucial difference between Gavison and Gans, then, concerns the limitations on the advantages of the dominant people in each of the two resulting states. Both believe that the Jewish people and the Palestinian people have rights to self-determination, which should be respected and implemented politically. Both believe that the two peoples have reason to have political control over territories that currently are contested. Gans is more critical than Gavison about how extensive Israel's rights to the land were at key points in her history, but both now support the existence of two contiguous states. Where they differ most of all, however, is that while both take Zionism to express a secular ideology for the Jewish people, Gavison argues that the privileges and advantages for the Jewish people in Israel ought to include all kinds of cultural and symbolic domains, while Gans limits those privileges and advantages severely, basically to "security and demographic" matters. In this way, Gans is more attentive to the needs and interests and integrity of Israel's non-Jewish and minority citizens; in a sense, his sense of nationalism is more attenuated than Gavison's is. Alternatively, Gavison's liberalism is more attuned to communitarian considerations, issues of cultural and religious identity, and the role of cultural and symbolic features in a liberal polity.

I doubt that we can pinpoint with any accuracy how Levinas would place himself in this kind of debate. As I have argued, I think that the implications of the primacy of responsibility and care for others for social and political commitments would encourage him to be sympathetic to much that Gans and Gavison share. Perhaps the most telling point about his understanding of ethics and politics, however, is that it takes to be primary the welfare of particular others, those affected by public policies and regulations and especially those who are members of minority communities in a state that aspires to be liberal, democratic, and yet nationalist, and that this priority requires constant attention to how justly and humanely individuals are treated. In this spirit, Levinas is very much a particularist. Overarching programs, arguments, and policies are always, from his perspective, provisional; they must always be judged by participants at moments when circumstances are challenging and must be considered in detail. This particularism means that there is no way to determine once and for all how Levinas would adjudicate the differences between Gavison and Gans. Still, the fact that Gavison is more open than Gans to the psychological and symbolic roles of cultural practices and artifacts makes her position a bit more attractive. There is more room in her view for flexibility and nuance. At the same time, Levinas would no doubt find appealing Gans's commitment to as much egalitarianism between majority and minority citizens as one can manage, restricted by and large only by security interests of the state as a whole. It may be, then, that Levinas would feel less bound by the arguments each brings in behalf of maximal equality of treatment for all or responsible dominance for the majority national community than he would be bound to the universality of the state's responsibilities to and for all its citizens, both majority and minority, and indeed all who are present within it, including as well non-citizen refugees, temporary inhabitants, migrant workers, and others.

I have returned frequently to Levinas's claim that it is not unimportant to know that a society is founded on charity and love and not on the war of all against all. In general, as we conclude our discussion of Gavison, Gans, and Levinas, I return to this statement. In this context, it means that it is not unimportant to hold that Israel is a Jewish and democratic state and to agree with Gavison and Gans about what would be required concretely for Israel to meet that standard to be based on a conception of persons as infinitely responsible for one another rather than on a conception of rights. Why does this difference make a difference? There is, especially in Gavison's conception, a deep tension between the liberal dimension of her view and the communitarian dimension. At crucial points in her arguments, she calls upon the importance of one's national, ethnic, or religious identity to one's growth and development and flourishing as a person. She regularly balances this with a claim about fairness and equal treatment, at times arguing that opportunities to enhance one's identity must be provided fairly to all citizens or as fairly as one can in a nation-state where the state is taken to give a privileged position to the national identity. But Gavison's claims about identity and nationhood are never provided with a secure normative foundation, surely not a morally normative one. Acquiring, maintaining, and enhancing one's sense of identity are assumed to have normative force, but in fact they can best be understood psychologically, as facts about our nature as persons. For Gans as well, even when he turns to the distinctiveness of peoples and historical considerations relevant to that distinctiveness, he does little more than take for granted the significance and importance of national differences. What Levinas provides is a conception of Jewishness—as a commitment to act responsibly toward one another, with a sense of justice and concern, and as a commitment to shape a society based on such attitudes of care and duties toward others—that is normative in and of itself; its normativity resides in the face-to-face relation itself. Awareness of the primacy of interpersonal relationships and attentiveness to living according to their ethical character are central to Judaism and hence, for Levinas, to Zionism as a Jewish political ideology.

If so, for Levinas, there is no deep tension between Israel's Jewishness and her democratic character and commitment to human rights. In a sense, these arise from the very same normative sources, from our nature as ethical beings, as infinitely responsible for and to one another. To be sure, this leaves Levinas with the problems of arguing in behalf of all those aspects of Jewish life that one might call cultural or ritual or celebratory and to defend their presence as dominant in the Jewish state's public culture. But, I would argue, this obligation is less onerous and easier to meet than the one with which Gavison is left, which involves the lingering suspicion that her conception of Jewishness and her commitments to Jewish cultural life expressive of a secular Jewish lifestyle are too lean, too lacking in seriousness and depth, to support any serious sense in which Israel is Jewish and not, as some argue, Israeli— where this stands for a nationality that draws upon Jewish history and symbols but is not, in any serious sense, identical with Jewishness.[77] In virtually every essay in which Gavison turns to these issues, she makes a strong case for rejecting a "theocratic" interpretation of Judaism, by

which she means an understanding of Judaism as halakhic and as rest-
ing on highly contested metaphysical foundations, most notably a commitment to God's existence and the role of God in human affairs and in
history. Gavison in fact argues that it is one of Israel's singular purposes
to advance the career of a secular Judaism that is primarily cultural and
is akin to a national identity. But to many this watered-down conception of Jewishness has only a contingent connection with Judaism and
Jewish history. What Levinas's conception of Judaism provides is a non-
theocratic sense of what Jewishness means and yet one that has serious
implications for social and political life. Moreover, it brings with it the
grounds of a normativity that applies both to Israel's Jewish character
and to its aspirations regarding democracy and human rights. This is no
mean accomplishment.[78]

NINE

ETHICS, POLITICS, AND MESSIANISM

In a well-known interview, Richard Kearney asked Emmanuel Levinas if the "ethical criterion of the interhuman" were not employed by him as a "sort of messianic eschatology." Levinas objected to the expression "eschatology" and yet accepted the proposal that the "ethical relation with the other" is messianic, but only when properly understood. That is, he rejected the idea of a historical *eschaton*, an end or goal, whether we think of it as a face-to-face exposure to an absolutely other, God, or as the completion or perfection of our face-to-face encounters with human others. Ethics has no end; it is not about a historical telos. As he put it, "I have described ethical responsibility as *insomnia* or *wakefulness* precisely because it is a perpetual duty of vigilance and effort that can never slumber." The key word here is "perpetual." Love, he says, has something incessant and impermanent about it. He refers to the image of Talmudic sages going from meeting to meeting, always discussing the law, in this life and the next, without end. Love or the ethical is like this process that demands ongoing wakefulness and attention.[1] If ethics is messianic, it is an episodic messianism that is never complete, and if politics ought to meet ethical standards, it too requires attention and correction, moment to moment.

Moreover, if ethics is messianic, its immediate agent is the person who reaches out to accept and care for another person. That is, we are all messianic agents but only when we act in response to the claims of others upon us. If the coming of the Messiah is a miracle and somehow grounded in divine action, it is so in a very special way. Furthermore, if it is a political event, it is political only insofar as the everyday and political can be more ethical than it currently is.

Levinas's comments in the Kearney interview, then, provide us with a sketch of his revisionary understanding of what he calls elsewhere the "popular" opinion among Jews about the coming of the Messiah. That popular opinion takes the Messiah to be a member of the House of David, who is appointed and sent by God to redeem the Jewish people from worldly injustice and suffering. The Messiah is widely believed to be a political figure who will rule over a reestablished Jewish state during a period characterized by peace and abundance. While classical and medieval texts do not present a uniform picture of the Messiah, his coming, and the conditions that lead to his arrival and that mark his reign, such a popular view can be culled from those texts. Often, moreover, rabbinic texts take the days of the Messiah to be separated from preceding social and political history by a catastrophe or cataclysmic event, and they are at most equivocal about the role of human conduct in precipitating the Messiah's advent.

Levinas's messianism, if we can call it that, has human action play a central role, and it is not tied to a linear or teleological interpretation of history. His view is dramatically different from the popular one, and it hardly sounds like the messianism found in traditional Jewish texts. Why does Levinas admit to calling these views "messianic"? What roots them, if anything does, in traditional Jewish treatments of the coming of the Messiah and the days of the Messiah?

In several places, Levinas discusses traditional Jewish texts on messianism and interprets them in his own terms. Looking at these discussions of classic rabbinic texts, from the Talmud and from Maimonides, would help to show how Levinas appropriates the vocabulary of messianism in a distinctive way. There are several features of traditional Jewish messianism that will be important to us: the political character of the Messiah; the relationship between the days of the Messiah and the world to come; the relationship between ethics and politics; the historical conditions that bring the Messiah; the role of divine agency and human conduct in the coming of the Messiah; the sense in which Zionism is a messianic movement; and the relationship between history and the coming of the Messiah. Here I want to look at one of those texts, the commentaries on Tractate Sanhedrin.[2]

In *Difficult Freedom*, Levinas includes two sets of his Talmudic commentaries from 1960 and 1961, when he delivered them at the third and fourth conferences of Jewish intellectuals, organized by the French section of the World Jewish Congress. The commentaries refer to four passages from the final chapter of Tractate Sanhedrin.[3] Levinas admits that the notion of messianism in Judaism is "complex and difficult," even if popular opinion encourages us to think that it is simple. But, he notes, the popular conception is not satisfying to the thinker. "One has failed to say anything about the Messiah if one represents him as a person who comes to put a miraculous end to the violence in the world, the injustice and contradictions which destroy humanity but have their source in the nature of humanity, and simply in Nature."[4] At this stage, it is not immediately clear what about this popular representation is unsatisfying, but Levinas does take it to betray the genuine teaching of messianism. Moreover, he even goes so far as to say that in our post-Enlightenment and post-Emancipation world, it is a view of the coming of the Messiah that makes it hard for Jews to take it seriously. Hence, his own account can be understood as one way in which the idea of messianism can be recovered for Jews today in a responsible and compelling way.

In "A Religion for Adults," Levinas argues for a mature view of Judaism and against childish views, which he associates with magic and mystification;[5] here, when he charges the popular view of messianism with concretizing it, with treating it as the result of a divine miraculous act that involves the appointment of a messianic redeemer, he is similarly charging popular Judaism with childishness, with a failure of maturity, a failure to understand the structures and features of our lives to which the messianic idea gives expression. Such understanding requires teaching and learning of a serious sort and a kind of disclosure and explication, or articulation that is probing and rational. His commentary is devoted to such a procedure, even if, as he says here and regularly says, it is produced by someone who has not studied for a lifetime the Talmudic literature but does bring to it his own philosophical and intellectual interests and training.

HISTORY AND THE MESSIANIC ERA

Let me begin with the question, how is the messianic era related to history? The question can mean many things, of course. It could be asking a qualitative question: is the historical situation such that its goodness warrants the coming of the Messiah, or is it a period of suffering and injustice that requires a divine act to rectify it and bring it to a close? Or the question could be asking: is the messianic era a continuation of history, or does it mark a break with it? Or it could be asking about the role of human conduct in bringing on the messianic advent: is human action necessary to do so or at least in some way sufficient, or is it irrelevant to the coming of the Messiah? Moreover, insofar as history is the scene of human action, including social, economic, political, and ethical conduct, does the messianic era incorporate a continuation of any one or any number of these human actions? It will become clear that to address this cluster of issues, Levinas takes the discourse about a messianic agent to be a *figure* for a particular kind of human conduct, its importance, its desirability, and its role in history and everyday life. To show this, then, let me turn first to Levinas's commentary on a text from the Babylonian Talmud (BT), Sanhedrin 97b–98a.

As Levinas notes, the text records a controversy between two prominent Amoraim, Samuel and Rab. The question that the text raises, as Levinas sees it, is: "Is the coming of the messianic era conditional or unconditional?"[6] Rab claims that history has arrived at the moment for redemption; everything has been accomplished—"history is over," as Levinas puts it, and all that remains is the need for repentance and good deeds. Samuel responds that it is sufficient for a mourner to keep his period of mourning.

For Rab, then, in the third century, all the conditions for the coming of the Messiah have materialized.[7] The only thing left is for individual human initiative to provide repentance and good deeds; this is up to "the individual effort that can be produced in full self-control." Levinas adds an important insight: "Moral action, *the individual's work*, is not alienated by a history that naturalizes it and, consequently, does not have to attempt to impose itself by taking the detour of politics and having recourse to reasons of State."[8] What does this mean? The point of Rab's view, as Levinas understands him, is that the messianic era requires moral action, which is up to the individual to accomplish, and is not "alienated" by naturalistic history, by the forces of politics. It is not excluded by that history, nor is it co-opted by it. What does Levinas mean by the contrast between moral action and politics? Typically, for Levinas, politics is the domain of ideology and institutions, of self-interest and power. His point is that history as the domain of politics does not rule out morality, nor does morality have to subordinate itself to political power and control. It can operate independently; it need not yield to political manipulation or accommodate itself to political modes of implementation. This is Rab's point; morality is a matter of the individual's "full self-control."[9] As Levinas puts it, "To bring a just course to triumph, one is not obliged to become politically allied to assassins." One need not become hostage to power. "All the predestined dates have passed: good deeds are efficacious. That is the Messiah."[10] Here I take it that what Levinas means is that the individual's moral actions are independent from political power, institutions, and ideological commitments. Such personal acts of kindness and compassion are messianic; nothing more is necessary. Politics and political accomplishments are not required. This is Rab's teaching.

But it is not Samuel's. For him, "political realities" are important. "Only messianism can undo the destructive effects they wreak on a moral life. For him, in a word, *messianic deliverance cannot ensue from individual effort* which it makes possible only in terms of efficacity [sic] and harmonious play."[11] But how is this lesson got from Samuel's enigmatic statement about a mourner keeping the period of mourning? Levinas proposes that we first ask who the mourner is, and he suggests that there are three options.

The first option is that it is God who mourns—or, as Levinas suggests, "objective will, which directs history, is in mourning," that is, "*the objective order of things cannot remain eternally in check*: it cannot remain eternally in a state of disorder; things will work out, and they will do so objectively."[12] And this will happen without the need for any special individual effort that is comprehended within this objective order. Rather it is all up to God, the mourner, to deliver the order of history and reconcile all difficulties and problems. Or, in secular terms, the natural, historical order will resolve its own political problems.

The second option is that the mourner is Israel, a people that suffers and calls for redemption. It is this suffering that is the precondition for redemption. Like Rab, Samuel, on this reading, posits a "moral event at the source of deliverance," but it is not repentance. Rather it is suffering, that is, the condition of deliverance is not a moral action but a moral condition, so to speak. On this view, then, the individual is not the direct cause of deliverance but rather a second cause, Levinas says. It is not the individual's conduct that brings the Messiah; it is her suffering that elicits the Messiah's coming. Moreover, as Levinas says, this suffering, "while laying hold of the individual . . . is received from the outside." In later essays, Levinas portrays suffering as something that assaults the self, targets her, and comes from the outside; suffering is an other. Here he associates it, in an allusion to the Holocaust, with martyrdom "suffered by Israel throughout the terrible years, as throughout its whole history" and hence with an "unmerited dignity" that exists between life and "the dignity of the victim who . . . suffers absurdly the repercussions of historical necessities."[13]

On both of these readings of Samuel's enigmatic response, the condition for the messianic coming is not individual action. On one, it is the self-correcting order of the political itself; on the other, it is the suffering that calls for that coming from another source. But there is a third reading, one that Levinas finds in the Maharsha, a seventeenth-century commentator; it is that the mourner is Israel, but her suffering does not alone bring redemption without some positive action on her part.[14] That suffering also requires repentance, which is the direct cause of deliverance. "In the economy of being, therefore, suffering has a special place: it is not yet moral initiative, but it is through suffering that *a freedom may be aroused*."[15] On this third reading, then, the freedom of Rab's proposal is joined with the suffering of the second reading of Samuel's: man suffers and then, through that suffering, emerges as morally free. There is, as Levinas puts it, a reconciliation of outside intervention in salvation with human agency; Samuel, to the Maharsha, appreciates that redemption incorporates the outside condition and the internal agency, good deeds.

But there is a fourth option for the question of who mourns: that it is the Messiah. In support of this reading, Levinas calls upon another Talmudic passage, a famous one, which reports a conversation between R. Joshua ben Levi and Elijah.[16] R. Joshua asks Elijah when the Messiah will come, but Elijah cannot answer. He tells R. Joshua to ask the Messiah, who, he says, is sitting at the city gates, among the lepers. The other lepers undo all their bandages at once, treat their wounds, and then re-bandage themselves, except for the Messiah, who treats only one wound at a time, lest he be delayed unduly when the time comes for him to appear as the Messiah. R. Joshua recognizes him, rushes over to him, and asks when he will come. His answer is, "Today." And when R. Joshua reports this to Elijah and wonders if this is not false, Elijah refers to Psalm 95:7: "Today, if you will hear his voice." Here, Levinas says, we have a Messiah who suffers. But redemption, the messianic coming, requires more than this suffering; the suffering of humankind and the suffering of the Messiah are not sufficient. Everything depends upon human beings. History is completed, the conditions are ripe, but God's agency is not automatic. It comes only with human action.

In the light of these three readings of Samuel's proposal—together with the fourth he proposes—Levinas notices that the debate between Rab and Samuel portrays a pair of alternatives: "Either morality—that is to say, the efforts made by men who are masters of their intentions and acts—will save the world, or else what is needed is an objective event that surpasses morality and the individual's good intentions."[17]

These texts deal with the coming of the Messiah; here Levinas speaks of deliverance or salvation. Implicitly, he is carrying forward the idea that history is constituted by political and economic problems that will be resolved in the messianic era. Hence, in this summary of the debate between Rab and Samuel, Levinas is distinguishing two views about what constitutes the messianic coming, two views about what the figure of the Messiah means. One is that the Messiah refers to a redemption constituted by the moral conduct of individuals; the other is that the messianic redemption is an extra-human political event, the outcome of divine agency. This distinction, moreover, synthesizes two dichotomies, between human and divine agency and between moral redemption and another sort, perhaps political.

From what Levinas says elsewhere about the fundamentally ethical character of human existence and about the way in which the Talmud regularly harbors the ambiguity of such polar opposites, we can conclude, perhaps, that what he takes the Talmud to be saying is that the redemption from history's political and economic problems requires conduct of a different order that is nonetheless a matter of human freedom. It is moral conduct but also has about it an element of the transcendent. Messianism is, we might say, acts of responsibility in response to the suffering of others. This reading is no simple recovery of the trope of working and waiting, a dichotomy that might be found in the debate between Rab and Samuel. Not so for Levinas, who takes seriously both poles and reads them in the light of a distinction between morality, on the one hand, and politics and economics, on the other. The human condition cannot neglect either the embodied and natural dimension of human experience or the transcendent and moral dimension, or, to use Robert Brandom's terms, that we are both sentient and sapient beings.[18] But redemption or messianism is the work of our transcendent character, the way in which we respond to suffering with free and responsible action in behalf of justice.

The text at BT Sanhedrin 97b continues this debate between the Amoraim Rab and Samuel, moreover, by recalling an older debate between two Tannaim, first-generation sages, R. Eliezer and R. Joshua. R. Eliezer says that if Israel repents, she will be redeemed, but if not, not, and this seems to anticipate Rab's position. R. Joshua adds, however, that if they do not repent, God will send a cruel ruler, a Haman, who will persecute Israel so that she will then repent and be redeemed. Here we seem to have a version of the Maharsha's reading, that it is an objective state of affairs that will bring suffering and give rise to free moral conduct. Hence, it might seem that the Tannaitic version of the debate, more explicitly than the Amoraic version, shows that Rab's and Samuel's positions are very close.

But there is more to be said. We have a version of the Tannaitic debate from the Baraita, a Tannaitic collection not included in the Mishnah, compiled in the second century by R. Hiyya and R. Oshaia, as Levinas reports. Here we have R. Eliezer's position about the necessity of repentance with a proof-text from Jeremiah 3:22, "Return, ye backsliding children, and I will heal your backslidings." As Levinas paraphrases it, when the return, the repentance, has occurred, the Messiah will come; salvation depends upon human action.[19] To this R. Joshua objects by citing Isaiah 52:3, "Ye have sold yourselves for nought; and ye shall be redeemed without money," and by pointing out that Israel's crime was idolatry and that the redemption will come "without money," that is, without repentance and good deeds. That is, as R. Joshua reads the Isaiah text, since—or when—the sin that Israel has committed is idolatry, then the redemption will be gratuitous and unconditional—a sign of God's boundless compassion for Israel perhaps. But to this R. Eliezer responds by citing Malachi 3:7, "Return unto Me, and I will return unto you," which confirms that redemption depends upon repentance. In this battle of proof-texts, however, R. Joshua rejoins with Jeremiah 3:14, "That I am master over you: and I will take you out of a city, and two of a family, and I will bring you to Zion," which seems to imply that no repentance is required. But Levinas points out that R. Joshua has either forgotten or suppressed the beginning of the verse, which is the word "Return"; R. Joshua's reading is that the verse confirms the unconditional character of the redemption. To this R. Eliezer answers with Isaiah 30:15, which he strains to read as requiring repentance, and so the debate continues, until R. Eliezer is silent; when R. Joshua cites Daniel 12:7 as proof of unconditional redemption, R. Eliezer has nothing more to say. Levinas asks why. He wonders what the Talmud means by allowing this debate to come to an end, even though one can easily imagine many further texts that could be cited on both sides. He refers to this debate as a "strange text," but what is it that makes it strange? Is it the content, the verses cited, or the fact that it is allowed to end so abruptly?

Levinas advises that the reader turn from the abstract positions— the contest between the necessity of repentance and the possibility of unconditional redemption—to the biblical passages themselves that were cited along the way. In the first stage, the text from Jeremiah 3:22 uses the word "heal" to characterize the redemption, and Levinas interprets this verb to mean that the condition to be redeemed is a "radical corruption" that requires medication that would be "ineffectual without some initial effort on the part of the sick person." What is essential here, he argues, is the depth of the corruption; the mere application of an external drug is inadequate. "Nothing can penetrate a person closed in on himself by evil. He first of all has to get a grip on himself in order to be healed from outside. Precisely, *because evil is not simply a 'backsliding,' but a profound illness in being, it is the sick person who is the first and principal worker of his own healing."* What lies behind such a reading, then, is an assumption about sin—that it is not merely an external act but rather an act of deep rebellion; it is a "breaking with the eternal order, a free being in selfish isolation."[20] R. Eliezer's view, then, presumes that redemption and the coming of the Messiah are about the overcoming of such sin, of an evil of the soul, so to speak, of a fundamental attitude about the human condition and its exclusivity, the rejection of transcendence in favor of a form of solipsism or egoism. That is, it is about a transformation in one's being, and this requires in some way a turning of the self in a new direction, a move toward reconciliation. If that reconciliation is figuratively a reconciliation with God but in fact with other persons, who call out to us to relieve their suffering and to care for their needs, then the redemption will involve a recognition of the suffering that confronts the self and its free, responsive, and responsible act to relieve it. Still, R. Eliezer's position emphasizes the importance of the free act of the individual.

As Levinas now points out, R. Joshua's reply emphasizes the other condition, the depth of the attitude that lies behind the sin in the first place. R. Joshua calls the "lapse" that lies behind the sin, "idolatry," which is the foundation of all "moral depravity" in R. Joshua's conception of Judaism. Why is the evil as deep as Levinas says it is? Why is it a "profound illness in being"? Because it is grounded in idolatry. Levinas then says, "An offence committed against man proceeds from a radical evil."[21] The expression "radical evil" comes, in part, from Kant, and for him it refers to action in affront of the moral law. Levinas appropriates it for what to him is the most serious flaw, the abandonment of the other person or the wrong committed against her. Here, moreover, there is no unilateral, unconditional reconciliation and recovery. The offense can be overcome only if the offended party offers pardon but demands reparation from the offender. In the ultimate case, when the offense is against God, it is He that must offer pardon, and only then He must demand reparation. But what does the offender need? A change of character, which requires true education. "External intervention" is insufficient, but it is nonetheless required; what is required is a new understanding, good deeds, and "an attempt at regeneration that comes from the individual." Hence, this is why R. Joshua is as right as R. Eliezer. "Beyond the corruption of evil, he perceives an intellectual flaw which can and must be redeemed from outside."[22] For Levinas, this dialectic—of the call from the other and the response of the self—mirrors the structure of the face-to-face, which is the ethical character of all human social existence. It is both an external call and an internal response. Without the free and moral response of the self, there is only unrequited appeal or overwhelming demand; without the appeal and demand, there is only the free play of the ego. Only together is there genuine ethical existence for persons with one another.

But the debate continues as R. Eliezer cites the famous verse from Malachi 3:7. Levinas's comment is, in one way, clear but also, in another way, rather obscure. He says that "here R. Eliezer once again affirms the eternal requirement of morality: the total *reciprocity* between free people, the equality found between freedoms. . . . It is in the name of such freedom that man's salvation must have its origins in man." On the face of it, the text refers to the human return or repentance that calls forth the divine return in response. On the one hand, Levinas says, the lapse that is sin requires help from the outside: "true knowledge cannot be self-learned"; on the other hand, redemption from sin requires a human act: "sin can be atoned for only from within."[23] But this reading is enigmatic. What does the necessity for redemption, for the coming of the Messiah, of the human act of repentance have to do with the *reciprocity* between free people? What does it mean to say that true knowledge cannot be self-learned? What does it mean to say that man's move toward God is reciprocated with God's move toward man?

For Levinas, salvation or messianism or redemption refers to acts of justice, and these acts are conducted in behalf of others, serving their needs and reducing their suffering. True knowledge involves the understanding of what the other demands of me; it cannot be learned without attentiveness to the claim of the other. On the other hand, it is a knowledge that is realized only in the self's taking that responsibility seriously and acting on it. The equality of free agents is grounded in the inequality of the other's claim upon the self; Levinas says this often. But this does not neutralize the self's freedom; it makes it possible. Real freedom is only possible in response to the pleas and commands of the other; this is what spontaneous freedom is all about. It is what Kant had in mind by autonomy; for Levinas, it is a freedom grounded in heteronomy. In short, the true education of character, the act of self-recovery, only arises from one's own act of self-understanding and then repentance. But this act of recovery involves an awareness of the claim that the other person makes upon the self and a commitment to responding to it; it involves learning to become a humane, caring, and just person and abandoning the impulse to self-satisfaction that may have dominated one's sensibility prior to this conversion.

R. Joshua, we recall, responds to R. Ezekiel with a quotation from Jeremiah (3:14), which Levinas interprets as a corrective to a notion of unilateral and unbounded freedom. Redemption is not wholly up to man; it is not solely facilitated by human freedom. The relationship with the other is not one-sided; it is like an engagement or a conjugal union or a marriage. "Doesn't freedom rest on a preliminary commitment to the being with regard to whom one puts oneself forward as free?"[24] Some translators take the verse to say: "Return, backsliding children, for I am a master to you," but others take *ba'alti va-hem* to mean "I am a husband to you" rather than "I am a master to you." Clearly, Levinas is one of these latter, who takes the relationship of God to the children of Israel to be that of husband to spouse. Even in rejecting God, the people has accepted Him; the freedom to return is grounded in this prior acceptance, in the relationship that is background for all one's acts. But this acceptance, this background relationship, is nothing other than the face-to-face that characterizes all social relationships, of the individual and God, the individual and the state, as Levinas points out, and more.

Once again, R. Eliezer responds with a verse, this time Isaiah 30:15, "In returning and rest shall ye be saved." That is, salvation—redemption and messianism—requires human repentance. But what does "rest" mean here? What does rest have to do with redemption? It is the prerequisite of repentance and return, for it stands for the tranquility and leisure that make the freedom of thought possible,[25] and that freedom of thought is what brings repentance, a change of heart, and with it redemption. But, as R. Joshua proposes, what of all those who have no such leisure, who cannot count on the conditions for such self-examination and self-awareness? His reference, Isaiah 49:7, refers to the poor, the peasants, the workers, and the despised of the earth, who have no such peace in order to reflect and so forth. Surely they require an unconditional redemption, a gift of salvation, "outside intervention, whether in the shape of the Messiah or revolution or political action,"[26] in order to bring them redemption without their prior free and intentional conduct.

Finally, we have R. Eliezer's last textual support, Jeremiah 4:1. What distinguishes this verse from his earlier claims is that here there is an "if." God will return, but only if man repents. But will he? And, more importantly, what if he does not? Levinas calls this a "dramatic turn," for it raises the question "What will happen in fact if men do not return to God?" to which Levinas responds, "The Messiah will never come, the world will be turned over to the wicked and atheist belief that it is governed by chance, and evil will triumph." That is, the conditional character of Jeremiah 4:1 incorporates within the notion of morality as the work of absolute freedom the possibility of nihilism, of an "immoral world—that is to say, the end of morality." Thus far, the debates that Levinas has been examining seem to have assumed that the Messiah will in fact come; the questions that are raised concerned the conditions for that arrival, and they are raised to assist humankind in preparing for that arrival or in bringing it about. What this claim of R. Eliezer adds is the contingency of the Messiah's coming; it does not treat human freedom as expressed through the act of return or repentance as merely a sufficient condition for that antecedent that leads to the messianic era but rather treats it as a necessary condition. Moreover, it introduces the possibility that it will never be provided, so that the Messiah will indeed never come. Levinas puts this succinctly: "Absolute morality [requires] absolute freedom. This creates the possibility of immorality."[27] It is precisely for this reason that R. Joshua in his response calls upon Daniel 12:7, which, as Levinas reads it, announces unconditional redemption on a fixed date.[28] The weight here, then, is not on the fact that the Messiah will come at God's behest but rather that he will in fact come, that his coming is guaranteed; the date is already fixed. Here is a belief in the triumph of the good, as Levinas calls it, in hope. The belief in God and the belief that the Messiah will come are coordinated beliefs, and with this commitment, Judaism proves to make a claim the point of which is similar to Kant's point in his *Second Critique* with his argument for the role of God and religion within morality.

As Levinas points out, R. Eliezer offers no response to R. Joshua; he is silent. For his commitment to absolute freedom seems to fly in the face of the "absolute certainty of the defeat of Evil" and hence in the face of God. But God is necessary for all, for immorality and for the certainty that morality will triumph over it. In order to believe this, one must believe that whether or not man does anything, the Messiah will come. Levinas finds in this, the truth revealed through R. Joshua's citation and that revealed through R. Eliezer's silence, a pure understanding of God. In his earlier essay "A Religion for Adults," Levinas defends an adult conception of God and dismisses as childish imagery of God as an agent. Here he takes this moral teaching about God, as indicative of the triumph of the good, and as a corrective to a childish conception of the Messiah as incarnate, a clear allusion to Christianity and its conception of Jesus as the Christ, as the Messiah. "God emerges here in His purest essence, one distant from all imagery of incarnation, through the moral adventure of humanity. God is here the very principle of the triumph of good. If you do not believe this, if you do not believe that in any case the Messiah will come, you do not believe in God."[29]

Furthermore, this outcome of the debate between R. Eliezer and R. Joshua explains the "famous paradox that the Messiah will come when the world is wholly guilty."[30] Levinas is referring here to R. Yohanan's claim that the son of David will come only in a generation that is either altogether righteous or altogether wicked (BT Sanhedrin 98a). On the one hand, of course, this might suggest that God will send the Messiah when he is most needed or when human effort has failed completely. That is, R. Yohanan might be telling us why God will send the Messiah. But what Levinas takes this to mean is that "even if the world is absolutely plunged in sin, the Messiah will come." He is interested not in why the Messiah will come but rather in that he will come. The belief in God is a belief that the good will ultimately triumph. We have learned, of course, that for Levinas the Messiah is a figure that represents the human accomplishment of justice. Hence, the belief in God is the belief that ultimately humankind will act in behalf of others and rectify injustice, to some degree, in some ways; absolute evil will never be victorious as long as human beings are capable of acting. Freedom may make evil possible, but it will also, we can be certain, realize the good.

But while R. Eliezer is silent, the debate, as we have seen, recurs with Rab and Samuel and, as Levinas says, is still alive. God—as Levinas understands rationally what God means—is at the core of Judaism. But the link between God and the Messiah is ethics. We may hope for its accomplishment and the triumph of the good, but the debate is not resolved: the gap between hope and certitude remains.

MESSIANISM, ETHICS, POLITICS

One of the outcomes of Levinas's reading of this debate is that the moral conduct that constitutes the messianic coming is not completely dissociated from politics. At any given moment, there are social and political problems that can be solved only through the efficacy of individual moral conduct. But such conduct, acts of kindness and justice, do not erase the social and political structures of our lives.[31] They redeem them and correct them. In this sense, the messianic times are ethical and political at the same time. Moreover, they do not mark an age that arrives when history has run its course; rather they are moments within history—redemptive or messianic moments.

Levinas arrives at this conclusion from reading a text in BT Sanhedrin 99a that records a controversy between R. Yohanan and R. Samuel about the difference between the days of the Messiah (*yemot ha-Mashiah*) and the world to come (*olam ha-ba*). The text begins by citing a statement by R. Hiyya bar Abba in the name of R. Yohanan: that the prophets prophesied about the days of the Messiah and not about the world to come, which, according to Isaiah 64:4, is beyond human apprehension. That is, as Levinas notes, the text formulates a "classic Jewish thesis . . . that there is a difference between the future world and the messianic era."[32] Or alternatively, there is a progression envisaged by R. Yohanan, from history to the messianic era, but the world to come is of a different order.

Levinas characterizes this conception of history more fully. Prophecy concerns two kinds of problems and corresponding promises: political and social. There are the injustice and alienation caused by "the arbitrary workings of political powers in every human enterprise," on the one hand, and "the power the rich hold over the poor," which leads to "social injustice," on the other. According to R. Yohanan, the messianic era will bring the eradication of both. Hence, messianism brings the rectification of historical ills. But what of the world to come? Levinas reads R. Yohanan as saying that it seems to "exist on another level." Whereas the messianic era concerns social achievements, the future world deals with personal ones, "a personal and intimate order, lying outside the achievements of history."[33]

Thus far, then, Levinas reads Sanhedrin in a traditional way. Prophecy, Judaism, is about "the Good of the community and the public order." It teaches about justice and is not, as Levinas puts it, an insurance company. "The personal salvation of men, the discrete and intimate relationships between man and God, escapes the indiscretion of the prophets."[34] Steven Schwarzschild, defending a view of messianism that he finds best articulated in Hermann Cohen, argues in a similar fashion, that in Judaism messianism concerns the ethical, broadly speaking, and is not a matter of personal salvation.[35] He similarly reads Maimonides as distinguishing the messianic age from the world to come in terms of a distinction between social, political accomplishment and personal salvation, but he views the latter in Aristotelian terms and hence more favorably as the accomplishment of theoretical understanding, of supreme knowledge of God and nature. Levinas reads R. Yohanan's view this way, although, I believe, he has in mind particularly Christianity, in which the ideal of salvation is personal and not social.

As Gershom Scholem argues in his famous essay on the messianic idea in Judaism, there is in Judaism a distinction between apocalyptic, catastrophic messianism, which is often associated with utopianism, and a more historical type, which is often restorative.[36] The paradigm of restorative, historical, and even rational messianism is Maimonides, who regularly cites—and he is not alone—both R. Yohanan's statement and the text that Levinas now turns to, which follows the previous one. R. Yohanan is said to have differed with Samuel, who said, "This world differs from [that of] the days of the Messiah only in respect of servitude to [foreign] powers."[37] That is, for Maimonides, there is nothing transcendent or apocalyptic or discontinuous about the messianic age. But how, then, does Samuel's view differ from R. Yohanan's?

Strictly speaking, their views do not oppose one another. R. Yohanan's claim is about the referent of prophetic promises, while Samuel's claim is that history and the messianic era differ with regard to one detail, the subordination of the Jewish state or the Jewish people to alien powers. But Levinas could interpret them in order to dramatize their conflict. He reads Samuel to mean that in the messianic era, there will be an end to "political violence." Since he had read the substance of the prophetic promises as including both political and social problems and promises, he could now identify the difference between R. Yohanan and Samuel as a difference regarding the role of social injustice. But instead, Levinas seems to take his cue from Maimonides, that the two can be reconciled, by asking if there is not more to the servitude to foreign powers than political violence in a narrow sense, the "political servitude suffered by" the people of Israel in the Diaspora.[38]

That is, Levinas wonders if political violence is not more serious. He proposes that the messianic era is the "high point of history" when "politics no longer presents an obstacle to man's moral enterprise," and he asks, "Can the end of political violence be separated from the end of social violence?" Could Samuel really think that the political solution can be separated from the social one?[39] Levinas looks for a text that might be used to provide Samuel with a reason for his claim. The text comes from BT Shabbat 63a; it repeats Samuel's claim and adds a biblical proof-text: "For the poor shall never cease out of the land" (Deuteronomy 15:11). Hence, Samuel clearly thought that political justice would be joined by social justice; he did not believe that messianism would only rectify the problem of political violence. It would also rectify the problem of social justice. Therefore, we must not be too quick to conclude that the solution to social injustices is what distinguishes R. Yohanan's view from Samuel's.

But if this is right, how do they differ? To Levinas, their difference must lie in the positive contribution of the messianic era. Or, alternatively, their difference concerns the way in which R. Yohanan and Samuel understand poverty and economics. The former treats them as a historical accident, to be removed in the messianic era; the latter treats them as essential features of human existence in the messianic era as much as in history. Hence, Samuel's special contribution is that he appreciates something important about human social existence and what the messianic era will bring to it. As Levinas puts it, R. Yohanan conceives of the messianic era as inaugurating a life of pure contemplative or active life, of "pure and gracious spiritual life," perhaps one of "absolute knowledge or artistic action or friendship . . . above the political and the social." To him, "the poor man . . . is merely the accident of a regrettable historical regime."[40] Samuel, on the hand, realizes that the messianic era does not leave economics behind; it does not eradicate poverty and need. What it does is to remove the political impediments to genuine giving; it makes such giving real. In Samuel, then, we find evidence for a central Levinasian belief, that morality is the sphere of responsibility to the other person, who is always the poor one, the vulnerable and destitute. Relationship with the other person is always a matter of giving, of offering; it is always a response to the claim of the other's face, as it were. The world to come may open up new possibilities, but the messianic does not yet *know* them. It is still part of history, and its character is essentially ethical, moral. R. Yohanan sees beyond history, beyond human life, incarnate and needful, to something spiritual and detached; Samuel does not.

Levinas tries, I think, to redeem R. Yohanan's otherworldliness, his sense of detachment from the concrete, the economic, the worldly. He calls his vision "an ideal of total grace and harmony, an ideal exempt from any drama" and from any effort, pain, suffering.[41] But does Levinas take such an ideal to be more lofty, more worthy, or simply a fantasy?

The text in Sanhedrin goes on to cite two further lessons reported by R. Hiyya bar Abba in the name of R. Yohanan, and Levinas now turns to them. In both cases, the lessons use the device that R. Yohanan already employed to distinguish the messianic era from the world to come. That device is the scope of prophecy. He distinguished between that to which the prophetic teachings apply and that which, according to Isaiah 64:4, is known to God but not to any human being, what "the eye hath not seen." The first of the two lessons uses this device to distinguish repentant sinners from the perfectly righteous; the second uses it to distinguish "him who marries his daughter to a scholar, or engages in business on behalf of a scholar, or benefits a scholar with his possessions" from the scholars themselves. In all these cases, then, R. Yohanan sees a limit to human understanding and a restricted domain to which prophecy applies and hence which is accessible through revelation. As we have seen, the messianic era falls within the latter purview; it is related to history and to a philosophy of history about which the prophets have informed us through their teachings and promises.

Levinas, in line with traditional readings, associates these pairs of distinctions. Prophetic promises apply to the messianic era and to the repentant sinners, who "inherit the messianic era." The perfectly righteous, on the other hand, inhabit the world to come; they are those whose lives are "without drama" and are "without contradiction." Levinas calls this the "ideal of a disincarnated and gracious spirit." Furthermore, as we have learned, the messianic era is a time when daily economic life and its problems are solved through acts of generosity and justice; hence it is a time when family life, one's business, and one's possessions are dedicated to the scholar's life, to one who "has direct access to the Revelation and the knowledge of God."[42] Hence, although family, work, and law cannot themselves involve direct access to God, they can be elevated through the accomplishments of the messianic era to a higher level through the mediation of the scholarly life that they serve. This is R. Yohanan's view, then, that the messianic era is continuous with history; both involve social and political conditions. But the world to come is severed from them, for it leaves such conditions behind. The ideal of the scholar is of a life that is not concrete and incarnate; it is detached and spiritual and abstract.

Who is right—R. Yohanan or Samuel? Levinas notes that in the Talmud, regularly, both such contraries contain an element of truth. Typically, "thought oscillates between the two." "Does the spirit indicate a quasi-divine life that is free of the limitations of the human condition, or does the human condition, with all its limits and its drama, express the very life of the spirit?" That is, for Samuel the ideal is this-worldly; for R. Yohanan, it is otherworldly. For Samuel, there is nothing beyond the human condition; for R. Yohanan there is. For Samuel, politics and economics are essential to the human ideal; for R. Yohanan, they are accidental and historical. But, as Levinas notes, both conceptions find a place in Jewish thought, for humankind is expressed through both and not by one alone.[43]

Levinas pursues the discussion between R. Yohanan and Samuel, concerning the issue of merit (*zekhut*). In a sense, he turns here to the issue we already discussed, about the role of human action in bringing about the messianic era. Is the messianic coming something that man earns, or is it an act of unconditional divine grace? R. Yohanan takes it to be an outcome of human merit: "the political problem is resolved at the same time as the social problem, and their joint solution lies in the hands of man, since it depends on one's moral power."[44] As we have seen, this is a central issue for the Jewish conception of the messianic era, the role of human conduct in the advent of the Messiah. The issue is whether human conduct is a necessary condition for the messianic coming. Samuel, on the other hand, differs. For him, there is something other than the moral individual, something that must be suppressed or removed before the messianic era can begin. This is a radical break, as Levinas reads it. That is, the rule of alien powers, which is naturally taken to mean that Jews will live under foreign sovereignty, must come to an end, and this, Levinas presumes, is not something that the Jews themselves can accomplish. Moreover, if the Jew stands for all humankind, then the removal of powers alien to man must require something other than human moral conduct, an external agency, a "break" that is expressed by the figure of the Messiah.[45] The Talmud is not clear about the outside agency that will accomplish this removal; it might be God or a purely political act, an event within the political order. What is clear is that it is not itself a moral action with human agency. Hence, Levinas draws the contrast between R. Yohanan and Samuel this way: the former ascribes everything to human freedom and moral action; the latter admits a kind of political violence that stands between the two, between human freedom and the good. Once again, even though Levinas reads the Talmud as hovering between one view and the other, it seems clear that it is Samuel's view that is closer to Levinas's understanding of the social and ethical character of the human condition. For Levinas surely takes it to be the case that there is a kind of violence that separates human freedom and the accomplishment of the good.

Levinas's ethical messianism, as it is expressed in these commentaries on Talmudic texts, does not seem to be limited to Judaism and to Jews. It appears to be a universal view that applies to all history, all politics, and all human conduct. The popular views about Jewish messianism, however, as we have seen, take the Messiah to be a Davidic monarch who will reestablish a Jewish state and rule over it. Is the messianic idea in Judaism particularist or universalist or in some way both?

MESSIANISM: UNIVERSAL OR PARTICULAR?

Levinas addresses this issue in his comments on BT Sanhedrin 98b–99a. He begins by commenting on a passage from 98b: R. Giddal says in Rab's name that in the days of the Messiah the Jews will eat their fill, to which R. Joseph responds that this is obvious; should we think that just anyone will enjoy the rewards of the messianic era? If not Israel, then who? R. Joseph formulates his objection by referring to "Hilek and Bilek," which some commentators take to mean "any Tom, Dick, or Harry" or the first people who might come along. In this case, the phrase would mean anyone who happened to be alive when the Messiah comes; R. Joseph's point is that one must be worthy of the messianic rewards and hence obviously they would be restricted to Israel. In this respect, Levinas says, the messianic era is unlike the end of history, which will arrive for anyone alive at the time.

But according to another commentator, Hilek and Bilek refer to the judges of Sodom, and hence R. Joseph's objection would be that of course the messianic era comes for Israel; do you think it comes for the judges of Sodom? But, as Levinas explains, Sodom does not refer exclusively to a single place, the biblical city; rather it refers to a condition that is present everywhere, and hence the judges of Sodom are a universal presence— they act "under the sign of universality." They are "people who are still familiar with political life and the State; and according to the theoreticians of the end of History, people who act under the sign of universality act just for their era."[46] Hence, R. Joseph's point is that "the simple fact of acting under the sign of universality does not justify entry into the messianic era, and that the messianic era does not correspond solely to the universality entailed in a Law or a human Ideal. It also has a content."

Let me translate Levinas's somewhat enigmatic comments into another idiom. I believe that Levinas appreciates how the ethical responsibility that characterizes all human social existence occurs in a world of institutions and politics. But historically speaking, there is and has been a tendency for such institutions and for political life to be corrupt and oppressive, to be dominated by injustice and evil. Here Levinas makes this point by commenting that "evil can assume universal forms and become a State."[47] Moreover, such a state and its institutions threaten to overwhelm our lives, if it were not for the fact of human responsibility, the human disposition to morality and justice. The figure of the Messiah indicates the expectation and the hope that the universality of the political and the state will not triumph over humanity and justice. The content that Levinas refers to in the passage quoted above is the ethical content of human existence; the universality enshrined in the state and in law will not deserve the messianic coming. This is R. Joseph's point: to reserve the messianic era for Israel and to exclude politics and law are to endorse the primacy of the ethical for human existence and for history.

But, Levinas continues, if the messianic era concerns Israel, why say so? Is it not obvious? Why does R. Giddal bother to make such a claim? This is the point of the text that follows, which says that R. Giddal is speaking in opposition to R. Hillel, "who maintained that there will be no Messiah for Israel, since they have already enjoyed him during the reign of Hezekiah."[48] R. Hillel, cited only here in the Talmud, says this one thing, "no Messiah for Israel" (*ein Mashiah le-Yisrael*). But if Israel has already enjoyed the rewards of the Messiah in the days of Hezekiah, centuries before, what is left for her? Does R. Hillel mean that for Israel the Messiah has come, but for the other peoples the Messiah is still yet to come? Is the fact that there is no Messiah for Israel meant to be to Israel's credit, or is it in some way a caution or reprimand?

R. Hillel's thesis is rejected, Levinas points out, here by R. Giddal and later at BT Sanhedrin 99a, where it is repeated by R. Joseph, who responds, "May God forgive him [for saying this]." This certainly suggests a criticism of R. Hillel's thesis, a negative view of it. But, as Levinas points out, the Talmud would only report it if there was something positive to be said about it. "With one voice the commentators let R. Hillel know that if for Israel the Messiah has already come, this is because Israel is waiting to be delivered by God Himself. . . . R. Hillel's opinion is suspicious of the messianic idea or redemption through the Messiah: Israel awaits higher aspiration than that of being saved by a Messiah."[49] That is, Israel's redemption involves no mediation; it is the outcome of God's acts directly. Unlike Christianity, for example, Judaism foresees divine redemption without a Messiah; God's gift is Himself and not His son.

But Levinas does not immediately comment on this rejection of a mediator. Rather he first provides another interpretation of the idea that Israel surpasses the idea of messianism. This interpretation is based on a point made by Vladimir Jankélévitch, "that if the moral order is incessantly improving, this is because it is always on the move and never provides an outcome. . . . The notion of morality having an outcome is as absurd as the immobilization of time which it assumes." Levinas takes this point to mean that "deliverance by God coincides with the sovereignty of a living morality that is open to infinite progress."[50] In other words, Levinas suggests that the idea of the Messiah is tantamount to the idea that the moral project will come to an end; it can be completed or perfected. There will be a time when injustice will be eradicated and justice achieved. But this idea is antithetical to the very idea of morality: this is how Levinas understands Jankélévitch's point. R. Hillel's claim that there is no Messiah for Israel means that Israel is committed to morality as an infinite quest, an idea that we associate with Hermann Cohen, among others.[51]

Moreover, Levinas points out that he—following Chouchani, his Talmudic teacher and mentor—does not take Israel in a nationalistic or parochial way; "this does not concern only the historical Israel." Rather Israel stands for an "open elite," as he calls it, which is defined here as having the dignity of being delivered by God alone.[52] Hence, Israel stands for a particularity and indeed a Jewish particularity, but it is one that harbors universality.

Levinas adds, however, a second interpretation of R. Hillel's claim, and his interpretation is extremely important and does involve a return to the issue of mediation. R. Hillel, he says, occurs only once in the Talmud, and this thesis of his only once. But it carries great weight, for it expresses an old tradition within Judaism. That tradition concerns the character of the Messiah and the messianic deliverance. The Messiah is a man or a king. If he is a king, however, then the messianic deliverance is political and does not extend to individuals. Hence, "salvation by the king, even if he is the Messiah, is not yet the supreme salvation open to the human being. Messianism is political, and its completion belongs to Israel's past—that is the force of R. Hillel's position."[53] What Levinas is here saying, I believe, is that insofar as the coming of the Messiah is conceived as the return of the Davidic monarchy or of a political solution to human injustice, it does not yet touch the ultimate human salvation. Hence, such a political completion to the historical process lies, as it were, and with respect to the real aspiration of the individual, in the past. Levinas associates this evaluation of the political as qualified and of limited significance with the tension between the political and the religious that we find in the book of Samuel and in Samuel's resistance to the people's political aspirations. Samuel opposes replacing divine kingship with that of a human king, precisely because such a political move would replace the individual's direct association with his moral aspirations with a mediated variety, in which salvation is got by another, the human king. What Samuel advocates is the retention of divine kingship and "a direct link between man and God devoid of any political mediation." Moreover, this conception of an unmediated deliverance or redemption, opposed to the redemption of "limited duration" that is political, resists a "doctrine of the end of History which dominates individual destiny." What this means, then, is that redemption or salvation is not something that comes at the end of history; rather "it remains *at every moment* possible."[54]

Levinas's point is that Judaism's conception of the messianic era is not that of a period of time at the end of history; nor is it of a political solution to historical injustice or social problems. Rather the messianic realization can occur at any moment. Messianism is the accomplishment of each individual and occurs through her choices and actions and not through the mediation of politics and institutions. It is, in short, the possibility of morality at each and every moment. Messianism in this form, then, is a "fundamental possibility of Judaism," and even though the Bible portrays God as directing Samuel to yield to the people's pleas for an earthly king, it is the form of existence reflected in R. Hillel's thesis that is the real Jewish ideal. In this sense, there is something deeply true about the tradition that stretches from Samuel to R. Hillel and beyond. It is the truth of a kind of moral messianism of the moment, achieved by individuals on any occasion when they act in behalf of others and the claims of kindness and justice.[55]

One point of this critique of politics and the concept of a narrative history is that "messianism does not exhaust the meaning of human history for all the wise men of Israel."[56] There is more to human history than a satisfactory goal or end. At Sanhedrin 98b, the Talmud lists three views about what makes history valuable. Rab said that the world was created for David's sake; Samuel said, for Moses's sake; and R. Yohanan said, for the sake of the Messiah. Rashi explains: for David's sake means for the merit of David, who would in the future sing songs and psalms; for Moses's sake means for the sake of Moses, who would in the future receive the Torah at Sinai. That is, as Levinas points out, the Messiah is not King David, who is the author of psalms, where poetry and prayer mingle with one another, and hence in whose work art is brought into the world. With Moses, it is the Torah, the ground of morality, that is brought into the world. But unlike both, R. Yohanan takes the world and history to be meaningful only in virtue of history's end, the messianic era. That is, "the Messiah is still necessary to the world where there is already prayer and Torah," adoration and poetry and morality.[57] But, Levinas comments, while some believe this, not all do. And, we might argue, Levinas is one of those who do not.

Messianism, then, is not a parochial hope for the recovery of a Davidic state; it is a universal hope for all ages and all peoples. This is the theme of Levinas's final comments, on BT Sanhedrin 98b and what follows.[58] To begin with, the Talmud recommends a touch of realism; the preceding text continues with R. Simlai's quotation of Amos 5:18, which seems to suggest that "the day of the Lord" will be one of darkness and not light. At first glance, Levinas notes, Amos appears to be speaking to those who might seem to be innocent and yet to aspire for the day of the Lord. Amos suggests that they would be the first to be "annoyed by the establishment of justice on earth." That is, the day of the Lord—the messianic era—will appear to these people to be darkness; "the messianic dream, and even the simple dream of justice that so delights human foolishness, promise[s] a painful awakening."[59] "Men are not only the victims of injustice; they are also the perpetrators." People may be inclined to view justice as if in a dream; they fail to appreciate the "stark severity entailed by justice and judgment";[60] they are simply too naïve about who they are and what will be their plight.

But this reading of Amos 5:18 is too simple; the Talmud gives it a deeper meaning. Levinas points out that the darkness to which Amos refers calls attention to "the existence of souls incapable of receiving the light and ill-suited to salvation." R. Simlai compares the reactions of a cock and a bat to the coming dawn; the cock tells the bat that he looks forward to the light because he has sight, but the light offers no benefit to the bat, who is incapable of vision. As Levinas interprets the analogy, there is no such thing as an objective waiting for the Messiah. From a vantage point within the darkness of the night, some will look forward to the dawn, and others will not or should not; they lack the aptitude to appreciate the light and to benefit from it. Levinas calls this aptitude "the mark of intelligence." It is not given with the mere capacity to see in the light but requires what he calls a "nose" for light, a keenness of anticipation, an appreciation of what the benefits will be. This intelligence, he interprets, "knows the meaning of History before the event, and does not simply divine it after it has happened."[61] Or, to put it in terms of Levinas's philosophical anthropology, only some will appreciate the ethical character of all human existence and hence appreciate what salvation or messianism means; to them, totality without infinity is barren, a distortion, and oppressive. Hence, in R. Simlai's imagery,

> the bat represents one who does not see the light. . . . Darkness weighs upon it, unhappy it lies in darkness. But the light, alas, says nothing to it. This is the very image of damnation, provided that damnation is not added to evil as an external sanction, imposed by violence; provided that damnation is more deeply tragic than violence. The bat suffers from darkness, but the light will give it nothing.
> A cruel messianism. The Messiah is refused to those who are no longer capable of enlightenment, even if darkness weighs upon them.[62]

The Talmud, that is, and R. Simlai in particular, teaches us that there are those for whom the very notion of messianism, of redemption or salvation or deliverance, is meaningless. It offers nothing. Their souls are utterly blind to the gifts of light; they are dark souls, damned and evil souls, intrinsically. They are, in terms that Hannah Arendt used in *The Origins of Totalitarianism* and that Emil Fackenheim would later use as well, radically evil.

But the passage from Amos and R. Simlai's reading of it, then, seem to make messianism exclusive to those who are attuned to its benefits. As Levinas says, there is no objective messianism; only those attuned to its benefits genuinely wait for it. I said, however, that Levinas takes it to be universal; after all, if we are all potential messianic agents, surely it is universal in a sense. But, as we now see, as the text goes on, its parochialism or exclusivity seems to persist as well. Or does it? Levinas takes on just this issue.

R. Simlai's point is that the "truth is given only to the person who is ready inside"; the text now presents a teaching that suggests that the "truth is not universal in the logical sense of the term." This is what Levinas says is the point of a conversation recorded between R. Abbahu and a *min* (a heretic). The latter asks, "When will the Messiah come?" And

R. Abbahu answers, "When darkness covers those people who are with you."[63] A *min* is a heretic, an apostate; one can take his question to be hostile. Indeed, if he is a Christian, then he might very well be chiding R. Abbahu for the Jewish failure to appreciate a messiah who has already come. Or, as Levinas puts it, the question might be ironic: "Are you sure the Messiah has not already come?" If this is so, however, R. Abbahu's response is merciless, as Levinas claims. What it means is to exclude the heretic and his colleagues completely from the messianic deliverance. "When darkness covers those people who are with you" means "For you and your associates, the true Messiah will never come." Alternatively, it means that the truth of the messianic coming is not universal; it excludes some people completely.[64]

The *min* exclaims, "You have condemned me," to which R. Abbahu responds by quoting Isaiah 60:2: "For, behold, the darkness shall cover the earth, and gross darkness the people: but the Lord shall shine upon thee, and His glory shall be seen upon thee." R. Abbahu takes this citation to be sufficient as a response to the heretic's shock; nor, Levinas says, is Isaiah 60:2 any less universalistic than Amos 5:18, as it has been read, until one reads the verse that follows, Isaiah 60:3: "And nations shall come to your light, and kings to the brightness of your rising." To be sure, although the first verse seems to affirm divine deliverance for Israel, even when darkness covers the earth, the next verse extends that deliverance to the nations and their rulers. Moreover, as Levinas suggests, R. Abbahu has taken the darkness to be a condition of God's salvation—"the darkness is needed to create the light."[65] This is not a matter of the Jews celebrating their particular divine redemption, "their privileged triumph in the midst of universal desolation," for the next verse clearly includes "the whole of humanity" in what Levinas calls "political evolution." However, in an obscure conclusion to this set of reflections, Levinas takes this teaching of R. Abbahu, "the universality of the messianic coming," to be distinct from the "universality that might be called catholic, which is sought by political life and formulated by Aristotle."[66]

We have seen Levinas distinguish genuine messianism, which can occur at any moment through the agency of any one of us who is attentive to his or her responsibilities to others to alleviate suffering and attend to the other's needs, and a flawed conception of messianism as an end to the historical narrative, a messianism that is anchored in divine agency and is political. When Levinas here, interpreting R. Abbahu's conversation with the heretic, distinguishes between the universality of messianism and the catholicity of political life, is he drawing a somewhat similar contrast? Fortunately, Levinas stops to explain himself, to clarify what this political and historical march to universality means, and to explain what it means to say that when darkness covers the earth, the Messiah comes. "What is in fact the march towards universality of a political order?" He answers, "It consists in confronting multiple beliefs—a multiplicity of coherent discourses—and finding one coherent discourse that embraces them all, which is precisely the universal order. A coherent discourse is already open to the universal when the person holding it, who up until now has remained enclosed within his individual circumstances—though his discourse may have been coherent—concerns himself with the inner coherence of discourses other than his own, and so surpasses his own individual state."[67]

This situation or condition is both a political condition and the origin of philosophy. A political order or a person who is a member of such an order and who is committed to a particular political discourse or ideology is in such a situation when he turns to other discourses or ideologies and asks what his own discourse and these others share and how they differ and when he asks whether there is a discourse that is coherent internally and also comprehends both his own and others within a grander, embracing order. Levinas's vision is a very Hegelian one, in which the ultimate truth of reason and the ultimate unity of all into a world state at the end of history form a unity, the self-understanding of Spirit and its historical and political realization. On such a view, politics and philosophy are one.

According to this image, all peoples and nations are ultimately incorporated into a whole, a world state that is the dialectical outcome of historical, political development. But this Hegelian image can be contrasted with another. Here political life is "an infernal cycle of violence and derision." Here political life employs means for achieving its goals that unavoidably corrupt those very goals. Here the very grandeur of the political has lost its meaning, and hence that special people who has lived apart is not found among peoples with this political life; rather it is a "people capable of diaspora, capable of remaining outside, alone and abandoned." In this image, then, "you have a totally different vision of universality, one no longer subordinated to confrontation."[68] Levinas of course is referring in this passage to the Jewish people and to its non-political life, its contrastive, critical, and primordially ethical character. In view of this image, moreover, we can interpret the phrase "the darkness covers all your people" not to mean when heretics have vanished from the earth but rather to refer to a time "when silence falls on all those teachings that call [them] to fallacious confrontations, when all the prestige of exteriority fades and is as though it never existed."[69] The light that shines, when this darkness is lifted, is the truth of the teaching of responsibility, of the self's obligations to others to serve their needs and reduce their suffering. The realization for everyone of this teaching about human existence and its ethical character is the "real universality, which is non-catholic" and which consists in "serving the universe" and is called "messianism."[70]

Levinas asks if this teaching of the true or real universality of messianism is a dangerous conception. Is there a risk here of Judaism claiming for its own teaching a privileged universality? Is this a case of one conception of history dominating all others? Or does Judaism, on the other hand, "glimpse the dangers of the politicization of truth and morality?"[71] The one, the Hegelian conception, risks engulfing the totality of individuals and peoples within one dominant whole; the other does not, for it does not extend totality into a dominating whole but acknowledges difference through universal and unbounded responsibility. "The dangers of the politicization of truth and morality" are the dangers of Spinoza, Hegel, and their political legacy; Judaism and its teachings expose these dangers, which are the risks of permanent conflict and violence, seeking after power and accomplishing domination and oppression. It also counters such a conception of universality with an alternative, which aims at taking responsibility for the needs of others and responding to the claims of others that constitute our very selfhood.[72] Messianism, conceived in these terms, is universal, but it is not a bad universality.

RECOVERING THE MESSIANIC IDEA TODAY

I have tried to show how Levinas, through his reading of some Talmudic texts primarily from Tractate Sanhedrin, articulates his revisionary humanistic account of messianism. But even in this form, is messianism as an ethical and political commitment believable? Can Jews today—can anyone today—still affirm a messianic hope and take on a messianic task?

Finally, in the concluding pages of his commentary, Levinas asks if a post-Emancipation Judaism can still believe in messianism. His answer is that Zionism and the State of Israel show that it can; they constitute the heart of a Judaism that is the universal particularism that is required of such a post-Emancipation Judaism that is skeptical about the meaning of history. These are important reflections and yet obscure ones.

To believe in messianism, Levinas says, is to believe that "History has no meaning, that no reason makes itself manifest therein," that is, history in and of itself. Ever since the Enlightenment of the eighteenth century, it has been thought that reason realizes itself in history and hence that history is intrinsically rational. Hegel is the culmination of such a rationalist philosophy of history; for Hegel, politics and the state are the engines of history and its development to the ideal of self-realized freedom. Messianism, on the other hand, involves the belief that history is a chaos of "violence and crime" without respite and that what salvation or deliverance there will be must come to history from "outside," as a miracle, as a divine gift. Judaism in the rabbinic period and the Middle Ages held such a belief. But with the Enlightenment and then the Emancipation of the Jewish people, it would be strange to find Jews inclined to denigrate the political order in this way, "by refusing to grant political life a significance and a source of truth") and by denying any meaning to history. Rather, as Levinas notes, the modern Jew would be more inclined to dispense with messianism if he knew it required such presuppositions. He would be inclined, that is, to "embrace the accusation made by the enemies of Judaism against the apparent egoism or utopianism of Israel's messianic thought."[73] The argument is that Emancipation has enabled the modern Jew to play a serious political role in the world and that this benefit would have led the modern Jew to reject messianism rather than to compromise this gain.

Why believe this? Because, Levinas argues, Emancipation has meant more than changes of a social and legal kind; it has meant as well an "opening on to the political forms of . . . humanity," and in this regard,

it has "enabled [Judaism] to take history seriously."[74] Levinas's point
is that Emancipation has made it possible for the Jewish people and for
Judaism to take seriously politics as the arena for rational thought and
practical rationality, to play political roles, to contribute to political gov-
ernance, and hence to appreciate that history as the arena for political
conduct and development is meaningful. For this reason, "messianism in
the strong sense of the term [as the belief that all history is violence and
suffering and only a divine agent could redeem history from its plight]
has been compromised in the Jewish consciousness since Emancipation,
ever since the Jews participated in world history."[75] In other words, messianism involves the belief that history is ultimately "absurd," and insofar
as the "prophetic vision of truth" is messianic, any bourgeois belief in
"prophetic messianism" is completely hypocritical, Levinas says.

One might think, therefore, that Levinas in the end concludes that
messianism is no longer possible for the modern Jew. But this is not so.
His final remarks show exactly how the modern Jew can respect the
political and nonetheless cling to a messianic sensibility, how he or she
can retain utter particularity and yet also maintain universalism. "This
universalist particularism (which is not Hegel's concrete universal) can
be found in the aspirations of Zionism." That is, in the State of Israel we
have a unique synthesis of Judaism's historical particularity with its universalist aspirations, a unity of the political and the ethical, or rather, as
Levinas puts it, it is in this synthesis that one finds the "importance of the
Israeli solution" for the history of Israel.[76] This is what Zionism means.
More specifically, it is via the Jewish state that the Jew in a particularly
distinctive way faces the dangers of history within history. For years,
these dangers were the dangers of being persecuted—which means for
Levinas the dangers of being ethically responsible for others while at
the same time suffering from the persecution of others. This dual status—ethical and yet suffering—is now represented for the modern Jew
by the State of Israel.

Moreover, what the State of Israel is to Judaism overall, "vanguard
groupings" within the state are to the state itself. But what are these
vanguard groupings? Levinas suggests, in these final remarks, that from
his perspective they are the members of "remote frontier kibbutzim,"
people who are "indifferent to the seething world whose human values

they none the less serve," and whose "indifference [is displayed] in their daily lives, lives composed of work and risks."[77] Is it plausible, then, to assign this vanguard status or to locate this paradigm status to Labor Zionists, socialists, and communitarian workers? If so, then for Levinas these workers are not only representative of a genuine modern Judaism; they are also messianic agents, who bring universal justice to Jewish life as an expression of the truth that can rectify the agony of history and the suffering of humankind. In them, the truth of universal justice is realized. The State of Israel is a Jewish state insofar as it is the domain of a just society, and Judaism is a worthy way of life insofar as it advocates and practices the same justice that Israel and its laborers seek to achieve within the Israeli state and the Israeli society.[78]

Levinas here provides us with an intriguing account of how the messianic idea in Judaism can be used to link Jewish belief and the State of Israel. Many treat the return to the Land of Israel and political hegemony over that land as features of a conception of history in which that return and that hegemony are linked to the coming of a Messiah of the House of David, sent by God. Levinas has already argued that the notion of a messianic era is tied to Jewish views about history, politics, and redemption and that it is also to be understood as a *figure* for acts of human kindness, generosity, and justice. Levinas demythologizes the conception of a Messiah, takes it to be universal, and revises its link to politics and history. It is in the light of these views that we should understand his final comments about Zionism, the State of Israel, and messianism. For Levinas, there is a sense in which Zionism and the State of Israel are messianic, but it is not because the ruler of the state is destined to be a Davidic monarch, nor is it because politics of a normal kind has come to an end. Rather Zionism is about how politics can be conducted in an ethical, humane way and hence how an ethical society can be realized, if not everywhere, at least at some moments and in some places, wherever justice is realized in the relationships between persons, whoever they are.

Words like "redemption" and "messianism" recur in Levinas's works, philosophical ones as well as ones on Jewish experience and Judaism. Like other European intellectuals of the twentieth century—including the likes of Ernst Bloch, Georg Lukacs, Walter Benjamin, and Jacques Derrida—Levinas was deeply interested in history, politics, and ethics, where all three are conceived in very broad and embracing terms. Hence, words like "redemption" and "messianism" introduced into this domain the question whether human experience was historical in a narrative sense, whether history was governed by a grand plot and by ultimate aims or goals; it also registered a worry about human capabilities, whether social and political problems could be solved by human endeavor or not. Furthermore, in the spirit of Kant and of many others too, the vocabulary of messianism raises the question whether ethics and morality are developmental or progressive and if so, how ethical or moral progress might be related to political and social institutions, programs, and policies. Insofar as Levinas's philosophical thought exposes the ethical character of all human existence, one is naturally led to wonder what relation the ethical has to everyday conduct, to politics, and hence to history. Thinking about redemption and messianism, then, is in part thinking about such matters.

A CRITIQUE AND A RESPONSE

Martin Kavka has objected to this reading of messianism in Levinas's thinking.[79] According to Kavka, there is an "apocalyptic" or "catastrophic" element in Levinas's conception of the messianic that the reading I have given ignores or avoids. He accepts my interpretation as a reading of the early Levinas, but he contends that in the writings of the late 1960s and then in *Otherwise Than Being* and thereafter, Levinas abandons the terminology of messianism and replaces it with the terminology of skepticism. That change corresponds to the more political and pragmatic character of Levinas's later thinking about ethics and politics. Kavka's criticism is very germane to the overall themes of the present book; considering it will help to clarify the point to which we have come.

On my reading, the primary agency of the messianic is human, and it involves acting in ways that are attentive and responsive to the needs and well-being of others, to their particularity as others for whom and to whom I am responsible. In some cases, these will be discrete acts of acceptance and care; in other cases, however, they will be acts of a more social and political nature, responses to public proposals and policies, public critiques of laws and practices, and so forth. That is, in addition to episodic acts of concern for others, we engage in acts of ethical critique of social and political programs and positions. On such a view of messianism, history is not treated as linear, as a closed narrative with an articulated sense of its ultimate goal. Rather history is the worldly setting for our individual and collectives lives, in which we are continually engaged with others and in which each of us, individually and communally, seek to live justly and humanely, to the degree that we can. In a sense, the messianic in Levinas, as I have understood him, is episodic and discrete, but in another sense, messianic actions can be part of social and political discussion. They can be aimed at influencing and modifying institutional patterns and structures in order to make them more responsive to others and especially to those who are disadvantaged and in need, the destitute, homeless, and hungry, minorities and the unprotected, the uncared for.

On Kavka's reading of my interpretation, the crucial features are the following. To Kavka, as I have read him, Levinas neutralizes the messianic by humanizing it and by demythologizing the apocalyptic elements. For Kavka, one of the great virtues of Gershom Scholem's classic account of the messianic idea in Judaism is that it reminds us of this apocalyptic or catastrophic dimension of much of the messianic tradition in Judaism. On such a reading, there is a radical break or rupture between the historical, political lives we live and the days of the Messiah. But there are those who deny such a discontinuity; the classic case is Maimonides. And Kavka takes my reading to argue the same for Levinas. But, he claims, this demythologized and neutralized messianism is not Levinas's. For him, in the 1960s, Levinas was not altogether clear about how the messianic era is related to ethical action. In the 1970s and 1980s, however, he gave up talking about messianism and took up a vocabulary of skepticism, which he associated with the prophetic. This skepticism, in one way, expressed itself as a critique of conventional social and political institutions and programs and indeed as anarchist. Indeed, it expressed itself as a critique of cultural ideologies, without any commitment to redemption, but with the hope of opening up new conversations about how one ought to live. In short, Levinas gave up any messianism of the moment for a messianism that can be institutionalized but that is always open to change and revision. It has no determinate content, but it is an allegiance to such modification and to the unpredictable. In this way, messianism is not cheapened by becoming historical; it does not become prosaic by neutralizing the catastrophic and disruptive dimension. It is about keeping such moments alive and by encouraging a resistance to accepting standard categories and norms in favor of a constant search for the novel and the distinctive.

Kavka's objections to my interpretation of Levinas's conception of the messianic raise a number of serious questions. To clarify, as I read him, Levinas does humanize and demythologize the tradition idea of a personal Messiah, anointed and sent by God, to reestablish the Davidic monarchy, to resolve the social and historical crisis facing humankind, and to establish an ideal political regime. But this reinterpretation of the traditional figure of the Messiah is not to neutralize it, certainly not in Scholem's sense of that expression. To Scholem, neutralization involves shifting from the arena of history and politics to the personal, psychological arena and to intellectualize or spiritualize the notion of redemption or salvation. Levinas clearly does not appropriate the concept of messianism in this sense. Rather for him messianism refers to the decisions and actions of each of us as individual agents, when we act out of a sense of our responsibilities and obligations to acknowledge, accept, and care for others. I think that Kavka and I can agree about this.

Furthermore, even in his earlier thinking, of the late 1950s and 1960s, Levinas realized that such actions on our parts, which should be as responsive as possible to the ethical demands placed upon us by our relations with others, would always be political in one sense or another. And in some cases, such actions would occur in the contexts of political crisis and debate, when matters of law, policies, and public programs are at issue. To Levinas, all actions that are responsive to our obligations to protect and care for others are messianic; some take the form of public critique of platforms and ideologies and of current institutions and norms. In the 1970s and '80s, Levinas does not abandon the vocabulary of messianism. In several texts and interviews, he continues to use this expression. He does come to focus on its prophetic dimension and hence on its role as a form of ethical critique. But this critique is not without content, without commitments to an ideal. It is always about paying due attention to the needs and concerns of individuals and about reshaping institutions and reformulating laws and policies that will serve such needs, that will be grounded in the ideals of care, protection, generosity, love, and charity. As Kavka points out, such aspiration urges us never to allow institutions and practices to calcify, to become rigid, obstacles to revision or inflexible. But Levinas does not idealize revisability or unpredictability for its own sake, nor does he emphasize or privilege change just because it opposes existing categories or practices. We may learn from the past and recover lessons from it; indeed, we ought to, as long as what we recover encourages us to advance the claim of our interpersonal responsibilities. Messianism is not simply a figure for open interpretability; it is a figure for the hopes invested in each of us as moral and political agents.

Many commentators mistake Levinas's treatment of totality, and while I would not want to ascribe any confusion to Kavka, his reading of Levinas's conception of messianism as disruptive is susceptible to the error of treating his account of the face-to-face and infinite responsibility as unconditionally opposed to ideologies and institutions. I have argued that Levinas takes responsibility as the ethical basis of human existence, tied to our interpersonal relations, and our everyday lives, social and political, are interconnected. Each limits the other. Messianism expresses especially how the primacy of responsibility ought to limit, shape, and orient our social and political lives. This is as true for the early Levinas as it is for the later, and while it does invoke constant and ongoing attentiveness and critique, it does not imply anarchism or the privileging of unpredictability and flexibility for its own sake.

It is helpful, in conclusion, to place the idea of messianism in a different context or framework than that of the disruptive and the discontinuous, which is what Kavka takes from Scholem and what drives his reading of Levinas. Here I would like to appropriate a distinction that is introduced by David Schmidtz in order to frame his discussion of individual responsibility and the welfare state.[80] Schmidtz's essay, in his debate with Robert Goodin, seeks to explore what role individual responsibility does and should play in providing for their welfare. How much is their own responsibility, and how much, in particular, is the gov-

ETHICS, POLITICS, AND ZIONISM

ernment's responsibility? In discussing these matters Schmidtz points out that the crucial distinction is between what he calls internalized and externalized responsibility. "Responsibility," he says, "is externalized when people do not take responsibility: for messes they cause, for messes in which they find themselves. . . . We can speak of responsibility being externalized whether the messes result from mistake, misfortune, or . . . from business as usual. In contrast, responsibility is internalized when agents take responsibility: for their welfare, for their futures, for the consequences of their actions."[81] From the point of view of this distinction, what might we say about the traditional idea of messianism in Judaism? It is, we might say, the ultimate externalization of responsibility. To believe that no matter how good or bad history gets and in the wake of the greatest conflicts and worst catastrophes, all one's hope ought to be invested in a divine, miraculous intervention aimed at rectifying all that is wrong in history—this is an extreme form of externalizing responsibility for one's welfare, future, and actions. In the end, only God can save us, so to speak. It is this conception of moral and political responsibility that Levinas opposes. In one sense, then, what he seeks to argue is that when properly understood, the idea of messianism is not this idea of absolute externalization of responsibility. Rather it is an idea of the internalization of responsibility; our welfare, future, and so forth are up to us.

However, in another sense, messianism appreciates how external responsibility is. That is, philosophers like Schmidtz and Goodin are interested in our taking responsibility for ourselves, as long as and to the degree to which we are capable. Levinas, on the other hand, is not interested primarily in responsibility as taking upon oneself one's own actions and well-being. For him the human situation is constituted by infinite interpersonal dependency relations. As the beings we are, we are always dependent upon the attention, concern, and help of others, and this means that in social and political situations, we need the assistance of institutions and political agencies, laws, regulations, and programs. We cannot do without them. Moreover, it is the responsibility of each of us to do what we can and should to assist others, to take responsibility for them. In this sense, where responsibility is responsibility for others, messianism stands for all the externalization that is reasonable and beneficial; what it seeks to avoid is internalization that becomes abandonment or moral failure to protect and care for others.

In short, Levinas's idea of messianism is one that seeks to arrive at an understanding of responsibility, both accepting it and taking it upon oneself, that is neither too external nor too internal. And the nemesis, from a Jewish point of view, is a mythologized conception of messianism that is neither human enough nor humane enough. Levinas's messianism performs these tasks by being both ethical and political, both personal and political, and both individual and collective.

TEN

LEVINAS'S NOTORIOUS
INTERVIEW

There may be no more controversial comments associated with Emmanuel Levinas than his remarks during a radio interview, broadcast
on Radio Communauté on September 28, 1982, in the wake of the massacres in the Sabra and Shatila refugee camps in Lebanon near Beirut.
The interview was conducted by Shlomo Malka, and the interviewees
were Levinas and Alain Finkielkraut. A transcript was published in *Les
Nouveaux Cahiers*, but its notoriety, certainly for English-speaking audiences, was accelerated by the publication of an English translation,
included by Seán Hand in his *The Levinas Reader*, published by Basil
Blackwell in 1989.[1] Introducing the transcript, Hand explains the circumstances that led the Israeli Defense Forces to occupy West Beirut in
mid-September of 1982 and the events that followed:

> While the move into West Beirut was supposedly made in order to protect the
> Muslims from the revenge of the Phalangists [after the September 14 bombing
> in party headquarters in East Beirut that killed twenty six, including Lebanon's
> recently elected president, Bashir Gemayel, a Maronite,], the Israeli Defense
> Forces (IDF) actually introduced Phalangists into the Palestinian camps with
> the mission of clearing out suspected *fedayeem*, or Arab infiltrators, who carried
> out hit-and-run raids inside Israel. The Christian soldiers massacred several
> hundred people in Sabra and Chatila camps over a period of nearly two days
> with no intervention on the part of the IDF. At first [prime minister Menachem]
> Begin refused to set up a judicial inquiry, commenting in the *New York Times* on
> 26 September that "*Goyim* kill *goyim*, and they immediately come to hang the
> Jews."[2]

The massacre had occurred in four days, from September 15 to 18, and had
resulted in the slaughter of Palestinian and Lebanese men, women, and

children, numbering anywhere from eight hundred to several thousand.[3] Ariel Sharon and the Israeli military had asked the Christian militiamen to clear out PLO terrorists and Palestinian guerillas from the camps, although there was a long-standing hatred between the Phalangist Christians and the Muslim occupants of the camps. By Friday, September 17, it was known by Israeli military officials that a slaughter was under way, but the Phalangists were permitted to remain until Saturday morning and the massacre continued. No distinction was made between guerilla fighters, women, children, and the elderly.

In response to the efforts of Menachem Begin to dismiss charges of Israeli complicity in the massacres, a number of peace movements organized a massive rally in Tel Aviv on September 25. It was estimated that 350,000 people gathered in the plaza before City Hall in Tel Aviv. The rally was reported to have been the largest in Israeli history, and in the course of the many speeches given, there were calls for the establishment of a board of inquiry into responsibility for the events and numerous cries for Begin and Sharon to resign.[4] By September 28 Begin had in fact appointed a board of inquiry under the leadership of the chief justice of the Supreme Court, Yitzhak Kahan. Also, Thomas Friedman had on September 25 published in the *New York Times* a long and detailed article on the details of the four-day massacre, and on that same day reports of the Tel Aviv rally were widely circulated.

This was the situation when Malka, Finkielkraut, and Levinas met for their radio interview. It was less than two weeks after the massacres had occurred. Begin's resistance and the internal criticisms of him and his government in Israel were known, and reports were widespread of the massive rally in Tel Aviv. The board of inquiry was appointed that very day.[5]

In this chapter I will look carefully at the interview in order to try to understand what Levinas says and what it means, both in this historical context and also in the context of his philosophical views about ethics and the political. To accomplish this task, I will treat the interview as having five stages. I will refer to them in terms of these stages or steps: innocence and responsibility (EP, 290–92); political necessity and ethics (292–94); who is the other? (294); Israel and messianic mystification (294–95); and the truth of Israel and the soul of Judaism (295–97). First,

I will read and offer an interpretation of each stage.[6] In so doing, I will step back and ask some questions about the rhetorical character of the whole interview, about what Levinas says and does not say, and about how he might have chosen to present himself and how a listener might well have understood him as a result of the interview.

INNOCENCE AND RESPONSIBILITY

Malka begins by referring to a talk that Finkielkraut had recently given at a memorial (presumably for the victims of the massacres) in which he had introduced the expression "the temptation of innocence." Malka quotes what he describes as the "last main point of the talk": "We are split between a feeling of innocence and a feeling of responsibility, both of which are anchored in our traditions and our ideals. I do not know yet which of the two, innocence or responsibility, we will choose as Jews. But I believe that our decision will determine the meaning that we give to the ordeal of genocide" (EP, 290). With this challenge in hand, Malka turns to Levinas and asks him directly "whether Israel is innocent or responsible for what happened at Sabra and Chatila" (EP, 290).

On the face of it, this looks like a straightforward request for a judgment on Levinas's part regarding the culpability—legal and/or moral— of the Israeli government and the Israeli military and especially Ariel Sharon for the massacres that took place in the camps. Were they responsible or not? And to the degree that one takes the question to be direct and explicit, it certainly seems that Levinas avoids answering it. Notice that Malka treats innocence and responsibility as alternative evaluations or judgments, where we might generally distinguish between innocence and guilt; moreover, while we might be inclined to distinguish between this as a matter of law, say international law, and morality, Malka makes no such distinction. In other words, what might seem to be a clear and direct question upon first hearing in fact is not clear or precise. Furthermore, while Finkielkraut refers to an idea, which he later explicates, that he calls "the temptation of innocence," Levinas's own thinking focuses on the responsibilities, infinite and primary, that we all have one to another. One can easily imagine that when he hears Malka's question, even prior to considering how to answer it, Levinas worries that in order to clarify what is at stake in the question and indeed in a situation where one is being asked to judge responsibilities, it is first necessary to say something to clarify what he means by "responsibility." That is the term and the concept that would have leaped out at him as requiring clarification and elaboration.

As we turn to Levinas's response, we find him doing exactly this, albeit in a way that incorporates, in a way, his own answer to the question. As we shall see, however, because of what responsibility means for Levinas, his way of answering the question may appear to be a way of avoiding any judgment or at least of avoiding a serious judgment, one that involves taking responsibility. But, I would like to suggest, that is not his intent, and it is an unfortunate outcome of expecting from him something that he has no intention of providing.

Levinas begins by saying that "what gripped us right away was the honour of responsibility" (EP, 290). And it is clear from the context that the "us" he is referring to is Jews in France. This, he says, was "our" immediate reaction, and we react in this way "despite the lack of guilt here," that is, in the Jewish community in France. Explicitly, then, Levinas refers to an immediate, pre-reflective experience, the experience of responsibility for the acts of the criminals and for the suffering and pain of the victims, and he distinguishes this sense of responsibility—of the honor of it—from the question of guilt, for clearly there is no guilt here—that is, in France. This is not a matter of the perpetrator taking responsibility for what he or she has done; it is prior to that, more fundamental than that, and this is clear from what Levinas goes on to say about this responsibility.

After this beginning, Levinas's first comment continues to do three things, first to elaborate on this notion of responsibility, to say a word about its relation to innocence, and then to remark on its special connection to Judaism. First, the responsibility he is calling attention to is not everyday responsibility or accountability. It is more fundamental than that. It is "an original responsibility of man for the other person." Or, as he puts it more fully, it "constitutes every man's responsibility towards all others, a responsibility which has nothing to do with any acts one may really have committed. Prior to any act, I am concerned with the Other, and I can never be absolved from this responsibility" (EP, 290).

To begin the interview and to respond to Malka's initial question, then, Levinas does not answer the question directly. Rather he introduces the very special notion of responsibility-for-the-other-person, which he also calls the face-to-face, the infinite, transcendence, enigma, hostage, substitution, persecution, and much else. As he explores in his philosophical works, this responsibility is the self's subjectivity insofar as it is fundamentally related to each and every other person. It does not come into being, nor does it ever cease. To be sure, as a kind of transcendental condition of all our social and moral relations, it is manifest in everyday, ordinary life to different degrees. But at a fundamental or transcendental level, it is always present. Hence, for Levinas, the issue is not one of innocence *or* responsibility. Rather it is one of how our pre-reflective, pre-conceptual, and primordial responsibility, to which we are always attuned and in particular cases more vividly than others, is related to our innocence or guilt. For the basic responsibility does not depend upon what we do; it is a feature of what we are in our relatedness to all other persons.

Furthermore, the actuality of this primordial responsibility means that even someone innocent of any act is still responsible, and his or her responsibility is "no more light or more comfortable for all that." And, as he then remarks, "it doesn't let you sleep any easier." What this comment suggests, as I see it, is that even though French Jews are innocent of the crimes in question, they still must respond out of concern and obligation. What that requires is a concrete, practical matter, but the point is that there is a practical issue here that concerns how the responsibility of French Jews for the Phalangist actions and the suffering of the Palestinian victims might and should be expressed. This is what Levinas means when he says, "I would insist on this responsibility, even if I am not speaking of direct guilt" (EP, 290). Innocence would not absolve French Jews—or other French citizens, or others anywhere else—from responsibility. The latter cannot be erased; it must be expressed in some way or other.

Finally, this is a "responsibility that the Bible of course teaches us" (EP, 290). In other words, the ineradicable responsibility to others is a deep teaching of the Jew's fundamental texts. It is a central teaching of Jewish tradition. As he will later put it, it is the "soul" of Judaism. And since Levinas does not hesitate to speak here as a Jew, he surely takes this responsibility seriously for himself. He may seem to be avoiding taking responsibility, but in fact he is underscoring exactly why he as a Jew must do so, as a Jew but of course also as a Frenchman and as a human being.

With this, Levinas completes his first response, and the interview turns to Finkielkraut, who makes two points. Both concern Israel's role in the massacres and the response in Israel, by the government and by the people. In effect, Finkielkraut recalls the issues that he had raised in the talk to which Malka had referred and what he calls "the temptation of innocence." First, Finkielkraut points out that Begin at first had refused to set up a board of inquiry, saying that no one can teach Israel anything about morals. He then cites Meron Benvenisti, former deputy mayor of Jerusalem, historian, and political critic, who had pointed to this tendency toward self-righteous indignation about one's privileged moral status as a result of having been victimized by the Nazis as the "the ultimate moral wound the Germans inflicted on us." Finkielkraut refers to this tendency as the "temptation of innocence," and he suggests that it leads to a destructive dialectic. Once criticism of Israel is registered by parties whose intentions are self-serving, this bad faith provokes the Jewish conscience, which responds by falling back on this temptation toward self-righteous reaction. The result, he says, is that "criticisms of Israel are so intolerable that we devote all our time to those criticisms without always thinking about the acts that have been committed" (EP, 291).

This is Finkielkraut's first point. It is a very pointed warning about a form of displacement that often occurs when Israeli policy and practices are discussed. He focuses on the official Israeli response and the judgments of some of Israel's many supporters and advocates. Instead of considering the "acts that have been committed" with seriousness and a sense of concern, the focus of attention becomes the criticism itself, whether it is an expression of bad faith and whether Israel is not above being criticized by anyone as a result of the atrocities that the Jewish people have suffered. For Finkielkraut, this is a form of avoidance, as Stanley Cavell would call it, when what is needed is acknowledgment and love, that is, concern for those who have been injured. Indeed, Finkielkraut's use of the word "temptation" suggests that his warning is itself akin to Levinas's own warning, in his essay "Useless Suffering," that after the Holocaust, we are in a situation in which we ought no longer to be tempted by theodicies, by responding to suffering and assaults on human dignity and such by diverting our responses from concerned action in behalf of their victims in favor of more and more theorizing, more and more thinking.[7] In the case before us, Finkielkraut implies, criticism becomes the locus for how Israel and the Jews are being treated, and the issue of whether Israel is culpable or not, accountable or not, is shunted aside. Instead of being concerned with Israel's responsibilities toward the Palestinians and those who have suffered, the focus of attention is on Israel herself and the criticism of her. This is morally faulty, morally disturbing.

There is a context for Finkielkraut's worries. "By the summer of 1982, the association of Jews with Nazis" had become a regular feature of the French intellectual landscape. As Joan Wolf puts it, events like Sabra and Shatila and responses to it "turned Holocaust discourse on its head." Divided as they were over Israel's conduct, still "French Jews were virtually unanimous in their denunciation of the press's widespread deployment of Holocaust imagery to characterize the war."[8] The literary critic and novelist Philippe Sollers worried that to many "the Jew is the executioner," and by making such claims, the anti-Semites relieve themselves of feeling guilt and "secure for themselves a retroactive innocence."[9] Finkielkraut himself notices the irony that "one can hate the Jews by recourse to anti-Nazism."[10] And while he himself called for Begin's resignation, he was adamant that "the comparison between Israel and Nazism is still stupid and scandalous."[11] It is against this background of controversy and debate that Finkielkraut proposes his worry about the temptation to plead innocence on the basis of the Holocaust.

This is his second point: if the Jew is the "absolute victim," then what responsibility can the Jew have to others? Perhaps they have no obligations to others, or, as he alternatively puts it, "we have no room for any imperative other than self-defence" (EP, 291). Calling upon the Holocaust in this way is offensive; it is to use Auschwitz "to escape here from the demand of responsibility" (EP, 291), and with this remark, Finkielkraut turns to Levinas, asking how he would react to this temptation. In effect, the temptation is to exploit one's status as a victim, an object of atrocity and persecution, to privilege self-defense and political necessity as one's exclusive reasons for action and hence to avoid responsibility to the greatest degree possible. One can only imagine what Finkielkraut expected from Levinas as he turned to ask him his reaction to such a strategy.

Levinas's first response is to point out that most Israelis did not succumb to this strategy, and he applauds their courage and their commitment.

> First of all, to return to the facts, I'd like to remind you of the reaction of a great many Israeli Jews, the majority, I'd say. We here are not the only ones to have had this feeling of responsibility, there too [i.e., in Israel] they've felt it to the highest degree.... We ought absolutely to glorify this reaction, which is not morbid, but a moral one. It's an ethical reaction on the part of what I think is the majority of the Jewish people, the Israeli people, beginning with President Navon, who felt it immediately, and who was the first to demand a board of enquiry. (EP, 291)

Since the mass rally in Tel Aviv, protesting the government and calling for Begin and Sharon to resign, had just occurred, it is natural to take Levinas to be referring to this event as expressing this "feeling of responsibility." Furthermore, in terms of the dialogue with Finkielkraut, Levinas is responding to the suggestion—the implication of his remarks about the dialectic of bad faith and moral conscience and the temptation of innocence—that Israelis were by and large avoiding such a sense of responsibility. Levinas's first point is that in fact they were not; rather they acted out of just such a sense of responsibility.

Hence, when he then says, "Real innocence clearly arises in this feeling of innocence," what he means is that the hundreds of thousands at this rally, who certainly were innocent, nonetheless acted out of a sense of responsibility. Real innocence is not an avoidance of taking responsibility; it is acted out precisely by taking responsibility. For anyone familiar with Levinas's conception of the face-to-face, the ways we take responsibility for others—acknowledging and accepting them and acting in their behalf and out of a sense of responsibility for and to them—are unavoidable but not all of equal kind or character. Innocence is not failing to respond, but it is to respond in a certain way. Levinas says this explicitly: "Innocence is not the zero degree of conscience, but merely an exalted state of responsibility" (EP, 291).

At this point, then, Levinas has underscored the fact that the Israeli people have expressed themselves about the massacres and about taking responsibility by calling for the establishment of a board of inquiry and for proper judicial and political procedures. The protests and the outcries are acts of responsibility and not of avoidance. But Finkielkraut had argued that a fixation on victimization during the Holocaust had led many Jews to a kind of avoidance and self-righteous indignation. Does this mean that Levinas is recommending that the Holocaust has no relevance here? Moreover, is he recommending that if responsibility is unlimited and always present, there is no justification for political necessity, for the purposes of self-defense?

These are the questions that implicitly Levinas is answering in his next remarks. Here he underlines that the Holocaust must not be forgotten, but that its role cannot be to absolve Jews of all responsibility. To do so would be appalling. Moreover, to acknowledge the primacy of infinite responsibility is not to rule out practical and prudential considerations, especially, say, self-defense. With regard to the first issue, he says that no one has forgotten or should forget the Holocaust, but "that in no way justifies closing our ears to the voice of men, in which sometimes the voice of God can also resound. Evoking the Holocaust to say that God is with us in all circumstances is as odious as the words 'Gott mit uns' written on the belts of the executioners. . . . My *self*, I repeat, is never absolved from responsibility towards the Other" (EP, 291). Here Levinas takes himself to be repeating his initial point, that what he means by responsibility concerns every person and his or her particular relations with all other persons; responsibility is a transcendental, structural feature of all everyday relationships. It is always present, has always been present, and always will be present. The issue is how or in what ways it is taken up, affirmed or declined, in our everyday affairs.

But, and this is his second point, although responsibility is always present and we are always acting in terms of it, still there are considerations that weigh in behalf of self-defense and other prudential and practical purposes. This fact of our natural and historical existence, that we and those close to us may be subject to attack or assault and that therefore defense is sometimes required, introduces what Levinas calls, in a broad sense, "politics." This is what he says: "All those who attack us with such venom have no right to do so, and . . . consequently, along with this feeling of unbounded responsibility, there is certainly a place for a defence, for it is not always a question of 'me', but of those close to me, who are also my neighbours. I'd call such a defence a politics, but a politics that's ethically necessary. Alongside *ethics*, there is a place for *politics*." (EP, 292). This remark is an extremely important one. It makes a point that is central to Levinas's thinking, that ethics and politics, and all the expressions he uses for the underlying face-to-face and for everyday life—institutional, social, and practical—are coordinated, for the facts, so to speak, are coordinated. In the terms of his conversation with Finkielkraut, innocence and guilt, on the one hand, and responsibility, on the other, occur together. One is the primordial and binding, compelling substructure of all relationships; the other is the status of the self in his or her relationship with the injured other in everyday, historical affairs. But in larger terms, what this means is something that Levinas underscores time and again elsewhere: the ethical character of our interpersonal lives, in all its particularity, must occur alongside and together with the social and political character, in all their generality, of our everyday lives, and the latter is as necessary as the former. They are two dimensions, broadly speaking, of human existence as social and relational. When Levinas here talks about responsibility, he is talking about the ethical dimension; when he talks about self-defense and political necessities, he is talking about the political. This is so important a theme for him and one that is easily missed or confused that he here indicates that he will return to it.

The immediate context for this general issue, however, which is a philosophical one about human existence, is the Israeli response to the atrocities in the refugee camps and also the French response. One might think that Levinas has avoided this context and that he has avoided responding directly and candidly to Malka's question about who is responsible, specifically whether Israel is responsible. There are certainly different ways, even at this point in the interview, to interpret Levinas's responses thus far. One might think that he is avoiding any personal judgment and any personal commitment. But this is a very uncharitable reading of what has transpired to this point. An alternative would be to understand what has happened as meaning that the concrete question of Israeli responsibility or complicity requires, from his point of view and especially given the ways in which his own ideas are easily misunderstood, some preliminary clarification. The relation between innocence and responsibility provided Levinas with an opportunity to do just that, to focus first on the idea of responsibility by itself and then to clarify how innocence and responsibility are interrelated. Finally, it enabled him to move on to indicate that the relation between responsibility and innocence is one instance of a more general issue, the relation between ethics and politics, as he understands them. This is the point to which the conversation has now arrived. This is how I read what Levinas is doing in this early stage of the dialogue.

ETHICS, POLITICAL NECESSITY, AND ZIONISM

The next stage of the conversation is introduced by Finkielkraut, who picks up the thread of Levinas's responses and calls attention to the particularly political expression of prudential concerns and matters of self-defense. That is, Finkielkraut introduces the concept of *raison d'état*, or "reason of state." He makes a statement about what such political necessities mean and how they come into conflict with ethical concerns and then asks what Levinas thinks about these matters. His statement is this:

> Political necessities are held up as justification. These are necessities of which everyone in Israel is aware. But at the same time, it seems to me that the demonstrators who gathered in Tel Aviv, three hundred thousand of them, precisely wanted to rethink the relations between ethics and politics. It was as if a slippage had taken place, as if certain moral demands, certain ethical imperatives had been forgotten in the name of political necessity. And these people who are obsessed by the concern for security at the same time also manifested another obsession, an ethical concern, and what this demonstration seemed to be saying was that the two are incompatible, or that in any case they shouldn't come into open contradiction. (EP, 292)

The point of Finkielkraut's statement here is pretty clear. States regularly act with security concerns in mind. Israel in particular has, since her establishment in 1948 and indeed even before, treated security issues as primary. Self-defense and security are a central, if not the central, responsibility of governmental institutions and practices, and in embattled and threatened states, this fact is exaggerated. Finkielkraut suggests above, however, that it is one thing to take such responsibilities seriously and part of a state's justification; it is another to treat them as the state's exclusive interests and responsibilities. His observation is that the hundreds of thousands of Israelis who protested in Tel Aviv realized that this exaggeration or distortion may have taken place in Israel in the course of her first thirty or so years of existence and that moral concerns—obligations and interests—had been forgotten or occluded, obscured. This is the "slippage" he refers to. But they, the protestors, had become as "obsessed" by these moral responsibilities as the nation was by its political ones. Here he uses a very Levinasian vocabulary: our responsibilities for and to the other person are an obsession. They are an overwhelming burden that we can never fully satisfy; they are a passion—we are passive, an unconditional and undeniable desire.

How does he conclude? The demonstrators realize that the two, ethics and politics, should not come into contradiction. This moment of judgment about how to react to the massacres and what to say about the board of inquiry is a moment when—so it might seem—moral demands and political necessities come into conflict. But they cannot both stand together; they contradict one another and so to go on one must choose one or the other, and their conviction is that the moral demands must take priority. In principle, of course, the two need not conflict. Political decisions and actions might be compatible with moral demands; they might serve the purposes of justice and humane conduct. But here they did not. Sharon and others believed, they said, that the camps were hotbeds of radicalism; they harbored terrorists and guerilla fighters who were a threat to Israel and needed to be rooted out. Many, however, asked why Sharon was so confident about the threat, why it was necessary to slaughter women, children, and the elderly, and why, when the atrocities became evident, nothing was done immediately to bring them to a halt. Which was a more powerful reason to act? Which obligation was or should have been primary? And, to the demonstrators, what did this conflict expose?

Levinas's initial response to Finkielkraut is to clarify what this contradiction means, and once he has, he agrees with Finkielkraut's point. He then considers what this means for Israel and for Zionism. "I think that there's a direct contradiction between ethics and politics, if both these demands are taken to the extreme" (EP, 292). If either moral or prudential considerations are taken to be extreme or overwhelming, then the other simply cannot find any grip. This, I think, is what Levinas means. He is not concerned with contradiction in a logical sense or in some strict sense; rather he is concerned about the necessity of conflict in which only one can survive or only one can remain. If one or the other is a dominant reason, all things considered, and the other is nonetheless an option, they conflict and the one that is dominant will always overwhelm the other.

Furthermore, the justification for politics, for the apparatus of the state and its functions, is separate from or different from what underlies ethics. This is true widely and generally. But is it true of Israel? Are the purposes of the State of Israel by and large political issues of security and self-defense? Levinas says this:

> The Zionist idea, as I now see it, all mysticism or false immediate messianism aside, is nevertheless a political idea which has an ethical justification. It has an ethical justification insofar as a political solution imposes itself as a way of putting an end to the arbitrariness which marked the Jewish condition, and to all the spilt blood which for centuries has flowed with impunity across the world. This solution can be summed up as the existence, in conditions which are not purely abstract, that is, not just anywhere, of a political unity with a Jewish majority. For me, this is the essence of Zionism. It signifies a State in the fullest sense of the term, a State with an army and arms, an army which can have a deterrent and if necessary a defensive significance. Its necessity is ethical—indeed, it's an old ethical idea which commands us precisely to defend our neighbours. My people and my kin are still my neighbours. (EP, 292)

What does Levinas say here about the core of Zionism and its character as a state, with typical political and military institutions? Zionism is the solution for the Jewish problem, the problem of the precariousness of Jewish existence in a non-Jewish world, in which Jews have been subject to the persecution and oppression of anti-Jewish forces. Its aim is to create, in the Land of Israel, a unified state with a Jewish majority, capable of defending Jews from their enemies.[12] Levinas calls this a political idea with an ethical justification that is itself a political solution. The ethical justification is the defense of neighbors from harm and injury, where the neighbors are one's "people and kin."

For Levinas, then, there is a sense in which Zionism is about self-defense, protection, and security. This is indeed a political purpose. It is a political *solution*. But, at the same time, since the Jewish people have been subject to persecution, attacks, and assault by those who harbor a deep animosity to Jews and Judaism, that purpose is also an *ethical justification*. It is a way of taking responsibility for the life and well-being of others, where the others are one's own family and fellow Jews.

But to this point there is nothing novel about Levinas's Zionism; he is hardly the first to take Zionism to be a movement the goal of which is to solve the Jewish question. Moreover, if this were all that Levinas had to say about Zionism, the Jewish state would hardly differ from any other state, and Zionism would barely differ from the kind of state conceived by Hobbes and Locke, among others. But he does say more, and that addition begins when he points out that "there is also an ethical limit to this ethically necessary existence" (EP, 293). In short, Zionism is a move-ment for a political solution to the problem of anti-Jewish persecution only within certain ethical limits, and, he suggests, the demonstrators in Tel Aviv had appreciated when those limits had been transgressed. As the interview will go on to show, this awareness and expression, that the ethical limit of political conduct had been crossed, is the rally's central theme, for Levinas.

To develop this claim and to clarify it, Levinas continues by pointing out that this issue, of how ethics and politics come into conflict, is not just a theoretical or abstract problem. It arises in life, in actual experi-ence, and that is unfortunate, for it means that people will suffer. One might think that Levinas is being insensitive, for at this point, with his attention on the clarification of what Zionism is and how it is related to Judaism and the Jewish tradition, and as he tries to explore how ethical limits confront political decisions for the Jewish people and for Israel, he does not even mention the Palestinian suffering. On the one hand, it would have led his thinking in a different direction, but on the other, it is that suffering that is at issue. What he does instead is to elaborate his point about the conflict between ethics and politics not being an abstract point but having theoretical but concrete implications:

> And perhaps this is where we might find the solution to the universal human problem of the relationship between ethics and politics; the people "engaged" (*engage*) in this "contradiction" and for whom, despite the war, it is an everyday thought, is a people with a long ethical tradition. The events over there, which we would rather hadn't happened, will therefore take on a significance for the

general history of the mind. Perhaps that's where some light will be shed on the
matter, in the concrete consciousness of those who struggle and suffer.

I'm not saying that Israel is a State like any other, nor a people unlike any
other. I'm saying that in the political and moral ideal, in the Passion of this
war—and every time the Jewish people is implicated in an event, something
universal is always at stake—it's there that the relationship between ethics and
politics is being decided, it's there that "in and for itself," as philosophical jargon
puts it, it is being defined; alas, it's a dangerous game that's afoot. (EP, 293)

First, let me clarify what Levinas is saying in these remarks. The relationship between ethics and politics is illuminated by events and only then
theoretically. Or, at least, Levinas suggests that this might be the case. Of
course, we can imagine philosophers concocting scenarios and thought
experiments to clarify this relationship, but the fact is, Levinas seems to
be claiming, that the relationship is really only disclosed by how the two
conflict in experience and in events. Moreover, in this case, the Jewish
people, who are immersed in these events in Lebanon and in the camps,
are not only represented in a state; they also have an ethical tradition. It
is because they have such a tradition and at the same time make political
decisions that there should arise, at the level of everyday reflection and
conscience, a conflict. Now, we know that Levinas takes the responsibilities we have to others to be present for everyone, but in practice, in life, it
is only when an agent has the awareness and sensitivity to these responsibilities that what he or she might do can come into conflict with what
they require. And in this case, he believes, that is so. It is strange to hear
him refer to the Israeli agents—the government and military—as those
who "suffer and struggle," when the Palestinians are in fact the victims
in this case. But in general I think he is referring to the Jewish people as
a whole and in particular those in Israel, who suffer the animosity of her
neighbors and who are members of a persecuted people seeking stability
and security and peace.

Is this whole stretch of thinking a kind of avoidance? Does it enable Levinas to ignore or evade Malka's original question? One could
read Levinas this way, but we should remember that he has not directed
the conversation. It was Malka who first introduced the terminology of
innocence and responsibility, and it was both he and Finkielkraut who
have steered the conversation to Israel and Zionism. To be sure, Levinas
is making a choice. He has chosen to treat the current events in Lebanon

as an exemplification of a persistent trope, so to speak. They are events or moments when the ethical and political come into conflict. They do not discredit or falsify his conception of Zionism or of Judaism. Rather they are challenges that will regularly occur when a tradition with a strong ethical dimension takes up political arms in its own defense. There will be times when the political dimension of her behavior will transgress moral limits that she herself recognizes. That is what is happening with Israel in Lebanon, he says. Those events are ones "we would rather hadn't happened." The war itself, as a whole, the Operation for Peace in the Galilee and the siege of Beirut, are a "dangerous game." They may have been justified, militarily and politically, but the particular events at Sabra and Shatila, even if strategically warranted, were carried out in ways that clearly violated moral responsibilities. They were atrocities and should not have occurred. But war is a dangerous enterprise. There are risks that there will be actions, decisions, and events that one regrets, morally, and ones that one must take responsibility for. Levinas is cautious. He does not come right out and point a finger at the guilty parties. But he does not withhold his regrets and his recognition of responsibility, in the everyday sense of that word.

Finkielkraut continues with a possible objection. "Some would say" that there may have been a sound reason for Operation Peace for Galilee, consonant with a traditional conception of Zionism that goes back to Ben-Gurion and Herzl and articulated by Begin. To be sure, something has gone wrong, but it is an "aberration." "The copybook," he says, "has been blotted," that is, the neat handwriting has been marred with splotches or smears. But, the objector might say, this does not mean that because of Sabra and Shatila, everything is "cast in doubt." As he puts it, they will defend the massacres as an anomaly and criticize the protestors by saying that they are simply "noble souls" who have "the luxury of a pure conscience exempted from the mudpit of history" (EP, 293).

Levinas begins his response by calling attention to Begin's statement, which Finkielkraut had cited: "Jewish blood must not flow with impunity." Attacks on the Jewish people, in particular the PLO terrorist attacks on northern villages and cities in the north, from bases within southern Lebanon and especially the refugee camps, ought not to go unpunished, and it is this that in part precipitated the military operations in southern Lebanon. Levinas is aware of the statement and takes it to be significant, that is, he accepts the compelling concerns of security and self-defense. But he points out that these pragmatic and military considerations by themselves do not specify what political and military actions are justified and which are not. In fact, he notes that this very issue, what is justified and what not, is being debated with regard to the two stages of the military action, the operation in southern Lebanon and then the siege of Beirut. Then, however, comes Sabra and Shatila, and the massacres are a watershed. He calls them an "interruption," a favorite postmodern word for a decisive break or rupture. The earlier episodes of the military action and the war are of internal interest, he seems to be saying, but these events—the massacres and the atrocities—these reach out and have implications for everyone. He puts it this way:

> But the place where everything is interrupted, where everything is disrupted, where everyone's moral responsibility comes into play, a responsibility that concerns and engages even innocence, unbearably so, that place lies in the events at Sabra and Shatila. Everyone's responsibility. Over there, no one can say to us: "you're in Europe and at peace, you're not in Israel, and yet you take it upon yourself to judge." I think that in this case, this distinction between the ones and the others, for once at least, disappears. (EP, 293–94)

In short, Levinas takes Finkielkraut's supposed objection to be raised by Israelis and especially by Israelis in the military and in the government, who might be willing to admit that occasionally one gets one's hands dirty but that they hardly need any "detached" and "safe" liberals from abroad to tell them so. The argument is of the form, who are you to tell us about what war involves and sometimes requires? The mud pit of history is after all just that, a mud pit.

Levinas responds by distinguishing Sabra and Shatila from other events. It was momentous, a watershed, a disruption, and not just for Israelis and Palestinians, but for everyone, everywhere. It is one of those events that has world-historical significance. And for that reason, there is no relevant separation of them from us, of those over there and us over here. All of us are responsible for treating others with humanity and concern; all of us must be deeply affected by callous disregard for life and dignity, wherever it occurs and to whomever. It is everyone's business and not just that of the locals, the partisans. This is Levinas's point. It may very well have a general significance, but it is especially appropriate given his understanding of the universality and unbounded character of our interpersonal responsibilities.

This remark brings us to the end of the second stage of the conversation. Its central point clearly is to underline that while ethics and politics are coordinate dimensions of our lives, they can and do come into conflict. There are times when such a conflict is of universal significance, when it is momentous, and the massacre at Sabra and Shatila is one of those. It is a moment or site when the conflict between political necessity and moral conscience is exposed and where judgment and response are necessary.

WHO IS THE OTHER?

The conversation up to this point has been rather abstract. Finkielkraut and Levinas have discussed innocence and responsibility, ethics and politics, and the nature of Zionism. Along the way, I believe that Levinas has expressed his sympathy with those who rallied in Tel Aviv, calling for a board of inquiry to determine what exactly had happened in the camps and who was responsible. Clearly, many protesters believed that Ariel Sharon and Menachem Begin were among those responsible and that they should resign. Levinas does not commit himself to such extreme views, but he does indicate clearly that he feels responsible for the events, regrets their having occurred, and supports the call for such an inquiry. At the same time, much of the interview has focused on Israelis and Jews and their responsibilities in this situation. There has been no discussion about the victims and how one should view them. Levinas in particular has not indicated any sympathy or concern, sadness or grief or compassion. But of course these are all emotional reactions, and the discussion has been about moral reactions and in particular taking responsibility and making moral judgments.

Shlomo Malka has been absent from the interview since his initial remarks, but he now intercedes with the interview's most controversial question. As I have pointed out, thus far there has been no explicit discussion about the Palestinian refugees in the camps who were slaughtered. And, to be precise, even at this point Malka does not ask Levinas for his reaction to them and to their suffering. What he says is this: "Emmanuel Levinas, you are the philosopher of the 'other.' Isn't history, isn't politics the very site of the encounter with the 'other,' and for the Israeli, isn't the 'other' above all the Palestinian?" (EP, 294). Malka here asks two questions: first, does not the encounter with the other person, about which Levinas has said so much, take place in "history" and in "politics," and second, is not the Palestinian the Israeli's most preeminent other person? He does not ask explicitly how Levinas feels about the Palestinians, nor does he even ask whether the Israelis ought not to have special obligations to the Palestinians, although one might think that his second question implies that if the answer is yes, then this would be so. At one level, Malka may have asked these questions in order to supplement them later, once he has heard the answer, or alternatively he might have asked them with the intent of eliciting Levinas's judgment regarding his own sense of responsibility or more precisely his own judgment about Israeli responsibility. Perhaps he sought from Levinas a condemnation of Israel for having failed to act on her responsibilities toward the Palestinians and even more to have acted in direct conflict with them. In short, Malka may have intended to elicit an extreme condemnation of Israel from Levinas.

If this is so, then Levinas chose to avoid Malka's intent. It may be, however, that either Levinas did not interpret Malka this way or he took Malka quite literally, to be making a point about what the face of the other person means and how it should be applied to political and military enemies, such as Israelis and Palestinians. We do not know Malka's state of mind or Levinas's. It might have been that Levinas felt under pressure to express publicly an indictment of Israel that he was reluctant to express, or he may have felt that he had already made his own criticisms evident and found in the questions a bundle of confusions that needed to be addressed. In the end, we may never know exactly how Levinas understood Malka's questions. There are any number of things that he might have said and that we might want him to have said, but all of this is speculation and beyond our knowledge. What we do know is how he responded to them. This is what he said:

> My definition of the other is completely different. The other is the neighbour, who is not necessarily kin, but who can be. And in that sense, if you're for the other, you're for the neighbour. But if your neighbour attacks another neighbour

or treats him unjustly, what can you do? Then alterity takes on another character, in alterity we can find an enemy, or at least then we are faced with the
problem of knowing who is right and who is wrong, who is just and who is unjust. There are people who are wrong. (EP, 294)

To my ear, these remarks make a number of extremely important points.
Malka's questions belie a very central confusion about Levinas's terminology and one that no doubt, even in the 1980s, had already given rise
to widespread confusion about his thinking. This confusion involves failing to distinguish what we might call the *ethical other* from the *political
other*. It is a distinction that corresponds to the more general distinction
between the face-to-face, as an underlying structural feature of all our
second-person relations, and the various features and relationships that
constitute our everyday relations with others. The latter are diverse and
general; they are capable of being understood, named, classified, compared, and more. The former is the primordial second-person relatedness
that is wholly constituted by the self's responsibility to and for each
and every other person. When Levinas says that we are responsible for
everyone, he means this primordial sense of responsibility, and in this
sense everyone is an ethical other for everyone else. At the everyday
level, in the context of our complex network of interpersonal, social, and
political relationships, our status as political others is a matter of degree.
We are closer or more distant, more intimate or less, more closely associated with some than with others. Malka has confused these two senses
of otherness; he has taken ethical otherness to be political otherness. As
Levinas puts it, using the word "neighbor" for the other with whom we
have a face-to-face relation and to whom and for whom each is responsible, one is a neighbor no matter whether one is kin or one is an enemy.
But at the everyday level—what Malka calls history and politics—others come in different degrees and kinds. His remarks here call to mind
his frequent discussions of the third party, which is the other person,
alongside every self-other encounter, and a further person, again and
again. In short, once we have a plurality of persons and a vast network
of responsibilities, we have to identify, classify, organize, compare, and
evaluate the responsibilities of others and our own. Only at this level
will it turn out, based on our calculations and discriminations, who we
judge is right and who wrong, who just and who unjust. That is precisely

what a board of inquiry ought to determine as the representative of the Israeli democracy. Just because one is a family member or a close friend does not mean that one has more or less actual responsibilities toward him or her, and just because one is an enemy similarly does not, by itself, mean that one has more or less actual responsibilities. It will all depend on the particular features of the relevant parties, the situation, the needs of the people involved, and more. In short, if one understands Levinas's views correctly, he does not think that there is any prejudice in favor of concern for one's enemy.

To some, I am sure, this answer, which is very precisely addressed to the confusions in Malka's question, may seem to involve the avoidance I mentioned above. To some, that is, Levinas may seem to be addressing what he wants to hear and to be failing to address what Malka really was asking. On that matter, he is disturbingly silent, some might say, or intentionally negligent. But there is another way of understanding what Levinas is here saying. Remember that he has all but agreed with the judgment of the Tel Aviv protestors that called for a board of inquiry, and the task of such a board of inquiry is to determine who is right and who is wrong in the case of the Sabra and Shatila massacres, who has committed injustice and who not. Even if Malka was calling for an explicit indictment, Levinas was not about to give it, for that would be to preempt that inquiry. He has given us every reason to think that he regrets that the events ever occurred and that he believes an inquiry is mandatory. That is as far as he is going to go. Unlike some protestors, who called for Begin and Sharon to resign, Levinas will wait to hear the judgment of the Kahan Commission. Moreover, there is no prejudice built into his conception of our nature as selves responsible for each and every other that requires him or anyone else to be more or less sympathetic or concerned regarding any particular other person. This is what he means when he says above that when one neighbor attacks another, *then* we are faced with determining who is right and who wrong, and there will be someone who is wrong.

ISRAEL AND MESSIANISM

The conversation now takes a decidedly new turn. Earlier, Levinas had cautioned against a view of Zionism that was associated with messianism. Malka now returns to this point; he wants to probe what the events mean for Judaism, for Israel, and for Zionism. He asks both Finkielkraut and Levinas if they think that there is a risk in Israel of "a mysticism which can degenerate into politics."[13] Finkielkraut is first to respond, and he immediately points out that the real problem is not that Judaism might become degraded by becoming political—an old criticism of Judaism and of Christianity—but rather that "the risk that Israel runs is one of a too hasty and summary transformation of politics into mysticism" (EP, 294). Finkielkraut then explains that what he means is the risks associated with one of two tendencies. The first is the one Levinas has just explained, the risk of politics in Israel becoming a kind of worship of political necessity, eschewing any relevance for the critical role of the ethical. This would be a case of politics itself becoming a kind of ideology, a devotion to reason of state for its own sake.

But there is a second concern he has as well, and this concerns politics in Israel degenerating into religious mystification and extremism. Clearly, Finkielkraut has in mind the dangers of religious fanaticism, especially the kinds of messianic politics associated with Gush Emunim, the followers of Zvi Yehudah Kook, and those who are aligned with the movements to return to the ancient sacrificial system on the Temple Mount.[14] "But the other peril facing Israel," he says, "is not taking account of the everyday practicalities of politics, in forgetting that it's a specific domain in the life of men, and in preferring to read into it, in mystical fashion, the presence of God and the signs of Providence." To be sure, this is not about mysticism in any restricted sense. It is a warning about using a theological conception of providential history and divine agency, in particular a conception of messianism and messianic action, in order to understand current historical events and more importantly as a basis for how decisions are made and what actions are taken even in the political domain. "If there is a danger, it's not one of mysticism degenerating into politics, but rather of an ill-considered elevation of politics onto the level of mysticism, a confusion of the two spheres" (EP, 294–95).

Finkielkraut does not simply state this worry in abstract terms. He specifically ties it to reactions to the Six-Day War in 1967. He sympathizes with the enthusiasm for the Israeli victory and its inspiring character. But he notes that the responses ran precisely the risk to which he is here pointing: "We can't think enough about the effects of the 1967 victory on the Israeli psyche. The victory, in its scope and its speed, was so unexpected, so miraculous, that some couldn't resist seeing it as a messianic moment. So the Israeli government hadn't included the conquest of the West Bank on its agenda? Then that proves that we're living through the 'first pains of redemption', and that God is giving the Jews back the Promised Land" (EP, 294). The "miraculous" nature of Israel's military victory called forth this messianic response both within Israel and without. It provided evidence, for those disposed to interpret it as such, of divine intervention in behalf of ultimate historical goals. With such a response came the inclination toward a theological reading of history and hence of mystifying politics. In this respect, in recent Jewish history, the Six-Day War was a watershed. After it, and especially in the wake of the Yom Kippur War, messianic interpretations of Israeli political and military life became—and continue to be—increasingly prominent.

But what are the risks to which Finkielkraut is pointing? He does not say explicitly, but one can easily imagine what he has in mind. With such views come frequently several attitudes, all of which are dangerous. One is the idea that historical events are in God's hands and hence that there is no reason to oppose human crimes and horrific acts; God will take responsibility and will do what is necessary to oppose them. Politics, as a result, may be left to those with the most appalling motives and goals. A second belief is that if God is acting in history, one must act without restraint in behalf of what He recommends or favors, and this can lead, as it often has, to fanaticism and passionate action that is susceptible to misdirection and manipulation. A further view is that history is the drama of irrational and hyper-rational forces that warrant highly emotional involvement or avoidance on our parts, which regularly drives politics in fearful and horrific directions or abandons it altogether. And finally the theologizing of history often gives the political process over to extreme partisanship and intolerance and may very well point to fascism and totalitarianism as natural outcomes. In short, Finkielkraut may associate messianic politics with a step in the direction of narrowness, irrationalism, exploitation, and extremism.

Levinas does not agree with Finkielkraut's concern, at least not with regard to Israel, and in fact he calls Finkielkraut to testify against himself. That is, Levinas did not take the current situation in Israel to be evidence for a risk of messianic fanaticism. Rather he interpreted it differently and more positively. This is how Finkielkraut himself, in the course of his remarks, had described Levinas's interpretation of the meaning of the Tel Aviv demonstrations that occurred in the wake of the massacres: "As Emmanuel Levinas has just shown, we're now witnessing a passionate examination of the contradictions between ethics and politics, and of the necessity, that is both vital and almost impossible, of conforming the demands of collective action to fundamental ethical principles" (EP, 294). Here we have Finkielkraut's summary statement of what Levinas had indicated is the meaning of the Israeli protest demonstration in Tel Aviv as a response to the Sabra and Shatila massacres and the initial reaction of the Israeli government. In essence, for Levinas, the events in Israel were about the relationship between ethical principles and political actions. They were an expression of a democratic and liberal process of public self-examination and of collective conscience.

It is against the background of Levinas's earlier remarks and Finkielkraut's summary of them here that Levinas can pick up the conversation and say that when compared with other cases in world history, "you have less cause to worry about Israel's soul and political history" (EP, 295). Overall, one might not think that Levinas should have been so confident. Israeli history, especially during the past several decades, might very well make one worry that political necessities have become the privileged justification for political and military policy and that the fear of interpreting recent events and political programs messianically is very real indeed. But Levinas was making this statement not immediately after the Six-Day War and not in the 1970s when Gush Emunim was becoming a prominent political player in Israeli public and political life. Rather this was 1982, in the precise context of reflecting upon the massacres in the refugee camps and the mass protest rally in response to those events, and in this respect, his judgment may seem more justified. It was a moment when the limits of politics were exposed as ethical. Levinas now puts it this way: "Ethics will never, in any lasting way, be the good conscience of corrupt politics—the immediate reactions we've witnessed these last few days prove it; and transgression of ethics made 'in the name of ethics' is immediately perceived as a hypocrisy and as a personal offence" (EP, 295). What exactly are the "immediate reactions . . . [of] these last few days," and for what exactly are they evidence? Levinas makes sure that we are aware that the issue, for him, is about what the demonstrations and protests in Israel mean for Israel and for the relation between ethics and politics both in Israel and in general. Israelis have shown, he believes, that they will not stand for security at all costs. They will not settle, to use Avishai Margalit's expression, for a rotten compromise of increased security at the cost of performing acts of humiliation, degradation, and atrocity.[15] This is what Levinas means when he says that the lesson that is being learned, which Israel is learning from her own citizens, is that "ethics will never be the good conscience of corrupt politics." Security and peace cannot justify horrific political acts. Or, alternatively, it is "hypocrisy" to try to justify morally the transgression of morality.

There is a great deal that could and ought to be said about this claim, which needs to be clarified before it is seen as obviously true. But for Levinas, the central point is that ethics in his terms, the responsibilities each of us has for all others, the obligations to care and concern for others, is the standard by which political actions—and indeed all everyday actions—are to be judged. No political decision, policy, or action is perfect; none is completely and unqualifiedly just. But they can be more or less just, and showing others respect and concern is the central consideration in determining how well we have done or how poorly. This lesson is being demonstrated in the streets of Tel Aviv and throughout Israel, Levinas believes. Israelis—not all but some, and a significant number it is—will not allow themselves the luxury or the indulgence of treating all political necessities as final justifications for anything that their military and their government chooses to do.

THE TRUTH OF ISRAEL AND THE SOUL OF JUDAISM

There is something ironic about the interview. It has been less about the plight of the victims, the innocent Palestinian refugees slaughtered in the camps, and more about those who were complicit in the massacre. And it may seem to some that the slaughter has become a kind of pretext or opportunity for those complicit to redeem themselves by a process of self-judgment and self-examination. Is this itself hypocritical and self-indulgent? Does it end up using one's own transgressions as a device for enabling one to achieve some nobility?

Worries of this kind, I can see, might easily have already arisen, and they might only be exaggerated by the way the conversation now proceeds, largely between Levinas and Finkielkraut. Their attention is now focused exclusively on Israel, on Zionism, and on Judaism.

Levinas turns to the question of what relation there might be between Zionism and messianism. First, he dismisses—indeed has already dismissed—the idea that Zionism is a form of religious Zionism because it is an expression of traditional Jewish messianic expectations, "which sees in [Zionism] the first labour pains of the Messiah's birth" (EP, 295). He refers to this idea as "the simplistic image of messianism, which is dangerous as a political principle" (EP, 295). By "simplistic," I think Levinas means that it takes literally the traditional idea of a personal Messiah, anointed by God to reestablish a Jewish commonwealth at the end of history, an idea that for Levinas is simply a mythological or imaginative expression of the role of ethics in life and in history. But this does not mean, which is his second point, that Zionism has nothing to do with messianism. In fact, the Zionist struggle, as he calls it, is deeply messianic, but only when messianism in Judaism is reinterpreted in ethical terms: "I believe that Zionism comprises a genuine messianic element, which is the day-to-day life in Israel of Israel itself. It lies in hard work, the daily sacrifice made by people who've left secure positions and often abundance in order to lead a difficult life, to lead an ethical life, to lead a life which isn't disturbed by the values of our Western comfort. . . . I would say that in this sense one is closer to the Messiah in Israel than here" (EP, 295). What does this remark tell us about Levinas's own conception of messianism in Judaism, and how is this associated with Israel and life in Israel?

To begin, everyday Jewish life—in Israel, in France, indeed everywhere—is closer or further away from "the Messiah," that is, from a life that has messianic features. Messianism is not about the culmination of history, nor is it political. Furthermore, the image of a personal Messiah

292 ETHICS, POLITICS, AND ZIONISM

is a figure or trope for the role of human agency in realizing messianic goals. What are those goals? Levinas calls them here "an ethical life," and he contrasts it with a life lived by Western values that is secure and abundant and easy, not difficult and demanding. This is not much to go on, but it is a beginning.

At least by this time, Levinas had come to think that a commitment to messianism is expressed in everyday decisions and actions that manifest, to the greatest degree possible, one's sense of one's responsibilities to others. Hence, in political life, decisions and actions are messianic insofar as they create institutions and policies that advance such concerns for others, that seek to meet people's needs, to minimize their suffering and pain, and such. In this respect, all of our lives—Jewish or not—have a messianic potential and are governed by messianic purposes, and what is true for all of our lives is also true for all of our political institutions.[16]

But Levinas also tells us more. He says, in these remarks, that acting in a messianic fashion and becoming a messianically attuned society are not easy. They are hard work, and part of that work comes with sacrifice. One will have to give up thinking primarily of one's own interests and needs and try to turn more attentively to the needs of others first, not exclusively of course but at least first. In the above remarks, Levinas has in mind particularly the sacrifices that many Western Jews—and non-Jews to some extent when they too have emigrated to Israel—have made who have left "safe, secure, and abundant" lives in Western countries (most notably in Europe and North America) and moved to Israel as a matter of commitment. Given the overall view he has about the primacy of interpersonal responsibilities and messianic conduct, then, Levinas takes this sacrifice to be a concrete and real one of giving up privileges and luxuries for a harder life but also an ideological one, so to speak, of giving up an acquisitive and self-interest oriented worldview for one that takes the concerns and well-being of others to be primary. To be sure, these claims may sound overly idealistic and even romantic, but they are certainly compatible and even expressive of Levinas's larger philosophical views. Moreover, as Levinas understands the history of Zionism and the Israeli *halutzim* (pioneers), the life on kibbutzim, and in general the struggles of early Zionist settlers to make the "desert bloom" and to create a vibrant economy in Palestine, there is a good deal of truth in this. And it is a truth supported by his knowledge of the role of social-ism in the thinking of many Zionists. Times have changed, of course, and capitalism has overwhelmed the global economy and certainly the Israeli economy and life in Israel. But this would have been less appar-ent to Levinas in 1982 than it is to us today. At that time, the sacrifices and the accomplishments of the Israeli economy and the commitment to the common good and to a distinct way of life would still have had a powerful grip on Jews in Europe.

At this point in the conversation, Finkielkraut's next comment can be understood best as his way of supplementing Levinas's historical point. If Levinas has tried to explain the sense in which Israel is mes-sianic, Finkielkraut now adds that what Levinas has in mind is a dimen-sion of Zionism that people may have thought had been abandoned or forgotten or lost, and in this sense, the Tel Aviv rally and the sentiment in Israel might be taken to be a revival of this older view. Finkielkraut calls this "a reconciliation of the Israeli elite with its own country" (EP, 295). He associates this "elite" view of Zionism with "the truth of Israel" and suggests that with this demonstration in Tel Aviv, it is being revived, and with due humility and respect, the Jews of the Diaspora ought to endorse it and support it. This is what he says:

> By the word "elite," I don't simply mean, as in other Western countries, the intel-ligentsia or the technostructure. The Israeli elite is made up of kibbutz workers, of the intellectual world, and of the military aristocracy. From 1977 up until the demonstration of the 25 September, this elite suffered from a feeling deeper and more painful than simple political disappointment: it was almost an internal exile. People who felt they had built Israel no longer recognized Israel. Hearing them today, the three hundred thousand people of Tel Aviv have proved that the Zionism of Ben Gurion and Levi Eshkol is still alive. It's not euphoria, but it's no longer *estrangement*. (EP, 295)

This is Finkielkraut's view of course, and we do not know yet whether or to what degree Levinas would endorse it. What is the view? Basically, it is the view that Finkielkraut associates with the Labor Party, with Ben-Gurion and Levi Eshkol and the tradition, as he says, of the kib-butz workers and military aristocracy and the socialists and moderate, realistic nationalists of the Second Aliyah. The critical point, he notes, is that the movement to the right in Israeli politics that culminated in Men-achem Begin's and Likud's victory in 1977 had deposed and dispossessed this liberal and socialist view in favor of a combination of religious and nationalist fanaticisms and extremism. Finkielkraut takes the protest in Tel Aviv to be a reinstatement of this socialist, realistic, and responsible view or at least an indication that it is still alive. He warns against "euphoria" but recommends that at least the perceived estrangement and alienation may not be present to the degree that one might have thought. Finkielkraut does not clarify what about the rally testifies to this view, what about it speaks in behalf of the old Zionist tradition and against the extremism of the right, but it is not hard to imagine what he had in mind. At least part of his thinking must be that intelligence and humanity require that Israel not demonize the Palestinians so that no negotiation or consideration is possible, as Sharon and Begin clearly did. Also, he surely is speaking against aggressive military actions that involve great risk and also that may require a significant level of duplicity and manipulation on the government's part.

Levinas latches on to the phrase "the truth of Israel." It is, to him, not only a reference to a modern political ideology but has deeper, much deeper roots. His tone seems elevated as he links the phrase to the long and ancient tradition of Jewish texts, Jewish writings, and their central theme. This association, of course, between ethical conscience and the teachings of the Bible and Talmud, is a powerful one for Levinas, and the tone of his response here shows just how powerful it is:

> The truth of Israel! It's because a profound attachment to Israel—and to the new mode of life we find there—can only be found precisely in conformity with the heritage of our scriptures. Not enough has been said about this, not enough has been said about the shock that the human possibility of the events of Sabra and Chatila—whoever is behind them—signifies for our entire history as Jews and as human beings. It's not only our thought that we must defend and protect, it's our souls, and that which upholds our souls: our books! Yes, for Jews, this is an enormous question, and the supreme threat: that our books should be in jeopardy! The books which carry us through history, and which, even more deeply than the earth, are our support. (EP, 296)

First, let me clarify what Levinas is saying here, so that we can then address how one might respond to it. There is, Levinas claims, a truth about the State of Israel because there is a continuity between how life is lived there and the "heritage of our scriptures," the teaching of the traditional texts of Judaism. Moreover, that teaching is central to Judaism and to the Jewish purpose in history and also central to human life. Levinas does not make explicit here what that teaching is, but from his writings and thought it is clear what it is—the fact that human existence is fundamentally ethical and requires each of our being responsible to all others and acting in our lives out of a sense of this responsibility. For this reason, because this is the central teaching of the Bible and Talmud and of various literary works, such as the works of Shakespeare, Dostoyevsky, and others, this Jewish concern for the primacy of the ethical and moral is also the central concern of all of us as human beings.

If so, then the events at Sabra and Shatila—as he says, no matter who is "behind them"—are an enormous threat to the persistence and the vitality of Jewish life and of human life generally. They are an act of slaughter, of assault on the most vulnerable and innocent. They show disrespect for humanity and hence are acts that degrade and humiliate the human image. In the face of such atrocities, we must defend, he says, not only our ideas but also "our souls"—that is, our character and the way of life for which that character is the ideal—and this means too a defense of our education and our books, the sources upon which our education is based. It is all of this—the commitment to an ethical way of life, to education of character, and to the books and texts that are its resources—that is in "jeopardy." If events like Sabra and Shatila take place, we are all in trouble, and if they take place without any being held accountable, without any serious challenge, the trouble is that much worse.

This is what Levinas says, and it is a particular application of various themes in his philosophical and theoretical work. But to the listener, at this moment in time and in this conversation, what does it mean? And what does Levinas show by making this statement and emphasizing it as he does? As I have suggested earlier, Levinas's attention here is on the Jewish soul, as it were, and on the truth of Israel. This may strike some readers as a further case of his avoiding any serious engagement with the plight of the victims. To be sure, much of the interview has focused on the Israelis and the Jewish response to the events in Lebanon and then in Tel Aviv. But still, to focus exclusively on what the events mean for Judaism and for Zionism may seem insensitive, if not worse. There is, however, a rather traditional trope evident in his concern with the Judaism and with Israel. Ever since Socrates and Plato, including the Stoics and Kant, much moral philosophy has focused on what agents can do for themselves and what their intentions and their actions mean for any evaluation of their moral character. Levinas, when he says that the events are momentous no matter who is ultimately responsible in a moral and legal sense, is not saying that such responsibility is unimportant. What he is saying is that the events discredit Judaism, Zionism, and indeed all of us simply by having occurred; the issue of who should be held responsible and what the penalties should be is a further matter. But the events' importance morally speaking does not depend upon determining who was responsible. And the reason, for him, is that in a deep and fundamental sense, we are all responsible and the events challenge all of us.

Finkielkraut asks Levinas to elaborate on the centrality of Jewish books to the ethical tradition that has been placed in jeopardy, and Levinas answers by referring to two different passages in the Talmud. In other words, rather than theorize, he points to two texts that reveal the centrality of the ethical to which the crowds in Tel Aviv had testified and which had been put in question by the massacres in Lebanon. The first, he says, occurs three times in the Talmud:

> "Our masters have said: those that are offended without giving offence, those who are defamed without defaming, those who obey in love and rejoice in suffering, are like the sun that rises in its glory." And the metaphor of the sun rising in its glory is borrowed by the Talmudic scholars from Judges, chapter 5, the verse which ends the glorious song of the military victory of Deborah, as if the true light of the sun of victory shone only on those who can "bear defamation without defaming." Or as if all Deborah's military combat simply stood for a moral combat. (EP, 296)

The Talmudic apothegm that Levinas cites is a very famous one. As he says, it occurs three times in the Talmud and is regularly taken to mean that there is a level of obedience to God that involves suffering and pain and nonetheless rejoicing in obedience to Him.[17] This level of piety involves accepting offense and humiliation and nonetheless not reciprocating. But Levinas reads the burden falling on the metaphor from Deborah's song: "So may all your enemies perish, Lord. But may all who love you be like the sun when it rises in its strength [or glory]" (Judges 5:31). Real victory comes with those who act with the greatest moral probity and not with military victories. They are the ones who are really like the sun rising in its glory. Here, then, we have a Talmudic teaching that matches what Levinas takes to be the central theme of the current events in Israel, allegiance to the principle that when the ethical and the political come into conflict, the ethical is primary and must prevail.

It becomes immediately clear, I think, that Levinas takes this to be a central principle of Zionism. It is a way of formulating what he earlier called the "messianic element" in Zionism, and what is true of Zionism is also true of Judaism, and by implication it is true for us all and for all states. The reason I think that this is what he has in mind is that he follows this Talmudic reference with another that he introduces by saying that it will help "those who confuse Zionism—or the relationship to the world and to human beings that its message entails—with some sort of commonplace mystique of the earth as native soil" (EP, 296). That is, not only do the "books" of Judaism help us to understand what Zionism is; they also warn us against what it is not.

In this case, he turns to a passage from Tractate Arakhin in the Talmud. The text that Levinas paraphrases says: "Rabbi Elazar ben Parata teaches: Come and see how great the power of an evil tongue is! Whence do we know its power? From the spies: for if it happens thus to those who bring up an evil report against wood and stones, how much more will it happen to him who brings up an evil report against his neighbor!"[18] That is, if the Bible indicates that slander against land and inert objects will be punished, *a fortiori* the punishment for slandering one's neighbors will be that much greater. Levinas focuses on the *a fortiori* itself—"a person is more holy than a land, even a holy land, since, faced with an affront made to a person, this holy land appears in its nakedness to be but stone and wood" (EP, 297). In other words, Zionism is about our relations with others and what is required of us socially and interpersonally; it is not about the land. The Talmud—representing those books that bear the central message of Judaism and of Zionism—warns against privileging security issues and protection of the land, not to mention the idolatry of the land itself, which marked so much Israeli politics in the period after the Six-Day War. Vividly, Levinas underscores his central theme and what he takes to be the central theme of the massacres and the Israeli protestors' response to them, the primacy of the moral obligation to others over any political and geographical considerations.

PART FOUR

Defense

ELEVEN

LEVINAS AND HIS CRITICS

In the course of this book I have had occasion to notice various criticisms of Levinas, but I have not yet responded to them. To some readers I may have appeared defensive and overly generous to Levinas. My goal has been to show the various ways in which his account of human existence as fundamentally, primordially ethical provides Levinas with the tools for an ethical critique of social and political action, programs, institutions, and policies. For this reason, I do not apologize for the orientation or tone of the book, but I would be remiss if I did not take a moment to consider some of the more provocative and controversial critiques of his work. That is the purpose of this chapter.

My reading of Levinas does not indulge in dramatic or hyperbolic interpretation of his terminology. His various expressions for the face-to-face—from enigma and hostage to persecution, accusation, and substitution—and the extreme way in which he characterizes the claim of the other on the self, for example as a form of violence, are intended, I believe, to call attention to Levinas's break with the tradition of Western philosophy and its conventional expressions. And these expressions and others are suggestive; they recommend interpretations of the intersubjective relation between persons and the various dimensions of our social existence. But I have regularly urged caution about interpreting these terms and about how to understand Levinas's overall project and its implications. My transcendental reading of the face-to-face is a modest or deflationary one, and I am aware that many will find it insufficiently radical and for this reason a distortion of Levinas's thinking. Another consequence of my reading, however, is that I am able to defend Levinas against many of his most vigorous critics. The more extreme they read him, the more objectionable he appears to be. This is not always the case, but there are certainly examples of this dialectic among the work of his critics.

One criticism of Levinas that I think is completely false is the charge that he opposes the political unconditionally, in the sense that he opposes all political systems and institutions and is in effect a political anarchist. This reading is associated with the so-called turn from politics to ethics and also with thinking after the demise of the metaphysical. To be sure, Levinas does often call the face-to-face "anarchic," but this does not mean that it should replace the state and all political institutions. No such reading of Levinas can make sense of much of what he says about social groups, political institutions and policies, law, and so forth. For Levinas, there is no question that our lives are filled with rules, norms, institutions, categories of objects and persons, species, and general programs and organizations and that they should be and must be filled with them. What is all too often forgotten, however, is that all of these structures are constituted by and serve the lives of concrete, particular persons in interpersonal relationships. In this sense, Levinas is a kind of nominalist, but he is not for this reason an opponent of universality and generality; rather he warns that there are good universals and bad ones, and human life flourishes and is enriched when the universals—groups and norms and so forth—are continually attentive to the needs and claims of other persons on each and every one of us and to the responsibilities each of has to and for others. All of life is a matter of degrees of justice and humanity, and it is our duty to do what we can to organize and conduct our lives with the greatest sensitivity and acknowledgment we can cultivate toward others and their dependencies upon us.

Many critics do not see Levinas in this light. They have charged him with inconsistencies, myopia, and one-sidedness. In this chapter I want to turn to a few of these critics in order to clarify Levinas's ethical politics by exploring how he might and ought to be understood in response to them. In particular, I will look primarily at the criticisms of Simon Critchley, Howard Caygill, and Judith Butler and then at Gillian Rose's comments on him.[1]

If my account of Levinas is plausible and compelling, then the reading of someone like Simon Critchley is seriously mistaken from the outset. In his paper "Five Problems in Levinas's View of Politics and the Sketch of a Solution to Them" Critchley contends that the domain of the political and in particular the relation between ethics and politics is a primary location for critique of Levinas. He lists five areas where Levinas's political views are suspicious and problematic: "his classical conception of political friendship as fraternity, as a relation between brothers, between free equals who also happen to be male"; the linking of fraternity and "universalistic republicanism" with God; his androcentric bias and the derivative place of women in his political view; his prejudice in favor of the ideal of the family and the role of the son; and finally, the "vexed" role of the State of Israel where the ideal of justice is its primary goal and yet where the reality is one of violence and even oppression.[2] Critchley inclines toward reading Levinas very literally, as if his terminology about the family, fraternity, the son, the feminine, and Israel is meant in a very restricted way. I have tried to read Levinas in another spirit, not to paper over difficulties but rather to expose that to which he is really committed. On my reading, fraternity is not a relationship exclusively between brothers or even exclusively between men. Families are not the only interpersonal ways of living just and humane lives. Israel—both the people and the state—is not restricted to Judaism. It may be, as Critchley ultimately argues, that in Levinas's thinking there is a gap, a disturbance, between ethics and politics, but it is not present as a solution to any set of pseudo-problems. The gap is present because the ethical is a normative ideal in a sense and an always-compromised because always-accommodated ideal. The infinite demand of infinite others registers in ramified justice all the time. There is no pure justice; there are no perfectly accomplished responsibilities. All there is are adjustments, better and worse, more and less attuned to the claims made on us as individuals and, by extension, on us as societies. Critchley's anarchism gives up on too much too quickly. The serious question for Levinas does not concern his narrowness; rather it is why it is better to have a political system grounded on fraternity and the second-personal than to have one grounded on the individualist, self-interested, and rational foundations of the social contract. Levinas does not point to anarchism of any standard variety; he points to a more humane and decent society ordered by institutions shaped to respond in the best way to human needs and human suffering.

CRITCHLEY ON LEVINAS

I start, then, with Critchley. To begin, I warn that Critchley is not primarily and certainly not exclusively a critic of Levinas as much as someone whose views appropriate features of Levinas within a context in which deficits in Levinas's thinking and politics are identified and discussed.[3] In "Five Problems in Levinas's View of Politics and the Sketch of a Solution to Them," Critchley notes that his reason for turning to politics and Levinas is not to continue the "homage" that is so frequently paid to him but rather to engage Levinas critically. In this spirit, he turns to politics: "In my view, politics is the name of a critical point in Levinas's work, perhaps *the* critical point or even the Achilles's heel of his work."[4] The views represented in this paper were then elaborated in Critchley's controversial book *Infinitely Demanding: Ethics of Commitment, Politics of Resistance.*[5] My goal here is not to give a general overview of Critchley's own position; rather it is to identify and discuss his critical comments about Levinas's political thinking.

As the title indicates, in his essay, Critchley identifies what he calls "five problems" in Levinas's view of politics, that is, five problems with what Levinas says about politics. Critchley admits that the "passage from ethics to politics" for Levinas is a necessary one: "Ethics as the infinite responsibility of the face-to-face relation . . . entails, and has to entail, a relation to politics conceived . . . as the realm of legality, justice, the institution of the state, and everything that Levinas subsumes under the heading of *le tiers*, the third party."[6] In this regard, Critchley accepts the orthodox view, which is the one I have outlined earlier, and which takes the plurality of social existence to be as fundamental and determinative of our lives as the face-to-face itself. Here Critchley treats Levinas's account as a kind of deduction or derivation: starting with the face-to-face as foundational for each particular second-person encounter, Levinas arrives at an account of how social and political institutions, norms and rules, roles and duties, all arise when a third party is acknowledged to exist before the self, alongside each particular other person, and beyond that third party a plurality of others. Levinas calls this plural social situation with its rules and institutions "the political," and Critchley takes Levinas to be saying that the ethical must always occur as embedded within—as "incarnated in"—the political. "There has to be an incarnation of ethics in politics for Levinas."[7] So far, Critchley does not go beyond what is well-known, even if the notion of "entailment" or derivation is not wholly clear.[8]

Critchley uses the expressions "entailment" and "deduction" for the relation between the face-to-face in second-person encounters and the plurality of interrelated persons represented by the image of the "third party." It is worth a moment to distinguish what Levinas has in mind from other well-known approaches in Western political theory. Critchley's terms do not help to clarify Levinas's account. "Entailment" suggests that the foundational or primary relation is a sufficient condition for the existence of the political sphere with its various laws, institutions, and roles, but this is clearly not an accurate description of how the face-to-face second-person encounter is related to the plurality of interpersonal relations. The "third party" is added to the single other person, and the various norms and institutions thereby required to deal with the complexity of social relationships are also added to the immediacy and singularity of the face-to-face of the self with one other person. By itself, the ethical is not sufficient for the political.

Hence, if "deduction" means entailment, then it too is an inaccurate expression for the relation between ethics and politics. The face-to-face does not explain the existence of the political sphere in this sense. It does not explain the existence of the political sphere in the sense of Hobbes, say, or others in the contract tradition or even in the sense of the "divine right of kings" and paternalism, where some pre-political act is responsible for the state's institutions and their authority coming into being. The face-to-face does not "lead to" the political sphere in this sense. But "deduction" might be thought to explain something about that sphere if the word is taken in the Kantian sense. That is, if ethics is the result of a kind of transcendental deduction of a condition that is necessary for the actuality and even the possibility of the political, then there would be a sense in which ethics does explain politics. It explains to us or shows us or helps us to understand how the institutions and practices of the political sphere are possible, and specifically it shows why political norms, institutions, and so forth are themselves necessary, that is, why the human situation is significantly altered for the self by the presence of more than one other person. In particular, the fact of the face-to-face—of the other's claim upon the self, for each and every particular self-other encounter—explains the role of political policies, principles, and institutions. The latter provide summaries, guidance, and regularity concerning how the self should act toward multiple others. In a sense, then, the ethical provides us with a functional explanation of why the political sphere exists and what purposes it serves; it provides us with the "point" or purpose of the political. Moreover, insofar as the ethical is normative and motivating, it inclines us to act according to the norms and so forth of the political domain, and insofar as it sets a standard or ideal, the ethical constitutes a way of determining how successful or defective are the norms and policies of the political sphere and the ways that we act in terms of them.

With this clarification, then, we can understand what Critchley means by the "necessity" of the ethics-politics relation for Levinas. This "necessity," however, is accompanied by worries, and Critchley refers to them collectively as a "disquietude" or "a series of open questions with regard to the passage from ethics to politics," which he articulates in the "five problems" I have referred to.[9] The five rubrics are fraternity, monotheism, androcentrism, filiality and the family, and Israel. After he discusses these five rubrics or "problems," Critchley says, "My hope would be for a nonfraternalistic, nonmonotheistic, nonandrocentric, nonfilial, nonfamilial, and non-Zionist conception of the relation of ethics to politics," and later in the essay he refers to such a view as an "anarchist metapolitics," and he associates it with an argument "for the experience of conscience as the link between ethical responsibility and political action."[10] To summarize, then, Critchley takes the relation between ethics and politics in Levinas to be critical rather than constructive. Ethics does not give rise to politics; it is present in the political as a "disturbance" or disruption, a critical moment that calls the political to be true to itself and not false and "tyrannical."

To begin, my primary purpose is not to elaborate Critchley's solution as he sketches it in this paper and then develops it more fully in his

book *Infinitely Demanding*. I will have something to say about these matters shortly, but for the moment I want to ask how these five problems or
rubrics constitute a series of difficulties with Levinas's account of how
ethics is related to politics. More precisely, we might put the question
this way: how and why does Critchley object to a Levinasian politics that
is fraternal, monotheistic, androcentric, filial and familial, and Zionist?
And indeed is he right that Levinas takes politics in all of its manifestations to have these characteristics? Clearly, Critchley does not think
that what Levinas offers—most explicitly in *Otherwise Than Being*—is
a deduction or derivation of the political—the domain of justice, of law
and political institutions—from the ethical, that is, from the demand of
the other person or its claim on the self that registers as the self's infinite responsibilities to and for the other person. As I have pointed out,
Critchley would agree with us, I think, in taking the primary role of the
ethical vis-à-vis politics to be critical and not constructive. The issues
Critchley raises under the five rubrics or problems concern the specific
features of the political insofar as it is "grounded" in some way on the
ethical character of the face-to-face. How does Critchley read Levinas?
Has he been fair to him? And is he right to object to what Levinas says
about the political?

The first rubric that Critchley employs is fraternity. What is the objection that Critchley has in mind? It is that "at the level of politics, the
ethical relation is translated into what I would see as a classical conception of political friendship as fraternity, as a relation between brothers,
between free equals who also happen to be male."[11] Although this objection is not altogether clear, it appears to be the charge of Eurocentrism
that has often been leveled against Levinas. That is, politics, like ethics,
is the domain of "brothers," of those who are like one another. Levinas
too frequently claims that all of human culture and society is governed
by the Bible and the Greeks, by the teachings of Jerusalem and those
of Athens. But such a claim leaves out all those aligned with neither of
these cultural and literary traditions. Critchley later cites the oft-quoted
comment in which Levinas worries that Russia might cast its lot with an
"Asian civilization," a "yellow peril [that] is not racial but spiritual. Not
about inferior values but about a radical strangeness, strange to all the
density of its past . . . a lunar, a Marian past."[12] Critchley's objection, then,

is to Levinas's parochialism, his failure to appreciate human diversity and otherness, a failure that infects not simply his occasional journalistic comments but even more deeply his philosophical understanding of the face-to-face and its political extension. Is the first-person self responsible only for those like him or her, his brothers, other free and equal selves? And is this responsibility expressed politically only among others like ourselves, others who are free, with needs and vulnerabilities like our own? Is there not more to human interpersonal conduct than what is taught in the Bible and in Greek culture and literature? This, then, is the first criticism that Critchley levels at Levinas. I am not sure that it is exclusively or even precisely a criticism of Levinas's politics. Perhaps it is more accurate to say that it is a parochialism about his conception of the primacy of the ethical in Levinas's philosophical anthropology that is especially manifest when it is manifest in Levinas's conception of the political sphere. It is a parochialism, an elitism, a Eurocentric imperialism.

Critchley's second problem he calls "monotheism," which he clarifies as "the linking of fraternity to the question of God, and the idea that political community is or has to be monotheistic."[13] Or, as he then puts it, "the universality of fraternity is ensured through the passage to God." That is, fraternity for Levinas is universal, and this universalism is underwritten by taking the foundation of our obligations to one another to be based on a relation to the one God. That all human beings are created in the divine image makes of all a brotherhood of the worthy. Monotheism is the religious commitment that corresponds to a political fidelity to the idea of "universalistic republicanism." If fraternity, then, is a bias against those genuinely other than ourselves, then monotheism is a bias against those whose conception of the divine involves multiplicity and those who have no such conception at all. Critchley's second objection is that Levinasian ethics is a religious ethics.

Fraternity, Critchley notes, is also, as it happens, exclusively a male relationship. His third problem concerns this failure to appreciate and incorporate the insights of the feminine. He calls this Levinas's "androcentrism." "Relations of solidarity between women are thinkable only on analogy with fraternity—hence, sorority is secondary to fraternity, sisterhood is secondary to brotherhood."[14] Just as Levinas privileges European culture and a monotheistic West, so he privileges the perspective and the life of the masculine, especially in terms of its political implications.

The fourth objection concerns the special role the family plays for Levinas and the particular relationship between the father and son. As in the case of the other objections, Critchley is not simply noticing contingent or occasional preferences or tendencies on Levinas's part. What he claims is that the family and the filial relationship play fundamental and determinative roles in the way Levinas formulates the ethical and then elaborates how the ethical is present in the political sphere. Critchley cites Levinas's "invocation of the 'marvel of the family'" near the end of *Totality and Infinity* and refers as well to the major role that family, fecundity, paternity, the father-son relationship, and such play in its fourth part. There is something especially valuable about this nexus of features or elements; better than other social relationships and roles, they express the salience of the ethical, its effectiveness and its special domains. As Critchley notes, Levinas starts *Totality and Infinity* with the "violence of the state only to end with the family," and "it then becomes a question of linking the pluralism of the family to the political order."[15] But the family has no single shape and character in all cultures and in all periods, nor does it organize its members with the same relationships, nor indeed is it always an esteemed and privileged venue. And while paternity and sonship are especially valuable to some, they are not always the most valuable familial relationships and the ones that are the most elevating and worthwhile.

Finally, Critchley charges Levinas with identifying the political with Israel. He makes this point in a very precise way when he claims that this objection concerns "the *political fate* of Levinasian ethics, namely, the vexed question of Israel." What exactly does Critchley mean? He gives us a clue when he reminds the reader that "Israel might be said to have a double function in Levinas's discourse, as both ideal and real, as an ideal where ethical responsibility would be incarnated in social justice, and as a really existing state where justice is endlessly compromised by violence. The name 'Israel' is suspended, possibly fatally suspended, between ideality and reality, between holy history and political history." When ethics, as Levinas understands it, is present in the political sphere, the result Levinas calls "Israel," Critchley seems to be saying, but this could mean that the political is the ideal Israel or the political is the real Israel. To Critchley, one is a just state and a just society, the goal of political principles and institutions, but the other is an unjust state and a society wracked by violence, persecution, and oppression. Citing Caygill, Critchley calls this a risk, that the "name *par excellence* for a just polity" is also "the nonplace of the ethical relation to the other," and he uses as an image of this risk the fact that the very same Ariel Sharon who was found guilty by the board of inquiry after the Beirut massacres and was removed from his post later became the prime minister of the State of Israel. Moreover, he aligns this paradox, as it were, with the judgment that in the "neoimperialist" United States, which he groups together with Israel under the same rubric, the very president who sent the country into war in Iraq is fond of reading the Bible, the paradigmatic literary resource for the teaching of ethical responsibility and justice.[16]

In part, then, Critchley's indictment of the role of Israel in Levinas's thought, as the paradigmatic locale of the political, is based on Critchley's own interpretation of recent events in Israel and the conflict between Israel and the Palestinian people. The criticism he levels would lose its grip if his judgment about the conduct of the State of Israel, her government and military, were different. And one is not surprised to find him associating Israeli "neoimperialism," as he calls it, with the policies and conduct of the United States, an alignment of purpose and character long a feature of criticism of Israel at least since the 1960s. Thus, Critchley's criticism of the role of Israel for Levinas is not internal in the same way that his other criticisms are. To speak of Levinas's Eurocentrism or his privileging of familial and male relationships or his assumption that ethics must be tied to monotheism, these are all objections to Levinas's use of certain concepts, where the concepts are themselves not contested; their meaning is clear. What is at issue is their role for Levinas or the use to which he puts them. Are they illustrative terms or figures, or are they definitive and restrictive? Indeed, Critchley does call attention to precisely this distinction when he notices how Levinas, in the Talmudic lesson "Judaism and Revolution," among other places, uses the name "Israel" to refer to any people.[17] But when he does, Critchley risks collapsing two objections to Levinas. One is that he is one-sided, insensitive to genuine otherness, in terms of the values that he privileges and the concepts he employs; another is that he is, as it were, morally obtuse or misguided, insofar as he is utterly mistaken about who is the victim and the needy, who is the oppressor and the ethically bankrupt. One criticism is a criticism of Levinas as a philosopher; the other is a criticism of Levinas's moral judgment. One is a philosophical criticism; the other is a moral and political judgment.

Critchley does not hide his own moral and political position and the associations that draw his ire. Alongside his dislike for the policies and practices both of the United States and of the State of Israel, he targets France; he is as disturbed by the identification of Levinas's ethics with French republicanism and the French tradition as he is by its identification with Israel and Zionism. In part, what repels Critchley is the identification of Levinas's central insight about our infinite responsibilities to others with any particular tradition or with any particular political sphere. As he argues later in the paper and more fully in *Infinitely Demanding*, Critchley advocates a kind of anarchism, not perhaps a total rejection of the state but certainly a robust, vigilant, and radical critique of contemporary state actions.[18] But in part what repels him are the particular identifications that are most vividly possible, given what Levinas himself wrote and said, and preeminent in this regard are the State of Israel and France. It is hard to separate Critchley's special variety of anarchism—"a moment of *disincarnation* that challenges the borders and legitimacy of the state"—from his very extreme assessment of Israeli policy and conduct.[19]

There is an anarchism that opposes the state altogether; it argues against the necessity or even the desirability of the state and seeks to oppose it in every way. To this kind of anarchism, the state is never legitimate; it never, with any modifications, is capable of serving valuable, useful, and significant functions. This is not, I think, Critchley's form of anarchism. Rather he contrasts his own view this way:

> In my view, Levinasian ethics is not ethics for its own sake in the manner of what we might call "angelic" readings of Levinas, but nor is it ethics for the sake of the state, which we might think of as the right-wing Levinasian option, whether that is linked to the logic of Zionism or indeed a quasi-Gaullist, quasi-Chiracian argument for French exceptionalism. On my view, ethics is ethics for the sake of politics. Better stated perhaps, ethics is the metapolitical disturbance of politics for the sake of politics, that is, for the sake of a politics that does not close over in

itself, becoming what Levinas would call totality, becoming a whole. Following
Levinas's logic, when politics is left to itself without the disturbance of ethics, it
risks becoming tyrannical.[20]

I think that it is clear from a passage like this one that for Critchley the
state and the political are necessary. Ethics is not a flight into world-
lessness, nor is it a way of justifying or legitimating the state and the
political. Levinas is no Platonist or Gnostic, nor is he Machiavelli. One
option is insufficiently attentive to the political, the other insufficiently
serious about the ethical. Rather, both are necessary in the precise way
that the right attitude to ethics is to take it to be a constant critique and
reprimand of political principles, policies, and practices.

This is the work of the people, for Critchley, and hence it is the core of
a genuine democracy, in which "democratization is politicization . . . the
cultivation of . . . forms of 'dissensual emancipatory praxis' or what might
also be called *politicities*, sites of hegemonic struggle that work against
the consensual idyll of the state, not in order to do away with the state
or consensus, but to bring about its endless betterment."[21] If we ignore
the jargon in this passage and the allusions to other continental political
thinkers, we might focus on the final clauses—"not in order to do away
with the state or consensus, but to bring about its endless betterment."
This is ethical political critique that is neither utopian nor messianic in
any classical sense. It is not anarchist in a wholly oppositional sense.
It is not teleological or even progressive. It takes every instant, every
situation, every moment as having the potential to be better, more just,
more humane. As I have suggested elsewhere, it is a kind of episodic, particularist messianism, in which, as Walter Benjamin reminds us, every
moment has the potential of becoming the straight gate through which
the messiah enters into history—with the proviso, of course, that each
one of us is capable of being that messiah.[22]

I have been using Critchley's paper to help us to consider some of the
objections that have been made of Levinas and in particular of Levinas's
conception of the political and its relation to the ethical. One temptation,
which Critchley's paper discloses, is the temptation to treat Levinas's use
of various terminology, figures, concepts, and so forth in a very literal or
restricted way, and doing so leads many to object to Levinas's chauvinism, Eurocentrism, religious bias, and more. Another temptation, which

Critchley also exposes, is to read terms and concepts in Levinas as his way of symbolically referring to other equally objectionable ideas or domains. How much of what he says is detachable from a literal or restricted interpretation is certainly not completely clear. When Levinas speaks of the special role of the Bible and the Greeks for human experience, why not take him at his word? Does the "Bible" mean whatever texts or literary resources convey the centrality of interpersonal responsibility? Does the "Greeks" refer to whatever traditions elevate rational inquiry, thought and examination, science and philosophy? Or does the "Bible" simply refer to the biblical text, and the Greeks to Homer and Hesiod, Herodotus and Thucydides, Aeschylus and Sophocles, Plato, Aristotle and so on?

We have said enough about these matters, along the way, to enable us to set these questions aside and to focus instead on another issue that Critchley's critical reading of Levinas brings to the surface. This other issue is the distinction between two types of objections, those raised about his philosophical thinking internally, as I have put it, and those raised about his political judgments in particular cases or at least about the sometimes disturbing ways he expresses himself. Moreover, we might want to consider if these two types of objections are separate one from the other. Ought we to treat his political judgments to be somehow implied or derived from his philosophical views, so that objectionable political comments become, to some degree, reasons for questioning and perhaps even for rejecting his philosophical views?

Perhaps, however, my reservations about Critchley have missed the point. Critchley's various charges—concerning a kind of parochialism and Eurocentrism in Levinas—may not arise simply as a faulty and facile inference from Critchley's political judgments or as a simple failure to take Levinas too literally and with insufficient attention to his use of metaphors or literary figures. Worries like these may not take Critchley sufficiently seriously. Might we put Critchley's concerns this way: Levinas, whose thinking is rooted in a profound appreciation for difference, transcendence, and otherness, never seems to have avoided the faults of homogenization, of comprehension and imperialism? Levinas's own thinking suffers from a serious one-sidedness and a failure to expose itself to the very sense of unpredictability, undecidability, indeterminacy, and openness-to-the-other that it purports to advocate. And the locus of this failure or limitation is his claims about how ethics and politics are related. It is here—when it comes to political or concrete and everyday dealings with non-Europeans, with feminine and gender issues, and so forth—where Levinas's discourse and his statements belie his failure to take otherness with the utmost seriousness. These failures are not just verbal slips or unfortunate choices; they expose a deep failure or inadequacy or error.

I think that these issues are too large and too difficult for us to deal with them here in anything like a complete or satisfying way. But I can say this. At a critical moment in Levinas's thought, as I understand him, he asks where, in human experience and in human life, each of us as selves and agents engage with what is radically and wholly other, what transcends ourselves and our world, what does not threaten to annihilate us in this engagement, and yet what we nonetheless encounter or confront. This question arises for him when he appreciates that there are matters like pain and suffering and death that assault us as from the outside and are other than ourselves in some serious way. Certainly it arises for him or would arise for him when we try to understand how we grasp the radical evil of certain atrocities and suffering and yet go on thereafter. Levinas's conception of the face of the other person and of our infinite responsibilities to and for that other person and each and every other person is part of his response to this challenge—of an otherness beyond all relation to which we are nonetheless related.

In short, when confronted by the various ways in which our lives are shaped, comprehended, and articulated by ourselves and our societies, Levinas takes us also to be engaged with that which transcends us, which is other. And when he locates the character of that engagement or relation in our responsibility to the other person and then appreciates how it grounds and provides content for what we call ethics and morality, his understanding of the human condition takes on a foundational character, a character of being grounded in a way that we all share. Critchley, I take it, would object to such a foundational universality, and he would argue that Levinas's one-sided political choices indicate how such a view fails to appreciate how otherness—as expressed in our everyday lives—

occurs. To me, however, this objection is to rule Levinas's conception of our relation to transcendence out of court from the start and to confuse everyday otherness, which occurs in all kinds of historically and culturally conditioned ways, with absolute or unconditional otherness, which occurs for us all as a structural feature of all our interpersonal relations. It is the latter that Levinas calls infinite responsibility, substitution, and much else. While it is not unrelated to all our particular othernesses, our local differences, it must not be confused with them.

CAYGILL ON LEVINAS AND THE PALESTINIAN

In discussing Levinas's participation in the interview with Alain Finkielkraut shortly after the massacres in Sabra and Shatila, in September of 1982, I have already raised some of these issues. Many critics have said or suggested that in the interview Levinas failed to express his moral views with clarity and in a compelling way, and that his lack of sympathy for the plight of the Palestinian victims of the massacres was a serious moral failure. Moreover, there are those who have taken this criticism of Levinas's moral and political judgment to count against the cogency and coherence of his views about human existence and the primacy of the ethical.

Critchley may have serious qualms about aspects of Levinas's politics, but there is nonetheless a good deal of agreement between Critchley and Levinas and indeed much that Critchley appropriates from Levinas. At first glance, this also seems to be true of Judith Butler, whose recent work is importantly indebted to Levinas and yet with whose work she expresses serious dissatisfactions.[23] But before I turn to Butler, we ought to turn first to the most detailed and sharp criticism of Levinas's interview, that of Howard Caygill.

In chapter 10 I have attempted a close reading of the notorious interview after Sabra and Shatila as a preparation for now stepping back and asking what Levinas's contribution can be taken to mean. As I have mentioned, the dominant pitch of reactions to the interview has been negative. Many readers have found Levinas to be evasive, unresponsive, and possibly insensitive. To some, I am sure, his remarks may seem an aberration; to others, they indicate serious flaws in his thinking. We now have to consider what might be said about these different responses when considered against the evidence of what he did say and how we have understood the conversation.

One of the most detailed and at the same time critical accounts of Levinas's part in the conversation can be found in Howard Caygill's *Levinas and the Political*.[24] Caygill probably makes the strongest case we have that Levinas exposes himself to very serious criticisms in the interview, so it will be helpful to look carefully at his treatment. It is only one piece of an examination of Levinas's understanding of Zionism, but I think it can be read on its own. When points he makes allude or refer to earlier points, we can consider the relevance of earlier discussion in the book.

Caygill begins with a very partisan account of the events in southern Lebanon and Beirut. His description of the events is framed as evidence against "Levinas's view of the defensive view of the State of Israel."[25] When Caygill reports Menachem Begin's contentions that the operations in Lebanon were defensive and his comparison of the PLO with the Nazis, and when Caygill calls the massacres a war crime, he does so to discredit any claims that the overall operation was defensive in initial purpose. But of course he cannot show this; nor would Levinas had thought so, as Caygill realizes. For Caygill, the defense claim is a sham. But there were certainly security issues in play, and there is no reason to think that Levinas had reason to doubt them on September 28.

As Caygill moves on to discuss the interview, he says that Shlomo Malka's introduction "evok[es] the shock felt by Jewish communities throughout the world at the murders" and that "Levinas replied evasively to his opening question on whether Israel was innocent or responsible for the deaths at Sabra and Shatila—prejudging the question of guilt—'Despite the lack of guilt here—and probably there, too' (perhaps referring to France/the Diaspora and Israel/Lebanon?)—and then claiming the 'honor of responsibility.'"[26] Even these introductory statements are riddled with mistakes, lapses, and confusions, as our reading of Malka's first question and Levinas's response has shown. Malka gives a rather objective description of what had happened and certainly evoked no shock. Furthermore, Levinas did not evade Malka's question about innocence and responsibility. He began by doing what was, given his own views, necessary, by focusing on responsibility in order to make clear that while all are responsible, the issue of innocence and guilt had yet to be decided. He does not evade that question when he says that there is no guilt here—clearly in Paris—and probably not there—in Tel Aviv; this is surely unobjectionable. His point is that even when the issue of innocence and guilt is set aside, the question of responsibility does not go away, and the Israelis in Tel Aviv realized this and acted in behalf of it.

It is not long before Caygill, his paraphrase accurate but highly selective, finds his way to Malka's question about the Palestinians and whether they are, as the enemies of Israel, the most other and hence, by implication, deserving of the most concerned acceptance and aid. He describes Levinas's answer this way: "Faced with this unavoidable question that went to the heart not only of his philosophy but also of his political judgment, Levinas's reply is chilling and, to use his idiom, opens a wound in his whole œuvre."[27] He then quotes Levinas's reply, which we have discussed in detail above. Caygill's terms raise a number of questions. Why exactly should we—and Levinas—take Malka's question to go "to the heart not only of his philosophy but also of his political judgment"? And why is Levinas's reply "chilling"? Does it in fact "open a wound" in his entire project? Given our commentary and clarification of Levinas's response, what follows in Caygill's account can only impress the reader as a cascade of confusions and errors, all aimed at vilifying Levinas for his response.

Caygill does in fact see what Levinas is saying in the first words of his response, but he then makes a crucial mistake. He realizes that Levinas is distinguishing here between the ethical other and the political other or "between empirical and transcendental others," as he puts it. And he sees the possibility that Levinas is referring in his response to the empirical other, what I would call the political other or other persons in everyday experience. He calls this an "apologetic response" and suggests instead that "a harder thought is that Levinas's claim is rigorously consistent with his philosophy."[28] He says this, he argues, because Levinas must accept the inevitability of war. But what does he mean by "rigorously consistent"? And what are we to make of this?

As we have seen, Levinas's answer is composed of two parts. In the first, he calls attention to what he means by confronting the face of the other person and that the other person here is the ethical other or the

other who makes a claim on me and to whom and for whom I am responsible. In the second part, however, he introduces the third party, and this
means that we are in the regime of justice, as he calls it, in the domain of
ordinary life. Here the other person is classified, thematized, compared,
and such. This is clearly the everyday self, what Caygill calls "the empirical self." It is as certain as can be that here Levinas is in fact talking
about such others, everyday others. Only here are there enemies; only
here is there any question of degrees of responsibility and justice, and
so forth. When Caygill argues that to be "rigorously consistent" Levinas
would have to be talking in this second stage about the transcendental
or ethical other, he is simply distorting not only what Levinas says here
but also his overall thinking. Caygill worries who is the neighbor and
who is attacking whom. But this is completely clear; indeed can there be
any doubt? When your neighbor attacks another neighbor and even acts
unjustly—when as a Jew, he sees Israelis attacking Palestinians or vice
versa—then there is the issue of who is a friend, who an enemy, who is
just, and who unjust. That is, all such discriminations and classifications
are matters of how in everyday life the plurality of our social situation
occurs and how the various parties, all of whom one is responsible for
and to, engage with one another. This is simply an articulation of what
Levinas says in more abstract terms in *Otherwise Than Being*.[29] All of
Caygill's questions, the intent of which seem to be to make what is clear
confused and unclear, lead to the suggestion that the Palestinian is not
an other at all or is not the Israeli's other and indeed not the Jew's other.
This should be a *reductio* of Caygill's line of thinking and not a conclusion
worthy of anyone's attention. For Levinas, everyone's relationship with
each and every other person is one of responsibility but also one of claim
and petition; we are all others in the ethical or transcendental sense.

Caygill's unwillingness to follow up on the clarity of the distinction
between empirical and transcendental others, between ethical and political others, leads him to a further confusion. He next charges that the
problem of knowing who is right or wrong, just or unjust simply "reduces
ethics to the problem of knowledge." But this knowledge, he argues, must
be ethical and not simply "of tactical or strategic utility." And if so, then it
makes it that much harder, he says, "to identify in the other an enemy."[30]
Once again, Caygill takes Levinas to be talking about the face-to-face

as a transcendental structure, when, as we have seen, the course of the argument makes it clear that he is talking about the everyday or political domain, where discriminations between friend and enemy, just and unjust, and so forth are made and where the important knowledge is about how to respond to others, what to judge and what to do, and not about "moral knowledge" of what right and wrong are in any everyday sense. In all cases in everyday affairs, what is just and unjust and so forth is a matter of judgment based on weighing responsibilities, resources, and a host of other situational considerations. Caygill takes Levinas to be utterly confused about the underlying or primordial structure that grounds moral normativity, but he is not. Levinas is very careful to distinguish it from the much more contextual judgments we make in everyday life.

Caygill continues to make this same mistake or to perpetuate this same confusion. He notices Levinas's use of the notion of the messianic and associates it, as Levinas himself does, with sacrifice. He quotes Levinas's statement that many early Zionist settlers and also later immigrants "sacrificed" secure and comfortable lives for the challenges and the hardships of life in Palestine, and he asks if it were not more appropriate to apply the terminology to the victims in Lebanon who "were sacrificed by the state to its own pursuit of power. On this possibility, that of the idolatrous, sacrificial state, Levinas remained silent until his last words in the discussion."[31] The word "sacrifice," as many of the terms Levinas uses, has a crucial ambiguity. It is sometimes used for the self in terms of its relationship of unqualified devotion to and responsibility for the other person, as virtually synonymous with "hostage," "substitution," and any number of other expressions. But at the other times, "sacrifice" refers to the differential responses of people to the claims of others upon them; at times, we sacrifice for others to a great degree, at times to a lesser degree. Levinas's comments about the settlers in Palestine do not refer to primordial responsibility but rather to one expression of that fundamental obligation to others. Levinas's point about many Zionists is that they turned from lives devoted to self-interest and what he calls "egotism" to lives committed to justice and humanity toward others. To be sure, the Palestinian victims in the refugee camps were killed, indeed slaughtered. And if the reasons for it were about power and domination, then they were, in a sense, sacrificed to serve those purposes. But, as we have discussed, this judgment about Israel as a state and about her purposes in Lebanon was and is a controversial one, and there is no reason to think that Levinas felt that the case had been made. About this Caygill is right: Levinas does not commit himself to treating contemporary Israel as an "idolatrous, sacrificial state." He certainly believes that appalling events have occurred and that Israel and her military were implicated, but he also believes that more must be said about Israel and her character as a state and about this moment in which her political character and her moral character have come into conflict.

Caygill concludes his comments on the interview by calling attention to the final Talmudic passage to which Levinas refers and which Levinas interprets as meaning that the core of Zionism is the concern for justice and for others and not for the land, for "wood and stones." In other words, Levinas takes the Talmudic text from Tractate Arakhin to allude to the lesson he has advocated throughout the interview, that Zionism is facing a critical moment in Israel because the massacres and how Israel responds to them will reveal whether Zionism is being faithful to the primacy of the ethical over security issues and political necessities. Caygill helpfully notices that Levinas had discussed the theme of what one learns from the explorers who brought back a false report in another place, in *Nine Talmudic Readings* and in the specific reading entitled "Promised Land or Permitted Land," where the text under discussion is Tractate Sotah (34b–35a). There Levinas says:

> The explorers go toward this land so that this land will be shamed, so that
> the worshippers of this land—for example, the Zionists of that time—will be
> shamed. They have decided, in the name of truth, to confound the Zionists....
> We are among intellectuals, that is, among people to whom one tells the whole
> truth. The intellectual has been defined as the one who always misses the mark
> but who, at least, aims very far. Rabi has said that he is the one who refuses rea
> sons of State, that is, who tells the truth.[32]

The truth is that Israel and Zionism should be primarily concerned with justice and not with reasons of state. The Zionists who are shamed are those who do not think this but who worship "wood and stone," so to speak.

Caygill thinks that in 1982 Levinas takes the passage in Tractate Arakhin to claim that "holy land is but stone and wood compared to an offended person"[33] but that by alluding to the earlier discussion of the explorers, Levinas fails to appreciate the stronger point it makes. Caygill is right; the Talmudic reading of 1965 does make a stronger point. There Levinas says:

> There is no right that cannot be revoked. . . . Only those who are always ready to accept the consequences of their actions and to accept exile when they are no longer worthy of a homeland have a right to enter this homeland.—You see, this country is extraordinary. It is like heaven. It is a country which vomits up its inhabitants when they are not just. There is no other country like it; the resolution to accept a country under such conditions confers a right to that country.[34]

The exaggerated view of the Land of Israel aside, this point is wholly consistent with what Levinas has later said in 1982 about the priority of justice over land as the core of Zionism. In the interview we are discussing, Levinas uses the Talmudic text to underscore the fact that ethics is more important to Zionism than the land itself. In the earlier Talmudic reading, his point was that continued right to the land depends upon the degree to which Zionism is just and humane. I am inclined to think that the role of the land as an object of value in itself has changed between 1965 and 1982 because of the Six-Day War, the emergence of various Greater Israel movements, and especially the rise of Likud and the political right in Israel, for whom the land and security issues were considered unqualifiedly paramount. All of this raises the stakes for Zionism and for Levinas's conception of its nature, but about this Levinas does not say anything. His earlier and later remarks are by no means inconsistent, but they do raise a serious question about how worried he might have been in 1982 about the future.

One of the central themes in Caygill's criticism is that Levinas, in order to be consistent, must either be confusing his distinction between the empirical and the transcendental or be altering his views, as a result of unwarranted prejudice against the Palestinians and in behalf of Israel and Zionism. I have tried to show, however, that Levinas is not confused. He maintains his distinction and is careful about when he is referring to the face-to-face and the transcendental structure that underlies our moral responsibilities and obligations to others and when he is referring to the everyday, practical and political ways in which those responsibilities work out in the highly complex networks of social relationships that

DEFENSE

make up our lives. My result is that he is critical of Israel but cautious and guarded; he is not happy at all with what has happened, and he takes the moment to be a critical one for Zionism and for Israel. But he does not attack Israel or defend the Palestinians. Caygill takes Levinas to be either confused or morally suspect. Hence, we have a choice. We can read Levinas as coherent, consistent, and yet cautiously critical of Israel while also holding on to a fairly positive but not unsupported conception of Zionism. Or we can read Levinas as incoherent and confused, while failing to appreciate the depths of the atrocities and what they show about Israel, that it is a power-hungry, violent, criminal state whose actions are heinous and criminal by any serious standards.

There are those who have found it easy to side with readers like Caygill by choosing the latter alternative. Judith Butler, for example, has clearly done so.[35] But we should beware of where the burden of intellectual responsibility must first fall. The options I just laid out rest on two issues: (1) the coherence of the view Levinas presents in the interview and (2) the reader's own views about Israel and Zionism. The two issues are connected. Caygill, I believe, wants the reader to believe that his reading of Levinas supports his critical attitude toward Israel and Zionism.[36] But his reading of the interview is ungenerous and faulty, as I have tried to show. I would contend instead that a fair and careful reading of the interview supports the interpretation I have given, and what is compatible with it is the judgment that Levinas is concerned about Zionism and rightfully so, but that his views are neither inconsistent nor confused. Nor do they fail to appreciate the humanity of the victims of the massacres of Sabra and Shatila or the extent of the atrocities performed against them. These are extremely serious matters to him, and their occurrence calls attention not only to how political decisions and actions are subject to ethical critique but also how much depends upon responding in the most serious way to what has taken place—for Israel, for Zionism, for Jews and Judaism, and for others as well. This is what I contend. A responsible reading of Levinas's participation in the interview shows that his position toward the massacres and toward Israel is coherent and reasonable; he supports the Zionist idea and is disturbed by the current realities in Israel, sufficiently so that one wonders how he would respond to the developments that have occurred during the nearly twenty years since he passed away.

Moreover, the interview has larger implications for Levinas's ethical views and their relation to political decisions, actions, policies, and institutions. There is an argument against the relevance of Levinas's ethics to politics. We might summarize it this way:

1. If Levinas's account of ethics has anything to teach us about politics, then it should, surely after the massacres in 1982, lead to a severe criticism of Israel as a colonialist and criminal state.
2. Levinas's account, in the interview, does not lead Levinas to such criticism of Israel.
3. Therefore, Levinas's account of ethics has nothing to teach us about politics.

Readers like Caygill and Butler hold (1) to be true, but surely Levinas would not, and I cannot imagine anyone holding it without harboring in advance of turning to Levinas a very negative opinion about Israel as a state. Clearly (2) is true, but for me it is true because it ought to be true, while for others it is true only because Levinas himself has altered his view of ethics in unfortunate ways or because what he says in the interview is confused and inconsistent. My conclusion, then, is that the interview, while revealing, is not a firm justification for thinking that Levinasian ethics does or does not have significant political implications. But, on my reading, it does tell us something valuable. It shows that Levinas was sensitive to political issues and did believe that ultimately politics—as art, culture, religion, and all the rest of everyday life—serves moral ends. It can be judged in terms of the degree to which it succeeds in taking ethical considerations seriously and as primary and how well it brings them to realization in our political lives. The state, that is, is subject to ethical critique, and the response of nearly four hundred thousand Israelis in the streets of Tel Aviv in September of 1982 shows that this critique was in fact leveled against the Israeli government and military by her own citizens.

BUTLER'S LEVINAS AND ITS DISTORTIONS

It is time to turn finally to one of the most complex and provocative appropriations and criticisms of Levinas, by Judith Butler. Let me begin with what Butler appropriates from Levinas. Butler finds Levinas—in particular Levinas's notion of the face—valuable as a source for understanding second-person address, the way in which subjectivity occurs as the target of the other person's address or claim, and the character of moral authority.[37] This appropriation of Levinas, moreover, allows Butler to sketch what she calls "a possible Jewish ethic of non-violence" and to relate it to recent events.[38] I will return to this connection with Judaism shortly. Butler starts by analyzing various passages in which Levinas presents and portrays the face; she then concludes that "to respond to the face, to understand its meaning, means to be awake to what is precarious in another life or, rather, the precariousness of life itself. This cannot be an awakeness, to use his word, to my own life. . . . . It has to be an understanding of the precariousness of the Other. This is what makes the face belong to the sphere of ethics."[39] Butler is not here altogether clear about what makes the face ethical. She could mean that what makes the face ethical is the fact that it involves the subject's sensitivity or attentiveness to the lives of other persons or that it involves an awareness of the "precariousness"—the vulnerability and dependency—that marks their lives or that it concerns the subject's attention to this fragility of life itself, wherever one finds it. I am inclined to think that universality is not the issue for Butler; rather what she finds in Levinas is an original orientation toward the needs of others and not our own needs or claims or interests. But presumably this other-directedness is not sufficient to make a relation or claim ethical; what Levinas adds is that the subject's concern is for the other's life and for the way in which that life is not self-sufficient. It is precarious or dependent and intrinsically so. Life cannot sustain itself; it requires help from outside. From one perspective, each living being needs support and assistance; from another perspective, each living other needs the subject's support and assistance. The sheer fact of social existence carries with it this claim on the part of every other and aimed at every subject; before any other characteristic or feature, a person is subjected to this claim to support or assist each and every other person. Finally, Butler adds that the subject, as the target of this claim or dependency or fragility, is also tempted to kill the other. This strikes me as a mistaken reading of Levinas. Only once there is the claim to accept and assist, when there are many others, can there be a rule or norm, and only then can the self be tempted to follow that rule or not. Moreover, even prior to the formulation of any rule or command, only in everyday life are we sometimes tempted to ignore or neglect or harm the other person; at the level of the face—the transcendental level—all that is present is the claim and the responsibility, nothing more but also nothing less. Even one's concern for one's own existence, one's desire for self-preservation, comes on the scene later, as it were. If, as Butler wants to argue, the subject is torn by a desire not to be killed and a desire to kill the other, this occurs at the level of everyday life and not at the transcendental level of the face-to-face; it harbors no tension and no internal conflict.

Like Critchley, Butler wonders if this account—which Levinas expresses by associating the subject's response to the other with a response to the biblical commandment not to kill—does not refer to a "nefarious Eurocentrism," even if it also seems mistaken historically and empirically in identifying Europe as the locale in which ethics is primary.[40] Her worry, that is, concerns a parochialism, a prejudice, at the heart of Levinas's ethics, one that excludes or at least marginalizes all those not at home in Europe. Once again, as I suggested earlier, this judgment may be the result of reading Levinas too literally and too narrowly. Moreover, to worry that Europe is the wrong place to find the heart of the ethical because one finds in the actual Europe war and violence, imperialism and domination, this is to confuse what Europe means as a way of calling attention to the origin of ethical normativity with the question of how well or how poorly any region or nation or domain addresses its moral responsibilities.

How, for Butler, is Levinas's account of the face relevant to contemporary concerns? She identifies two issues. One concerns the relationship between representation and humanization; the other involves coming to understand how an ethic of nonviolence arises within the Jewish tradition, which Butler takes to be of special importance to those like herself who support what she calls "the emergent moment of post-Zionism within Judaism."[41] First, what does Butler mean by the relationship between representation and humanization? By "representation" Butler seems to mean the many ways in which persons or groups are depicted or portrayed or made manifest to us in everyday life. She suggests that there is a distinction to be made between those who are represented and those who are not and also between those who are capable of being represented and those who are incapable of such representation. For those who can be represented, some are humanized and some are not, when their presence in memory or imagination or public media demeans or belittles or degrades them. That is, the more vividly and positively that an individual or group is present in our imagination and in our thinking, the more our actions toward them treat them as human beings, as worthy of respect, acceptance, and generosity. The less they are represented to us—in memory, imagination, or thought—the less inclined we are to act toward them as beings worthy of respect. And if their representation is negative—demeaning or degrading or frightening—then this too would affect how we might treat them. Finally, if certain persons or groups are systematically excluded from the mechanisms of representation—by never being depicted in media, never being present in novels or films or magazines, or never being portrayed in television programs—then actions toward them are unlikely to treat them as beings worthy of respect or acceptance or generosity.

Against this background of possibilities, what role does Levinas's notion of the face—as a mode of representation—play? Even though Butler notices, in a footnote, that Levinas does distinguish between "countenance" and face, between the physical or gestural features that we sense or perceive and the face-to-face as a primordial relation of claim and responsibility, she seems to ignore this distinction in her efforts to make Levinas's notion of the face problematic and paradoxical. For Levinas, she argues, takes the face to humanize, even though there are depictions of the face that are degrading and dehumanizing. Butler wants to present us with a paradox or a tension, but she can only do so by ignoring the distinction between the everyday experience of the other person and the face-to-face as a transcendental-like structural relation between a subject and each particular other person. This enables her to ask, "How do we come to know the difference between the inhuman but humanizing face, for Levinas, and the dehumanization that can also take place through the face?"[42] Is Butler manipulating Levinas, or is she reading him for a different purpose? Both, I would say. On the one hand, Butler goes on to cite various cases in which the media especially frame and manipulate the visual representations of figures from Osama bin Laden and Yasser Arafat to Colin Powell and a group of young Afghan girls removing their burkas. In all these cases, and in so many others, the visual representations are organized with certain tacit intentions in mind and with the goal of shaping the reader's response. The camera, to Butler, was the imperialist of its reproductions; "we arranged for the face to capture our triumph, and act as the rationale for our violence, the incursion on sovereignty, the deaths of civilians." But clearly here the word "face" refers to the countenance, the visual presence, the photographic image, and so forth; it is not the Levinasian face. On the other hand, however, Butler seems aware of this: "Indeed, the photographed face seemed to conceal or displace the face in the Levinasian sense, since we saw and heard through that face no vocalization of grief or agony, no sense of the precariousness of life."[43] To be sure, when Butler here says that the manipulated media images can "displace" the Levinasian face, she does not fully appreciate that while that face—the claim of the dependent other and the self's infinite responsibility to the other person—can be concealed or hidden, made subservient or neglected, it cannot be wholly or totally erased and replaced by something else. It is, after all, a feature of all social relations and relationships. But she does seem to be aware that the everyday countenance or visage is not the face in a technical sense. Only by eliding or ignoring the distinction can one take the face itself to have a paradoxical relationship to humanization.

From this "ambivalence," as she calls it, Butler concludes that in the public images and photographic representations that she discusses we can see operative a kind of opposition or violence done to the face in the Levinasian sense. Rather than expose "scenes of pain and grief," "all of these images seem to suspend the precariousness of life; they either represent American triumph, or provide an incitement for American military triumph in the future. . . . And in this sense, we might say that the face is, in every instance, defaced, and that this is one of the representational and philosophical consequences of war itself."[44] Of course, Butler's anti-American judgement is based not on the Levinasian distinction between everyday representations and the face-to-face with the other person. It is grounded in her independent readings of these photographic images and their purposes, which she takes to be manipulative and defensive, propaganda for American militarism and imperialism and not genuine portrayals of terrorism, of unacceptable disrespect for women, and of the worthy protection of humane values. Such judgments are the weight-bearing dimension of Butler's account; the Levinasian account of the face-to-face, as she understands it, is the fulcrum on which the argument turns, but it is not the crucial or determinative aspect of it.[45]

As we have seen, Butler associates Levinas's face-to-face with an "understanding" of the "precariousness" of the other person's life. "Understanding" is much too cognitive a word for Levinas; "engage" or "encounter" is better. Levinas is interested in living with the other person in a relational nexus and not with moral epistemology. Furthermore, he more frequently refers to "vulnerability" than he does to precariousness. And it is not a generalized or blanket dependency; it is what I have called "targeted dependency." The other's neediness, his or her dependencies, is aimed at particular subjects. Moreover, it is not in any restricted sense a matter of the other's life or existence. To be sure, the sense in which the other's life depends upon the subject, for each and every subject, is an extreme, but it represents all aspects and degrees of dependency—for the other's sheer existence, for her quality of life, for her suffering and pain, for all that she is and does. It is as true to say that the subject is responsible for acknowledging the other, accepting her in the most undramatic and mundane ways, as he is to be responsible for the other's suffering and life—or death. Butler likes the more literal, limited, and radical reading, but that is not Levinas. It leads to an exaggeration of the other as the suffering other, the besieged or dispossessed, the radically disenfranchised masses. In fact, "face" calls attention to the subject's infinite responsibilities—unrestricted in every way.

Butler naturally, then, appropriates from Levinas an understanding of responsibility:[46]

> For Levinas, who separates the claim of responsibility from the possibility of agency, responsibility emerges as a consequence of being subject to the unwilled address of the other. . . . It [persecution but more particularly responsibility] returns us not to our acts and choices but to the region of existence that is radically unwilled, the primary, inaugurating impingement on me by the Other, one that happens to me, paradoxically, in advance of my formation as a "me" or, rather, as the instrument of that first formation of myself in the accusative case.[47]

In everyday life, we associate responsibility informally with all kinds of causality, and of course, in moral and legal contexts, we require that an agent is responsible for what he or she has done or for consequences of the agent's actions only if he or she chose voluntarily to act. The topic is complex and widely discussed, and there is no need to explore it here.[48] Levinas's technical understanding of responsibility, suffice it to say, involves taking us, as subjects or persons, to be responsible in some sense prior to the questions arising of the self's being held accountable in these everyday ways. Since the latter all involve the self's will or capacity to choose and act, then responsibility in Levinas's sense is a status prior to freedom and agency, and since, for Levinas, it arises when the other person in its sheer existence as confronting the self makes a claim of the self, responsibility is passivity of an ultimate kind. In religious terms, responsibility is the hallmark of a kind of Augustinian selfhood, which is characteristic of certain strands of rabbinic Judaism as well. Responsibility to God becomes, for Levinas, the unconditional responsibility to and for the other person. And everyday responsibility is typically for one's own actions, while Levinasian responsibility is to and for the other person.

This primordial responsibility can be clarified by revising our conception of the primordial scene of Western philosophy. If the primordial scene of traditional Western philosophy, when it comes to the subject or to selfhood, is the mature, rational adult, self-contained and self-transparent, reaching out and peering out from its seclusion at the world and at others in it, then the primordial scene of Levinas's philosophy is the newborn infant, utterly dependent upon the world around it and in particular upon his or her mother, not yet a locus of anything more than needs and yet to develop the capacity to see or experience the world in any structured or organized or articulate way. And what corresponds, from the side of the subject, to this utterly dependent newborn infant, is the utterly responsible parent—specifically the mother—whose time and resources, now that the infant is born, are wholly given over to the infant's needs and dependencies. With the birth of the infant, a woman becomes a caregiver, first and foremost. To be sure, when Levinas—in *Totality and Infinity* and earlier in *Time and the Other*—presents this primordial scene in his own terms, he does so with a highly male-oriented terminology of paternity and the father's responsibility to his son, but the gist of its significance for the notion of responsibility, which only becomes fully clear in *Otherwise Than Being* and the writings that preceded it, surely derives from the mother's unquestionable relation to the infant child. This revised primordial scene is the background to Butler's appropriation of Levinas's terminology. What, however, does she do with it?

First, Butler calls attention to the way in which Levinas characterizes this "impingement on me by the Other" as persecution or accusation. She makes the helpful observation that Levinas warns against treating these terms as features of a narrative or historical account; responsibility occurs prior to ontology and hence prior to history. There is no story that tells how and why the persecution occurs that produces the self's infinite responsibility. It is "a passivity before passivity" in the sense that it is "the precondition for the active-passive distinction as it arises in grammar and in everyday descriptions of interactions within the established field of ontology."[49] In particular, Butler claims that Levinas's reason for using the term "persecution" is because it is "unwilled" and subject to the imposition of the other; it is a persecution that is outrage. Surely, although she does not mention it, the usage is ironic. Here we have a persecution that is no persecution at all, for actual, everyday persecution is a restriction, a constraint, unjustified and illegitimate. And an accusation only applies when one is susceptible to being found guilty, when one is capable of being responsible. When one is not capable, there is no persecution; when there is no freedom, there is no bondage. And yet, for Levinas, the most serious, most basic persecution is just that—a limit without anything to be limited, a persecution that is not yet persecution, an accusation that is not yet an accusation.

Butler does not avoid the temptation to connect Levinas's usage, his calling responsibility the self's response to persecution, with the Nazi Holocaust and the persecution of the Jews. She does point out that Levinas does not mean that the Jews were somehow responsible for their own persecution, their own destruction.[50] To be sure, as Levinas himself says, the persecuted is responsible for the persecutor, but this is true in all cases. As a metaphysical matter, since one is responsible vis-à-vis every other, and since every other persecutes the self, the self is responsible to and for the one who persecutes it. At the everyday level, of course, persecution takes on another sense. It is oppression and domination, and while in a sense, then, I am responsible in principle, as it were, for the one who oppresses me, the facts of the particular situation may very well mitigate against my acting on that responsibility and, say, advocating for that oppression, assisting in it, or even condoning it. Butler calls it "the central dilemma . . . whether or not one may kill in response to persecution," but this case strikes me as no more paradoxical than any act of self-defense. If she means that it is obvious that one cannot kill the other person, whose persecution of me in the Levinasian sense makes me responsible for the other, then who could disagree? But if she means that it is obvious that one cannot kill someone who seeks to kill me, then who could agree?

Furthermore, when Butler says that Levinas "situates the particular nexus of persecution and responsibility at the core of Judaism, even as the essence of Israel,"[51] her failure properly to keep separate in her mind and in her reading of Levinas the transcendental persecution and responsibility that are the face-to-face and the actual persecutions and oppressions that occur or have occurred historically to the people of Israel allows her to slide into a critique of Levinas's blindness toward the Palestinians and what she takes to be his chauvinism. Butler comments on the concluding passage of Levinas's essay "From the Rise of Nihilism to the Carnal Jew," first published in 1968, in which Levinas takes the "ultimate essence of Israel" to be "its exposure to persecution" but clearly distinguishes this primordial persecution that is responsibility from the historical varieties when he says, "To be persecuted, to be guilty without having committed any crime, is not an original sin, but the obverse of a universal responsibility—a responsibility for the Other—that is more ancient than any sin."[52] Butler thoroughly confuses or mistakes the sense of what Levinas says, first by taking "Israel" to refer to the land of Israel (does she mean the state?) and the Jewish people, when in fact it is clear that it means the latter, and second by taking Levinas to be referring to historical sufferings rather than to the transcendental structure of the face-to-face, which is universal and characteristic of all social relationships, as Levinas clearly underscores. Butler is surely right to say that "it is clearly wrong to claim that only the state of Israel suffered persecution during those years—i.e., from 1948 to 1968—given the massive and forcible displacement of more than seven hundred thousand Palestinians from their homes and villages in 1948 alone, not to mention the destitutions of the continuing war and occupation." But Levinas never makes this claim. The persecution that he takes to be the ultimate essence of Judaism and the Jewish people is the central teaching of interpersonal responsibility, and while he may think that the long history of persecutions of the Jews as the target of anti-Jewish and anti-Semitic hatred is part of what warrants calling attention to this feature of the Jewish experience, surely it is not "curious," as she puts it, "that Levinas should here extract 'persecution' from its concrete historical appearances, establishing it as an apparently timeless essence of Judaism."[53] It is not curious at all for Levinas to take the suffering of the Jewish people as a barometer of how poorly Western cultures and states have done in taking responsibility for others and creating humane and just institutions. Nor would he ever say that only the Jewish people have ever suffered or that no other people could become the paradigm of such neglect or injustice. There are surely psychological and personal reasons why Levinas privileges Judaism and the Jewish people in his illustrations, examples, and even choice of terminology and expressions. But in addition there is certainly historical justification for treating the Jew as the traditional outsider and object of hatred in the Christian West and at least plausibility in his readings of Jewish texts as expressive of the centrality of justice and interpersonal concern.

Butler, like Critchley and many others, objects to what she calls Levinas's "blatant racism" regarding non-Western cultures and civilizations, and she charges him with the confusion—she also calls it a "vacillation"[54]—between the ontological and pre-ontological realms. She is not wholly clear about whether that confusion leads him to that bias or contributes to his justification for it. I doubt that one side here could convince the other about who is capitalizing on the ambiguity between the two types of persecution and on sliding from one domain to the other. Butler is convinced that it is Levinas, while I am convinced that she is the culprit here, exploiting the distinction by taking Levinas to have manipulated it for his own "racist" and biased purposes. If there is reason to side with one or the other of us, perhaps it might be found in the generosity in my view—both toward Levinas and by Levinas toward others. On my reading, Levinas appreciates that we all start, metaphysically and ethically, as it were, with infinite responsibility toward one another, and we all start by persecuting all others from the place of our own precariousness or vulnerability, our own dependencies. This is a structural, transcendental or metaphysical matter, so to speak. How that works out in everyday situations and hence in those passages where Levinas is called upon to focus on one people's sufferings or another's depends upon the context in which he makes his judgments, his purposes, and the information available to him, among many other considerations. On Butler's reading, Levinas purposely distorts his judgments by capitalizing on the ambiguity between ontological and pre-ontological terminology, ignoring Palestinian suffering and dishonestly promoting Judaism. But, as I have underscored and Butler certainly appreciates, being persecuted in the sense of being infinitely responsible for others and being persecuted as the target of the hatred and violence of others are two different things, albeit not unrelated ones. Levinas never says that infinite responsibility to others is the essence of Judaism because the people of Israel are historically the most persecuted of peoples. Nor does he ever say that infinite responsibility could not be or is not the essence of many peoples. To be an "essence" in the sense he employs is to be the highest purpose of a group's existence and historical destiny, to be its central task, and to be its primary teaching and mission—from its own point of view. It may be that responsibility to others is the essence of many peoples; *our* reasons for thinking so are wholly empirical and depend upon the evidence we have about what a tradition's texts teach and how a people conducts itself. Levinas's argument is not a priori, as Butler seems to think; he does not infer from historical persecutions to essential truth.[55]

Butler calls Levinas's judgment about the essence of Judaism "implausible and outrageous"; his words "carry wounds and outrages, and they pose an ethical dilemma for those who read them." Butler defends these judgments by claiming that Levinas is making "a given religious tradition . . . the precondition for ethical responsibility."[56] But on any reading, this is a preposterous way of understanding Levinas. Even if he does take responsibility to others to be the essence of Judaism, it need not be exclusive, and it hardly means that unless one is a Jew in the cultural, historical sense, one cannot be a just and humane person. But even if one thought that Levinas's words "wound" those who suffer who are not Jews, what is the dilemma in how the reader should react to this wounding? As a metaphysical matter, this does not alter the fact that each of us is infinitely responsible to and for all others, including those who do us harm and injury, and at the everyday level, this poses no particular dilemma. How to respond to those around us is always a matter of limitations and determinations, and dealing with those who harm us is no more difficult than is dealing with those whom we are tempted to ignore or who appear too distant to be of any concern to us.

Butler as much as says that Levinas portrays the Jewish people as a people of permanent victims. She takes him to say that this "historically constituted group of people are, by definition, always persecuted and never persecutory" and that is "to confound the ontological and preontological levels" and "to license an unacceptable irresponsibility and a limitless recourse to aggression in the name of 'self-defense'."[57] But, as I have already underlined, this charge can only be made if Butler herself, while realizing that in Levinas's thought there is a distinction between transcendental and everyday responsibility, confuses or ignores it in order to take Levinas to have done so. Moreover, she must read his notion of an essence or central feature in the most uncharitable way, with the result that she cannot accept that he does indeed have "a relation to Israel as a complex ideal," which is what she herself advocates.[58]

In her contribution to *The Power of Religion in the Public Sphere*—a dialogue in which she participated along with Jürgen Habermas, Charles Taylor, and Cornel West—Butler calls attention to her recent attempts "to consider the complex relationship between Judaism, Jewishness, and Zionism." Her paper is entitled "Is Judaism Zionism?"[59] Butler's project is to formulate a conception of Jewish identity and especially Jewish ethics that is not Zionist and may even be said to be post-Zionist and anti-Zionist.[60] In the essay, she does not refer to Levinas. Her primary interlocutor on the questions she raises about Jewish identity and Zionism is Hannah Arendt, and I do not want here to consider in any detail her use of Arendt or the account she gives of a non-Zionist conception of Jewishness.[61] But I believe that there is a point in Butler's work—which best presents itself in *Parting Ways* of 2012—where her formulation of a conception of Jewishness and Jewish ethics, her anti-Zionism and her defense of Palestinian nationalism, and her appropriation of Levinas intersect, and my goal is to clarify and discuss exactly what contribution the appropriation of Levinas on the face and on responsibility plays in that intersection, where her opposition to what she calls "Israeli state violence" is grounded in an ethic of "cohabitation as a norm of sociality."[62] For this reason, I want to say a few words about her essay about Judaism and Zionism.

The basic shape of Butler's account is clear. If Judaism and Zionism were somehow intimately tied together, then there would be no way of being Jewish while opposing Zionism. But, Butler wants to argue, there is a form of Judaism, call it a form of Jewishness, that opposes the Zionist ideology insofar as it has conducted a program of "Israeli state violence" against the Palestinian people. That form of Jewishness is grounded in a reading of Jewish sources that can be understood as expressing an ethic of cohabitation as a norm of sociality. The latter is inspired by the work of Arendt and Levinas and perhaps others as well. Hence, Butler presents herself as an advocate of an ethical Jewish identity that is anti-Zionist and affirms an ethic of cohabitation or responsible social existence.[63]

This is an outline of Butler's argument, and from it we can see that much of it is a function of particular empirical, political, and historical claims about Judaism, Jewish texts and teachings, and Zionism and Zionist practices. The role of Arendt, Levinas, and others, figures whose thinking inspires Butler's ethical views, is nonessential. She learns something from reading them, to be sure, and she is inspired by the fact that some of these figures identify themselves as Jewish, even if, in some cases, their Judaism is attenuated and not Zionist and sometimes critical of Zionism. But the role of these readings and appropriations is accidental to her argument, as it were.[64] What is essential are the particular political judgments she makes about Zionism and its violence toward others and the claims she makes for the Jewishness of the ethic of cohabitation she articulates. Butler is not the first to oppose Zionism, either as a militant political ideology and movement or in general as a messianic movement within Judaism or even as a commitment to Jewish integrity and security. Nor is she the first to claim allegiance to a Judaism that opposes various ideas, principles, or practices that one associates with Zionism in one form or another. But her anti-Zionism is distinctive, and it may be that what distinguishes Butler most of all are the vitriolic tone of her criticism of the State of Israel and its government that is reflected often in her work, even while she vigorously defends her view as Jewish, and the particular constellation of intellectual influences that she draws upon.

Within the context of this overall argument, what do we learn from Butler's essay? In particular, what do we learn about her criticisms of "Israeli state violence," as she calls it, and about her ethic of cohabitation? First, Butler explores a line of thinking that begins with Arendt's appreciation for the theme of dispersion and the scattering of divine sparks in Lurianic kabbalah that we find in a response to the publication of Scholem's *Major Trends in Jewish Mysticism* and continues through Arendt's appropriation of ideas of what I have called a kind of "episodic messianism" in Walter Benjamin's late theses on the philosophy of history. As I read Benjamin, the crucial point is that messianism, for Benjamin, is the task of the contemporary critic who exposes the true character of contemporary moments of suffering by juxtaposing them with recollections of past moments of suffering and danger and who then calls for a redemption of the present sufferings from occlusion and neglect and who ultimately sponsors the fight against oppression. This focus on fighting injustice and eradicating suffering from violence and oppression is, it seems to me, the core of what Arendt learns from Benjamin. But it is not what Butler takes to be central. For her, what is central to Arendt's appropriation is the idea of the exilic and, by implication, of the dispossessed and the stateless. I would agree that this is a central theme of Arendt's, but I would argue that it is not in Benjamin. What is in Benjamin is a concern with the universality of present suffering and the need to expose and eradicate it. No group, no people, no class or gender has cornered the market on suffering and injustice. Messianism is not about parochial redemption; it is about redeeming unjust suffering from occlusion and neglect, wherever it occurs. Although Butler does not mention it, this conception of the messianic is precisely the notion that we find in Levinas, whose conception of the universality of taking responsibility for others and the episodic or particularistic manner of so doing makes him one of Benjamin's genuine heirs.[65]

Moreover, Levinas—like Arendt—takes this task to be central—or even essential—to the existence of each and every state and hence it is central to the State of Israel. Where they differ is that Arendt opposes the very idea of a nation-state (and nationalism) precisely because it must deal and cannot deal effectively with minorities in its midst, while Levinas does not—at least in the case of the State of Israel. Indeed, one might say that this may be the greatest political challenge—for the political institutions of a state to care for all, including minority groups within its borders, while at the same time advocating for a particular mission and a particular national identity. This challenge is characteristic of the State of Israel—but not it alone.

As I indicated, Butler's most developed case for her Jewish ethic of nonviolence toward the other can be found in *Parting Ways: Jewishness and the Critique of Zionism*. In this work, she appropriates themes that she finds in the work of a range of authors, from Levinas, Benjamin, Arendt, and Primo Levi to Edward Said and Mahmoud Darwish. This is not the place for a critical engagement with the book and her argument as a whole. What I want to do is to focus our attention on how she draws on her indebtedness to Levinas, combines it with her messianic and ethical interpretation of Arendt, and puts the results to work in the service of her critique of Zionism as "Israeli state violence" against the Palestinian people. Completing this examination of Butler, my primary goal is to shed light on Levinas and to understand better the character of Levinas's ethical politics.

In the introductory chapter of *Parting Ways* Butler summarizes what she takes from Levinas this way:

> It is interesting that Levinas insisted we are bound to those we do not know, and did not choose, and that these obligations are, strictly speaking, precontractual. He was, of course, the one who claimed in an interview that the Palestinian had no face, that he only meant to extend ethical obligations to those who were bound together by his version of Judeo-Christian and classical Greek origins. In some ways he gave us the very principle that he betrayed. And this means that we are not only free, but obligated to extend that principle to the Palestinian people, precisely because he could not. After all, Levinas also gave us a conception of ethical relations that make us ethically responsive to those who exceed our immediate sphere of belonging and to whom we nevertheless belong, regardless of any choice or contract.[66]

Moreover, at this point, as we have hinted already, Butler associates Levinas's conception of the ethical with Arendt's notion of cohabitation, which she takes to be "a condition of our political life" that is "prior to contract and prior to any volitional act" and which, she emphasizes, calls attention to the fact that we are bound to live together "on the earth" with those who do not share a language or way of life with us,[67] that is, what I called our "political others." As I have tried to show and underscored in my discussion of Butler in this chapter, what we have here is Butler appreciating a distinction that Levinas makes between the transcendental and the everyday and yet claiming that Levinas "betrays" it at the very same time. Yet, in order to do this, she herself must acknowledge the distinction and then herself pay no attention to it in order to generate her criticism of Levinas. The critical moment comes when she claims that Levinas denies a face to the Palestinian other. If this means that to the Israeli the Palestinian who is his or her enemy has no transcendental face, that is, the Israeli citizen has no responsibility to or for the Palestinian, this reading of Levinas is completely false. And yet, if it means that even though the Israeli ought to be bound to treat the Palestinian with concern and justice in daily and political life, he or she may fail to, then this is a political judgment that may be true but justified. After all, in our daily lives, our comprehensive, infinite, and indeterminate obligations to others are always realized in a determinate way that depends upon our choices and the precise features of the situation.

But the fact is that there is good reason to think that Levinas himself did not abandon the Palestinians in the interview; to claim that he did is to read his comments in a decidedly one-sided and prejudiced fashion. Moreover, when Butler says that because Levinas did abandon the Palestinians, "we" are obligated not to do so, she has fallen into a complete non sequitur. Clearly, "we" do have an obligation to the Palestinian, but it is because we have infinite responsibility to each and every other person and has nothing to do with how Levinas acted or did not act. And if we judge that we should in everyday life act on that obligation and set aside other obligations, that depends upon the circumstances of our choice and other factors that might shape our conduct. It depends upon who "we" are and what our other ties, interests, needs, and concerns are, for the "conception of ethical relations," as Butler calls it, that Levinas has disclosed to us does not "make us ethically responsive to those who exceed our immediate sphere of belonging" exclusively; indeed, that is precisely what Levinas points out in the interview. Our primordial and fundamental ethical obligation to acknowledge and care for others applies to *all* others, the near as well as the far. One must not confuse the "ethical other" with the "political other," to use the terms I have introduced.

There is, in Butler, a bias against the "ties that bind us," so to speak. These ties—family ties among them and ties of intimacy and friendship—should play no political role. She makes this clear as she goes on to claim that Arendt's idea of the givenness of our living with diversity and plurality is at least part of why she is so opposed to genocide—surely one does not need such a reason!—and more importantly why she opposes the nation-state and nationalism. From this foundation, then, Butler derives a commitment to political forms that accept and deal with such diversity and forbid any acts that "destroy any part of the human population or . . . make lives unlivable." Hence, she can conclude, "if Arendt is right, then settler colonialism was never legitimate, and neither were the expulsions of indigenous populations on the basis of their nationality or religion, or indeed the continuing confiscations and displacements of the Palestinian people." Butler has used Arendt, with the preparation provided by her reading of Levinas, to slide into a criticism of the State of Israel as a Jewish state and of its treatment of the Palestinian people. "Zionism," she says, "has never found justification in principles of political equality and, for that reason, has never approached a substantive condition of democracy." Zionism is a nation-state, with a state religion, which is "the basis of the subordination, destruction, or expulsion of the indigenous."[68] What can we say about this line of thinking?

First, one does not need Arendt's notion of cohabitation with the stranger, so to speak, to have a reason to oppose ethnic cleansing, genocide, and such. Second, while Arendt may have opposed the nation-state for good reasons—although this opposition may not have been implied by her conception of cohabitation, clearly Levinas did not, and his willingness to countenance nationalism and to appreciate the challenges nation-states must face is not incompatible with the primacy of the ethical as he understands it. To put this matter in other terms, Levinas is neither a classic liberal, nor is he a communitarian, but he certainly does not deny that there is some truth in both. There is no simple, blanket rule for negotiating the tensions that may arise between moral duties and personal attachments, for individuals and for nations and even for nation-states. And finally, whether or not the pre-state Zionists were justified, politically, militarily, and morally in their policies and actions and whether the State of Israel is now justified or not regarding its treatment of minorities within the state and of Palestinians in the West Bank, Gaza, and elsewhere, these are matters that require particular judgments based on available information, an understanding of what has occurred, the needs and interests of the relevant parties, and more. They are highly contested matters. It is clear from what she says where Butler stands; she may or may not be justified. But to derive moral support for her own political judgments from the fact that Levinas has different ones and to claim that his judgments "betray" his own conception of the ethical, these are philosophical mistakes—and perhaps more, expressions of ill will toward Levinas or even duplicity. They do not enhance her position regarding the State of Israel. If they do serve a rhetorical purpose, it is to suggest that allegiance to the Jewish state is such a powerful, sinister drive that it even has the capacity to corrupt a thinker whose ethical scruples are exemplary. But to exploit this ploy is itself an expression of a failure of generosity toward Levinas and his ethical ideal. Honest criticism is one thing; vitriol is another.[69]

Butler's most extensive discussions of Levinas in *Parting Ways* develop the treatments we have already considered; they occur primarily in chapters 1 and 2. In chapter 1, for example, Butler introduces Levinas's notion of the face in order to provide a universal foundation for our ethical obligation to the other, as she puts it, but she immediately finds it problematic, since it means reading Levinas against himself, that is, "against his own Zionism and his refusal to accept that Palestinians make a legitimate ethical demand on the Jewish people." What is her reasoning? It is this:

> Philosophically, Levinas outlines an ethical scene in which we are obligated, under most situations, to preserve the life of the other—obligated by the alterity we encounter there. Upon closer inspection, however, it turns out that this scene, which would seem to obligate us universally, is restricted culturally and geographically. The ethical obligation toward the face of the other is not an obligation one can or does feel toward every face. . . . The ethical demand is not prior to notions of cultural autonomy, but is precisely framed and restricted in advance by certain notions of culture, ethnicity, and religion. . . . For Levinas, the prohibition against violence is restricted to those whose faces make a demand

upon me, and yet these "faces" are differentiated by virtue of their religious and cultural background. This then opens up the question of whether there is any obligation to preserve the life of those who appear "faceless"' within his view or, perhaps, to extend his logic, by virtue of not having a face, do not appear at all.[70]

There are a number of difficulties with this reading of Levinas, but suffice it to say that it trades on the very confusion between the face-to-face as a transcendental structure of all interpersonal relations and the degree to which the responsibility to care for a particular other is expressed in any given concrete, everyday situation that Butler elsewhere charges Levinas with making when she says that he is betraying his own view. But the simplest and indeed the most accurate way of saving Levinas from such a betrayal is to realize that he does not make it. He does keep these two distinct levels of human social experience, the transcendental and the ontological, separate. Butler does not, and so in this passage, she makes the claim—that there are some who are "faceless"—which is either completely false at the transcendental level or perfectly understandable, even if questionable in any given particular situation, at the ordinary or political level. This is not an objection to Levinas of any serious kind, and to raise it with the inflammatory expression of facelessness is to charge Levinas with inconsistency, where the most one can say is that in a particular case he might be too willing or not at all justified to abandon his obligation to care for and protect the other person. And since Butler is here alluding to Levinas's participation in the notorious interview we have discussed earlier, it is obvious to what service she is putting this erroneous reading, as an indictment of Levinas's Zionism and an apology for Butler's advocacy of the Palestinian people, whom she calls "the paradigm for the faceless."[71]

In the light of such a reading of Levinas, it is no wonder that Butler finds puzzling Levinas's shift from the messianic sensibility of the Jewish people to the "discussion of Israel as a historical place, people, and state." It is not the "arbitrary violence of historical events" and the long history of anti-Jewish persecution that has given to Jews their ethical mandate, and hence, while that mandate does have an ahistorical quality about it, there is no paradox in Levinas's taking it to be the destiny of the Jewish people to realize that sensibility in the world. For Levinas, the Zionist challenge is to bring that ethical sensibility to political realization and in this sense, as Butler quotes Levinas, "Zionism and the creation of the State of Israel mean for Jewish thought a return to oneself in every sense of the term, and the end of an alienation that lasted a thousand years." This is exactly what Levinas means when he says, once again in a passage that Butler quotes, "The State of Israel is the opportunity to move into history by bringing about a just world."[72] It is this vision or challenge that is the content of the "universalism embodied in a particularism" that Levinas advocates for the Jewish people. Butler reads these texts as evidence of Levinas's inconsistency and perhaps of his self-denial. For at this point she turns to Levinas's use of the vocabulary of persecution that we discussed earlier and makes the claim that Levinas confuses transcendental persecution with real, historical persecution. Her charge is that Levinas credits the "original responsibility" for others, which is essential to the Jewish people, as somehow founded on the historical persecutions that this people has suffered and then justifies the state because of its timeless destiny. "We are asked," she says, "to consider this historical political state as timelessly suffering persecution." And she also charges Levinas with making the preposterous claim that only the Jews have suffered, thereby neglecting to appreciate the persecution of the Palestinian people.[73]

The gist of these criticisms of Levinas, however, is that he thoroughly confuses "the preontological and the ontological" in his work. Butler goes on in chapter 1 to find this same confusion elsewhere in Levinas's writings, providing us, as I have indicated, with the bizarre spectacle of a critic of Levinas who takes him to have been making a central distinction that he then himself confuses and whose way of exposing these confusions is to make the very same confusion herself.[74] In the end, Butler objects to Levinas's privileging of the Judeo-Christian culture of Europe, and she associates his failure to acknowledge the historical sufferings of the Palestinian people with his admittedly dismissive and insensitive comments about Asia and others, comments that Critchley condemned for their parochialism and myopia. I do not want to defend Levinas and these comments, which should be read as cultural and political judgments (and highly unattractive ones at that) and not metaphysical or philosophical ones. But Butler herself sets the context for interpreting them, and philosophically speaking, that context is the distinction between the transcendental and the everyday levels of discourse. Surely, there are other ways to plead in behalf of what the State of Israel owes its minorities and its neighbors, even those with whom it has had long-standing conflict, than to claim that she somehow denies that her enemies are worthy of any respect at all and thereby makes a philosophical mistake with serious moral and political consequences.[75]

Let me conclude our discussion of Butler by looking at chapter 2 of *Parting Ways*, where she asks, what does the face command?[76] Butler begins by noting that the face carries an "interdiction against killing" the other and that while in one sense killing the face is impossible, in another it is possible and is done all the time, when people take up power in order to do others injury or harm or to fail to come to their aid. All this is a very thoughtful and accurate account of Levinas, and Butler caps it off by noting that there is a sense in which "the political supplants the ethical."[77] To be more precise, there is a sense in which it is always the case that the political is in tension with the ethical, just as the ethical always makes its claim on the political. This is what I have called the interdependency of the two, the fact that each limits the other.

Butler admits that "even though the social dimension of the political does not negate the ethical and its claim, it remains difficult to say in what way that ethical claim lives on in the social and political domain. . . . Does the face survive in the domain of the political? And if it does, what form does it take? And how does it leave its trace?"[78] Butler then makes the salient point that the presence of the face not only brings the duty not to kill or do harm or abandon, but it also brings the threat of the self's power and hence the risk that the subject will fail in meeting its obligation. "The face signifies the precariousness of the Other, and so also a damage that can be caused by my own violence," that is, the other person's dependency upon me and the possibility that I might fail to acknowledge and assist her when she confronts me.[79] In this situation, moreover, the very particular other does not issue a general command; rather "if I am obliged not to be indifferent toward the death of the other, this is because the other appears to me not as one among many, but as precisely *the one* with whom I am concerned." As Levinas says, in the text Butler cites to support her interpretation, from a 1986 paper entitled "Uniqueness" and reprinted in the collection *Entre Nous*, it is "as if the imperative went toward me alone." In addition, it is an imperative that comes from this particular other—as if from *it* alone. Hence, as Butler summarizes, "the face of the Other thus disrupts all formalisms." But, she then asks, shall we then think that this is a rejection of all formalisms, of all politics, and of law? No; this cannot be right, for the political and the general are necessary, as Levinas frequently says. Hence arises the question: How can the ethical remain in the political? How can the utterly particular still be present in the general and the formal?[80]

Butler's answer, in a sense, starts by making the point that we should begin with the political, as it were, and take the question to mean that "the ethical injunction, though 'prior' to the political domain, emerges for Levinas precisely within the terms of political conflict." That is, the ethical does not occur by itself. In my terms, the transcendental, ethical structure that underlies every second-person encounter always occurs within the context of a host of various other features and relations that characterize the social situation of the I and the other. The emphasis here is on two things: first that the political is already in place and second that the political is marked by conflict, by the possibility and threat that my power, my capacity for violence, carry with them with regard to the other. "The ethical emerges in the midst of a conflict already underway."[81] This situation of social conflict is the "necessary background" for the presence of the face of the other. Butler's point here is that the ethical arises out of a primal scene that is one of conflict, of fear and anxiety, about both being killed and oneself killing the other. What emerges from this is a commitment against violence, but it "does not come from a peaceful place, but rather from a constant tension between the fear of undergoing violence and the fear of inflicting violence. Peace is an active struggle with violence, and there can be no peace without the violence it seeks to check."[82] It is this understanding of Levinas's primal scene, Butler argues in a very illuminating way, that helps us to understand what it means to claim that "this command can be said to persecute me, to hold me hostage" and that "the face of the Other is persecutory from the start. And if the substance of that persecution is the interdiction against killing, then I am persecuted by the injunction to keep the peace."[83]

I agree with much of this reading of Levinas, and it is certainly illu-minating and plausible. But, with this in hand, Butler then takes Levinas to slide from these claims about how the ethical and the political occur together and how the ethical in a sense requires the political, and in particular social conflict, as a background condition, to the claim that it is the "historical experience of persecution" by the Jewish people that warrants our saying that the Jewish people is persecuted in the transcen-dental sense of commanded to oppose violence, to advocate for peace and justice. Now clearly this would be a confusion on Levinas's part; indeed, it is not a claim that he makes, as I have argued before, not in the essay "From the Rise of Nihilism to the Carnal Jew" and not elsewhere. And the reason is that for Levinas the interdependence of the ethical and the political is a transcendental condition and not a historical, everyday situation. Even primordially, that is, there is a tension in the subject's in-finite responsibilities, insofar as they must accommodate to the subject's freedom, his capacity to exert and utilize its resources for or against one other or another. Historical persecutions are not what make "the ulti-mate essence of Israel" universally responsible for others. One might certainly agree with Butler that this responsibility "entails . . . a struggle for nonviolence, that is, a struggle against the ethics of revenge, a struggle not to kill the other, a struggle to encounter and honor the face of the Other."[84] And it is certainly in the spirit of Levinas to take this to be an accurate way of describing the special task of Israel's existence. But this does not mean that Levinas must agree with Butler about how that re-sponsibility will express itself in everyday, actual situations, especially when it comes to the relation between the State of Israel and the Pales-tinian people. As we have already discussed, and Butler here repeats, she takes Levinas here to be betraying his own principles, and so what she proposes is "to think with Levinas against Levinas, and to pursue a possible direction for his ethics and his politics that he did not propose."

I have argued before that Levinas is not making one mistake with which Butler charges him; he is not confusing historical judgments with transcendental conditions. But what she says here might be read differ-ently. She might be taken to be saying that Levinas fails to be honest about how Israel has failed to live up to the ethical claim to nonviolence that is at the heart of her mission. That is, Butler may be claiming that

Israel has indeed persecuted and oppressed its own minorities and also the Palestinian people and that Levinas should have seen and admitted this "state violence" and condemned it. If this is her charge, then what is her evidence? Butler takes the judgment against the State of Israel to be transparent and unquestionable. Surely Levinas would not have agreed. But in the notorious interview after Sabra and Shatila, Levinas does not seem to question the guilt of Israeli military and political leaders, even prior to the outcome of the board of inquiry. Hence, the issue is whether Levinas was himself culpable of failing to condemn the state, and I have argued that there are many hasty assumptions being made by those who take Levinas's comments and his silences to warrant a judgment about his culpability; to these hasty assumptions Butler does not add any more substantive comments here in chapter 2 of *Parting Ways*.

Let me add one last point about Butler's appropriation and critique of Levinas in *Parting Ways*. In chapter 2, she has given us a very interesting account—largely an uncontroversial one—of how ethics and politics are interrelated for Levinas. To be sure, she is not as careful as one might be and should be about distinguishing between the status of this interdependence at the transcendental level and its status and character as it functions in everyday life. But she does state quite clearly that there is something fundamental about both the way that politics depends upon ethics and about how ethics depends upon politics. Indeed, she makes an interesting case for thinking that one reason for Levinas's calling the face-to-face "persecution," "accusation," and "hostage" lies in the fact that ethics as an admonition and command to seek peace must be understood against the background of the conflict between the self and the other, and this means against the background of a conflict and an anxiety or fear both regarding the other's life and well-being and also about one's own temptations, that is, the temptation to accede to power and to become a killer. In the sense that one's potential to be a violent agent or even a killer is at issue for oneself and that the other challenges that potential and that temptation, one is being accused or persecuted by the other—but in a good sense, of course. Butler might have added that this background conflict is part of what politics means for Levinas, that it is already present transcendentally in every social encounter, and that it is part of what it means to say that the other is present at a height, that is, it is part of the asymmetry between the subject and the other. If all of this is correct—and I am inclined to think that it is—then the distinction between friend and enemy, in a certain sense, is built into every interpersonal encounter from the beginning, or, to put it differently, both internally within each of us and interpersonally between any two of us, there is a conflict between ethics and self-interest, between power and violence, on the one hand, and love and peace, on the other. These are always in tension, always in conflict, in every second-person encounter. Ethics only makes sense as a response to this conflict.

Fortunately, Butler does not infer from this account that the everyday conflict between friend and enemy is therefore already a transcendental condition of social existence and therefore the ethical obligation is always to prefer the enemy to the friend, the other to myself, the other's needs to my freedom and power. That, indeed, would be a non sequitur; it would be to read features of our everyday life back into the transcendental conditions for its possibility. Often Butler's readings of Levinas and her criticisms of him capitalize on just such a confusion. Here she does not make it, and for that I commend her. By and large, if one could summarize it this way, Butler's appropriation of Levinas is often insightful and informed, while her criticisms of him—which are primarily about his political judgment—capitalize on her making just the mistakes or confusions that she charges him with making.

A FINAL CRITICISM

In this chapter I have focused primarily on the criticisms of Levinas and of his thinking about ethics and politics that can be found in the work of Simon Critchley, Howard Caygill, and Judith Butler. I have done so because what they say is distinguished by very insightful and compelling interpretations of his work and thought together with characteristic criticisms of him, made in the service of independent agendas worth taking seriously. I leave it to others to consider critically the objections or difficulties raised elsewhere by Richard Rorty, Alain Badiou, William Paul Simmons, John Drabinski, and others. But there is one final criticism that I would like to introduce, in part because it has been influential and in part because it raises a question that we have not discussed explicitly: the relation between Levinas's ethics, the place of ethics in a post-metaphysical situation, and the role of law.

In her book *Mourning Becomes the Law,* Gillian Rose challenges the turn to ethics after the rise of postmodernism and a post-metaphysical situation and argues for the centrality of politics and theology. In particular, Rose argues that Levinas erred in privileging ethics to law and politics, and she treats his argument as characteristic of a deep contemporary mistake, one that accepts the dichotomy of Athens and Jerusalem only to advocate for a flawed understanding of the latter. Rose paints with broad strokes, and I want neither to give an overview of her portrait nor to work out details she left in outline. My goal is much more focused: to locate exactly what role Levinas plays in her narrative.

Historically, the task of evaluating the possibilities of traditional metaphysics and then of locating practical reasoning and morality within the resulting account fell to Kant. Famously—to give a caricature—he discovered in autonomy and rational self-determination the ground of moral normativity that was required once the commands of a transcendent God were discredited as the traditional locus of that source. The first readers and then critics of Kant were not persuaded by his challenge to metaphysics, nor were many who followed. But, in the waning years of the nineteenth century and into the twentieth, the worries that we associate with nihilism, relativism, historicism, and skepticism concerning values and especially moral value generated a host of responses to the question of the possibility of ethics and morality. Neo-Kantianisms, *Lebensphilosophie*, positivism, naturalisms, and on and on, with the challenge always in the wind, contributed to a variety of responses. Rose's essay—concerning the return to ethics in the wake of postmodernism and utilizing what she calls an aporetic method of reading—takes place as a late twentieth-century reflection on this problematic. Drawing on Rorty and others, she paints a picture of exhaustion in political theory after the libertarian-communitarian debates and sympathizes with the judgment by Rorty that the best alternative left to us is to become "ironic liberals." Eschewing foundationalisms and realism, we nonetheless at the very least oppose unqualifiedly cruelty and torture, and yet we find ourselves in a fragmented and conflicted situation.[85] In the first chapters of her book Rose explores what is possible for talking about the Holocaust and for understanding Judaism at a time when the search for a new ethics after the failure of traditional metaphysics has not succeeded and with the decline of orthodoxies in political theory and theology. Eventually, she finds her way to a conception of "activity beyond activity," a view of "learning, growth, and knowledge as fallible and precarious, but risk-able" in a time of the broken middle, a view that she finds in the work of Maurice Blanchot.[86]

Rose calls upon Levinas at the conclusion of her first chapter, which is based on a lecture entitled "Athens and Jerusalem: A Tale of Three Cit-ies," as part of her inquiry into a postmodern Judaism. Rose identifies a trend in recent philosophy and religious thinking that is characterized by accepting the traditional dichotomy between an Athens of "knowledge, power, and practical reason" and a Jerusalem of love and true commu-nity. This trend or development mourns the loss of Athens and advocates for a new Jerusalem, but this, she claims, is a fantasy, a delusion. "To op-pose the new ethics to the old city, Jerusalem to Athens, is to succumb to loss, to refuse to mourn, to cover persisting anxiety with the violence of a New Jerusalem masquerading as love."[87] What Rose finds disturbing in this strategy is that it accepts the terms of modernism, the old dichoto-mies of love and justice, ethics and politics, and more, and takes the one alternative to be a compelling response to the failure of the other. It is a form of Platonism, bad Platonism. This kind of thinking, philosophical or religious or both, "[hopes to evade] the risks of political community" with a kind of asceticism that Rose calls "Levinas's *Buddhist* Judaism" and to which she opposes "rabbinic Judaism."

One can tell from Rose's description of this *Buddhist* Judaism that she finds it singularly unattractive and even dangerous. It is otherworldly, for all of its claim to be concrete and social, and while it makes Judaism somehow very appealing to philosophy, it does so at the cost of cutting both off from real, conflicted, unreconciled, and "risky" politics and daily life. Rose reads Levinas as advocating for a selfless mysticism, but this is a mistake, she argues, both about what postmodern philosophy ought to be and also about what Judaism has been and might be. To Levinas's pri-oritizing of passivity, she opposes activity; to Levinas's "plac[ing of] eth-ics beyond the world of being and politics," she opposes confronting the political world with all its uncertainties and dangers; to Levinas's anti-cognitivism, she requires a struggle for knowledge and understanding, risking mistakes but serving the ongoing actions that life requires of us. Finally, to Levinas's making of Judaism "the sublime other of modernity" and "invest[ing it with an] other-worldly beatification," Rose "immerse[s] Judaism in the difficulties of modernity."[88] This is a Jewish anti-Platonism but one with a post-Hegelian twist; the world and the politics that are Judaism's venue resist any confidences and are riddled with risk. This is a post-Holocaust world, one that claims response but is forever fragmented and endangered.

This brief sketch, then, encapsulates Rose's critique of Levinas or at least some features of it. For our purposes, what is central is the special role that politics and law and ordinary life play for any contemporary philosophical view and any religious view that is worth taking seriously. Rose is writing in 1993, and it appears that there is at the time an orthodoxy about how to read Levinas. It takes Levinas to be an apologist for an other-worldly passivity that can be found in particular moments when the other person's claim brings to the self a responsibility that is "inconceivable and not representable, because it takes place beyond any city."[89] No wonder Rose calls this a *"Buddhist"* Judaism. No wonder she calls this passivity "sublime." Either there is an orthodoxy about this reading of Levinas, which helps to give it its "canonical" status, or Rose is the author of such a reading, which she takes to explain its popularity and its status. Whichever is the case, the outcome is the same. For Rose, unless there is a political dimension to Levinas's ethics, it cannot properly engage with the political world we live in and cannot provide the content for a responsible picture of Judaism.

I agree with this conclusion but only because I disagree so completely with Rose's depiction of Levinas's *Buddhist* ethics. In this regard, Rose exposes a serious shortcoming among many of her most vigorous critics, and that is to claim that Levinas's ethics has no political dimension or political application. If I am correct, Critchley and Butler at least do not stoop to such a mistaken reading of Levinas; nor do Caygill and others. For them, Levinas's ethics or his political judgments are flawed because one or the other or both are too parochial, too biased, insufficiently sensitive to actual others, and so forth. To Butler, Levinas's writings are filled with confusion. But nowhere do we find what is so vividly present in Rose's comments, the mistaken view of Levinas's ethics that takes it to be wholly detached from the urgencies and dangers of ordinary life and everyday politics. In this chapter, I have considered these various criticisms, not simply in order to expose their weaknesses, although I have tried to do that, but primarily to use them as an additional lens to clarify further the character of Levinas's ethical politics as I have described it in earlier chapters.

CONCLUSION

Social and political philosophy consider the principles for designing a system of norms, institutions, and practices that ought to organize the lives of individual persons living together in groups. There are various values that such principles should express and that the system itself should exemplify. Among such values are security of the individual citizens, stability, fair treatment of all, some measure of equality, and such. While there are doubtless many ways to frame this project, a particularly helpful one is to portray it as an effort to promote and protect general and group interests as well as the needs and interests of individuals. Putting the task of political philosophy this way leaves a good deal of room for interpretation, but it is helpful. Thomas Nagel calls it the "central problem of political theory" and describes it as "the familiar [problem] of reconciling the standpoint of the collectivity with the standpoint of the individual."[1]

Nagel gives this familiar problem an illuminating twist. He treats it as a problem internal to the self, as a problem about how to incorporate into one program two standpoints that the self takes toward itself, others, and the world around it. These are the "impersonal standpoint in each of us [that] produces a powerful demand for universal impartiality and equality" and "the personal standpoint [that] gives rise to individualistic motives and requirements which present obstacles to the pursuit and realization of such ideals."[2] In short, Nagel examines a variety of tensions in political philosophy that occur as tensions within our very selfhood.

Levinas, as I have described him, seems aware in his own way of both of these tensions and even, one might say, takes them to be characteristic of the human condition. One way of putting this would be to notice that for Levinas, insofar as each of us relates to each particular other person, we do so both with unconditional and with conditional responsibility. In our interpersonal relations, the other is both an utterly particular second person and at the same time a completely general third person.[3] Each other person is to the self both utterly particular and entirely general; we are called upon at once to treat others in terms of their distinctive needs and interests and in terms of values such as "impartiality and equality." In part, this coincidence of orientations or standpoints, to use Nagel's terminology, expresses how neither ethics nor politics occurs by itself. Both are always present, even if, in our world, after the horrors and atrocities of the twentieth century, ethics has often been occluded and hidden from view.

To lift the veil of such hiddenness is one role of Levinas's ethical politics. His account privileges the ethical—understood as the infinite responsibilities we have to and for one another—partly because there is so much evidence that attentiveness to it has been lost or at least obscured, but only partly. Another reason for focusing so much of his attention on the ethical—as relational, characterized by infinite responsibilities, and utterly particular—is that it is a given of the human condition and not something ultimately derivable from a natural or rational fact. It is original, or what Levinas would call "primordial."

I have shown that Levinas's conception of the ethical led him to appreciate how it always occurs as both present in and also as an ideal for our everyday experience and in particular for our social and political lives. It both makes possible and orients those lives, but about this—and hence about how others depend upon us and how we are responsible to and for them—we need constant reminding. This is one task of the ethical critique of the political. One way that Levinas is fond of to express this task is to point out that it is not unimportant for us to know that society is founded on "charity" and responsibility and not on "the war of all against all." We are not ultimately competing, acquisitive atoms; rather we are responsible agents of care for those dependent upon us.

As Nagel shows, it is not easy to reconcile our personal motives and interests with the claims of impartiality and equality. By and large, he writes from within the Kantian tradition, and so what he finds when he considers our "personal standpoint" are sometimes very distinctive interests and projects but also morality and moral principles grounded in our autonomy. Levinas's conception of selfhood differs. For him, our individual selfhood is originally filled up with otherness, so to speak. We are, as he puts it, "substitution" for the other, deputies or surrogates or proxies first and foremost. The more attentive we are to the claims and demands made of us by others, the more we bracket or set aside our self-interestedness. But this is not something that we do for the generalized other or the universal principle; it is something we do for the other person in all his or her particularity. For Levinas, the tension between the personal and the impersonal within us is not between altruism and self-interest; it is deeper than that. The tension concerns how generality can by its very nature ignore or threaten morality. It is necessary and can serve the ethical or it can distort or destroy it. One purpose of ethical critique is to warn us when politics becomes ideology and despotism and when it veers from the path of liberal, welfare democracies, with their commitment to the well-being of all.

In this book I have developed these themes by reading carefully what Levinas has written and said on the ethical and the political. By and large, what he calls for is a reorientation, a different way of understanding the human condition and our relations with others. Education is fundamentally Platonic; it leads us to see things differently. But Levinas produces no systematic account like those of Rawls or Habermas, nor the kind of concrete detail one finds in Arendt or Honneth or Fraser or others. Levinas is more a "metaphysician" than a social or political theorist. He provides hints in various places—in his occasional writings, interviews, and Talmudic readings—about what his "ethical metaphysics" led him to see. But that is all. For us, these hints yield a kind of heuristic and a pedagogy, encouraging us to view the urgencies and crises in our own lives in a distinctive way. It leaves us with a task, a challenge for our daily lives and for social and political theorists who find Levinas's argument for the centrality of interpersonal responsibility important and compelling.

NOTES

PREFACE

1. See Michael L. Morgan, *Discovering Levinas* (Cambridge: Cambridge University Press, 2007), 261, citing Richard Rorty, *Achieving Our Country* (Cambridge, MA: Harvard University Press, 1998), 96–97. The passage is quoted by Simon Critchley, "Metaphysics in the Dark," *Political Theory* 26, no. 6 (1998): 806.

2. Seyla Benhabib, "Ethics without Normativity and Politics without Historicity: On Judith Butler's *Parting Ways: Jewishness and the Critique of Zionism,*" *Constellations* 20, no. 1 (March 2013): 150–63.

3. Levinas also finds the primacy of the ethical in Kant, but more often he refers to his thinking as a new form of Platonism rather than a new form of Kantianism. For its appreciation of transcendence and the preeminence of a goodness that lies beyond thought and language, the Platonic tradition has a powerful attraction for Levinas, even if his appropriation of it is deeply concrete and historical. For a criticism of Levinas's reading of Plato's Form of the Good, see Michael L. Morgan, "Plato, Levinas, and Transcendence" (forthcoming in a volume on Levinas as a reader to be edited by Sarah Hammerschlag and published by Indiana University Press).

4. Richard J. Bernstein, "Evil and the Temptation of Theodicy," in *The Cambridge Companion to Levinas,* ed. Simon Critchley and Robert Bernasconi (Cambridge: Cambridge University Press, 2002), 252–67; also in Richard J. Bernstein, *Radical Evil: A Philosophical Interrogation* (Cambridge: Polity, 2002), ch. 6, 166–83.

5. Sarah Cooper has written insightfully about the Levinasian dimension of the Dardenne brothers' films; see Sarah Cooper, "Mortal Ethics: Reading Levinas with the Dardenne Brothers," *Film-Philosophy* 11, no. 2 (August 2007): 66–87. The best book I know of on the Dardenne brothers is Joseph Mai, *Jean-Pierre and Luc Dardenne* (Champaign-Urbana: University of Illinois Press, 2010). See also Philip Mosley, *The Cinema of the Dardenne Brothers: Responsible Realism* (New York: Wallflower Press, 2013).

1. TEARS THE CIVIL SERVANT CANNOT SEE

1. This orientation to Levinas leads to anarchism or asceticism, neither of which, I believe, is acceptable as a reading of Levinas. For a clear and succinct statement of the anarchist option, see Simon Critchley, *Infinitely Demanding: Ethics of Commit-*

ment, *Politics of Resistance* (London: Verso, 2007), 119–23.

2. See John Drabinski, "The Possibility of an Ethical Politics: From Peace to Liturgy," *Philosophy and Social Criticism* 26, no. 4 (2000): 49–73, esp. 49–57. Drabinski does note the difference between his view and that of Critchley, who claims that the political is necessary for the ethical; see 53 and note 7.

3. Ibid., 53. See also Emmanuel Levinas, "Ideology and Idealism," in *The Levinas Reader*, ed. Seán Hand (Oxford: Basil Blackwell, 1989), 247–48: "There is need for a state. But it is very important to know whether the state, society, law, and power are required because man is a beast to his neighbor (*homo homini lupus*) or because I am responsible for my fellow. It is very important to know whether the political order defines man's responsibility or merely restricts his bestiality. It is very important, even if the conclusion is that all of us exist for the sake of the state, the society, the law." We shall come back to this important point. As Drabinski puts it, "Is the legal justice of the state necessary for the protection of one from another, or is it necessary as an extension of my responsibility for the neighbor?" ("The Possibility of an Ethical Politics," 53). He notes that Levinas is recalling Thomas Hobbes's famous question posed to William, Earl of Devonshire in the dedication to *De Cive* in 1651; the phrase is from Plautus's *Asinaria*. Man is both a beast and a child of God. See also Drabinski, "The Possibility of an Ethical Politics," 58: "Against the tradition that grounds the universality of law in an extension of *my* interests, Levinas' law establishes a protection of the rights of the singular Other."

4. Drabinski takes up the early genetic account that Levinas seems to endorse, where justice or the face-to-face is the origin of law and the state (ibid., 54); see Emmanuel Levinas, "Uniqueness," in *Entre Nous: Thinking of the Other*, trans.

Michael B. Smith and Barbara Harshav (New York: Columbia University Press, 1998), 195–96, but notice that justice here is said to "explain" the state, and there are different types of explanation. I do not take explanation here to be genetic, identifying an origin in some temporal sense, but rather teleological, in a sense.

5. I have discovered four Levinas references to this Talmudic text, Babylonian Talmud, Rosh Ha-Shanah 17b–18a: "Interview with François Poirié," in *Is It Righteous to Be?*, ed. Jill Robbins (Stanford, CA: Stanford University Press, 2001), 69 [1986]; "Responsibility and Substitution," in *Is It Righteous to Be?*, 231 [1988]; "The Other, Utopia, and Justice," in *Entre Nous*, 230 [1988]; and "In the Name of the Other," in *Is It Righteous to Be?*, 194 [1992]. The references are all to comments in interviews, and, as the dates indicate, they are all quite late in Levinas's career. There is an allusion to the Talmudic passage in "The Awakening of the I," in *Is It Righteous to Be?*, 183–84. For an earlier text on a similar theme, see Emmanuel Levinas, "An Eye for an Eye," in *Difficult Freedom*, ed. Seán Hand (Baltimore: Johns Hopkins University Press, 1990), 146–48. Robert Gibbs has discussed this Talmudic reference and the role of the judge in confronting the defendant, together with a paper by Robert Cover, "Violence and Word," in "Verdict and Sentence: Cover and Levinas on the Robe of Justice," in *Essays on Levinas and Law: A Mosaic*, ed. Desmond Manderson (Basingstoke, UK: Palgrave Macmillan, 2009), 95–110.

6. In the earliest reference I have found, in his long interview with François Poirié in 1986, Levinas says that in terms of an "appeal to mercy behind justice," the Talmudic text provides an "illustration, not an example" of this point. Two years later, he refers to the text as "Judaism—in the guise of a parable," and he calls upon it to clarify "the State in which justice is not separate from mercy" and a "surplus of

charity over justice." In the interview "The Other, Utopia, and Justice," also in 1988, he notes that this "Talmudic apologue" shows how the "possibilities of mercy" fully belong to the "work of justice." Finally, in 1992, he interprets this text to mean that "charity can accomplish a lot, even after a rigorous justice has been passed." (For citations, see references in note 5 above.)

7. Levinas, "In the Name of the Other," in *Is It Righteous to Be?*, 194. See also Levinas, "Interview with François Poirié," in *Is It Righteous to Be?*, 69: "Before the verdict, no face; but once the judgment is pronounced, He looks at the face."

8. Levinas, "Interview with François Poirié," in *Is It Righteous to Be?*, 68.

9. Ibid., 69.

10. Levinas, "The Other, Utopia, and Justice," in *Entre Nous*, 231.

11. Levinas, "In the Name of the Other," in *Is It Righteous to Be?*, 194. As I note elsewhere, Annabel Herzog alludes to this when she says that Levinas has ethics say "yes" to the state and justice say "no" to it. This bad conscience is expressed in that "no."

12. See, for another treatment, Emmanuel Levinas, "Diachrony and Representation," in *Entre Nous*, 165–68. The essay dates from 1985.

13. "The Paradox of Morality: An Interview with Emmanuel Levinas," in *The Provocation of Levinas: Rethinking the Other*, ed. Robert Bernasconi and David Wood (London: Routledge, 1988), 171, 174.

14. For a clear account, see Levinas, "Responsibility and Substitution," in *Is It Righteous to Be?*, 230.

15. Levinas, "The Paradox of Morality," 175.

16. In the interview with Poirié, Levinas expresses the same point by saying "if, ultimately, the unique ones have to enter the genus, why then insist so much on the uniqueness?" He answers, "As long as the State remains liberal its law is not yet completed and can always be more just than its

actual justice" ("Interview with François Poirié," in *Is It Righteous to Be?*, 68). This is the consciousness that the justice on which the state is founded is an "imperfect justice."

17. Levinas, "The Paradox of Morality," 175.

18. As I pointed out earlier, this is the point of Drabinski's discussion of origin and explanation; justice explains what the state (and law) is for ("The Possibility of an Ethical Politics," 54–55). Left to itself, as he says, "politics . . . is tyrannical."

19. See Emmanuel Levinas, "Being-Toward-Death and 'Thou Shalt Not Kill'," in *Is it Righteous to Be?*, 132: "Hobbes says that it is precisely *from* this reciprocal hatred that one can come to philosophy. That is to say, without love for the other, we can therefore teach a better society in which allowance is made for the other. This would be a politics capable of leading to an ethics. I believe, conversely, that politics must be held in check by ethics: the other does concern me."

20. Derrida says that ethics and politics disturb one another; they engage in a "double bind." Ethics provides the ground for a critique of justice, and justice is necessary for realizing ethics. See Jacques Derrida, *Adieu to Emmanuel Levinas* (Stanford, CA: Stanford University Press, 1990), 20, 33; cited by Annabel Herzog, "Is Liberalism 'All We Need'? Levinas's Politics of Surplus," *Political Theory* 30, no. 2 (April 2002): 204–5.

21. Levinas, "In the Name of the Other," in *Is It Righteous to Be?*, 194.

22. Levinas, "The Paradox of Morality," 175.

23. Levinas, "The Paradox of Morality," 175. Levinas also refers to it, as a lesson of Akiba's reading, in "The Other, Utopia, and Justice," in *Entre Nous*, 231.

24. Levinas, "The Paradox of Morality," 177–78.

25. Elsewhere, Levinas uses the expression "the adventure of a possible holiness";

see "The Other, Utopia, and Justice," in *Entre Nous*, 231.

26. In "Responsibility and Substitution," Levinas says, "The State can always review its laws and its justice. Is this concern for reconsideration—for amelioration—not in effect the essence of democracy and of the liberal State, the sign of a mercy and charity that breathe there? An effort in view of an always better law.... When the State lays claim to an unvarying justice that is logically deduced, one must suspect Stalinism and fascism" (*Is It Righteous to Be?*, 230–31).

27. Levinas, "The Other, Utopia, and Justice," in *Entre Nous*, 229–30. Here he also uses the expression we have seen "the bad conscience of justice." See also Levinas, "In the Name of the Other," in *Is It Righteous to Be?*, 194.

28. As Herzog indicates, Levinas says that those limits that the state confronts are called "surplus, religion, peace, or charity, a commitment toward a *utopia*" ("Is Liberalism 'All We Need'?," 219). Also, citing Critchley, Herzog compares Levinas's critique of the state with Benjamin's form of "redemptive critique" (219–20). She notes moreover that this challenge does not mean that politics needs to become other than it is, but rather that it must make room for the kinds of responsibility that it cannot deal with itself. Jill Stauffer has a nice statement of how ethics and politics limit one another and how the relation between them is one of oscillation and ambivalence; see Jill Stauffer, "Productive Ambivalence: Levinasian Subjectivity, Justice, and the Rule of Law," in *Essays on Levinas and Law: A Mosaic*, 76–91, esp. 85–89. I also find a congenial account of this oscillation between ethics and politics in William Paul Simmons, *An-archy and Justice: An Introduction to Emmanuel Levinas's Political Thought* (Lanham, MD: Lexington Books, 2003), chs. 4–5.

29. Emmanuel Levinas, *Otherwise Than Being* (Pittsburgh: Duquesne University

Press, 1998), 159–60. For a similar formulation, see Emmanuel Levinas, "Peace and Proximity," in *Basic Philosophical Writings*, ed. Adriaan T. Peperzak, Simon Critchley, and Robert Bernasconi (Bloomington: Indiana University Press, 1996), 169.

30. Emmanuel Levinas, *Ethics and Infinity: Conversations with Philippe Nemo* (Pittsburgh: Duquesne University Press, 1985), 80.

31. Herzog, "Is Liberalism 'All We Need'?," 204–27.

32. See Robert Bernasconi, "Extra-Territoriality: Outside the State, Outside the Subject," in *Levinas Studies: An Annual Review*, vol. 3, ed. Jeffrey Bloechl (Pittsburgh: Duquesne University Press, 2008), 61–77. For discussion, see ch. 6 in this volume.

33. In "Ideology and Idealism" Levinas says, "In the social community, the community of clothed beings, the privileges of rank obstruct justice" (*The Levinas Reader*, 243–44). This opposition to rank and inequalities is part of why Levinas favors democracies, I take it. Drabinski takes these considerations to mark a tendency to violence ("The Possibility of an Ethical Politics," 62). Critchley focuses on the role of justice in democracy, which he calls "ethics in practice"; see Simon Critchley, *The Ethics of Deconstruction*, 2nd ed. (West Lafayette, IN: Purdue University Press, 1999), 239. For discussion, see Drabinski, "The Possibility of an Ethical Politics," 67–68, who discusses the distribution of power in a democracy and calls for a radical redistribution by giving power to minorities and not simply allowing power to attach to the majority. The same goes for wealth, as he also discusses (68), where he encourages redistribution at a loss without expectation of return—a kind of sacrifice. Levinas entitles one of his Talmudic lessons "Beyond the State in the State," in *New Talmudic Readings*, trans. Richard A. Cohen (Pittsburgh: Duquesne University Press, 1999), 79–107.

34. Herzog argues that Levinas says both "no" to the state and justice and "yes" to them, and although I think she may have much more in mind, what she says is certainly akin to what I mean here when I say that he claims that the liberal state seeks to be just and yet realizes that there is always more to be done. Also, what she says is akin to what I note is the violence of the state that accompanies its justice. See Herzog, "Is Liberalism 'All We Need'?," 212–13. She says, "In revealing hunger and demanding a solution for it, ethics both controls and appeals to politics" (213); I would say, "In revealing the infinite vulnerability and need of the other for me and for each and every person, and demanding that we find a means for dealing with that vulnerability, ethics directs and appeals to politics." In a sense, democracy is the alternative between tyranny and religion or, we might say, between tyranny and anarchy.

35. For discussion of how Levinas is committed to liberalism and to what degree, see Herzog, "Is Liberalism 'All We Need'?"

36. I do not read Levinas as intrinsically destabilizing, as Drabinski does. He takes the idea of "extravagant generosity" very seriously and reads Levinas or provides a Levinasian reading that encourages expenditures at a loss for public works—in terms of political power and wealth, at least. See Drabinski, "The Possibility of an Ethical Politics," 68–69. My reading does not foreclose on such a dramatic orientation to Levinas, but it does not require it. Political critique does have content, but it does not require anarchism or revolution.

37. Levinas, "Diachrony and Representation," in *Entre Nous*, 166–67.

38. Herzog emphasizes the political sense of representation to identify those who in practice are in fact unrepresented; see Herzog, "Is Liberalism 'All We Need'?," 216–17. Herzog refers to those who once were present and who now, in

politics, are re-presented, but, she says, the "dying of the hungry and persecuted Other" are lacking in presence; i.e., "many others lack the presence that is re-presented in politics" (217). This is Herzog's way of saying that politics is not always just or as just as it should be. To say that there are those who are not present is to say that there are laws and policies that do not attend to the face of the other, their vulnerability and needs. She claims that "the real *problem* is the absence of nonrepresented people" (217), which means that too often laws and policies are insensitive to many people and omit to attend to the needs of many people. In other words, there are "tears that the civil servant does not see," as I explain later.

39. Drabinski uses Levinas's term "liturgy" for what he calls an "ethical politics." Liturgy, a term that originated in ancient Greece, means an act of expenditure that is made for public works at a loss to oneself. It is an act of extraordinary generosity. I am happy with the term, but I disagree with what Drabinski seems to require for an "ethical politics." See Drabinski, "The Possibility of an Ethical Politics," 66ff. See also Emmanuel Levinas, "Reality Has Weight," in *Is It Righteous to Be?*, 163: "You know, the rights of man are nothing new; we already find their traces in Cicero. Much more important to me is that the rights of the other come before my own. That is much more important. We must understand that the rights of the other do not only begin with the defense of my own rights."

40. See Levinas, "Responsibility and Substitution," in *Is It Righteous to Be?*, 230. See Levinas, "Peace and Proximity," in *Basic Philosophical Writings*, 169; and *Otherwise Than Being*, 159–61.

41. Drabinski, in "The Possibility of an Ethical Politics," calls Levinas's project a "peace for the Other" that seeks to "secure the Other's place in the sun" (58), and he asks if such a "politics of peace" is suffi-

cient for an "ethical politics." Does it lead to the excess of giving, "the extravagant generosity" that Levinas refers to? Drabinski claims that it does not, and he argues this by showing that Levinas is insufficiently conservative (58 and following). In a way that is closer to my own view, Herzog makes the point this way: what kind of a state do we need that does not leave out those who are unrepresented? "The state . . . should be established *for* the sake of those who do not, or cannot, fight for their being, those who are defeated and cannot send representatives. . . . The legitimacy of politics should not consist in its relation to its participants but, on the contrary, in its responsibility for . . . its *absentees*" (218). Understood properly, this is a helpful formulation: politics should focus not on those who are adequately represented but rather on those who are not; moreover, it should focus on the dimension of our lives that is hidden or occluded by representation, our vulnerability and very particular needs and dependencies.

42. Margalit distinguishes decency from justice, following a suggestion of Sydney Morgenbesser. Levinas, too, distinguishes ethics from justice—in his mature vocabulary—but for different reasons, I think, as we shall see. Margalit also distinguishes a decent from a civilized society. In the former, the institutions do not humiliate; in the latter, people do not, even if the institutions do. See Avishai Margalit, *The Decent Society* (Cambridge, MA: Harvard University Press, 1996), 1–2. One might think that Levinas would only be interested in promoting the latter, i.e., concrete acts of interpersonal decency, but my point here is that he is also interested in promoting institutions that treat people without humiliating them and with due respect and humanity.

43. That is, it avoids humiliating its citizens and others "under its jurisdiction." See Margalit, *The Decent Society*, 150. With regard to citizens, the important issue is

that no citizens or groups of citizens are treated badly or considered "second-class citizens." If the state is an ethnocultural nationalism, then the minority cultures are treated with respect. On the relation between justice and decency, see *The Decent Society*, 271–91.

44. Margalit characterizes humiliation as excluding the victim from the family of humanity and thus of degrading the person, and this involves, at one level, either rejecting an encompassing group or excluding a person from such a group when he or she has a legitimate right to be a member. See Margalit, *The Decent Society*, 135–43.

45. Margalit, *The Decent Society*, 119. Cf. Richard Rorty, *Contingency, Irony, and Solidarity* (Cambridge: Cambridge University Press, 1989), 90: "A recognition of a common susceptibility to humiliation is the only social bond that is needed." Also see Rorty's distinction between agents of love and agents of justice: Richard Rorty, *Consequences of Pragmatism: Essays 1972–1980* (Minneapolis: University of Minnesota Press, 1982), 203.

46. See Margalit, *The Decent Society*, 280–81: "Efficiency . . . involves only the probability of obtaining a just pattern of distribution, and not a humane manner of distribution. The distribution may be both efficient and just, yet still humiliating. . . . Justice may lack compassion and might even be an expression of vindictiveness. . . . It is not enough for goods to be distributed justly and efficiently—the style of their distribution must also be taken into account."

47. Another difference between Margalit and Levinas is that Levinas has a kind of theory in terms of which our everyday, social and political, institutions and conduct should be evaluated, whereas Margalit denies that he has a theory. Margalit says that he is offering a story about a decent society, a utopia in terms of which reality can be criticized. See Margalit, *A*

Decent Theory, 288–89. Given Margalit's description of different kinds of theory, Levinas's is what he would call a Gödelian theory, as we have in Rawls.

48. See Levinas, "Transcendence and Height," in *Basic Philosophical Writings*, 23.

2. JUDAISM, ZIONISM, AND THE STATE OF ISRAEL

1. Annabel Herzog, in order to clarify the "double bind" between ethics and politics, discusses several of Levinas's "confessional" texts: "The State of Caesar and the State of David" and "Politics After!" in *Beyond the Verse*, passages in the Talmudic commentaries on messianism in *Difficult Freedom*, and "Judaism and Revolution" in *Nine Talmudic Readings*. See Annabel Herzog, "Is Liberalism 'All We Need'?: Levinas's Politics of Surplus," *Political Theory* 30, no. 2 (April 2002): 213–15. For a very informative discussion of the role of the Holocaust and the State of Israel in public discussion in France after 1967, see Joan B. Wolf, *Harnessing the Holocaust: The Politics of Memory in France* (Stanford, CA: Stanford University Press, 2004).

2. An intriguing parallel to Levinas's silence with regard to the victims of West Beirut is Camus's silence regarding Algeria. For discussion, see Tony Judt, *The Burden of Responsibility: Blum, Camus, Aron and the French Twentieth Century* (Chicago: University of Chicago Press, 1998), 133–34.

3. Emmanuel Levinas, "Means of Identification" (1953), in *Difficult Freedom*, trans. Seán Hand (Baltimore: Johns Hopkins University Press, 1990), 50–51.

4. Levinas, "The State of Israel and the Religion of Israel," in *Difficult Freedom*, 216–20 (originally 1951; in *Difficult Freedom* 1963).

5. Ibid., 218.

6. Ibid., 219.

7. Levinas often makes it clear that there is an element of capitulation or assimilation to Zionism, an acceptance of Western principles and the sense of rootedness in nationality and soil. Judaism is something more elevated than this, and only insofar as Zionism is committed to that supplement, that elevated dimension, is it true to itself as a movement to realize Judaism in political institutions and in a national life. See Levinas, "Assimilation Today" (1954), in *Difficult Freedom*, 257–58.

8. See Levinas, "Space Is Not One-Dimensional" (1968), in *Difficult Freedom*, 263–64: "It is not because the Holy Land takes the form of a State that it brings the Reign of the Messiah any closer, but because the men who inhabit it try to resist the temptations of politics; because this State, proclaimed in the aftermath of Auschwitz, embraces the teaching of the prophets."

9. Levinas, "From the Rise of Nihilism to the Carnal Jew," in *Difficult Freedom*, 225.

10. Ibid., 224: "But, for nations as for people, moral sovereignty is experienced as the faculty of dying for an idea." See also "How Is Judaism Possible?" (1959), in *Difficult Freedom*, 250: "The State of Israel, whatever the ephemeral political philosophy of its greatest workers, is not for us a State like any other. It has a density and depth that greatly surpass its scope and its political possibilities; it is like a protest against the world."

11. Levinas, "From the Rise of Nihilism to the Carnal Jew," in *Difficult Freedom*, 221.

12. Ibid., 222.

13. Emmanuel Levinas, *Beyond the Verse: Talmudic Readings and Lectures* (Bloomington: Indiana University Press, 1994) (originally 1982). The essays are "The State of Caesar and the State of Israel" (originally 1971), "Politics After!" (originally 1979), and "Assimilation and New Culture" (originally 1980).

14. Levinas, *Beyond the Verse*, xv.

15. Ibid.

16. Ibid.

17. Ibid., xvi.

18. Ibid., xvii.

19. Ibid.

20. Ibid., 193.

21. Ibid., 194.

22. Ibid., 195.

23. In commenting on this essay, Herzog cites the following description of the peace that followed Sadat's visit: "For what is 'politically' weak about [this peace] is probably the expression both of its audacity and, ultimately, of its strength. It is also, perhaps, what it brings, for everyone everywhere, to the very idea of peace: the suggestion that peace is a concept which goes beyond purely political thought" (Levinas, *Beyond the Verse*, 195). This is what I have called an "ethical peace" and not simply a peace that is the cessation of war.

24. "Israël: éthique et politique," *Les Nouveaux cahiers* 71 (Hiver 1982–83):1–8; "Ethics and Politics," in *The Levinas Reader*, ed. Seán Hand (Oxford: Basil Blackwell, 1989). For a detailed examination of the interview, see ch. 10 below.

25. Israeli sources claim that it was no more than eight hundred; Palestinian reports take the total to be up to three thousand.

26. Shalom Achshav, Peace Now, had been founded in 1978, but the rally in 1982, in which it played a role alongside other peace movements, brought it to prominence and was arguably its first major accomplishment.

27. The commission, formally called the *Commission of Inquiry into the Events at the Refugee Camps in Beirut*, delivered its report on February 8, 1983. It is available in English as *The Beirut Massacre: The Complete Kahan Commission Report* (Princeton, NJ: Karz-Cohl, 1983).

28. John Drabinski, like so many others who read this interview in a very critical spirit, wonders how Levinas has moved from the "widow, orphan, and stranger" to "people" and "kin," as if this marks a shift in Levinas's thinking and a confusion or mistake on his part. As I try to explain,

this is not Levinas's mistake; rather it is Levinas's attempt to call attention to an easy mistake often made of his thinking, the confusion between political others and the ethical other. See John Drabinski, "The Possibility of an Ethical Politics: From Peace to Liturgy," *Philosophy and Social Criticism* 26, no. 4 (2000): 58–59. From Levinas's remarks, Drabinski concludes that failing to be a kin or being an enemy "establishes a boundary that bars Palestinians from the work of ethics" (59). As I will show, this reading of Levinas is so remarkably ungenerous and strange that one wonders what leads otherwise sensitive readers like Drabinski to engage in it. Rather than read Levinas's philosophical work on its own terms and then to read this interview in the light of the former, Drabinski chooses explicitly to use the interview in order to reread various of Levinas's later essays, e.g., the essay on human rights and the rights of the other.

29. "Ethics and Politics," in *The Levinas Reader*, 294, 292.

30. Ibid.

31. Ibid., 295. And as Levinas goes on to point out, since Zionism and the State of Israel have, for him, a messianic character, the day-to-day lives in Israel are invested in the ethical task, and it is a hard and challenging one. Sabra and Shatila are a shock to this task and to the hopes invested in it.

32. In *Parting Ways: Jewishness and the Critique of Zionism* (New York: Columbia University Press, 2012), Judith Butler says that in the interview Levinas says that "the Palestinians have no face" (227n24). I am baffled by such a claim, which shows a complete lack of understanding of Levinas. I take it that Butler is interpreting Levinas's response to Malka's question about Levinas's views and the otherness of the Palestinians. I have shown what Levinas's response clearly means. He is pointing to an ambiguity in the idea of the other, between its political and its ethical

senses, and I would venture that this confusion is precisely what Butler expresses. What lies behind or motivates her confusion, however, is another story. We return to this issue shortly.

33. Sol Goldberg has pointed out to me that compassion and even pity are not necessarily positive responses to suffering and pain. Nietzsche warns that approaching others with these attitudes may be demeaning and that the objects of such compassion may feel resentment or humiliation as a result. But the important point is that Levinas understands that at the everyday or practical level, many factors enter into one's judgments and actions toward others. Being attentive to the particular circumstances of a situation and to the humanity of the others involved, however, does not prejudge their claim upon each of us, but many contextual factors determine how one eventually decides to act and how one does act. Levinas's point is that there are moments when what has occurred and the weight of the other's humanity, etc., are in conflict. Levinas's views do not preclude deliberation, reflection, and judgment; they provide one reason for engaging in them and a particular orientation toward them.

34. Drabinski seems aware that the face-to-face does not by itself provide contextual information about who we are and who the others are, but he then claims that this is a flaw for Levinas and not simply the fact that our moral sensitivity is always embedded in our natural and everyday lives. See John Drabinski, "The Possibility of an Ethical Politics," 61–62. In a sense, his argument is an anarchist one; a stronger Levinasian reading would put the universality of law into question. And part of his strategy for such a reading is to build socio-political features into the very notion of alterity, i.e., to argue that the materiality of persons—gender, race, class, etc.—is already built into the otherness of the other person. He takes this idea

from Luce Irigaray's reading of Levinas; see Luce Irigaray, "Questions to Emmanuel Levinas," in *The Irigaray Reader,* ed. Margaret Whitford (Oxford: Blackwell, 1993), 185. It is a mistake. The petitionary and commanding presence of the other person in all his or her particularity is all there is to the face-to-face; everything else is politics, so to speak. See Drabinski, "The Possibility of an Ethical Politics," 64.

35. Howard Caygill, *Levinas and the Political* (London: Routledge, 2002), 192. See ch. 11 below.

36. Ibid.

37. See ch. 3 in this volume.

38. Caygill, *Levinas and the Political,* 192.

39. See Butler, *Parting Ways,* 83–101; Judith Butler, *Precarious Life: The Powers of Mourning and Violence* (London: Verso, 2004), 128–51.

40. Butler, *Parting Ways,* 23.

41. Ibid. See also ibid., 24: "Unwilled proximity and unchosen cohabitation are preconditions of our political existence." Butler draws on the thought of the important political philosopher Hannah Arendt, author of *The Origins of Totalitarianism, Eichmann in Jerusalem,* and a number of other influential works. For critical discussion of Butler's appropriation of Arendt, see the review essay by Benhabib cited in note 42 below.

42. For an important critique of Butler's interpretation of Arendt, see Seyla Benhabib, "Ethics without Normativity and Politics without Historicity: On Judith Butler's *Parting Ways. Jewishness and the Critique of Zionism,*" *Constellations* 20, no. 1 (2013): 150–63. Also, see chs. 8, 10, and 11 in this volume.

43. See Ruth Gavison, "Can Israel Be Both Jewish and Democratic?," cited from the Social Science Research Network (Jan. 1, 2011): http://papers.ssrn.com/so13/papers.cfm?abstract_id=1862904, an adaptation of chapter 1, "Conceptual Compatibility and Justifiability, in Principle, of a Jewish and Democratic State," in *Israel*

as a Jewish and Democratic State: Tensions
and Prospects (Jerusalem: Van Leer, 1999)
(Hebrew); Chaim Gans, A Just Zionism:
On the Morality of the Jewish State (Oxford:
Oxford University Press, 2008), 65ff. See
also Alan Wolfe, "Israel's Moral Peril,"
The Chronicle of Higher Education: The
Chronicle Review, March 25, 2012, quoted
from the online version.

44. For such criticism from within Is-
rael and the Jewish community, see Atalia
Omer, When Peace Is Not Enough: How the
Israeli Peace Camp Thinks about Religion,
Nationalism, and Justice (Chicago: Univer-
sity of Chicago Press, 2013); Mordechai
Bar-On, In Pursuit of Peace: A History of the
Israeli Peace Movement (Washington, DC:
U.S. Institute of Peace Press, 1996); Tamar
Hermann, The Israeli Peace Movement: A
Shattered Dream (Cambridge: Cambridge
University Press, 2009); Shlomo Ben-Ami,
Scars of War, Wounds of Peace: The Israeli-
Arab Tragedy (Oxford: Oxford University
Press, 2006). See also the works of Baruch
Kimmerling, Uri Ram, David Grossman,
David Schulman, Adi Ophir, Orin Yifta-
chel, and Yehouda Shenhav. See Laurence
J. Silberstein, ed., Postzionism: A Reader
(Brunswick, NJ: Rutgers University Press,
2008); Ephraim Nimni, The Challenge of
Post-Zionism (London: Zed Books, 2003).

45. For further discussion of Levinas
on rights, see ch. 5 in this volume.

46. Of course, not all such opportunities for a "personal approach" will end up
involving humane behavior. Or, another
way of putting this is that while all bureaucracies are not bad, all personal contact is
not good. For a helpful discussion of this
point, see Avishai Margalit, The Decent
Society (Cambridge, MA: Harvard University Press, 1996), 212–21.

47. Critics of Israel will surely find
this approach to developing a critique to
be unsatisfying and perhaps even obfus-
cating. It requires a keen attention to the
complex details of the situation, policy, or
conduct that is being subjected to scru-

tiny. And weighing or comparing options
and possibilities offers no firm or rigid
criteria for acceptability or legitimacy.
There is no fixed calculus for carrying out
such deliberations and no fixed scale for
weighing responsibilities. Understanding
and sensitivity grow with and are shaped
by experience. But there is a difference between a critique based on the foundational
impulse to protect rights and freedom and
a critique based on the foundational impulse to acknowledge and care for others.
And that is what I am trying to clarify.

48. See Emmanuel Levinas, "In the
Name of the Other," in Is It Righteous to
Be? Interviews with Emmanuel Levinas, ed.
Jill Robbins (Stanford, CA: Stanford University Press, 2001), 197–98: "I have personally never leaned toward an active Zionism. However, for me this is not merely
a political doctrine. Nor is it a state like the
others, rife with conflict and subject to the
requirements of the moment. Is not the
ultimate finality of Zionism to create upon
Israeli soil the concrete conditions for political intervention, and to make or remake
a state in which prophetic morality shall be
incarnate, along with its message of peace?
. . . Israel represents a security in a world
where politics count, and where the cultural depends upon the political."

49. Much of what Levinas takes to be
characteristic of a democratic regime is
widely held to constitute the democratic
ideal. To be sure, states aspire to democratic practices and institutions to different degrees and succeed only to some
degree or other. Israel has been widely
conceived as democratic in terms of some
of what Levinas has in mind; this is true
of the UN Resolution 181 of 1947 and the
declaration of the state's foundation in
1948. To be sure, of course, there are critics
who deny that it has been successful. Or
they might be willing to accept that while
Israel once aspired to democratic principles and achieved them to some degree,
recently she has failed more regularly to

put them into practice. Levinas's attitude is traditional and optimistic, to be sure, but it need not be dismissed as mindless romanticism; it is or can be sober and realistic, even if it is positive and optimistic. Moreover, his approach to Zionism might be seen to be one way in which one could coordinate a commitment to Judaism and Zionism with loyalty to the ideals of French identity. For discussion of the issue of "dual loyalties" see Wolf, *Harnessing the Holocaust*, 53–62.

50. Levinas, "The State of Israel and the Religion of Israel" (1951), in *Difficult Freedom*, 218.

3. THE THIRD PARTY

1. In *Otherwise Than Being* (Pittsburgh: Duquesne University Press, 1998), it is what Levinas calls "obsession," "accusation," "persecution," "hostage," "proximity," and "substitution." His continuing engagement with this primordial and determinative relationship between persons proceeds through elaborations of his changing vocabulary.

2. Simon Critchley has his own way of calling attention to the centrality of this relationship as the critical one for Levinas, in terms of the roles of anarchy, the third party, ambiguity, and reduction; see Simon Critchley, "Anarchic Law," in *Essays on Levinas and Law: A Mosaic*, ed. Desmond Manderson (Basingstoke, UK: Palgrave Macmillan, 2009), 203–11.

3. Philippe Nemo quotes this passage from *Totality and Infinity* (Pittsburgh: Duquesne University Press, 1969), 57–58, in a question to Levinas about political philosophy in *Ethics and Infinity: Conversations with Philippe Nemo* (Pittsburgh: Duquesne University Press, 1985), 79.

4. There are several helpful accounts of the role of the third party in Levinas's thinking. See, e.g., John Drabinski, "The Possibility of an Ethical Politics: From Peace to Liturgy," *Philosophy and Social Criticism* 26, no. 4 (2000): 49–73; Jill

Stauffer, "Productive Ambivalence: Levinasian Subjectivity, Justice, and the Rule of Law," in *Essays on Levinas and Law: A Mosaic*, 76–91, esp. 85–89; William Paul Simmons, *An-archy and Justice: An Introduction to Emmanuel Levinas's Political Thought* (Lanham, MD: Lexington Books, 2003), chs. 4 and 5; Robert Bernasconi, "The Third Party: Levinas on the Intersection of the Ethical and the Political," *Journal of the British Society for Phenomenology* 30, no. 1 (1999): 76–87, reprinted in Claire Katz with Lara Trout, eds., *Emmanuel Levinas: Critical Assessments of Leading Philosophers*, vol. 1 (London: Routledge, 2005), 45–57.

5. Levinas, *Totality and Infinity*, 213.

6. Levinas reiterates this point, that community and fraternity are not biological categories or relationships, later in *Otherwise Than Being*; they are the unity of a society organized by justice. See *Otherwise Than Being*, 159. And it is because of this that our social lives have the meaning, the ethical meaning, that they do. "My relationship with the other as neighbor gives meaning to my relations with all the others."

7. Levinas, *Totality and Infinity*, 214.

8. Martin Buber, *I and Thou* (New York: Scribner's, 1970), 94.

9. As I have just shown, this is not to say that prior to this Levinas had not appreciated the role that multiplicity and complexity play in our daily lives and how the face-to-face is only given to us in the context of that life. See *Totality and Infinity*, 213 (cited by Drabinski, "The Possibility of an Ethical Politics," 55, and Annabel Herzog, "Is Liberalism 'All We Need'? Levinas's Politics of Surplus," *Political Theory* 30, no. 2 [April 2002]: 204), where Levinas already mentions the third party. See also *Totality and Infinity*, 300, where Levinas says that the face-to-face "aspires to a state, institutions, laws." The I becomes a We as the face-to-face becomes a collectivity and achieves universality (see

Drabinski, "The Possibility of an Ethical Politics," 55–56). Cf. Simon Critchley, *The Ethics of Deconstruction*, 2nd ed. (West Lafayette IN: Purdue University Press, 1999), 233.

10. Levinas, *Otherwise Than Being*, 16.

11. Ibid. "It is on the basis of proximity that being takes on its just meaning" (ibid.).

12. Ibid.

13. It is not a genetic account, then, and not a derivation. But it can be said that the face-to-face or charity does explain language, conceptualization, comparison and discrimination, classification, rationality, institutions, generalization, and such. It provides the reason why these activities and structures are worthwhile or valuable by identifying what ultimate purpose they serve. In a world of human beings with networks of social relationships, it explains what these functions enable us to perform—to respond to others and the claims they make upon us.

14. Without due attentiveness to the humanity of the other, the state is tyrannical. Or, as Drabinski reminds us (citing Levinas, "Uniqueness," in *Entre Nous: Thinking-of-the-Other*, trans. Michael B. Smith and Barbara Harshav [New York: Columbia University Press, 1998]), "the prophetic voice reminds the judgment of the state that the human face is concealed in the idea of the citizen"; John Drabinski, "The Possibility of an Ethical Politics," 56. This is part of what social and political critique means for Levinas—the reminder that each citizen is essentially, fundamentally one to whom each and every one of us is responsible.

15. Levinas, *Otherwise Than Being*, 153–62, esp. 156–62. See also Bernasconi, "The Third Party: Levinas on the Intersection of the Ethical and the Political," 76–87, reprinted in Katz with Trout, *Emmanuel Levinas: Critical Assessments of Leading Philosophers*, vol. 1, 45–57.

16. Levinas, *Otherwise Than Being*, 157.

17. See ibid., 158: "In the comparison of the incomparable there would be the latent birth of representation, logos, consciousness, work, the neutral notion *being*."

18. Ibid., 157.

19. This is my paraphrase of what Levinas argues in *Otherwise Than Being*, 157. See also Levinas, "Peace and Proximity," in *Basic Philosophical Writings*, ed. Adriaan T. Peperzak, Simon Critchley, and Robert Bernasconi (Bloomington: Indiana University Press, 1996), 168: "But the order of truth and knowledge has a role to play in this peace of proximity and in the ethical order it signifies. To a great extent, it is the ethical order of human proximity that gives rise to or calls for the order of objectivity, truth, and knowledge. Which is extremely important for the very sense of Europe; its biblical heritage implies the necessity of the Greek heritage." It is what I meant earlier when I said that the ethical order explains how generalization, language, institutions, politics, and so on, are worthwhile.

20. Levinas, *Otherwise Than Being*, 157.

21. Ibid., 158.

22. Ibid. See also ibid., 160: "And it is because the third party does not come empirically to trouble proximity, but the face is both the neighbor and the face of faces, visage and visible, that, between the order of being and of proximity the bond is unexceptionable."

23. Ibid., 159.

24. See ibid., 160: "It is the necessary interruption of the Infinite being fixed in structures, community and totality."

25. See Onora O'Neill, *Towards Justice and Virtue: A Constructive Account of Practical Reasoning* (Cambridge: Cambridge University Press, 1996).

26. Ibid., 159.

27. Ibid., 159–60.

28. Harry Frankfurt, in "Equality as a Moral Ideal," points out that equality and liberty are much more widely discussed than fraternity, even when it is claimed

that equality, for example, is indispens-
able for "fraternal relationships among
the members of society." See Frankfurt,
"Equality as a Moral Ideal," in *The Importance of What We Care About* (Cambridge:
Cambridge University Press, 1988), 137 and
esp. 137n6.

29. Levinas, *Otherwise Than Being*, 160.

30. Ibid., 161.

31. Ibid., 160.

32. Ibid., 161.

33. Ibid., 162.

34. See, for another treatment, Levinas,
"Diachrony and Representation," in *Entre
Nous*, 165-68. The essay dates from 1985.

35. Levinas, *Ethics and Infinity*, 99.

36. Levinas, *Ethics and Infinity*, 80.

37. See also Emmanuel Levinas, "The
Other, Utopia, and Justice," in *Is It Righteous to Be? Interviews with Emmanuel Levinas*, ed. Jill Robbins (Stanford, CA: Stanford University Press, 2001), 205-6, for a
further formulation of these same points
about the third party, responsibility, and
justice. It is a situation that leads to "a reciprocity of rights and duties" (206).

38. Levinas, "The Proximity of the
Other," in *Is It Righteous to Be?*, 214.

4. ETHICS AS CRITIQUE

1. In the debate, in the 1840s, about
the nature of philosophy, one response was
to take the primary role of philosophy to
be critical. There is a good introduction
to this notion of philosophy as critique
in Frederick C. Beiser, *After Hegel: German Philosophy 1840-1900* (Princeton:
Princeton University Press, 2014), 22-28.
An important source for this conception
of philosophy is the Transcendental Dialectic in Kant's *Critique of Pure Reason*.

2. Michael Walzer, *Interpretation and
Social Criticism* (Cambridge, MA: Harvard
University Press, 1993).

3. See Richard S. Bernstein, "Foucault: Critique as a Philosophical Ethos,"
in *Critique and Power*, ed. Michael Kelly
(Cambridge, MA: MIT Press, 1994), 213.

See also 217-21 for an analysis of three
criticisms of Foucault—by Nancy Fraser,
Charles Taylor, and Jurgen Habermas—in
terms of the question of the ground of critique.

4. This is characteristic of Foucault,
for example, and also the Frankfurt
school. James Tully follows them in
"Public Philosophy as a Critical Activity,"
in *Public Philosophy in a New Key*, vol. 1,
Democracy and Civic Freedom (Cambridge:
Cambridge University Press, 2008), ch. 1;
see 37n38, where Tully focuses on "forms
of oppression in an era of globalization—
inequality, exploitation, domination,
racism, deliberative democratic deficits,
and rights abuses." To Tully, this mode of
political thought or public philosophy is
oriented around freedom and domination
rather than on justice and fair treatment.
By "power," I mean "coercive force" or
"domination." Levinas, of course, takes
the face-to-face to involve violence, but it
is a beneficial violence and not coercive
or injurious in a negative sense. This language of violence for Levinas is part of the
metaphorical description that he uses to
distinguish the sense of burden and obligation to others that is, for him, foundational for all moral normativity.

5. Avishai Margalit, in *The Decent
Society* (Cambridge, MA: Harvard University Press, 1998), 287-88, has a brief account of immanent critique, and he notes
that his own account of a decent society
and its aims, to reduce humiliating and degrading institutions and practices, is not a
theory at all and hence not a critical theory
that aims at liberating citizens from judgments that are based on a false or mistaken
view of social and political relationships.
Rather what he proposes is a story about a
cluster of concepts that produces a picture
of a utopia through which to criticize reality (289).

6. One manifestation of this dimension of Levinasian critique is what might
be called "the temptation of theodicy,"

about which Levinas wrote in "Useless Suffering," trans. Richard A. Cohen, in *The Provocation of Levinas*, ed. Robert Bernsconi and David Wood (London: Routledge, 1992). After the Holocaust, he argued, we live in a time of the end of theodicy. Theodices are any theoretical or explanatory attempts to place and understand suffering within a conceptual scheme or system. The temptation is to overindulge this interest in explanation and understanding or to be satisfied with it, or even to be deterred or deflected from direct acts of assistance to the needy and suffering by paying too much attention to the project of gaining such knowledge or understanding. I will discuss this further below.

7. Walzer, *Interpretation and Social Criticism*, 21.

8. Ibid., 35–39.

9. Walzer's paradigm in the book are the biblical prophets and most notably Amos. See ibid., ch. 3, "The Prophet as Social Critic" and esp. 89: "Amos's prophecy is social criticism because it challenges the leaders, the conventions, the ritual practices of a particular society and because it does so in the name of values recognized and shared in that same society." Walzer cites Raymond Geuss, *The Idea of a Critical Theory: Habermas and the Frankfurt School* (Cambridge: Cambridge University Press, 1981), 63: "A critical theory is addressed to members of *this* particular social group . . . it describes *their* epistemic principles and *their* ideal of the 'good life' and demonstrates that some belief they hold is reflectively unacceptable for agents who hold their epistemic principles and a source of frustration for agents who are trying to realize this particular kind of 'good life.'" See also Tully, "Public Philosophy as a Critical Activity," 28–29.

10. Walzer, *Interpretation and Social Criticism*, 40.

11. Ibid., 40–41. Walzer cites Marx and Engels, *The German Ideology* (New York: International Publishers, 1947), 40–41.

12. Walzer, *Interpretation and Social Criticism*, 46–47.

13. Ibid., 64.

14. Geuss, *The Idea of a Critical Theory: Habermas and the Frankfurt School*, 1–2.

15. See John McDowell, *Mind and World* (Cambridge, MA: Harvard University Press, 1994); John McDowell, *Mind, Value, and Reality* (Cambridge, MA: Harvard University Press, 1998; and Samantha Ashenden and David Owen, eds., *Foucault Contra Habermas: Recasting the Dialogue between Genealogy and Critical Theory* (London: Sage, 1999), and the debate between them over the nature of critique.

16. Avishai Margalit, *The Decent Society* (Cambridge, MA: Harvard University Press, 1996), 1–2.

17. Ibid., 9.

18. Ibid., 24. Cf. 44–48, 51–53, where Margalit distinguishes self-respect from self-esteem and dignity.

19. Ibid., 112, and the whole of ch. 6.

20. Ibid., 104. He does not refer to Primo Levi's remarkable description in *Survival at Auschwitz* and *The Drowned and the Saved*, but he might have. The crucial point is that the humiliated person feels that his very humanity has been denied or rejected. Cf. 119–22. Humiliation always involves shame, but not vice versa, as Margalit explains on 130–33.

21. Ibid., 141 and 135–43.

22. Ibid., 194–96 and, specifically on minorities and their relation to a dominant group, 198–99.

23. Ibid., 212–13.

24. Ibid., 215. See also 236–37.

25. Michael Ignatieff, in his account of his experience in the Canadian parliament, gives a vivid description of the problems of government bureaucracies and the efforts he and his staff expended in trying to intercede in behalf of his constituency: "What representing my fellow

citizens also meant—and this was a major discovery—was that I had to defend them against the incompetence and indifference of government itself. . . . As citizens showed up in my constituency office with their tales of passports delayed, visas withheld, tax files mislaid, my staff and I would pick up the phone and try to help. Every representative has to develop a staff with networks deep inside municipal, provincial and federal bureaucracies. Thanks to them, we fixed thousands of problems for the people in my district. They were often tearful with gratitude when we resolved some Kafkaesque imbroglio with a bureaucrat. . . . The reality of government service delivery was something to see: often dilatory, arbitrary and just plain inefficient. A citizen seeking a service, after all, is claiming a right, not a privilege, but the citizens who ended up in my office often had the cowed look of people caught in a labyrinth of rules beyond their comprehension. . . . A few of them were far from innocent, but most were just dispirited by encounters with a government they were told was there to serve them. . . . Liberals like me, who believed in an empowering government, failed to appreciate what it was like to beg for visas, to queue in a government office, to be kept waiting by a computerized government answering service or to hang around a mailbox every day for a late pension or employment insurance cheque. . . . Once the liberal state fails to treat citizens with respect, citizens conclude that the less they have to do with it the better" (Michael Ignatieff, *Fire and Ashes: Success and Failure in Politics* [Cambridge, MA: Harvard University Press, 2013], 104–6).

26. Margalit, *The Decent Society*, 214 and ch. 14.

27. Ibid., 231.

28. Margalit uses a nice midrash to show that in Judaism the rabbis sought to reduce the motivational role of pity toward the poor and to elevate the poor even as they sought assistance and sup-

port. The rabbis said, "God stands with the poor person at the door" (Leviticus Rabbah). But, as he goes on to show, not only is "mercy" as a motivating factor itself in tension—both ennobling to the giver and demeaning to the recipient—it also "vacillates between pity and compassion" (Margalit, *The Decent Society*, 231–32). Margalit goes on to discuss Nietzsche's famous critique of pity (232–33, 234–35) and Spinoza's as well (233). The central theme is to replace pity with a concern for dignity and self-respect, both for the giver and for the recipient. Part of the difference, for Margalit, as for Levinas—although for different reasons—is that in a welfare society, giving is a response to entitlement. See ibid., 240. For a brief but helpful comment on how welfare societies utilize bureaucracies that can become impersonal and oppressive, see Thomas McCarthy, "The Critique of Impure Reason: Foucault and the Frankfurt School," in Kelly, *Critique and Power*, 252–53.

29. Margalit, *The Decent Society*, 223–24.

30. Margalit makes a useful distinction between a welfare society "in which voluntary, or quasi-voluntary, organizations provide" welfare services and a welfare state "in which the state is [their] provider" (ibid., 225). It is an interesting question whether Levinas would recommend one over the other when there is the option. Margalit uses the state to illustrate the society in respect to distributing welfare.

31. Ibid., 235.

32. Richard M. Titmuss, *Essays on the Welfare State*, 3rd ed. (London: Routledge, 1976) (orig. 1950). See also Titmuss, *The Gift Relationship* (New York: Vintage Books, 1972); and David Reisman, *Richard Titmuss: Welfare and Society*, 2nd ed. (New York: Palgrave, 2001).

33. Margalit, *The Decent Society*, 241–42.

34. Ibid., 242–43. Margalit gives several other reasons for a possible disanalogy, but the ones I mention here are sufficient to

make one wary of using blood donation as a paradigm of welfare distribution.

35. Ibid., 244–45.

36. Ibid., 246.

37. Margalit describes the just society in Rawlsian terms. He puts the question this way: "Is it possible to have a just society that is not a decent society?" (ibid., 271). The connection between the two types of society is not obvious. A just society ought to be decent, but it may not always manage to be so (271–72).

38. Ibid., 273. "If humiliation means damaging people's self-respect, then it is clear that a necessary condition for the just society is that it should be a society that does not humiliate its members" (ibid.).

39. See ibid., 274–81.

40. The film, *Close to Home* (*Karov labayit*, 2005), was directed by Dalia Hagar and Vidi Belu.

41. See esp. Tully, *Public Philosophy in a New Key*, vol. 1, *Democracy and Civic Freedom*, chs. 1–3. Also see Bernstein, "Foucault: Critique as a Philosophical Ethos," in Kelly, *Critique and Power*, esp. 217–21.

42. See James Tully, "To Think and Act Differently: Comparing Critical Ethos and Critical Theory," in *Public Philosophy in a New Key*, vol. 1, *Democracy and Civic Freedom*, 76–83: "[Foucault's historical studies] do not provide a normative ideal in accordance with which citizens measure their practices and act. Although a genealogy certainly frees citizens from false legitimating beliefs about their practices, they are left to develop the reasons and shared will to act themselves. Rather, a genealogy provides a toolkit for understanding the relations of knowledge, power, and ethics in which they think and act, the contingent and arbitrary aspects of these arrangements, the possibilities of modifying them and the effects of modification in practice" (83).

43. See ibid., 119–31, where he discusses this objection to Habermas's critical

theory, that it is utopian; see esp. 119–22. Agreement or deliberation by giving and receiving reasons, not under some coercive influence, becomes a kind of regulative ideal for Habermas. In a sense, Levinas's understanding of the infinite responsibilities we have for and to one another underlies such interpersonal, communicative deliberation. For the observation that Habermas's notion of an ideal of rational discourse is utopian, see McCarthy, "The Critique of Impure Reason: Foucault and the Frankfurt School," in Kelly, *Critique and Power*, 264–65.

44. In a critical examination of Foucault, Nancy Fraser identifies various features that she claims are essential to any kind of social criticism. These include whether it identifies forms of domination, is capable of judging between better or worse regimes and institutions, can distinguish between positive and negative forms of resistance, and can illuminate what sort of social and political change is desirable. Levinasian critique can be understood to fulfill these functions, albeit in very particular ways, although his critique is aimed not at violence and domination in particular but rather at failures of responsibility, broadly speaking, i.e., poverty, injury, suffering, and loss that result from the failures of peoples and institutions to care for people and for one another. See Nancy Fraser, "Michel Foucault: A 'Young Conservative'?," in Kelly, *Critique and Power*, 195.

45. See Bernstein, "Foucault: Critique as a Philosophical Ethos," in Kelly, *Critique and Power*, 228–29.

46. Emmanuel Levinas, "Useless Suffering," trans. Richard A. Cohen, in *The Provocation of Levinas*, ed. Robert Bernasconi and David Wood (London: Routledge, 1992), 161. Another English translation of the essay, originally published in 1982 in French, appears in *Entre Nous*, trans. Michael B. Smith and Barbara Harshav (New York: Columbia Univer-

sity Press, 1998). I cite Richard A. Cohen's translation of 1992.

47. Ibid., 163.

48. For Levinas's formulation of this point, see ibid., 164. This paragraph is Levinas's universalization, as he puts it, of Emil Fackenheim's response to the horrors of Auschwitz, which he articulates as the 614th commandment that Jews are forbidden to give Hitler any posthumous victories. See Emil L. Fackenheim, *God's Presence in History* (New York: New York University Press, 1970), ch. 3.

49. Levinas, "Useless Suffering," in *The Provocation of Levinas*, 164.

50. Ibid., 165.

51. Ibid.

52. But if there is a critical edge to Levinas, it errs on the side of the particular. Albert Camus makes a similar point; see Tony Judt, *The Burden of Responsibility: Blum, Camus, Aron, and the French Twentieth Century* (Chicago: University of Chicago Press, 1998), 131, where Judt cites Camus, as reported in *Le Monde*, December 14, 1957, as having said, "I have always condemned terror. Therefore I must condemn a terrorism operating blindly on the streets of Algiers, for example, and which one day may strike at my mother or my family. I believe in defending justice, but first I will defend my mother." The quotation is cited by Olivier Todd, *Albert Camus: Une vie* (Paris: Gallimard, 1996), 700.

5. RESPONSIBILITY FOR OTHERS AND THE DISCOURSE OF RIGHTS

1. This central commitment to subjectivity and alterity or the second person goes back to Fichte at least and also to Hegel. But it reaches a distinctive and important level in Levinas.

2. Emmanuel Levinas, *Otherwise Than Being* (Pittsburgh: Duquesne University Press, 1998), 159–60. For a similar formulation, see Emmanuel Levinas, "Peace and Proximity," in *Basic Philosophical Writings*, ed. Adriaan T. Peperzak, Simon Critchley,

and Robert Bernasconi (Bloomington: Indiana University Press, 1996), 169.

3. Emmanuel Levinas, *Ethics and Infinity: Conversations with Philippe Nemo* (Pittsburgh: Duquesne University Press, 1985), 80.

4. See Simon Caney, "Global Poverty and Human Rights: The Case for Positive Duties," in *Freedom from Poverty as a Human Right*, ed. Thomas Pogge (Oxford: Oxford University Press, 2007), 275–302.

5. What kind of a difference does Levinas have in mind? James Griffin, in his book on human rights, takes the discourse of human rights to pick out our status as normative agents and to identify characteristics, features, etc., that everyone must respect in terms of this status. He says that morality could do without this discourse, but it is useful. It makes a practical difference to us to have it available and to provide it with this kind of determinateness. Having this discourse available is not necessary, theoretically or systematically. But it does have practical utility for everyday purposes, including political ones. Is this what Levinas has in mind when he says that it is not unimportant to know whether society and the state are founded on one conception of who we are as selves rather than another one? See James Griffin, *On Human Rights* (Oxford: Oxford University Press, 2008), 94.

6. We should keep in mind that while Levinas seems to be referring generally to the use of the notion of rights to identify the significance and function of the state and to play the central role in political critique, he might also have in mind the more specific notion of human rights that has increasingly, at least since the late 1970s, become the core device for justifying international humanitarian efforts and critique and for registering concerns with the privileges of sovereignty. There is a recent plethora of empirical and conceptual work on human rights and especially a revisionist historiography that seeks to clarify

when, in the twentieth century, the human rights discourse as we know it came into being and under what conditions and for what purposes. See Lynn Hunt, *Inventing Human Rights* (New York: W.W. Norton, 2007) and Samuel Moyn, *The Last Utopia: Human Rights in History* (Cambridge, MA: Harvard University Press, 2010) for two watershed discussions of the history of human rights discourse. A central theme of Moyn's important work is how late the emergence of human rights as a "moral vernacular" occurred and how much it contested the primacy of the anticolonialism of the postwar period with its core commitment to the self-determination of peoples. Much can be explained by keeping an eye on this shift from nationalism to internationalism and all it implies for the precedence of morality over politics. A central venue of this shift is the State of Israel and especially its conflict with the movement for Palestinian sovereignty. Moyn takes this shift to be a replacement of various failed utopian visions with another that is more realistic and more minimalist (121).

7. In part, Levinas wants us to appreciate how different it would be to establish a society and political world in the spirit of responsibility from what it would be to establish them in the spirit of the priority of extensive rights and liberties that require protection and endorsement. One society would be a society of socially and communally attuned members with a strong sense of solidarity and commitment, with a willingness and disposition to sacrifice for others and for the community as a whole. The other society would be a society of individuals seeking to be as independent and self-sufficient as possible, thinking primarily of what can be got through initiative and personal growth and development. Mary Ann Glendon, in a very compelling account of the impact of legal decisions and discourse on public perception, criticizes America for the domination

of the latter profile and the lack of a sense of civic pride and responsibility; see *Rights Talk: The Impoverishment of Political Discourse* (New York: Free Press, 1991). Glendon emphasizes the individualist and isolationist dimensions of rights talk and argues that the legal profession, the practice of law in America, and legal education play major roles in educating Americans to a way of life that fails to appreciate our responsibilities to others.

8. It is important to appreciate that while Levinas, at times, seems to suggest that what I am calling a rights discourse is regularly associated with a kind of Hobbesian individualism of competing, atomistic persons, at other times he appreciates how social and relational rights can be. For an excellent statement of this relational character of rights, see Duncan Ivison, *Rights* (Montreal: McGill–Queen's University Press, 2008), 21.

9. See Samuel Moyn, *The Last Utopia: Human Rights in History* (Cambridge, MA: Harvard University Press, 2010).

10. A rights vocabulary introduces two features of our interpersonal relations that might seem to be in tension. On the one hand, the bearer of rights is dependent upon those obligated to him or her; she cannot do without the addressee, needs him or her, and hence is somehow incomplete or deficient without her or him. On the other hand, the rights bearer takes herself to be owed something; she deserves to be treated with concern, to be protected and provided for. Some features of the rights relationship turn on the sense of dependence, some on the sense of worthiness or desert. Levinas is fully attentive to this duality. In essays such as "Transcendence and Height" (in *Basic Philosophical Writings*), it emerges as the two senses of responsibility and the notion of height—the other person calls out to me from below and from above, as both a petitionary and a ruler. The face-to-face is constituted of

both plea and command. All of this is reflected in the ambiguity of rights.

11. I am thinking of Moyn's central thesis in *The Last Utopia* and subsequent writings about the special role of human rights discourse in international relations since the late 1970s.

12. Griffin notices this shift in international law, from considerations of national interest to those of morality, in *On Human Rights*, 205. See especially his reference (205n18) to Allen Buchanan, *Justice, Legitimacy, and Self-Determination* (Oxford: Oxford University Press, 2004), where Buchanan develops a moral account of international relations in contrast to the dominant view based on national self-interest. Griffin argues that without a secure and precise moral foundation, human rights would lack sufficient determination, and international law based on them would lack "explanatory capacity" and "action-guiding authority" (206).

13. See my *Discovering Levinas* (Cambridge: Cambridge University Press, 2007) and also my "Agencies of Redemption," in *The Cambridge History of Jewish Philosophy*, vol. 2, *The Modern Era*, ed. Zachary Braiterman, Martin Kavka, and David Novak (Cambridge: Cambridge University Press, 2012), 465–97.

14. Moyn, Lynn Hunt, and other historians have investigated human rights historically and politically. Philosophers such as James Griffin, Charles Beitz, and John Tasioulas have investigated human rights philosophically, although their accounts all, to one degree or other, take into consideration the role of human rights within the international human rights movement.

15. James W. Nickel, *Making Sense of Human Rights*, 2nd ed. (Malden, MA: Blackwell, 2007), 22–33, esp. 24–26. To qualify as a human right, the interest or condition must be serious enough and weighty enough to warrant its being an overriding consideration in our reasoning. Nickel cites Henry Shue's comment that

human or basic rights specify "the lower limits of tolerable human conduct" rather than "great aspirations and exalted ideals." But this suggests that they are always about negative conditions to be removed, protected against, or avoided, whereas it is clear that there are some human rights that point to conditions to be provided. See ibid., 36.

16. Mary Ann Glendon, in *A World Made New: Eleanor Roosevelt and the Universal Declaration of Human Rights* (New York: Random House, 2001), 75, quotes Ghandi and Chung-Shu Lo, who both suggest that the Universal Declaration of Human Rights should include language of duty as well as of rights, in their responses to the questionnaire from the UNESCO philosophers' committee.

17. For the moment, I want to ignore the possibility that Levinas would take the addressees of human rights and the agents of responsibility to differ. In a sense, for Levinas, each and every one of us is the agent of infinite responsibilities insofar as in each and every relationship we have, we are infinitely responsible to and for the person to whom we are related. In the case of human rights, as the hallmark of the international human rights movement, the primary addressees are governments, while governmental agencies and nongovernmental agencies are also secondary addressees. By and large, while such rights are intended to protect individuals, those bound to respect them are institutions or agencies and not other individuals. However, I think that we can interpret the two views to be closer than it might seem from this comparison. See Nickel, *Making Sense of Human Rights*, 38–41.

18. Nickel, *Making Sense of Human Rights*, 70.

19. Near the conclusion of her engaging account of the historical developments that led to the Universal Declaration of Human Rights, Mary Ann Glendon notes that the conception of rights that most of

the participants had in mind was not the individualist, Hobbesian model found in Anglo-American discussion, but rather the more communitarian conception that is more compatible with Asian and African traditions. See Glendon, *A World Made New,* 277.

20. See Griffin, *On Human Rights.*

21. See, e.g., Nickel, *Making Sense of Human Rights,* 186–87 and passim.

22. I will discuss these papers shortly and also a very instructive Talmudic lesson in which Levinas discusses economic rights and duties and especially the rights of the worker that an employer must respect and fulfill.

23. Nickel, *Making Sense of Human Rights,* 185 and passim.

24. Emmanuel Levinas, "The Prohibition against Representation and 'The Rights of Man,'" in *Alterity and Transcendence* (New York: Columbia University Press, 1999), 121–30 (originally published in 1981 in the proceedings of a colloquium at Monpellier on the "Prohibition against Representation"); "The Rights of Man and Good Will," in *Entre Nous: Thinking-of-the-Other,* trans. Michael B. Smith and Barbara Harshav (New York: Columbia University Press, 1998), 155–58 (originally published in 1985 in an anthology on the indivisibility of the laws of man); "The Rights of Man and the Rights of the Other," in *Outside the Subject* (Stanford, CA: Stanford University Press, 1994), 116–25 (originally published in 1985 in the same anthology on the indivisibility of the laws of man); "The Rights of the Other Man," in *Alterity and Transcendence,* 145–49 (originally published in 1989 in a volume on the "rights of man" in question). I will not discuss the last of these papers, which basically recapitulates the content of the third section of the long essay "The Rights of Man and the Rights of the Other."

25. "The Prohibition against Representation and the 'Rights of Man'" is ten pages in the English translation *Alterity and Transcendence;* the references to rights all come in about two and a half pages (127–29). In the republication of the essay in *Alterity and Transcendence,* Levinas dedicates it to the memory of Adélie Rassial, a young French artist and photographer, who died of cancer in 1983 at the age of thirty-five. In her later years she became interested in psychoanalysis; her husband Jean-Jacques Rassial was a psychologist and psychoanalyst. The essay was originally published in the proceedings of a conference on the prohibition against representation, held at Monpellier in 1981; Rassial (née Hoffenberg) was one of the organizers of the conference. Various themes in the essay—the role of representation and art, the relationship to death, God and religion, and more—suggest Levinas's attention to the conference's themes. The reason for his introduction of the theme of rights and especially the "rights of man" is not clear to me, although by the late 1970s and 1980s the human rights discourse was widely used, and Levinas may have felt the need to show how it is related to his thinking about the face and the primacy of the ethical.

26. Later in the essay Levinas will say, "The epiphany of the face . . . interrupts the unity of the 'I think' in each person who, unique, is awakened to a non-transferable responsibility for the first person who comes along. A gratuitous responsibility: independent of what I may or may not have committed" (ibid., 129). This responsibility for the other is not based on anything I have chosen or done, nor is it something I can avoid or defer or alienate.

27. Ibid., 126–27.

28. Ibid., 127–28.

29. Ibid., 128–29.

30. Levinas, "The Rights of Man and Good Will," in *Entre Nous,* 155–58; "The Rights of Man and the Rights of the Other," in *Outside the Subject,* 116–25. Both

were published in the same collection of papers on the indivisibility of the rights of man in 1985.

31. Levinas, "The Rights of Man and Good Will," in *Entre Nous*, 156.

32. Ibid.

33. Ibid.

34. Ibid., 157.

35. Ibid., 157–58. The reference is to Descartes, *Passions of the Soul*, articles 153 and 156.

36. In the final paragraph, Levinas refers to the classical claim that the rights of man, natural rights, are grounded in divine command. As he had in the earlier essay, he interprets this as a figure for the fact that the ground of natural rights is our relation to transcendence, i.e., the responsibility for the other person and the face-to-face. In brief, respect for human rights occasions talk about divine revelation and divine command. In dealing with natural rights, one is dealing with norms or rules that serve to enhance our responsibilities toward one another. Understanding this is in effect to hear the word of God. See Levinas, "The Rights of Man and Good Will," in *Entre Nous*, 158.

37. Levinas, "The Rights of Man and the Rights of the Other," in *Outside the Subject*, 116–17.

38. Ibid., 116.

39. Ibid., 118.

40. Ibid., 118–20.

41. Ibid., 121.

42. One finds this strategy especially in Nickel, *Making Sense of Human Rights,* and Charles R. Beitz, *The Idea of Human Rights* (Oxford: Oxford University Press, 2009); also see James Griffin, *On Human Rights.*

43. Levinas, "The Rights of Man and the Rights of the Other," in *Outside the Subject*, 120.

44. For an excellent account of the process that led to the United Nations vote on the Universal Declaration of Human Rights, see Glendon, *A World Made New.*

The various documents that led up to the final version and then the final Universal Declaration are printed as appendices to Glendon's book; see 271–314. René Cassin, a French representation on the committee responsible for preparing the document, produced an important draft. Cassin was president of the Alliance Israélite Universelle for thirty-three years, beginning in 1943; Levinas knew him well, and it is likely that Cassin's involvement with the United Nations was one way in which Levinas was informed about and tied to the international human rights movement. See Jay Winter and Antoine Prost, *René Cassin and Human Rights* (Cambridge: Cambridge University Press, 2013).

45. Levinas, "The Rights of Man and the Rights of the Other," in *Outside the Subject*, 120.

46. All of these documents can be found in Nickel, *Making Sense of Human Rights*, 191–242.

47. Levinas, "The Rights of Man and the Rights of the Other," *Outside the Subject*, 120.

48. Ibid., 121.

49. L.W. Sumner, *The Moral Foundation of Rights* (Oxford: Oxford University Press, 1987), 11–12.

50. Levinas, "The Rights of Man and the Rights of the Other," in *Outside the Subject*, 122.

51. Ibid., 123.

52. Ibid.

53. See Michael Walzer, *Interpretation and Social Criticism* (Cambridge, MA: Harvard University Press, 1993); for Walzer, the biblical prophets are the paradigmatic engaged social critics.

54. See 2 Samuel 11–12.

55. See Robert Bernasconi, "Extraterritoriality: Outside the State, Outside the Subject," in *Levinas Studies*, vol. 3, ed. Jeffrey Bloechl (Pittsburgh: Duquesne University Press, 2008), 61–77.

56. Levinas, "The Rights of Man and the Rights of the Other," in *Outside the Subject*, 124.

57. Ibid.

58. Ibid., 124–25.

6. LIBERALISM AND DEMOCRACY

1. See Plato, *Republic* 8–9.

2. Levinas does not, I believe, raise the question of whether there should be a state at all. That is, the question of anarchism never comes up for him, and the reason is that ethics and politics require one another, as I have tried to explain earlier in this book. For a brief and helpful discussion of liberalism as one of several ways of responding to the state—alongside pure democracy, anarchy, Marxism, and others—see Raymond Geuss, *History and Illusion in Politics* (Cambridge: Cambridge University Press, 2001), 128–31.

3. Robert Bernasconi, "Extra-Territoriality: Outside the State, Outside the Subject," in *Levinas Studies: An Annual Review*, vol. 3, ed. Jeffrey Bloechl (Pittsburgh: Duquesne University Press, 2008), 61–77. Another version of the essay appeared in *Journal of Chinese Philosophy* 35, no. 5 (2008): 167–81. All references here are to the version in *Levinas Studies*.

4. See Emmanuel Levinas, "The Rights of Man and the Rights of the Other," in *Outside the Subject* (Stanford, CA: Stanford University Press, 1993), 123; "Peace and Proximity," in *Alterity and Transcendence* (New York: Columbia University Press, 1999), 144. See also, Levinas's comment in "The Awakening of the I," in *Is It Righteous to Be?*, ed. Jill Robbins (Stanford, CA: Stanford University Press, 2001), 186; his endorsement of democracy in "In the Name of the Other," in *Is It Righteous to Be?*, 195; and "The Other, Utopia, and Justice," in *Is It Righteous to Be?*, 206; "Responsibility and Substitution," in *Is It Righteous to Be?*, 230.

5. Emmanuel Levinas, "The Other, Utopia, and Justice," in *Entre Nous: Thinking-of-the-Other*, trans. Michael B. Smith and Barbara Harshav (New York: Columbia University Press, 1998), 239–40; also in *Is It Righteous To Be?*, 206.

6. Emmanuel Levinas, "Reflections on the Philosophy of Hitlerism," in *Unforeseen History* (Urbana: University of Illinois Press, 2004), 16. Also *Critical Inquiry* 17, no. 1 (Autumn 1990): 62–71. References here are to *Unforeseen History*.

7. Levinas, "Reflections on the Philosophy of Hitlerism," in *Unforeseen History*, 15–20 passim.

8. Bernasconi, "Extra-Territoriality," 65. The text Bernasconi has in mind and examines is the preface Levinas wrote for a French translation of Mendelssohn's book *Jerusalem* of 1783, in which Mendelssohn articulates a political philosophy for the liberal state, formulates an account of the relation between church and state, and argues for the continued significance of Judaism and the Jewish people in the context of a liberal state. Levinas's preface was originally published in 1982. The English translation appears as "Moses Mendelssohn's Thought" in *In the Time of the Nations* (Bloomington: Indiana University Press, 1994), 136–45.

9. Levinas's preface to the translation by Dominique Bourel takes up several themes: Mendelssohn's liberalism and political philosophy, the role of his liberalism in the assimilation of the subsequent centuries, its relation to Zionism, and the justification for Judaism as a religion of ceremonies and religious practices. Bernasconi focuses all of his attention on Mendelssohn's political philosophy as Levinas understands it. For our purposes here, I will do the same.

10. Bernasconi, "Extra-Territoriality," 65.

11. Ibid., 67. Levinas mistakenly identifies Altmann as a professor at Harvard University; in fact he taught at Brandeis. Altmann's essay appeared in Hebrew in *Daat* in the summer of 1980; it was also published in a supplement to the *Lessing Yearbook: Humanität und Dialog*, ed.

E. Bahr, E. P. Harris, and L. G. Lyon (Detroit: Wayne State University Press, 1982), 37–65.

12. See Bernasconi, "Extra-Territoriality," 69.

13. The crucial pages in Bernasconi's essay are pp. 67–68, and those in Levinas's preface are pp. 137–38.

14. See Bernasconi, "Extra-Territoriality," 69–70.

15. Ibid., 70–71.

16. See ibid., 70–74.

17. Ibid., 70–71, citing Moses Mendelssohn, *Jerusalem* (Hanover, NH: University Press of New England, 1983), 59.

18. Bernasconi, "Extra-Territoriality," 72.

19. See Levinas, "Moses Mendelssohn's Thought," in *In the Time of the Nations*, 138: "But the so very demanding Mendelssohnian ideal of freedom and the rights of man, the splendor of which dazzled the Jews of the liberal world of the nineteenth century, who recognized in it something close to their own prophetic traditions— that ideal remains dear to their hearts, despite the course of events and the fragility of Europe's democratic institutions, which were unable to prevent two world wars, fascism, and Auschwitz."

20. Levinas, "The Rights of Man and the Rights of the Other," in *Outside the Subject*, 123.

21. Annabel Herzog, "Is Liberalism 'All We Need'?," *Political Theory* 30, no. 2 (April 2002): 205, where she cites Levinas, "Reflections on the Philosophy of Hitlerism," *Critical Inquiry* 17, no. 1 (1990): 63.

22. See Herzog, "Is Liberalism 'All We Need'?," 206, where she cites Simon Critchley but confuses these issues by failing to appreciate exactly what Levinas's endorsement of democracy means.

23. Ibid., 207.

24. Ibid.

25. Herzog's discussion of representation within democratic politics does not distinguish clearly between representation as conceptualization and representation as proxy; see Herzog, "Is Liberalism 'All We Need'?," 216–17. Either Herzog simply allows the ambiguity to slide past or she intentionally plays on the ambiguity. Under either interpretation of what she is doing, the ambiguity is a problem for her reading. What starts as a discussion of representation as conceptualization ends with the statement "There are actual people who are not and cannot be represented, who stay outside representation" (217). One cannot be completely sure what Herzog wants the reader to understand what "representation" here means. But what follows in the next paragraph, the discussion of people who are actually present and those who are not, suggests, I think, that Herzog means political representation.

26. Emmanuel Levinas, *Otherwise Than Being* (Pittsburgh: Duquesne University Press, 1998), 159, cited by Herzog, "Is Liberalism 'All We Need'?," 217.

27. Herzog, "Is Liberalism 'All We Need'?," 217–19.

28. See ibid., 219–20. The unrepresented include "actual hungry people who never are, who cannot be taken into account" (221). By this time, Herzog clearly wants the reader to take "representation" to be political and to think of the other person in her vulnerability and weakness as defining a class of people. Elsewhere I have called this the confusion of the political other with the ethical other. Note also that like Bernasconi, Herzog glosses the notion of the beyond-liberalism with the idea of the trace, although for Bernasconi it is the notion of prophecy and a Mendelssohnian liberalism that is akin to the trace. In general, this is to be expected. The trace is an idea intended to illuminate the relation between everyday or ordinary experience, on the one hand, and the face-to-face, on the other. In terms Levinas uses in his essay "Substitution" and *Otherwise Than Being*, it is a figure for the relation between the Saying and the Said. In our terms in this discussion, it is one

way of portraying how ethics and politics
are interrelated.

29. If one values stability and permanence, however, then democracy would
be seen as the worst of regimes, as it was,
for example, by Plato, for whom truth and
beauty were associated with order and
permanence and hence with a domain that
was itself not subject to change, the domain of the Forms. See *Republic* 8.

30. Levinas, "The Awakening of the I,"
in *Is It Righteous to Be?*, 183–84. See also
"Responsibility and Substitution," in *Is It
Righteous to Be?*, 230, which is from 1988.

31. Ibid., 184.

32. For all his affection for Platonism,
this is an area where he and Plato most
clearly disagree.

33. See Geuss, *History and Illusion in
Politics*, 3.

34. Ibid., 8.

35. Ibid., 110–11.

36. See ibid., 113–19.

37. See ibid., 120–22.

38. Ibid., 123.

39. See ibid., 123, and for serious doubts
and an effective rebuttal, 123–24. In a later
discussion, Geuss suggests that rights are
one way that a liberal state accepts the
risks of having an independent governmental apparatus, while feeling the need
to protect citizens from possible oppression by it; see ibid., 131–38. But liberalism
has a strained relationship with rights, as it
does with democracy.

40. Ibid., 124–25.

41. In the "Conclusion" of *History and
Illusion in Politics*, Geuss argues that the
flexibility of democracy is in tension with
the firmness and stability that a regime of
rights seeks to establish. He is thinking, of
course, of "subjective" rights of the person,
whereas to Levinas, rights are ultimately
based on rights of others toward the subject, but qua rights, they still are norms
and hence seek stability and regularity.
See ibid., 154.

42. It is important to keep in mind that
for Levinas the ethical critique is a critique
of politics and political life, not of political
philosophy; moreover, it is not a critique
from ethical philosophy but from the
ethical, its priority and its compellingness.
See ibid., 156–62, and see Geuss's references to figures like Rorty, Williams, and
others on p. 156.

43. See Levinas, "In the Name of the
Other," in *Is It Righteous to Be?*, 194–95.
This interview is from 1990. For a fascinating and thoughtful discussion of the
history of democracy, see John Dunn,
Democracy: A History (New York: Atlantic
Monthly Press, 2005). Dunn makes a
number of distinctions helpful to understanding what role democracy plays for
Levinas. One is between democracy as
a form of government and as a political
value. The modern history of "democracy"
as the word for the best form of political
life, which begins with the French Revolution, is really about how some sense of
popular legitimacy can be combined with
an aspiration to equality. Levinas's understanding of democracy as responsive
to its own incompleteness as a political
aspiration to justice and humanity suits
the sense of "democracy" as a term for a
political value or ideal and yet one that
aspires to equality. See Dunn, *Democracy*,
19–20, 184–88, and passim.

7. TEACHING PROPHETIC POLITICS

1. For a list of the annual *Colloques
des intellectuels juifs de langue française*,
from the first in 1957 until 1989, when
Levinas last attended the meetings, see
Robert Gibbs, *Correlations in Rosenzweig
and Levinas* (Princeton, NJ: Princeton
University Press, 1994), 175. He delivered
twenty-four Talmudic lessons at these col-
loquia, twenty-three of which have been
translated. There are several helpful essays
on the lessons, but a comprehensive study
of them, in their historical situations, is a
desideratum. Ethan Kleinberg is working

on a book on the Talmudic lessons, and Annabel Herzog is also working on a book based on readings of them.

2. See Emmanuel Levinas, "As Old as the World?," in *Nine Talmudic Readings*, trans. Annette Aronowicz (Bloomington: Indiana University Press, 1990), 72: "It deals with the organization of the supreme court, the Sanhedrin. In what way is it connected to the theme of our colloquium, on the need that the world may have of Judaism? I will try to show this." But then, Levinas goes on, "I need not have given it any thought: a Talmudic text, even when it does not try to prove it, always proves that Judaism and the Jews are necessary to the world." As I indicated, in addition to adding detail and concreteness to the notion of an ethical or prophetic politics, these Talmudic lessons exhibit how Judaism can provide literary resources for ethical and hence political education.

3. See ibid.

4. Ibid., 75.

5. Ibid., 76.

6. Ibid., 77–78.

7. There is no right to national sovereignty specifically in the Universal Declaration, but if one combines articles 15, 17, and 21, the right to a nationality strongly suggests that the community of the nationality has a right to self-determination in a location over which it shall have sovereignty.

8. Levinas, "As Old as the World?," in *Nine Talmudic Readings*, 78.

9. Ibid., 79–80.

10. Ibid., 80.

11. Ibid., 81.

12. The mitzvot are taken to be the separation in one's soul that prevents one from falling into sin, which facilitates the resistance to temptation. Levinas takes this to be the point of Resh Lakish's response to the objection. See ibid., 83–84.

13. Ibid., 85.

14. Ibid., 85–87.

15. Ibid., 87.

16. Ibid. Levinas remarks that this is what the Jewish tradition teaches and that "its exposure to persecution is perhaps only a fulfillment of this teaching—a mysterious fulfillment" (ibid.). In other words, the central lesson of infinite responsibility to and for others is taught by the Jewish textual tradition and by Jewish history itself, through its failure.

17. Levinas, "Judaism and Revolution," in *Nine Talmudic Readings*, 97. In an aside, Levinas comments that "last May we welcomed the disadvantaged mostly in the universities," referring of course to the student revolt of May 1968 and the ways in which many actually provided for those in need among the student activists.

18. Ibid., 98.

19. Levinas studied with the enigmatic, itinerant Talmudic savant Monsieur Chouchani or Mordechai Chouchani from 1947 to 1949. For a brief summary of Chouchani's influence, see Jacob Meskin, "The Role of Lurianic Kabbalah in the Early Philosophy of Emmanuel Levinas," in *Levinas Studies: An Annual Review*, vol. 2, ed. Jeffrey Bloechl (Pittsburgh: Duquesne University Press, 2007): 55–58.

20. Levinas, "Judaism and Revolution," in *Nine Talmudic Readings*, 98–99.

21. Ibid., 99.

22. Ibid., 100.

23. In the preface, I discussed briefly the recent film by the Dardenne brothers *Two Days, One Night*, which presents a contemporary example of how the responsibilities and demands associated with employment work out in a very complex and problematic employment situation.

24. See Levinas, "Judaism and Revolution," in *Nine Talmudic Readings*, 101.

25. Ibid., 102.

26. Ibid.

27. Ibid., 103.

28. Ibid., 104.

29. See especially Emmanuel Levinas, *Totality and Infinity* (Pittsburgh: Duquesne University Press, 1969), 158–68.

30. Levinas, "Judaism and Revolution," in *Nine Talmudic Readings*, 104.

31. Levinas makes the association of work here with his account of work in *Time and the Other* and *Totality and Infinity* all but explicit as he summarizes this positive valuation of work: "The rights and dignity of man are derived from his condition as worker. Work belongs to the order of light and reason. The time of work, as Resh Lakish sees it, is not the time of frustration or alienation, is not cursed time. In a world in which work appeared as a mark of servitude reserved for the slave, Resh Lakish wants to see it as the perfection of creation" (Levinas, "Judaism and Revolution," in *Nine Talmudic Readings*, 104). Levinas's point here is also part of an anti-Marxist polemic, I think.

32. Ibid., 104.

33. Ibid., 104–5.

34. This is from the Talmudic text, cited by Levinas, ibid., 105.

35. See Seth D. Armus, *French Anti-Americanism, 1930–1948* (Lanham, MD: Lexington Books, 2007). Also, Jean-François Revel, *Anti-Americanism* (San Francisco: Encounter Books, 2004); Denis Lacorne, Jacques Rupnik, and Marie-France Toinet, *The Rise and Fall of Anti-Americanism: A Century of French Perception* (New York: St. Martin's Press, 1990).

36. Levinas, "Judaism and Revolution," in *Nine Talmudic Readings*, 105–6. Spinoza's first kind of knowledge—sensory and empirical knowledge based on imagination—is the most inferior form of knowledge or cognition. See Ethics IIP43S.

37. Levinas, "Judaism and Revolution," in *Nine Talmudic Readings*, 106.

38. The Talmud's words, cited by Levinas, ibid.

39. Levinas, ibid.

40. Ibid.

41. Ibid., 108.

42. I do not think that for a French philosopher, writing in the 1960s, the whole issue of collaboration and resistance dur-ing the Vichy years of World War II could be very far from his mind or the minds of those in the audience. The problem of Vichy, collaboration and resistance, pervades postwar French intellectual life and indeed public life. See Henry Russo, *The Vichy Syndrome: History and Memory in France since 1944* (Cambridge, MA: Harvard University Press, 1994).

43. Levinas, "Judaism and Revolution," in *Nine Talmudic Readings*, 108.

44. Ibid., 109.

45. The Talmud, cited by Levinas, ibid., 110.

46. Levinas, ibid., 109.

47. Ibid., 110.

48. Ibid., 109–10.

49. Ibid., 110.

50. Ibid.

51. Ibid., 111.

52. Ibid., 112.

53. See ibid.

54. Ibid.

55. The Talmud, cited by Levinas, ibid., 113.

56. One might consider as well Hannah Arendt's treatment of complicity and the *Judenrate* in *Eichmann in Jerusalem*. Levinas no doubt had the French situation and the issue of collaboration in mind, but by the late 1960s the storm caused by Arendt's account might very well have been known in France as well as in North America and Israel.

57. Levinas, "Judaism and Revolution," in *Nine Talmudic Readings*, 113.

58. Ibid.

59. Ibid., 114.

60. See Scholem's famous remarks about living in deferment and the messianic idea in Judaism, in "Toward an Understanding of the Messianic Idea in Judaism," in *The Messianic Idea in Judaism and Other Essays* (New York: Schocken Books, 1971), 35.

61. Levinas, "Judaism and Revolution," in *Nine Talmudic Readings*, 114.

62. Ibid.

63. Ibid., 115.

64. Ibid., 115–16. There is another piece of text that continues the discussion of Rabbi Eleazar and the theme of collaboration with the Romans, but I have chosen to treat it as a coda to the main discussion and will end with the letter from Levinas's friend, whom I believe was Maurice Blanchot. I thank Simon Critchley for identifying the letter's author.

65. Ibid., 115.

66. From Blanchot's letter, cited by Levinas, ibid., 115–16.

67. Levinas, ibid., 115.

68. Ibid., 116.

69. See Levinas, "Cities of Refuge," in *Beyond the Verse: Talmudic Readings and Lectures* (Bloomington: Indiana University Press, 1994), 34–52.

70. Ibid., 38.

71. Ibid., 36.

72. Ibid., 38.

73. Ibid.

74. Ibid. "The beginning of the Talmudic extract that we have chosen gives us the sense of the problems faced in the cities in which men like ourselves live. It concerns, as you will see, cities which bear witness to a very high level of civilization, and to a humanism which is certainly authentic. But it is a completely different mode or potential of spirituality, a new attention to the human."

75. Ibid., 39.

76. Ibid., 40.

77. Later Levinas will say, "There are cities of refuge because we have enough conscience to have good intentions, but not enough not to betray them by our acts" (ibid., 50). In other words, we want to help others, not to injure them or cause them harm and suffering, but our desire to act towards others in these ways is not perfect or complete. It has flaws and weaknesses; therefore, we need to protect society from our failures, so to speak. Of course, this might be more than irony. It might be unconscious self-protection.

78. See ibid., 41–42.

79. Ibid., 43–46.

80. Ibid., 51–52.

81. Ibid., 52.

82. See Levinas, "The Sixty-Nine Nations," in *In the Time of the Nations* (Bloomington: Indiana University Press, 1994), 92–108.

83. Levinas, "The Nations and the Presence of Israel," in *In the Time of the Nations,* 97.

84. Ibid., 97–108.

85. Ibid., 97–98.

86. Ibid., 98–99.

87. Ibid., 99.

88. Ibid., 100.

89. Ibid., 99–107, esp. 100, 101, and 103.

90. Ibid., 103.

91. Ibid., 104.

92. Ibid., 107.

93. The Talmud, cited by Levinas, ibid., 108.

94. Levinas, ibid., 108.

95. Levinas, "Promised Land or Permitted Land," in *Nine Talmudic Readings,* 61.

96. Ibid., 62.

97. Ibid., 63.

98. Ibid., 65–66.

99. Ibid., 66.

100. Ibid., 67.

101. Ibid., 69.

102. Here we have a strong indication that Levinas would agree with Gavison, Gans, and a host of contemporary commentators about the rights of the Palestinian people and the need to take seriously the existence of a Palestinian state alongside the State of Israel. See ch. 8 in this volume.

103. Levinas, "Beyond the State in the State," in *New Talmudic Readings,* trans. Richard A. Cohen (Pittsburgh: Duquesne University Press, 1999), 94–95.

104. Ibid., 95.

105. Ibid., 96.

106. Ibid., 106–7.

8. ZIONISM AND THE
JUSTIFICATION OF A JEWISH STATE

1. Levinas, "The State of Israel and the Religion of Israel," in *Difficult Freedom*, trans. Seán Hand (Baltimore: Johns Hopkins University Press, 1990), 216–20 (originally 1951; in *Difficult Freedom* 1963).

2. Ibid., 218.

3. Ibid., 219. For Levinas, Zionism is more than a platform for and a movement in behalf of national liberation; it is an opportunity to realize the very essence of Judaism. On the paradoxes associated with national liberation movements, see the engaging and fascinating discussion by Michael Walzer, *The Paradox of Liberation: Secular Revolutions and Religious Counter-revolutions* (New Haven, CT: Yale University Press, 2015).

4. On the complex and multifaceted history of Zionism as a political ideology, see Alain Dieckhoff, *The Invention of a Nation: Zionist Thought and the Making of Modern Israel* (New York: Columbia University Press, 2003).

5. Levinas, *Beyond the Verse: Talmudic Readings and Lectures* (Bloomington: Indiana University Press, 1994) (originally 1982). The essays are "The State of Caesar and the State of Israel" (originally 1971); "Politics After!" (originally 1979); and "Assimilation and New Culture" (originally 1980).

6. Levinas, *Beyond the Verse*, xv.

7. Ibid.

8. Ibid., xvi.

9. Ibid., xvii.

10. Ibid.

11. Levinas, "The State of Caesar and the State of David," in *Beyond the Verse* (Bloomington: Indiana University Press, 1994), 177–78.

12. Ibid., 180.

13. Ibid., 180–81. Levinas cites extensively from Maimonides's account, "which is notable," he says, "for its rationalist sobriety" (181). Levinas also refers to this ideal as a kind of Platonic one for its commitment to the realization in the world and history of an eternal ideal.

14. Ibid., 183: "But if the Messianic City is not beyond politics, the City in its simplest sense is never this side of the religious."

15. Ibid., 183. Levinas says: Israel "is aware of the temptation, within itself and around it, of the war which pits everyone against everyone else." This is a reading, indirectly, of *Pirke Avot*, "Pray for the welfare of the government, since but for the fear thereof men would swallow each other alive" (cited on 183).

16. Ibid.

17. Ibid., 184.

18. Levinas reviews the themes of the Babylonian Talmud, Baba Metzia 53b and the story of Rabbi Eleazer helping the Romans with local thieves, Jews among them, and being criticized for it by Rabbi Joshua bar Karhah.

19. Levinas does not take this dismissal of the political literally; it is a figurative way of expressing the "temptations of the political." It is as if the rabbis were saying: If one could, one ought to want to transcend the political and attain some kind of otherworldly salvation, but of course one cannot.

20. In a footnote, we learn that the lecture was delivered at the nineteenth colloquium of the French Jewish Intellectuals held in Paris on October 25–26, 1970.

21. Levinas, "The State of Caesar and the State of David," in *Beyond the Verse*, 187.

22. Ibid., 187.

23. For discussion, see below and the discussion of the work of Ruth Gavison and Chaim Gans especially.

24. Levinas, "Politics After!," in *Beyond the Verse*, 188.

25. Ibid., 189.

26. Ibid.

27. Ibid., 191.

28. Ibid., 192.

29. Ibid.

30. Ibid.

31. Ibid., 193.
32. Ibid.
33. Ibid., 194.
34. Ibid.
35. Ibid., 195.
36. Levinas, "Assimilation and New Culture," in *Beyond the Verse*, 196–97.
37. Ibid., 197.
38. Ibid, 198.
39. Ibid.
40. Ibid., 199.
41. These are phrases Levinas uses in "Assimilation and New Culture," in *Beyond the Verse*, 200. I call special attention to the phrase "the temptation of assimilation," which is akin to the "temptation of theodicy" and means something like the "temptation of universality."
42. Levinas, "Assimilation and New Culture," in *Beyond the Verse*, 200.
43. Ibid.
44. Ibid., 200–201.
45. Ibid., 201.
46. Much of what Levinas takes to be characteristic of a democratic regime is widely held to constitute the democratic ideal. To be sure, states aspire to democratic practices and institutions to different degrees and succeed only to some degree or other. Israel has been widely conceived as democratic in terms of some of what Levinas has in mind; this is true of the UN Resolution 181 of 1947 and the declaration of the state's foundation in 1948. To be sure, of course, there are critics who deny that it has been successful. Or they might be willing to accept that while Israel once aspired to democratic principles and achieved them to some degree, recently she has failed more regularly to put them into practice. Levinas's attitude is traditional and optimistic, to be sure, but it need not be dismissed as mindless romanticism; it is or can be sober and realistic, even if it is positive and optimistic. Moreover, his approach to Zionism might be seen to be one way in which one could coordinate a commitment to Judaism

and Zionism with loyalty to the ideals of French identity. For discussion of the issue of "dual loyalties," see Joan Wolf, *Harnessing the Holocaust: The Politics of Memory in France* (Stanford, CA: Stanford University Press, 2003), 53–62.
47. See Ruth Gavison, "Can Israel Be Both Jewish and Democratic?," cited from the Social Science Research Network (Jan. 1, 2011): http://papers.ssrn.com/so13/papers.cfm?abstract_id=1862904, an adaptation of chapter 1, "Conceptual Compatibility and Justifiability, in Principle, of a Jewish and Democratic State," in *Israel as a Jewish and Democratic State: Tensions and Prospects* (Jerusalem: Van Leer, 1999) (Hebrew); Chaim Gans, *A Just Zionism: On the Morality of the Jewish State* (New York: Oxford University Press, 2008), 65ff. I also refer to several papers by Gavison and to her recent report to Tzipi Livni on the constitutional anchoring of a vision statement about Israel's Jewish and democratic character. References will be provided in subsequent notes.
Originally I had hoped to place Levinas in conversation with both Ruth Gavison and Chaim Gans. Gans's *A Just Zionism* provides a meticulously argued view that is well worth comparing with Levinas's ethical commitments, but for reasons of space, I limit myself here largely to a comparison with Gavison. I want to thank Chaim Gans for providing me with an early version of his translation of his Hebrew book *A Political Theory for the Jewish People* and Ruth Gavison for an English version of her Hebrew book *Israel as a Jewish and Democratic State*. In Gans's recent book, he calls Gavison a "hierarchical" Zionist and distinguishes the view, which accepts the privileged or dominant national status in a nation-state, from his own, which he calls "egalitarian" Zionism and which is distinctive in that advantages given to a dominant nation should be limited to considerations pertaining to achieving equality in the state. As I think

will become clear, Levinas's Zionism would elide the difference, I believe; I will say a bit more about this shortly.

48. Gavison often refers to these topics of public tension and debate, especially with regard to the place of Arab Israelis in Israel. See, e.g., Ruth Gavison, "Jewish and Democratic? A Rejoinder to the 'Ethnic Democracy' Debate," *Israel Studies* 4, no. 1 (1999): 58; "The Jews' Right to Statehood: A Defense," *Azure* 15 (Summer 2003): 107–8n28. For discussion of the Law of Return, Jewish settlement within Israel, and education, see Gavison, "The Jews' Right to Statehood: A Defense," 95–97.

49. The importance of paying sufficient attention to empirical, historical factors and not reduce the problem to one of conceptual clarification is the central theme of Gavison, "Jewish and Democratic? A Rejoinder to the 'Ethnic Democracy' Debate," 44–72. As she puts it, the problem is that the debate about whether Israel is or is not an ethnic democracy "presents issues that to me are primarily political and normative as matters of theory and conceptual analysis" (47), where the notion of the political has a concrete and historical valence. This requires "the adequate description of Israeli reality and its moral and political perspectives" (49).

50. For Gavison's objections to claims that democracies must be neutral, see Gavison, "Can Israel Be Both Jewish and Democratic?," 132–33. For her discussion of Jewishness as requiring that the state be a Torah state, governed by halakhic standards, see Gavison, "Can Israel Be Both Jewish and Democratic?," 133–34. On the one hand, Jewishness need not mean the kind of theocratic rule that would prevent the state from being democratic; on the other, theocracies are not necessarily nondemocratic to some degree or other. See also Gavison, "Jewish and Democratic? A Rejoinder to the 'Ethnic Democracy' Debate," 60–61; "Reflections on the Meaning and Justification of 'Jewish' in

the Expression 'A Jewish and Democratic State'," in *The Israeli Nation-State: Political, Constitutional, and Cultural Challenges,* ed. Fania Oz-Salzberger and Yedidia Z. Stern (Boston: Academic Studies Press, 2014), 145–46.

51. See Gavison, "Democracy and Judaism—Between Conceptual Analysis and Public Discourse," in *The State of Israel: Between Judaism and Democracy,* ed. Joseph E. David (Jerusalem: Israel Democracy Institute, 2003): 331–59.

52. See Gavison, "Can Israel Be Both Jewish and Democratic?,"135: "Israel is a Jewish state in the sense that it has a Jewish majority, which will enable it to control immigration and security in a democratic state. Giving Jews their own state was seen [in 1947] as an implementation of the universally recognized principle of national self-determination. Israel committed itself to grant all Jews a right to return to their homeland, and saw this commitment as a central part of its raison d'être. At the same time, Israel undertook to grant its non-Jewish citizens full and equal rights in the emerging state." Gavison elsewhere expresses concerns about to what degree Israel has failed in this latter effort for a variety of reasons and in various ways. See also Gavison, "Jewish and Democratic? A Rejoinder to the 'Ethnic Democracy' Debate," 53–54.

53. On Gavison's comments on neutrality, a subject of much controversy, see Gavison, "Can Israel Be Both Jewish and Democratic?," 132–33, 139–40.

54. See Gavison, "Reflections on the Meaning and Justification of 'Jewish' in the Expression 'A Jewish and Democratic State'," 150–51.

55. Gavison, "Can Israel Be Both a Jewish and Democratic State?," 137–38.

56. Gavison makes a useful comparison with how blacks in the United States have been treated and how they feel about membership in American society; see ibid., 138–39. For a statement of Gavison's

criticism of Israeli policies and practices, see Gavison, "Jewish and Democratic? A Rejoinder to the 'Ethnic Democracy' Debate," 58–59, 64–66. Also see Gavison, "The Jews' Right to Statehood: A Defense," 94–98; "Reflections on the Meaning and Justification of 'Jewish' in the Expression 'A Jewish and Democratic State'," 152–58, for a discussion of culture and language, i.e., multiculturalism in Israel and the role of Arabic, alongside Hebrew, and 158–60, on the importance of avoiding discrimination of minorities and the privileging of Orthodoxy and Jewish law.

57. Arguing for this claim is the burden of Gavison, "Can Israel Be Both Jewish and Democratic?," 141–48; see also Gavison, "The Jews' Right to Statehood: A Defense," 70–108.

58. This justification is the central theme of Gavison in ibid.

59. For a good discussion of how these factors contribute to the specific determinations of the right to self-determination for the Jewish people, see ibid., 74–77. See also Gavison, "Reflections on the Meaning and Justification of 'Jewish' in the Expression 'A Jewish and Democratic State'," 137–41.

60. This strikes me as a very important feature of Gavison's argument. The Jewish people's right to self-determination may have been general and always applicable, but the realization of that right in a political state in a specific territory depended upon the growth of a majority and the costs to the others living in the territory or region. Hence, the right to establish a state in a particular place is in part a historical matter; as events change, so does the moral situation. This is true both for the Jewish people in this case and for the Palestinian Arabs. Gavison talks about the necessity for Jews to establish a "massive Jewish community in some territory" in several places; see, e.g., "Can Israel Be Both Jewish and Democratic?," 142–43.

See also Gavison, "The Jews' Right to Statehood: A Defense," 78–86.

61. Gavison, "Can Israel Be Both Jewish and Democratic?," 142: "A people may claim a right to self-determination in that territory in which it is, and has been for some time, a majority. Even under these circumstances, one people's right may be defeated by the interests and rights of members of other peoples living in that territory." See ibid., 143–48. On the situation when Zionism established the early settlements in Palestine, see ibid., 144–45. Gavison takes the situation then to be a conflict of liberties: "In terms of the politics and international law of self-determination, Jews indeed did not have a right to self-determination in Palestine at the turn of the 20th century. But they did have the liberty to seek to establish a population-base that would give them the right, just as the local Arab population had the liberty to try to resist this settlement, predicting full well the implications of the enterprise for their life" (ibid., 144). If indeed the Arab population had conceived of itself as a nation or people at the time, with a majority in the territory, it could be said to have had the right to establish itself, and a right can be defended in ways that a liberty cannot. Gavison does not call attention to any Arab right at the time. Chaim Gans notes that the Arabs had more than a liberty; they also had a "fully fledged right" (*A Political Theory of the Jewish People* [Oxford: Oxford University Press, forthcoming], ch. 3, 106 ms). See also Gavison, "Jewish and Democratic? A Rejoinder to the 'Ethnic Democracy' Debate," 54–55; and for Gavison's most detailed historical account of the right of the Jewish people to political self-determination in Palestine, see Gavison, "The Jews' Right to Statehood: A Defense," 78–85; see also Gavison, "Reflections on the Meaning and Justification of 'Jewish' in the Expression 'A Jewish and Democratic State'," 142–45. She also

discusses the changing Palestinian reality and the right to self-determination of the Palestinian people; ibid., 86–88.

62. Gavison, "Can Israel Be Both Jewish and Democratic?," 145–46.

63. Ibid., 146. See also "The Jews' Right to Statehood: A Defense," 77–88.

64. Ruth Gavison, "Constitutional Anchoring of Israel's Vision: Recommendations Submitted to the Minister of Justice," in *Defining Israel: A Forum on Recent Attempts to Determine Israel's Character*, part 1, "The Report," *Marginalia* (Los Angeles Review of Books, 2014), online, 4.

65. See ibid., 11–15, for Gavison's argument against a constitutional anchoring of the vision. See also Gavison, "Democracy and Judaism—Between Conceptual Analysis and Public Discourse," 342–43, 349, 355–58; Gavison, "Reflections on the Meaning and Justification of 'Jewish' in the Expression 'A Jewish and Democratic State'," 158–60.

66. Gavison, "Constitutional Anchoring of Israel's Vision," 12.

67. Ibid., 13.

68. Ibid., 14.

69. Ibid., 15. See also Gavison, "Reflections on the Meaning and Justification of 'Jewish' in the Expression 'A Jewish and Democratic State'," 159: "Democracy makes the Jewish character of the state contingent on the preferences of the majority, and requires that the state should grant the minority actual freedom to convince the majority to change its opinion. This conclusion does not necessarily imply that the state should be defined, in law or in constitution, as a Jewish state, or that explicit declarations will be made about the implications of the state's Jewishness. In fact, it seems to me preferable that such definitions not be included in law or constitution. These questions are not a legal matter, and frequently declarations are unnecessarily alienating when the reality of the situation is sufficient. Additionally, the inclusion of declarations such as these

in laws transfers the power to decide such issues to the courts invoking the human rights discourse or constitutional interpretation. Ideally, these questions should not be resolved by courts in this manner."

70. As I mentioned earlier, in the Israeli film *Close to Home* (2005), two 18-year-old girls serve in the IDF and patrol the streets of Jerusalem, stopping Arabs to check credentials and carrying out body searches, requiring women to strip and expose themselves. They carry out their duties with no sensitivity whatsoever. Those they confront are degraded and mistreated. These young women perform their tasks with a kind of indifference and lack of regard that is offensive to watch. In one particular scene, when one of the women, in a booth, asks a Palestinian woman to strip, she shows no sympathy at all for how degrading it will be, and when the woman objects, she ignores her comments and proceeds, as if nothing had occurred. The girls exemplify the way young Israeli soldiers become accustomed to treat the Arabs and Palestinians in their midst. It is just this kind of indifference and humiliation that Levinas would find deeply disturbing about how minorities are treated in Israel.

71. See Gavison, "The Jews' Right to Statehood: A Defense," 95–96.

72. Gavison, "Democracy and Judaism—Between Conceptual Analysis and Public Discourse," 345–47.

73. See *A Political Theory for the Jewish People*, passim. For a sketch of Gans's classification, see "The Zionism We Really Want: A Third Way to Look at the Morality of the Jewish Nationalist Project," *Haaretz*, Sept. 3, 2013, online at Haaretz.com.

74. See Gans, *A Political Theory for the Jewish People*, ch. 3, 3 ms.

75. Gans argues, both in *A Just Zionism* and in *A Political Theory for the Jewish People*, that historical considerations that tie the Land of Israel to a sense of Jewish

identity warrant the people's seeking to establish political hegemony in that territory, and furthermore the persecutions in Europe, culminating in the Holocaust, warrant doing so even if the land is occupied at the time. Gans gives the example of someone who is mortally wounded who has the *remedial right* to break into a pharmacy after hours to obtain life-saving medicines. See passim, especially in *A Political Theory of the Jewish People*, ch. 3, 122 ms and 148n72. Moreover, Gans argues that the "medicine" is either unique in this pharmacy or better than in any other available one. In a note (149n73), Gans refers to his response to Føllesdal and Perlmann's critique in the symposium on *A Just Zionism*—that the necessity defense and the evidence for current urgency and danger override the objections to the establishment of the state in the given territory. Hence, the role of the Holocaust and persecutions from the nineteenth century on, at least, is important to provide a ground for such necessity. It also indicates the limits of the land to be appropriated, Gans argues, although I am not sure that his argument is compelling, since the emergency points to the protection needed in the future, and the population involved might significantly increase as history goes on and as events occur that might alter the danger and its scope.

76. For a preliminary overview of "egalitarian" Zionism, see Gans, *A Political Theory for the Jewish People*, ch. 3, 109–10 ms. Gans develops his account in ch. 3.4, 109–33 ms. Gans argues that the dominant people's advantages in the state in which it is the majority should be limited by two constraints, first by applying only to security and demographic issues and not matters such as education or representation in the symbols of public culture, second by not leading to human rights violations. See *A Political Theory for the Jewish People*, ch. 3.4.4, 130–32; and Gans, *A Just Zionism*, 133–38.

77. Something similar applies to Gans as well, whose conception of Judaism and the Jewish people is similarly a conception of a cultural, secular identity.

78. Insofar as Levinas has a conception of Judaism that facilitates understanding how Israel can be both Jewish and liberal-democratic, he is similar to others—like Buber, for example—whose redefinition of Judaism makes possible a form of Zionism that is ethical, political, and religious all at once. Gavison's category of the theocratic lacks the subtlety necessary to distinguish various views of Judaism that are historical and political, on the one hand, and yet respect transcendence, on the other.

9. ETHICS, POLITICS, AND MESSIANISM

1. Emmanuel Levinas and Richard Kearney, "Dialogue with Emmanuel Levinas," in Richard A. Cohen, *Face to Face with Emmanuel Levinas* (Albany: State University of New York Press, 1986), 30–31.

2. The texts I have in mind are the Talmudic commentaries on passages from BT Sanhedrin 97b–99a from 1960 and 1961 that are available in Emmanuel Levinas, *Difficult Freedom: Essays on Judaism*, trans. Seán Hand (Baltimore: Johns Hopkins University Press, 1990); the Talmudic commentary on BT Yoma 10a from 1979 that is published in Emmanuel Levinas, *Beyond the Verse: Talmudic Readings and Lectures* (Bloomington: Indiana University Press, 1994); and Levinas's paper "The State of Caesar and the State of David," which appeared in the *Proceedings of the Colloquium of Rome* in 1971 and is also published in *Beyond the Verse*.

3. The texts are BT Sanhedrin 99a, 97b–98a, 88b, and 98b–99a. Levinas points out that they are printed in the order of his presentation and not the order in which they occur in the Talmud.

4. Levinas, *Difficult Freedom*, 59.

5. Levinas, "A Religion for Adults," in *Difficult Freedom*, 11–23.

6. Levinas, *Difficult Freedom*, 69.

7. Ibid.

8. Ibid.

9. While it is Rab's point, it is not one that Levinas himself will commit to. Morality for him has priority, but it always operates in a political setting, broadly speaking.

10. Levinas, *Difficult Freedom*, 69.

11. Ibid.

12. Ibid., 70.

13. Ibid.

14. The Maharsha is Rabbi Samuel Eliezer Halevi Eidels (1555–1631), a famed Polish rabbi, whose *Hidushei Halakhot* is printed with the Talmud.

15. Levinas, *Difficult Freedom*, 71.

16. The previous passage is from BT Sanhedrin 97b; this passage is from 98a.

17. Levinas, *Difficult Freedom*, 72.

18. Robert B. Brandom, *Making It Explicit* (Cambridge, MA: Harvard University Press, 1998), passim.

19. Levinas, *Difficult Freedom*, 73.

20. Ibid., 75.

21. Ibid.

22. Ibid., 76.

23. Ibid.

24. Ibid.

25. Ibid.

26. Ibid., 77.

27. Ibid.

28. Ibid., 75, 77.

29. Ibid., 77.

30. Ibid.

31. See Levinas, "The State of Caesar and the State of David," in *Beyond the Verse*, 180–83: "The epoch of the Messiah can and must result from the political order that is allegedly indifferent to eschatology and preoccupied solely with the problems of the hour. This political world must, therefore, remain related to the ideal world." Levinas cites passages from Maimonides's *Mishneh Torah*, Genesis Rabbah, and BT Shabbat 11a in order to show that while "the Messianic City is not beyond politics, the City in its simplest sense [viz. the city as a political venue] is never this side of the religious," i.e., "although Israel would see itself as descended from an irreducible fraternity, it is aware of the temptation, within itself and around it, of the war which pits everyone against everyone else" (183).

32. Levinas, *Difficult Freedom*, 60.

33. Ibid.

34. Ibid., 60–61.

35. Steven Schwarzschild, "On Jewish Eschatology," in *The Pursuit of the Ideal: Jewish Writings of Steven Schwarzschild*, ed. Menachem Kellner (Albany: State University of New York Press, 1990), 209–28.

36. Gershom Scholem, "Toward an Understanding of the Messianic Idea in Judaism," in *The Messianic Idea in Judaism and Other Essays on Jewish Spirituality* (New York: Schocken Books, 1971), 1–36.

37. Levinas, *Difficult Freedom*, 61.

38. Ibid.

39. Levinas puts it this way: "Does Samuel announce a capitalist paradise in which there is no more war, no more military service, no more anti-semitism, in a way that leaves savings untouched and the social problem unsolved?" (*Difficult Freedom*, 61). Levinas here shows in inclination toward socialism, I think, and perhaps even Marxism.

40. Ibid., 62.

41. Ibid., 63.

42. Ibid.

43. Ibid., 64.

44. Ibid.

45. Ibid., 65.

46. Ibid., 81.

47. Ibid.

48. Ibid. Levinas points out that this is not the famous Hillel but nonetheless a Tanna, before the second century, who is cited only this once in the Talmud.

49. Ibid., 82. Rashi, on R. Hillel's thesis on BT Sanhedrin 99a, comments, "Rather the Holy One Blessed Be He will rule Himself and He will redeem them alone."

50. Ibid., 82–83.

51. That ethics has no end, as we have seen, is a view that Levinas holds regarding his own view of the ethical; see the first paragraph of this chapter and Levinas's comment during the interview with Kearney.

52. Levinas, *Difficult Freedom*, 83.

53. Ibid.

54. Ibid., 84.

55. Levinas summarizes this account of R. Hillel's point in "The State of Caesar and the State of David," in *Beyond the Verse*, 185–86.

56. Levinas, *Difficult Freedom*, 84.

57. Ibid., 85.

58. Ibid., 91–96.

59. Ibid., 91.

60. Ibid., 92.

61. Ibid.

62. Ibid.

63. Ibid., 93.

64. Why is this what it means to say that the Messiah will come only when "darkness covers those people who are with [the *min*]"? I take it that R. Abbahu's point is that the Messiah will never come for heretics (Christians?) as long as they are alive; it will come only once they have all passed away. That is, I read "darkness covering over someone" as meaning once they are dead. But I am not sure of this reading, only that the point of R. Abbahu's claim is that there are those, like the heretic, for whom the Messiah will never come.

65. Levinas, *Difficult Freedom*, 93.

66. Ibid., 94.

67. Ibid.

68. Ibid.

69. Ibid., 94–95.

70. Ibid., 95.

71. Ibid.

72. Levinas uses a famous midrash to provide an image for this distinction. The midrash portrays the first man as being as large as the universe, for some "from the earth to the heavens" and for others "from the east to the west." Levinas takes the latter to represent the Hegelian synthesis of the political and the former to represent the Jewish view, of a first man who is as tall as the gap between heaven and earth. "It signifies above all that Israel does not measure its morality by politics, that its universality is messianism itself" (ibid.).

73. Ibid.

74. Ibid., 95–96.

75. Ibid., 96.

76. Ibid.

77. Ibid.

78. In "The State of Caesar and the State of David," Levinas calls this goal of Zionism a "monotheistic politics"; see pp. 186–87.

79. See Martin Kavka, "Reading Messianically with Gershom Scholem," in *Rethinking the Messianic Idea in Judaism*, ed. Michael L. Morgan and Steven Weitzman (Bloomington: Indiana University Press, 2015), 404–8.

80. See David Schmidtz and Robert E. Goodin, *Social Welfare and Individual Responsibility: For and Against* (Cambridge: Cambridge University Press, 1998).

81. Ibid., 8.

10. LEVINAS'S NOTORIOUS INTERVIEW

1. "Israël: éthique et politique," *Les Nouveaux cahiers* 71 (Hiver 1982–83): 1–8.

2. "Ethics and Politics," in *The Levinas Reader*, ed. Seán Hand (Oxford: Basil Blackwell, 1989), 288. Further references to this translation of the interview will be marked in the text as EP.

3. Israeli sources claim that it was no more than eight hundred; Palestinian reports take the total to be up to three thousand.

4. Shalom Achshav, Peace Now, had been founded in 1978, but the rally in 1982, in which it played a role alongside other peace movements, brought it to prominence and was, according to some, its first major accomplishment.

5. The commission, formally called the Commission of Inquiry into the

Events at the Refugee Camps in Beirut, delivered its report on February 8, 1983. It is available in English as *The Beirut Massacre: The Complete Kahan Commission Report* (Princeton, NJ: Karz-Cohl, 1983).

6. I am going to read the interview the way we read a Platonic dialogue, closely, in detail, and critically. To be sure, it is an interview and not a written text, but I am assuming that Levinas saw the final version before it was published and that it was edited and not an unedited transcript.

7. Emmanuel Levinas, "Useless Suffering," trans. Richard A. Cohen, in *The Provocation of The Provocation of Levinas,* ed. Robert Bernasconi and David Wood (London: Routledge, 1988).

8. Joan B. Wolf, *Harnessing the Holocaust: The Politics of Memory in France* (Stanford, CA: Stanford University Press, 2004), 101.

9. Philippe Sollers, in *Le Quotidien de Paris,* August 13, 1992, cited by Wolf, *Harnessing the Holocaust,* 101.

10. Wolf, *Harnessing the Holocaust,* 101.

11. Alain Finkielkraut, in *Liberation,* September 24, 1982, cited by Wolf, *Harnessing the Holocaust,* 103–4.

12. This conception, that the Jewish problem of the Jews in Europe could be solved by establishing a political entity with a Jewish majority, goes back to Herzl and is associated with Jabotinsky and Ben-Gurion. See Ruth Gavison, "Israel as a Jewish and Democratic State," 119–21, 142–43, cited from the Social Science Research Network, "Can Israel Be Both Jewish and Democratic?" (Jan. 1, 2011): http://papers.ssrn.com/s013/papers.cfm?abstract_id=1862904. Gavison cites Yoram Hazony, "Did Herzl Want a Jewish State?," *Azure* 9 (2000). Ahad Ha'am criticized this very thin conception of Israel as a Jewish state by arguing that if it would solve the problem of Jews, it would not solve the problem of Judaism in the modern world.

13. Malka is citing from an article by Monsignor Aaron Jean-Marie Lustiger, archbishop of Paris from 1981 to 2005, in *Débat.* The next year, in 1983, he was appointed cardinal. Born a Jew from Polish survivors of World War I, Lustiger always considered himself a Jew, but one who had taken up Christianity to educate the world in God's ways. For the Jewish community, he was a controversial and problematic figure.

14. There are vast number of papers and books dealing with this subject. I especially think about the works of Menachem Friedman, Aviezer Ravitzky, Menachem Kellner, Ian Lustig, Motti Inbari, and others. There are several essays that touch on these themes and worries in Michael L. Morgan and Steven Weitzman, eds., *Rethinking the Messianic Idea in Judaism: Historical, Philosophical, and Literary Perspectives* (Bloomington: Indiana University Press, 2014).

15. See Avishai Margalit, *On Compromise and Rotten Compromises* (Princeton, NJ: Princeton University Press, 2013).

16. See above, chapter 9.

17. The Talmudic statement occurs in the Babylonian Talmud, Shabbat 88a, Gittin 36b, and Yoma 23a. The principle is called *ha-ne'elavim ve-einam olvim* (those who are insulted but do not insult). They are suffering servants of God, so to speak. But Levinas reads the text differently. He focuses on the fact that it alludes to the last verse of Deborah's song and the image of the sun rising in its glory but only after the military victory has occurred.

18. Babylonian Talmud, Arakhin 15a–b.

11. LEVINAS AND HIS CRITICS

1. In an earlier draft of this book, I included a chapter that dealt with feminist criticisms of Levinas, feminist readings of him, and the similarity between the overall orientation of his thinking to the ethics of care that has emerged from feminist thinking. I have deleted that chapter

in part because I take the work of writers such as Stella Stanford, *The Metaphysics of Love* (London: Athlone Press, 2000) to have responded in a convincing and significant way to many of the feminist criticisms of Levinas. The writings of various care theorists make clear the ways in which Levinas's focus on responsibility for others is similar to an ethics of care.

2. Simon Critchley, "Five Problems in Levinas's View of Politics and the Sketch of a Solution to Them," *Political Theory* 32, no. 2 (April 2004): 173–75. I turn to a more developed discussion of Critchley's important paper shortly.

3. In a sense, Judith Butler's use of Levinas is similar; she is indebted to his work but takes it to be deficient or flawed in certain ways. Unlike Butler, however, Critchley is both a critic and one of the most illuminating and helpful readers of Levinas. See below.

4. Ibid., 172–85, esp. 173.

5. Simon Critchley, *Infinitely Demanding: Ethics of Commitment, Politics of Resistance* (London: Verso, 2007).

6. Critchley, "Five Problems in Levinas's View of Politics," 173.

7. Ibid., 175.

8. Later in the essay, Critchley calls this "passage" or "entailment" a "deduction of politics from ethics, from the other to all others, from *autrui* to *le tiers*" (ibid., 177). Critchley defends this connection against Derrida's charge that Levinas never makes clear how it is made (178), but he later refers to it as a "moment of *disincarnation* that challenges the borders and legitimacy of the state" (182). I will say something about what Critchley means by this shortly.

9. Ibid., 173.

10. Ibid., 177, 182, 184n18.

11. Ibid., 173.

12. Emmanuel Levinas, "Dialectics and the Sino-Soviet Quarrel," in *Unforeseen History* (Urbana: University of Illinois Press, 1994), 108 (originally 1968). See

Critchley, "Five Problems in Levinas's View of Politics," 175–76.

13. Critchley, "Five Problems in Levinas's View of Politics," 174.

14. Ibid.

15. Ibid.

16. Ibid., 175.

17. Ibid., 175–76.

18. As Critchley goes on to describe this "anarchist metapolitics," it involves inventive, highly particularized decisions and actions that are "singular, situational, and context dependent." This emphasis on responding to the "other's decision in me" or "the demand of the good experienced as the heteronomous opening of autonomy" reflects a "relation between ethics and politics that is both nonfoundational and nonarbitrary." There is invention and distinctiveness at the same time that the demand comes from the other. See ibid., 180. I am reminded of a famous passage in Buber's *I and Thou* where Buber formulates what he calls the religious antinomy, in which the experience of God is both an experience of everything being up to the agent and yet the experience of the agent's being singled out and given over to the divine other. See Martin Buber, *I and Thou* (New York: Charles Scribner's Sons, 1970), 145.

19. For some summary, initial comments on this "anarchist metapolitics," see Critchley, "Five Problems in Levinas's View of Politics," 182–83.

20. Ibid., 182.

21. Ibid., 183.

22. See Michael L. Morgan, "Levinas and Messianism," in *Rethinking the Messianic Idea in Judaism*, ed. Michael L. Morgan and Steven Weitzman (Bloomington: Indiana University Press, 2014), 195–225; and Michael L. Morgan, "Time, Messianism, and Diachrony," in *Discovering Levinas* (Cambridge: Cambridge University Press, 2007), 208–27. See also Simon Critchley, *Infinitely Demanding*, 92–94, 119–23, where Critchley elaborates

the "anarchist metapolitics" he sketches in this paper.

23. See Judith Butler, *Precarious Life: The Powers of Mourning and Violence* (London: Verso, 2004), ch. 5; *Giving an Account of Oneself* (New York: Fordham University Press, 2005), esp. ch. 3; "Is Judaism Zionism?" in *The Power of Religion in the Public Sphere*, ed. Eduardo Mendieta and Jonathan VanAntwerpen (New York: Columbia University Press, 2011), 70–91; *Parting Ways: Jewishness and the Critique of Zionism* (New York: Columbia University Press, 2012), esp. chs. 1, 2, 4, and 5.

24. Howard Caygill, *Levinas and the Political* (London: Routledge, 2002), 190–94.

25. Ibid., 190.

26. Ibid., 191.

27. Ibid., 192.

28. Ibid.

29. See above, chapter 3.

30. Caygill, *Levinas and the Political*, 193.

31. Ibid.

32. Emmanuel Levinas, *Nine Talmudic Readings*, trans. Annette Aronowicz (Bloomington: Indiana University Press), 56.

33. Caygill, *Levinas and the Political*, 194.

34. Levinas, *Nine Talmudic Readings*, 69.

35. See below, the section of this chapter on Butler, for further discussion of Butler's use and criticisms of Levinas.

36. It is too risky to begin with a negative or critical view of Israel as a colonialist or military state and argue that Levinas ought to have acknowledged and expressed such a judgment if he had any integrity at all. Such an approach smacks of outright bias. It is safer and more responsible intellectually to argue that a reading of what he shows is riddled with inconsistencies or confusions, presumably caused by his desire to avoid the critical appraisal of Israel. For a very balanced and detailed comparison between Israel and other democratic regimes, see Alexander Jakobson and Amnon Rubenstein, *Israel and the Family of Nations: The Jewish Nation-State*

and Human Rights (London: Routledge, 2009). The charges against Israel as a criminal state are highly tendentious and should not be employed as an argument against Levinas.

37. See Butler, *Precarious Life*, 129–31.

38. Ibid., 131.

39. Ibid., 134.

40. Ibid., 135–36.

41. Ibid., 140. As I indicated, I will turn to this Jewish dimension of Butler's recent thinking shortly; for now I focus on the role that Levinas and especially the face play in Butler's critique of American militarism and the way in which the media serve it.

42. Butler, *Precarious Life*, 141. See also 161n6. Butler also comes close to making the distinction clear on p. 144, where she says, "It is important to distinguish among kinds of representability. In the first instance, there is the Levinasian view according to which there is a 'face' which no face can fully exhaust, the face understood as human suffering, as the cry of human suffering, which can take no direct representation. Here the 'face' is always a figure for something that is not literally a face. Other human expressions, however, seem to be figurable as a 'face' even though they are not faces." Butler is incorrect to call the face-to-face a figure. It is a real albeit transcendental dimension of all human encounters and relationships. But it is not identical with all the other ways in which the subject and the other person confront one another. She goes on to say that in fact the face is not representable, which is correct.

43. Butler, *Precarious Life*, 142.

44. Ibid., 142–43.

45. This is evident from Butler, *Precarious Life*, 144–51, where the Levinasian vocabulary becomes almost an afterthought and Butler foregrounds her criticism of the way in which corporate and media interests orchestrated the depiction

of the American attack on Iraq in order to support American exemplarism.

46. Here the primary text is Butler, *Giving an Account of Oneself*, 84–101.

47. Ibid., 85.

48. Of particular interest, see Gary Watson, *Agency and Answerability: Selected Essays* (Oxford: Clarendon Press, 2004); R. Jay Wallace, *Responsibility and the Moral Sentiments* (Cambridge, MA: Harvard University Press, 1998).

49. Butler, *Giving an Account of Oneself*, 87.

50. Ibid., 92–93.

51. Ibid., 93.

52. Emmanuel Levinas, "From the Rise of Nihilism to the Carnal Jew," in *Difficult Freedom,* trans. Seán Hand (Baltimore: Johns Hopkins University Press, 1990), 225. Originally published as "De le montée du nihilisme au Juif charnel," in I. Schneersohn (ed.), *D'Auschwitz à Israël* (Paris: Centre de Documentation Juive Contemporaine, 1968), 244–49. See Butler, *Giving an Account of Oneself*, 93.

53. Butler, *Giving an Account of Oneself*, 93–94.

54. Ibid., 94.

55. In these paragraphs I am trying hard to identify with some precision and clarify exactly what Butler is claiming about Levinas and about his portrait of Judaism and the Jewish people. This task is not made any easier by the imprecise and highly rhetorical ways in which she expresses herself in these pages of *Giving an Account of Oneself*. I may not be reading her correctly, but she is certainly not being helpful. A sentence like the following shows how careless is her presentation: "The problem, of course, is that 'the Jew' is a category that belongs to a culturally constituted ontology (unless it is the name for access to the infinite itself), and so if the Jew maintains an 'elective' status in relation to ethical responsibility, then Levinas fully confuses the preontological and the ontological" (94). In one sense, of course,

being Jewish is an everyday, cultural and religious category, but the parenthesis in this sentence begs the question completely—since it is certainly possible and even likely that Levinas does treat the term "the Jew" as a name for anyone who is especially attentive and responsive to the claim of the other person and the demands of justice and humanity. Moreover, to say so, that is, to say that the Jew is one who is especially attentive to "ethical responsibility," does not disclose a confusion but instead shows exactly how precise Levinas is being about the distinction between everyday persecution and that primordial persecution that is universal. And even if Levinas is confused, surely it is not entailed by any fact about the Jewish people but at best by some other claim that Levinas himself makes. No fact of the matter about Judaism implies that Levinas is confused about anything—by itself.

56. Butler, *Giving an Account of Oneself*, 95.

57. Ibid., 96.

58. Ibid., 96.

59. The event was held in Cooper Union, in New York, on October 22, 2009; the book *The Power of Religion in the Public Sphere*, by Judith Butler, Jürgen Habermas, Charles Taylor, and Cornel West, ed. Eduardo Mendieta and Jonathan VanAntwerpen (New York: Columbia University Press) was published in 2011. Reworked, the material in this paper appeared subsequently in chapter 5 of Butler's *Parting Ways: Jewishness and the Critique of Zionism* (New York: Columbia University Press, 2012).

60. For a survey and discussion of reactions within the Jewish community to Butler's work on Jewishness and Zionism, see Shaul Magid, "Butler Trouble: Zionism, Excommunication, and the Reception of Judith Butler's Work on Israel/Palestine," *Studies in American Jewish Literature* 33, no. 2 (2014): 237–59. I want to thank Shaul Magid for making this essay available to

me prior to its publication. My focus here, of course, is not on the political and historical impact of and responses to Butler's work. Rather I am interested in how Butler uses her appropriation of Levinas's work and thought within the context of her account of a Jewish ethics that is post-Zionist and anti-Zionist.

61. There is a very good critique of Butler's reading and use of Arendt in Seyla Benhabib's review of *Parting Ways*; see Seyla Benhabib, "Ethics without Normativity and Politics without Historicity: On Judith Butler's *Parting Ways. Jewishness and the Critique of Zionism*," *Constellations* 20, no. 1 (March 2013): 150–63. I want to thank Seyla Benhabib for allowing me to see her review long before its publication and for the conversation and e-mails that had so much to do with my reasons for engaging with Butler's work and for writing this book on ethics and politics in Levinas. Benhabib basically accepts Butler's reading of Levinas but objects to her interpretation of cohabitation in Arendt. The account adumbrated in this essay is developed and extended in *Parting Ways*.

62. Butler, "Is Judaism Zionism?," in *The Power of Religion in the Public Sphere*, 74.

63. Although not presented in this schematic way, Butler's basic argument is set out in the introduction to *Parting Ways*, 1–27. An issue that I do not take up, which she considers extensively, is the universal character of the ethic that is derived from Jewish sources and yet must be translated into an idiom that can be understood and accepted by all.

64. To a degree, this is an exaggeration. Why? Because an essential feature of the argument would be for Butler to show that her conception of an ethic of cohabitation and of nonviolence toward the other person is found in Jewish sources. Without showing this, she has failed to make the case that her ethic is a Jewish one. To my knowledge, she never does this. Instead she points out that various features of such

an ethic can be found in thinkers who make such features part of their own views and/or explicitly associate them with Judaism. This is the case with her appeal to Arendt, to Buber and Yehuda Magnes, and to Levinas. For this reason, these appropriations take the place of the appeal to traditional Jewish sources and hence are not inessential. It is all the more puzzling, if not simply ironic, to find her criticism of Levinas focusing on his claim that attentiveness and commitment to the centrality of the ethical as infinite responsibility to be targeted on this very claim.

65. See Butler, "Is Judaism Zionism?," in *The Power of Religion in the Public Sphere*, 80–83.

66. Butler, *Parting Ways*, 23.

67. Ibid., 23.

68. Ibid., 24.

69. Unfortunately the book is filled with the latter, along with much excellent and provocative analysis of Benjamin and others. For example, is it necessary or even justified to say that "Zionism . . . [has a] structural commitment to state violence against minorities?" (see Butler, *Parting Ways*, 32). What evidence could show this to be true in all its generality? What would a "state commitment" require in order to carry out "violence" systematically against all minorities? This sounds like Arendt's account of Nazi fascism and Stalinism as regimes of total domination that seek to eradicate all difference and hence as paradigmatic totalitarian regimes. Is it surprising that in the same sentence Butler associates Zionism with "Hitlerian politics"? This is no longer responsible analysis and argument; it is polemics and nasty polemics to boot.

70. Butler, *Parting Ways*, 39.

71. Ibid. When Butler says that "we have not yet seen a study of the 'faceless' in Levinas" (ibid.), one can only respond that only someone with no idea of what Levinas is saying might provide one. That no such study exists is a good sign. If the

reader of Levinas takes the word "face" always to have its technical sense, then there is no such thing as a faceless person; at the transcendental level, each of us has a face-to-face relation with each and every other person. And if we do allow a non-technical, everyday use of the expression, then there are always going to be degrees of such a relation. To put this in the terminology of Levinas's later work, in everyday life, our responsibility to others is always a matter of degree and of kind. It is not a matter of either/or but always of how much and in what way.

72. Ibid., 42–43. The quotes from Levinas are from *Difficult Freedom*, 164.

73. Butler, *Parting Ways*, 45–46, and see our earlier discussion of the passage from *Difficult Freedom* and the essay "From the Rise of Nihilism to the Carnal Jew."

74. See Butler, *Parting Ways*, 46ff.

75. In the section of chapter 1 entitled "Who Has a Face?" Butler begins with a highly evocative and rhetorical version of this criticism, that there is in Levinas a loss of all sensitivity to the plight of the dispossessed other outside of Judaism and Christianity: "There is no nameable Islam here, there is no nameable Arab here, only something vaguely *Asiatic*, without a face, threatening engulfment, but also threatening the people whose elected task it is to carry universality and so threatening universality itself." Butler charges Levinas with a kind of metaphysical xenophobia. She calls it an "Ashkenazi presumption that underwrites the Levinasian ethical scene" (ibid., 48).

76. I should acknowledge the fascinating and compelling readings Butler gives of Benjamin and also her important if controversial reading of Arendt, but these are parts of the book that we do not need to consider for our purposes, which is to examine critically her appropriation and critique of Levinas.

77. Butler, *Parting Ways*, 54–55.

78. Ibid., 55. This, of course, is the central question of this book; Butler has a clear picture of how the political arises, according to Levinas, and what the ethical means by itself. What she is asking here is what the ethical means for the political. Robert Bernasconi has written thoughtfully on this theme, and as I say, my efforts in this book are in part aimed at explaining how Levinas would answer the question.

79. Ibid., 56.

80. For this paragraph, see ibid., 56–57.

81. Ibid., 57–58. Butler returns here to a discussion of Jacob and Esau that she already initiated in *Precarious Life* and to which she here refers.

82. Ibid., 58–59.

83. Ibid., 59.

84. Ibid., 61.

85. See Richard Rorty, *Contingency, Irony, and Solidarity* (Cambridge: Cambridge University Press, 1989).

86. See Gillian Rose, *Mourning Becomes the Law: Philosophy and Representation* (Cambridge: Cambridge University Press, 1996), 7–14, esp. 13–14, and then ch. 5.

87. Ibid., 36.

88. Ibid., 37–38.

89. Rose then concludes the sentence with the caveat "even though Levinas insists that it is social and not sacred." Ibid., 37.

CONCLUSION

1. Thomas Nagel, *Equality and Partiality* (Oxford: Oxford University Press, 1991), 3.

2. Ibid., 4.

3. Jean-Luc Marion, in a comment to me after a lecture on these matters, described his understanding of Levinas's concept of the third party along these lines; I think that this is very helpful. The face of the other is both utterly particular and universal. For Marion's reading, see his paper on the third party in *Figures de phenomenology* (Paris: J. Vrin, 2012).

INDEX

"Quest for Liberty in Moses Mendelssohn's Political Philosophy, The" (Altmann), 129

Rab, 231–35, 241, 247–48, 251, 388n9
racism, 23, 37, 128
radical evil, xi, 237, 253, 314
Rashi, 251
rationalism, 129
rationality, 5, 6, 16, 133, 203, 366n13
Rawls, John, 5, 61, 82, 93, 354, 361n47
reciprocity, 59, 88–89, 238, 367n37
redemption, 254, 259–60, 262; end of
    history and, 231, 251; episodic messian-
    ism and, 97; from history and politics,
    195; with and without a Messiah, 249;
    messianic, 234; radical evil and, 253;
    repentance and, 236, 238, 239; revelation
    and, 118; suffering and, 233, 234, 235, 237;
    unconditional, 240
"Reflections on the Philosophy of Hitler-
    ism" (Levinas), 127–28, 134, 135–36
refugees, 96, 105, 137, 211, 225
relativism, 185, 348
religion, 3, 57; the state and, 22, 26, 129, 133;
    "wars of religion," 6
"Religion for Adults, A" (Levinas), 230, 241
Renaissance, 114, 115
repentance, 13, 17, 236, 238, 240
representation, 34, 36, 53, 366n17, 374n25;
    biblical prohibition against, 109; hu-
    manization and, 325–28; plurality and,
    16; of social existence, 54; social ex-
    istence and, 107; third party and, 52;
    unrepresented people in democracy,
    137–40, 377n25, 377n28
Republic (Plato), 69, 126
responsibility, xiii, 3, 7, 25, 32, 354; as cen-
    tral Jewish teaching, 21, 158, 190, 204,
    379n16; conditional and unconditional,
    353; decent society and infinite respon-
    sibility, 71–81; everyday life/experi-
    ence and, 9, 328–29; externalization
    of, 264–65; of the face-to-face, 11–12;
    failures of, 177; innocence and, 269–70;
    Jewish identity and, 22; justice and, 12,
    53–54, 58; limits on, 91; messianism and,
    235, 256, 264–65; mutual, 49; negotiated
    and qualified, 59; order of, 14; political

order and, 356n3; politics and, 52; pri-
    macy of, 18, 28, 51, 105–6, 224, 263; rights
    discourse and, 92–106; social/political
    institutions founded on, 17, 353; toward
    Sabra and Shatila victims, 29, 268–83;
    unbounded, 50; utopian element of, 67;
    as "word of God," 109
"Responsibility and Substitution" (Levi-
    nas), 358n26
revolution, 161–62, 165, 168, 359n36; ethics-
    politics relation and, 175–76; Judaism
    threatened by, 173–74; non-violence
    and, 172; the state and, 166
rights discourse, 38, 364n47; discourse of
    responsibility and, 92–106; individu-
    alism and, 372n8; interpersonal rela-
    tions and, 372n10; Levinas's apparent
    rejection of, 107. *See also* human rights
"Rights of Man and the Rights of the
    Other, The" (Levinas), 112–23, 127
Rorty, Richard, ix, 347, 348
Rose, Gillian, 3, 302, 348–51, 395n89
Rousseau, Jean-Jacques, 93
Rubinstein, Amnon, 206

Sabra and Shatila massacre, 20, 28–29, 281,
    315; Holocaust discourse and, 272; inno-
    cence or responsibility of Israel for, 268;
    Kahan Commission Report on, 267,
    286, 346, 389n5; Levinas's comments
    on, 29–31, 266; number of victims, 28,
    266–67, 362n25, 389n3; redemption of
    those complicit in, 290–91; as threat to
    Jewish ethical tradition, 295–96; as war
    crime, 316. *See also* Tel Aviv peace move-
    ment protest
Sadat, Anwar, 20, 26–28, 135, 197, 199–200,
    205, 362n23
Said, Edward, 337
Samuel, Rabbi, 231–35, 241–47, 388n39
Sanhedrin court, 153, 154, 158, 379n2
Saying and Said, 46–47, 48, 57, 58, 59
Scanlon, Thomas, 67, 93
Schmidtz, David, 263–64
Scholem, Gershom, 172, 199, 243, 261,
    262, 336
Schwarzschild, Steven, 243
science, 55, 114, 115, 147, 152, 201; "Greeks"
    and, 313; natural sciences, 69; rights

MICHAEL L. MORGAN is Chancellor's Professor Emeritus in Philosophy and Jewish Studies at Indiana University Bloomington and the Jerahmiel S. and Simone S. Grafstein Visiting Professor of Philosophy at the University of Toronto. He is author of *Dilemmas in Modern Jewish Thought* (1992), *Interim Judaism* (2002), and editor (with Steven Weitzman) of *Rethinking the Messianic Idea in Judaism* (2014), all published by Indiana University Press. He is also author of *Beyond Auschwitz* (2001), *Discovering Levinas* (2007), and *Fackenheim's Jewish Philosophy: An Introduction* (2014).

CPSIA information can be obtained at www.ICGtesting.com
Printed in the USA
BVOW08s0924050516

446909BV00003B/41/P